ANXIOUSLY ENGAGED

ANXIOUSLY ENGAGED

A BIOGRAPHY OF

M. RUSSELL BALLARD

SUSAN EASTON BLACK | JOSEPH WALKER

DESERET
BOOK

SALT LAKE CITY, UTAH

All photos courtesy of the Ballard family, unless noted below. Used with permission.

Page 3, photo by Ron Pope; pages 4, 6, 167, 191, 194, 227, 229, 249, courtesy of the Church History Library/© Intellectual Reserve, Inc.; pages 251, 264, 278, courtesy of the *Church News*; page 287, © The Church of Jesus Christ of Latter-day Saints; pages 312, 353, photos by Suzanne Drysdale; pages 314, 320, 356, photos by Ravell Call, *Deseret News*; pages 316, 336, photos by Jeffrey D. Allred, *Deseret News*; page 338, photo courtesy of the Vatican; pages 344, 348, photos by Richard Holzapfel.

Library of Congress Cataloging-in-Publication Data

Names: Black, Susan Easton, author. | Walker, Joseph, 1955– author.
Title: Anxiously engaged : a biography of M. Russell Ballard / Susan Easton Black, Joseph Walker.
Description: Salt Lake City, Utah : Deseret Book, [2021] | Includes bibliographical references and index. | Summary: "A biography of Elder M. Russell Ballard, the acting president of the Quorum of the Twelve Apostles in The Church of Jesus Christ of Latter-day Saints"— Provided by publisher.
Identifiers: LCCN 2021016447 | ISBN 9781629729541 (hardback)
Subjects: LCSH: Ballard, M. Russell, 1928– | Quorum of the Twelve Apostles (The Church of Jesus Christ of Latter-day Saints)—Biography. | Mormon Church—Apostles—Biography. | LCGFT: Biographies.
Classification: LCC BX8695.B319 W35 2021 | DDC 289.3092 [B]—dc23
LC record available at https://lccn.loc.gov/2021016447

Printed in the United States of America
Lake Book Manufacturing, Inc., Melrose Park, IL

10   9   8   7   6   5   4   3   2

CONTENTS

PREFACE

As President M. Russell Ballard travels throughout the world as Acting President of the Quorum of the Twelve Apostles of The Church of Jesus Christ of Latter-day Saints, he says one of the questions he is often asked is this: "When is there going to be a biography of your life?"

"I never know what to say in response," he said during an interview in early 2020. "As I look back on my life, I see an assortment of experiences, individuals, institutions, situations, and circumstances that have had significant influence upon me. My life has been filled with highs and lows, ups and downs, good things and bad—just like every other life.

"I have experienced things that have given me the greatest joy I could possibly imagine, and I have also experienced things that have taken me to the very depths of sorrow," he continued. "There are times in my life at which I look back and laugh, and times that the mere memory of it moves me to tears."

But in President Ballard's mind, none of that is particularly unusual. "You can say the same thing about your life," he told his interviewer, "and so can everyone I know."

He explained: "My life has been a great life for me, and I have loved . . . well . . . almost all of it. But I've never felt that there was anything especially extraordinary about my life that would make people want to read about it."

On various occasions Deseret Book approached President Ballard about the possibility of a biography, but it wasn't until Susan Easton Black mentioned the topic to him that he relented.

When asked about his change of heart about participating in a biography project, he said: "As I have advanced into my nineties, I have found myself wondering if perhaps by not supporting a biography of my life I am missing an important opportunity for teaching, and for bearing witness to the world of God's goodness, patience and love.

"I'm not so very different from others—as I see it, I'm pretty common and ordinary," he said. "But in ninety-two-plus years, this common, ordinary man has had some rather remarkable experiences through which I have learned extremely valuable and worthwhile lessons that have shaped me as a special witness of the Lord Jesus Christ. If I can share these experiences in such a way that readers can understand what I've learned and see the hand of the Lord in my life, maybe it will help them to better understand the lessons of their own lives and to see how God has been there for them as well."

This, then, has been the clearly understood objective for all those who have worked to capture the essence of the life and ministry of M. Russell Ballard: to document the realities of his life—including both the successes and the failures—so that others can see in his experiences elements into which they can tap with their own experiences. The hope is that readers can experience learning, growth, understanding, and connection.

A number of people have been instrumental in compiling, researching, writing, and editing this biography. Of special note are the four women who have assisted President Ballard during his apostolic ministry: Dorothy Anderson, Carolyn Hyde, Emily Merrell, and Suzanne Drysdale. Through the years, these hardworking, faithful women have spent countless hours compiling journals, scrapbooks, and timelines to help document and record President Ballard's life. Sister Hyde actually wrote an early biography that was circulated only among Ballard family members and friends. This early biography was the foundation upon which this volume was built. Susan Easton Black, a friend of President Ballard's and a well-known historian, did a great deal of research, conducted a number of important interviews, and pushed the project further down the road. Another longtime friend, Joseph Walker, also added meaningful input. And Deseret Book's senior editor, Emily Watts, finally brought the project home. President Ballard would like to express his sincere appreciation to Sheri Dew for all she has done to see this book to its completion.

"I am profoundly grateful to all of these dear people for their help and encouragement along the way," President Ballard said as the project moved toward completion. "I give them all of the credit, but none of the blame. If there are errors, they are mine, probably due to insufficient understanding or lapses in memory. Everything that has been written here has passed under my eyes and been approved by me. Therefore, I alone am responsible for the content of this book."

And so, he continued, "this is my story, offered in the sincere hope that the reader will find in these words a connection that will bind us as celestial siblings, God's children sent to earth to have a lifetime of experiences that will mold us and give us direction as we work together to find our way back to our heavenly home."

CHAPTER ONE

FAMILY MATTERS

I n 1990—five years after he was ordained an Apostle in The Church
of Jesus Christ of Latter-day Saints—Elder M. Russell Ballard
visited Nauvoo, Illinois, on Church business. Now a small village
just across the Mississippi River from Iowa, Nauvoo was once—150
years earlier—a bustling city of some significance regionally as the
headquarters of the Church. Nauvoo was also significant to Elder
Ballard personally, as many of his progenitors had been instrumental in
turning a small town that was called Commerce into Nauvoo (derived
from the Hebrew word for "they are beautiful"), which in 1844 boasted
a population of 12,000,[1] making it one of the largest cities in Illinois
at the time.

And so Elder Ballard was troubled by what he saw at the Smith
Family Cemetery in Nauvoo, in which a number of his ancestors were
buried. Indeed, it wasn't much of a cemetery at all—just "a flat granite
marker which only identified the graves of Joseph, Emma and Hyrum
Smith [Elder Ballard's maternal great-great-grandfather]."[2] The sur-
rounding grounds were also the final resting place for nearly two dozen
other Smith family members, including Joseph Smith Sr. and Lucy

Mack Smith, but none of their graves were marked. The grounds had not been well kept through the years, and Elder Ballard could see that they needed a lot of attention. He felt this need even more keenly when he received a copy of a letter from Emma to her son Joseph Smith III, dated December 2, 1867—more than twenty-three years after her first husband, Joseph, and his elder brother Hyrum were martyred in Carthage, Illinois. In the letter, Emma wrote: "I have always felt sad about the neglected condition of that place. . . . I have got twenty-five dollars that no one has any right to but myself. . . . I feel anxious to apply that money on the graveyard. After I have done that I think we can ask our Smith relations to help mark Father's and Mother's graves, if no more."[3]

It is not Elder Ballard's nature to see a problem and hope that someone else will take care of it. And so he approached Wallace B. Smith, who was at the time president of the Reorganized Church of Jesus Christ of Latter Day Saints (now known as the Community of Christ), which owns the cemetery property. Even more important to this discussion, however, was the fact that President Smith was a direct descendant of Joseph Smith. As a direct descendant of Hyrum Smith, President Ballard felt it was appropriate for him to meet with his distant cousin and say, "We need to do something about this."

Together they decided to form the Joseph Smith Sr. Foundation. Ultimately, Elder Ballard was responsible for raising more than $500,000 toward this effort among Smith family descendants. "Hyrum's love for Joseph should serve as an example to all of us as we reach out with Joseph's posterity in this joint effort," Elder Ballard wrote to Hyrum Smith's descendants.[4] So many generous donations were received that the cemetery was turned into a garden-like park with trees, grass, flowers, lights, fencing, and a brick walkway. "A stately headstone for Joseph, Emma, and Hyrum was put in place," said Karl Ricks Anderson, a historian and educator who has helped the Church acquire many historical properties in the area. "When the graves of

Graves of Joseph, Emma, and Hyrum Smith

Joseph Smith Sr. and Lucy Mack Smith were located, headstones were placed there."[5] A portion of the funds raised through this effort assures the costs of maintaining the cemetery in perpetuity.

More than a thousand people, including two hundred descendants of Joseph Smith Sr. and Lucy Mack, gathered in the cemetery for the dedicatory services on August 4, 1991. President Wallace B. Smith dedicated the cemetery, saying that it "finally constitutes a fitting memorial to those principal figures of the Restoration and provides an appropriate setting for their repose."[6] Elder Ballard said in his remarks, "I am grateful that on the day of resurrection they will rise up and have no question as to whether or not their posterity loved them. I think we have demonstrated by our combined efforts our deep love and affection for those whom we honor by the improvement of this cemetery."[7]

"Creating the cemetery was not an easy task," Anderson said, referring to how it required cooperative effort from groups of people who have struggled in their relationships previously. "Elder Ballard's skill in working with people was greatly evidenced as he often expressed his desire to be a peacemaker in the family, much as was his ancestor Hyrum

Mary Fielding Smith   *Hyrum Smith*

Smith. He tried always to look for the good in others. When there were differences, he could see beyond them. . . . He was able to put people ahead of projects. And now the result of his energy and his intense desire to bring the Smith family together to do this good thing for their ancestors is there for the world to see and appreciate."[8]

Fifteen years later, Church President Thomas S. Monson observed that "M. Russell Ballard is justifiably proud of his ancestors." And, he added, "they would also be very proud of him because of the manner in which he speaks of them and emulates them."[9]

For his part, President Ballard never really thought of his ancestry as a matter of personal pride or entitlement. Yes, he knew that his mother, Geraldine Smith, was a direct descendant of Hyrum and Mary Fielding Smith. And he knew that her father was an Apostle (Elder Hyrum Mack Smith) and her grandfather was Church President Joseph F. Smith. He was also well aware that his father, Melvin R. Ballard, was also the son of an Apostle—Elder Melvin J. Ballard—with a pioneer heritage extending back for generations. But these people weren't important to President Ballard because of their prominence, titles, or positions. They were important to him because they were his family, and, as far as he was concerned, that was the only thing that really mattered, for him or for anyone else.

"I believe the mission statement for mortality might be 'to build an eternal family,'" he said during the October 2005 general conference of the Church. "Here on this earth we strive to become part of extended families with the ability to create and form our own part of those families. That is one of the reasons our Heavenly Father sent us here. Not everyone will find a companion and have a family in mortality, but everyone, regardless of individual circumstances, is a precious member of God's family.

"The gospel and the Lord's plan of happiness and salvation should remind us," he continued. "What matters most is what lasts longest, and our families are for eternity."[10]

Melvin and Geraldine Ballard

With an ancestry of prophets, apostles, and faithful women who dedicated their lives to the cause of Christ, one would naturally assume that M. Russell Ballard grew up in a home where gospel topics dominated conversations and scripture reading and family prayers were the norm. One would also logically assume that he had front-row seats at general conference, enjoyed family home evenings discussing the Restoration of the gospel of Jesus Christ, and worshipped together with his family each Sunday.

But such was not the case.

"As far as sitting down together and reading the scriptures or studying the gospel as a family, that just didn't happen," said Elder Ballard.[11] Nor did his family go to church together. They rarely even mentioned the unique fact that both of his grandfathers—Melvin J. Ballard and Hyrum Mack Smith (who died more than ten years before M. Russell Ballard was born)—were much-admired Apostles. "For some reason

M. Russell Ballard's grandfathers, Melvin J. Ballard (left) and Hyrum Mack Smith

I have never been able to understand, my father and mother never taught me what it meant that Grandfather Ballard [with whom he had an intimate and loving relationship as a little boy] was an Apostle of the Lord Jesus Christ."[12] His sister Ann added, "I did hear Russ say once, 'You know, I just wish Dad had taken me to hear Grandpa speak or sing. He could have done that for me, and he didn't.'"[13]

Melvin Russell Ballard, the father of M. Russell Ballard, was born in Logan, Utah. His father, Melvin J. Ballard, was away, having been called to serve in the Eastern States Mission with B. H. Roberts while Martha was expecting their child. Melvin R.'s young life was spent living in different places as his father fulfilled various Church callings and assignments in Utah and Oregon. When he was old enough to be called on a full-time mission, he was assigned to the Northwestern States Mission, over which his father was already presiding at the time.

Following his mission, he worked for a time in Oregon, then returned to Salt Lake City to work on the business side of the Church-owned *Deseret News* newspaper. It was the "Roaring Twenties," an era bursting with opportunity for a bright young man with entrepreneurial talents. With dreams of future prosperity and the possibility of economic expansion all around him, Melvin married Hannah Marie Covey, daughter of Stephen Covey and Hannah Saunders, in the Salt Lake Temple on May 30, 1920.

Melvin supported his new wife as the city circulation manager of the *Deseret News*. Largely through his efforts and innovative ideas, the circulation of the *Deseret News* increased from 12,000 to more than 34,000 subscribers almost overnight. Melvin also talked the *Deseret News* management into funding equipment for a wireless station and a voice transmitter atop the *Deseret News* building on South Temple and Main Street. Melvin foresaw the day when Church members would gather in their places of worship to hear from the President of the Church via the wireless station. The wood and tin radio shack built on top of the *Deseret News* building was the beginning of KSL Radio.[14]

Melvin's career might have been linked with the *Deseret News* for many years had not his father-in-law, Stephen Covey, encouraged him to go into business for himself, even offering to put up the money to start a new entrepreneurial venture. Covey was himself a successful businessman who would later found Covey's Little America, a gas station, café, and motel in Wyoming. It was through this inspiration and backing that Melvin found his way into the automobile business, where he would spend the rest of his professional life.

Things were going wonderfully well for the young Ballard family until Hannah fell ill and died two months after their first child, Betty Marie, was born. Difficult days followed as twenty-six-year-old Melvin tried to adapt to life as a single father. He moved in with his parents

Melvin R. and Geraldine Smith Ballard

so his mother could help with the baby. His business relationship with his father-in-law became awkward and was eventually terminated as he launched out on his own as the regional distributor and dealer for Nash Motors Company, an America automobile company based in Kenosha, Wisconsin.

Eventually he met and fell in love with Geraldine Smith, the orphaned daughter of Elder Hyrum Mack Smith and Ida Elizabeth Bowman. Although she was seven years Melvin's junior, they found they had much in common besides being the offspring of Apostles. And it was said that she possessed "qualities that impressed and persuaded anyone to approach her with the utmost courtesy and respect," and she had a "queenly bearing," "poise," and "ever present innate charm."[15]

Like Melvin, Geraldine spent her youth in the mission field. At age nine she journeyed with her parents to England, where her father presided over the European Mission of the Church. Geraldine attended the Liverpool College for Girls, a private school owned and operated by the Church of England. She recalled that first thing in the morning as the other girls were repeating the catechism and singing hymns in Latin, she sat alone in a corner listening.

With the outbreak of World War I in 1914, shortly after the Smiths arrived in England, Geraldine was often asked to accompany her mother as she traveled around the mission to help organize British Relief Societies to support the families and soldiers impacted by the war. Just ten years old, Geraldine was terrified by the sights of smoldering remains of bombed-out buildings in London following the German strategic bombing campaign by airships and airplanes. But she didn't back away from what she saw as her duty, and she joined the Relief Society sisters in rolling bandages, making mittens, and knitting socks.

Geraldine and her family returned to the United States in 1916 when the Church missions in Europe were closed. With Salt Lake City becoming her home once again, a sense of peace returned to Geraldine. But that peace was short-lived. In 1918, when she was only fourteen years old, both her father and her mother died—her father from a ruptured appendix and her mother from complications following the birth of her brother, Hyrum. It was her mother's single sister, Aunt Margaret Bowman, who took care of Geraldine and her siblings, supporting them as a seamstress. Because of the selfless care of Aunt Margaret and a scholarship to the University of Utah, Geraldine was able to pursue her education.

On February 26, 1926, twenty-one-year-old Geraldine Smith was married to twenty-eight-year-old widower Melvin R. Ballard in the Salt Lake Temple, with President Anthony W. Ivins, First Counselor in the First Presidency, officiating.[16] At the same time, Geraldine instantly became a mother—the only mother Betty Marie Ballard would ever know. Two and a half years later, Geraldine would bear a child herself.

CHAPTER TWO

"SOMETHING SPECIAL GOING ON HERE"

In 1928, while the nation looked to US President Calvin Coolidge to lead the country through an era of peace and prosperity and cheered on Charles Lindbergh for receiving the Medal of Honor for his 1927 solo trans-Atlantic flight from New York to Paris, Melvin and Geraldine were looking forward to the birth of their first child—who, it turned out, would be their only son. Little Melvin Russell Ballard Jr. was born on Monday, October 8, 1928, in the LDS Hospital in Salt Lake City, a small city with a population of fewer than 140,000.

"When Russ was born, I think Mother understood that there was something special going on here," his sister Ann later said. "Mother always dealt with him as though he was special. And rightfully. As everything has unfolded I can see that maybe she understood."[1]

Just four days after he was born, Russell—he was always known by his middle name—was given his name and a blessing by his paternal grandfather, Elder Melvin J. Ballard. That blessing was filled with prophetic promises of service to the Lord.

As a toddler, Russell lived with his parents in a neighborhood of young families at 1399 Butler Avenue near the University of Utah. At

Russ as a toddler

the time, his father was owner of Ballard Motor Company. The Great Depression that began with the stock-market crash in 1929 disrupted the Ballard family lifestyle, but not as much as it did to so many others. Salt Lake City was hit particularly hard during the economic downturn; at the peak of the Great Depression, unemployment in the city reached 61,500 people, or about 36 percent of the population. Jobs were scarce, but somehow there were still people with money to purchase cars. Though the Nash Motor Company scaled back production during the 1930s, it had not closed its doors—fortunately for the Ballards. With Melvin's genius for business and Geraldine's willingness to rent out a room in their house, the Ballard family weathered the financial downturn and were able to hold on to their home.

However, the Great Depression led to an unfortunate spiritual turn for Melvin and Geraldine. Melvin "became so involved in the business community and in the struggle to support a family during the Great Depression . . . that for a time it pulled him away from activity in the Church," President Ballard recalled.[2] His parents' withdrawal from Church activity, however, did not prevent Russell from attending worship services or praying with his mother and occasionally his father. His parents taught him to work hard, tell the truth, and understand his responsibility to family and neighbors. They always encouraged him to do the right thing for the right reason but allowed him to decide for himself whether or not he would be involved with the Church. Even as a child with less-active parents, there was never any doubt for Russell about that.

Russell was slight of build and younger than most of the boys in the neighborhood. He remembers being the victim of what some called "friendly pranks." His being a finicky eater and wanting everything to be clean and orderly added fuel to the pranks, as did his concern that nothing sticky touch his hands. Attending the Stewart Training School, a model school located on the University of Utah campus, gave him welcome relief from the pranks, but due to illness, Russell missed too many school days and needed to repeat kindergarten at the Wasatch Grade School the next year. The one event he remembers from his second year in kindergarten was a field trip to a dairy farm. All the children were invited to milk a cow. Russell was the only one in his class who was able to get the cow to give a few drops of milk. "As I look back on it," said President Ballard, "any milk that I was able to extract from the cow was by pure luck."[3]

As a student at Wasatch Grade School, one of Russell's daily highlights was walking with Scottie—a black, brown, and white collie—to and from school. Scottie walked with Russell down Butler Avenue to University Street and across Reservoir Park to a red light at South Temple and Thirteenth East. The dog would sit and watch as Russell crossed at the light and walked the next three blocks to the school.

When the school day was over, Russell would often find Scottie waiting by the stoplight to walk him home. Needless to say, boy and dog were inseparable friends.

Throughout grade school, Russell not only grew in stature but, according to his younger sister Ann, he became a "very outgoing, gregarious person."[4] He had an acting debut, playing the part of Tommy Miller in the Theta Alpha Phi Players' production of Eugene O'Neill's *Ah, Wilderness!* at the University Theater, under the direction of his mother's brother, Joseph F. Smith, the oldest son of Hyrum Mack and Ida Elizabeth Bowman Smith. A Salt Lake newspaper review of *Ah, Wilderness!* stated that cast members, including Russell Ballard, "deserve special commendation."[5] But acting wasn't something he wanted to pursue. So *Ah, Wilderness!* was both the beginning and the end of his acting career.

In 1936, his father purchased property in Lambs Canyon, about thirty minutes east of Salt Lake City in the beautiful Wasatch Mountains. Wildflowers, streams, and heavy stands of aspen and spruce dotted the landscape. Melvin's plan was to build a cabin on his property, working primarily on weekends—including Sundays. Melvin built the cabin out of lumber from the crates in which Model T Fords were shipped to his car dealership. The cabin was sturdy but not aesthetically appealing. As it turned out, the cabin was never finished, but working on it was a relaxing outlet for Melvin, whose definition of "fun" was just a different kind of work than what he did to earn a living. For everyone else—especially his only son—the cabin was just work. President Ballard said, "One of my father's drives was that he didn't really know how to relax."[6]

One time when Russell was with his father at the cabin, Melvin decided to siphon gasoline out of the car so that he could run the power generator. The hose he used for siphoning flipped out of the car's gasoline tank. President Ballard recalled:

> Gasoline poured out into Dad's eyes, and he couldn't see a thing. I grabbed his hand and walked him over to where there was an outdoor water faucet and got him down on the ground. I told him to hold his nose and then turned the water on and pushed

his eyes open so the water could run across his face and his eyes. It took some time, but his vision finally cleared. On that occasion my dad said how grateful he was that he hadn't been up there alone.[7]

Grandfather Ballard occasionally visited the family at the Lambs Canyon cabin. He built a kiva, an Indian ceremonial structure, back amongst the trees and took his grandchildren there and told them stories. After his grandfather told stories, Russell recalled, he took sticky pine pitch from a tree, chewed it into a kind of white-colored gum, and shared pieces with the children. President Ballard mused, "These are wonderful memories of a loving, caring grandfather."[8]

On Russell's eighth birthday, Grandfather Ballard took him to the Rialto Theater in downtown Salt Lake City to see a Walt Disney cartoon featuring Mickey Mouse and Donald Duck. "As soon as the lights went off, Grandfather fell fast asleep," said Russell years later. He remembered feeling "a little embarrassed because he was sleeping quite noisily. I couldn't understand how anybody could sleep through a Walt Disney movie. I watched the show through, and it started the second time. I finally had to wake him up and tell him that the movie was over."[9]

Decades later, the exact same thing happened to Russell when he was a General Authority himself. "I recall coming home from a conference assignment and listening to my children as they lobbied to go see *Star Wars* at the Center Theatre in Salt Lake City," he said. "I thought that would be fine and was assured it was a good movie. We went to the movie, the lights went off, and I fell fast asleep. My children still wonder how it is possible that Dad could sleep through *Star Wars*. Now I can tell you that it is an occupational hazard when you're a General Authority. Whenever the lights go off, he will fall fast asleep. I didn't understand that when I was eight, but I understand it now because a Grandfather made a precious memory."[10]

At age eight, Russell was old enough to join the neighborhood's very own Butler Avenue Bulldogs football team. Occasionally, the Bulldogs would attend University of Utah football practices, longing for the day when they too might wear the red-and-white uniforms.

More importantly, however, Russell was old enough to be baptized. Wanting her son to have a successful interview with the bishop, Geraldine coached Russell on questions his Church leader might ask. Russell listened with real intent to her answers. To say that he was well prepared for his interview is an understatement. "I passed with flying colors," President Ballard recalled.[11] All the questions asked of him were the same questions his mother had prepared him to answer.

On October 31, 1936, M. Russell Ballard was baptized by his great-uncle John Bowman in the font of the Salt Lake Tabernacle on Temple Square. He was confirmed a member of The Church of Jesus Christ of Latter-day Saints by his grandfather Ballard.

As Russell grew in stature, his father grew in reputation. Melvin became one of the most successful Nash Motor distributors in the nation. His Ballard Motor Company was awarded the "Nash 10 Point Award," a recognition from the Nash Motor Company that customers at Ballard Motors could expect "the finest service available anywhere."[12]

The Nash slogan, "Give the customer more than he has paid for," fit Melvin's marketing approach. The Nash cars lived up to the slogan with innovations in the straight-eight engine, twin spark plugs, and nine crankshaft bearings. With mid- to low-priced cars that offered four-wheel brakes, Nash was such a success among Utah consumers that "month after month all the cars that could be produced were sold before they left the factory floor."[13]

But all of that success came at a price: Melvin was spending more and more time at work, and less and less time at home with his family. So, despite his busy schedule as a General Authority, Grandfather Ballard looked for opportunities to spend time with his grandchildren. On one occasion, Grandfather Ballard took Russell and his cousin Barbara to a circus. President Ballard recalled, "Grandfather had a bag of peanuts. He would take a peanut in the shell and break it in half, giving one half to each of us. Then he would eat a full one and begin the process again until the peanuts were gone."[14]

Russell was ten when his beloved grandfather drove his car from New York to Salt Lake City after preaching the gospel throughout the eastern United States. "When he came into the driveway of his home at 80 North Wolcott, he collapsed," recalled President Ballard. "He was rushed to the LDS Hospital, where he was found to have acute leukemia. He never came out of the hospital. He went in and out of a coma. As I have had it told to me by my father, who was there, Grandfather pushed himself up in bed, looked into his hospital room as though he were addressing a congregation or a group, and said clearly, 'And above all else, brethren, let us think straight.'" The statement "Let Us Think Straight" has become President Ballard's personal motto. A plaque with the saying sits in his office. "I don't go into my office any day of the week that I don't see those words, and I find that they help me a great deal," he said.[15]

Russell was at the mortuary for the family prayer and took the opportunity to kiss his grandfather goodbye. This was the first time that Russell saw his father weep. The Salt Lake Tabernacle and the Assembly Hall were filled to overflowing for the funeral. Several hundred people stood on the temple grounds listening to the funeral services over the loudspeaker.

"For some reason, it had never occurred to me that my grandfather Ballard meant anything to anyone else," President Ballard recalled. "He had always just been Grandpa to me. But at his funeral, I saw thousands of people to whom he was obviously someone very special and important. That was a revelation to me, and the first step for me on the road to understanding what it meant to be an Apostle of the Lord Jesus Christ."[16]

Following his grandfather's death, Russell became very close to his grandmother Ballard, who called him "Bussy." Asked where that nickname came from, President Ballard smiled and shrugged his shoulders. "I never thought to ask her," he said, almost apologetically. "That was just her name for me, and I never questioned it." Grandmother Ballard was a woman of great faith and commitment to the Lord, and she had a powerful influence on shaping Russell's desire to know more about the gospel and the apostolic ministry of his grandfather.

Russell also learned the way all young people learn: through trial and error. One time, on a vacation to San Francisco, the family stopped at Wendover, Nevada, to put gasoline in the car and pick up something to eat. While his parents were taking care of those things, young Russell wandered around the store at which they had stopped, and he noticed a row of slot machines in one area of the store. He watched as people put money into the slot machines—and occasionally took money out of them. It looked kind of interesting and fun, especially when the numbers lined up on the machine and the lights flashed and the bells rang and money came trickling out. So he took a dime out of his pocket, put it in a slot machine, and pulled the handle. To his utter delight, there was an explosion of light and sound as dimes came flying out of the machine. Russell was thrilled until the manager of the store ran breathlessly toward him, exclaiming, "You can't do that! You're too young!"[17] Although the manager told him he could keep the dimes, they weren't worth the stern lecture he received from his parents. That was his first and last experience with slot machines—and, in fact, with gambling of any kind.

Another stern lecture came from Miss McCoy, the principal of Wasatch Grade School. But this lecture wasn't about the evils of gambling; it was about the fistfight Russell had gotten himself into. "To tell the truth, I don't remember what the fight was about, but evidently we were both pretty upset about something," President Ballard recalled years later, shaking his head slowly at the memory. "But I do remember how disappointed Miss McCoy was in me. That probably hurt more than any of the punches that were thrown. I wasn't the kind of boy who got into fights. And yet, there I was."[18] Instead of having the two boys sit there and rethink their actions, the principal named Russell and the other boy co-captains of the Junior Police Corps and handed them Junior Police bandelos to be worn each day. The boys were told to arrive early for school so they could assist the younger children as they crossed the street. At the end of the school day, their duty was the same. With energy redirected, the two boys forgot all about their fight and became fast friends. Years later, Elder Ballard set apart his friend as a mission president.

When Russell was ordained a deacon by a ward member, John Bjarneson, on March 16, 1941, there was a marked change in his behavior. His sister Ann recalled, "At some point Russ determined that he could not be at the cabin every Sunday. . . . I can remember thinking, 'Why isn't Russ here helping build; he should be doing this.' . . . I really did not understand that he needed to be in church fulfilling his Aaronic Priesthood responsibilities."[19]

When war broke out in Europe in 1939, it seemed so far away. The United States remained neutral, so life continued in Utah as it had been before. However, that changed on Sunday, December 7, 1941, when thirteen-year-old Russell returned home from priesthood meeting to learn from his mother that Pearl Harbor had been attacked by the Japanese Imperial Navy.

Suddenly, it seemed that his whole world was thrust into chaos.

World War II would be the deadliest conflict in human history, with millions of fatalities, strategic bombing, death by starvation and disease, and eventually the use of atomic bombs. The Ballards felt the effects of rationing and saw many family members and acquaintances head off to war—some of whom never returned home.

Though it was a frightening, formative time for teenaged Russell, life for his family at 1399 Butler Avenue was much the same as it had always been. The family supported the war effort in any way they

Russ with his sisters. Left to right, front row:
Ann, Chaunie; back row: Betty, Russ

could, participating in neighborhood scrap drives and rationing clothing, meat, and gasoline along with everyone else.

While his father was required to work long hours away from home keeping his business running during this challenging time, Russell took on extra duties around the house—including adding coal to the furnace and caring for the yard—and around the neighborhood. Those who were close to him could see the emergence of the energetic entrepreneurialism that dominated most of the rest of his life.

"There was money to be made by working on neighbors' yards," his sister Ann recalled. "I can remember him having jobs cutting lawns even when he was quite young. He was an entrepreneur from the beginning. I think it was just part of him and part of what he learned from Daddy."[20]

When Russell moved on to Bryant Junior High at 800 East and First South, he quickly made many friends and was involved in student government.[21] As is so often the case for young people, those friends became vitally important to him. Indeed, President Ballard acknowledges today that it was his peer group that kept him active and involved in church. He wanted to be in church on Sunday because his friends were there. He participated in most of the Aaronic Priesthood activities in the University Ward and attended a few Scout camps largely because his friends did. Plus, it helped that he really liked his youth leaders. When the secretary of the ward's Aaronic Priesthood program, Brother Stewart, suddenly died from a heart attack, Russell remembers that he had "the impression that I ought to do something nice" for the man's widow:

> I didn't know what I could do, but I went to her home to visit her. . . . As I walked onto her front porch, I noticed that the paint was all chipped and peeling off. It occurred to me that somebody ought to paint the porch for her. I went back to my father and said, "Will you buy the paint if I paint the porch?" He was glad to do it. I went down and painted her porch. . . . She never forgot that I had painted her porch, and I never forgot what a great pleasure that was for me.[22]

One of the youth leaders Russell especially liked was John L. Firmage. Brother Firmage drove a Fleetwood Cadillac and liked to fill his car with Aaronic Priesthood boys and take them down to Welfare Square to nail together shipping crates and storage boxes. When they finished, Brother Firmage drove them to Farr's Ice Cream Parlor and bought the boys all the ice cream they could eat. "And I don't mind telling you, I could eat a *lot* of ice cream back then," President Ballard said years later. For the rest of his life, going to get ice cream—or, in his later years, frozen yogurt—remained the ultimate reward for a job well done and the perfect way to celebrate friendship.

Ice cream and fun times helped Russell maintain a slight sense of normalcy in the face of the pall cast over the entire world by the horror and devastation of war. It was a constant presence, something that kept people constantly on edge, even those who lived in the relative security of the mountains of Utah. This was especially true after his father was required to register for the military draft at age forty-five. At first Melvin thought it was a mistake, or maybe a joke someone was playing on him. The war effort couldn't be going so badly as to require calling up a battalion of middle-aged used-car salesmen—could it? But there it was, in the harsh black-and-white of a letter from the War Department: the tentacles of World War II had now reached him.

Once he had registered with the Selective Service System, the possibility of being drafted and sent off to fight in Europe or in the islands of the South Pacific weighed heavily on Melvin. It wasn't that he was afraid, nor was he unwilling to do his patriotic duty to his country. But he had invested so much of himself—his time, his talents, and his undivided attention—on building and maintaining his business that it was difficult to imagine himself doing anything else for any period of time.

"He was an absolutely brilliant man," President Ballard said of his father. "Probably as good a businessman as I've ever been acquainted with in my life."[23] Melvin was admired for his deep sense of responsibility to his employees and for adding all the benefits to his employees' paychecks offered by the Utah Automobile Dealer Association, an association he organized and of which he served as president for many years. Eventually he expanded his business horizons to include real-estate ventures and property management, subdividing large acreage into individual lots in the Salt Lake area. Of him, one man wrote to President Ballard, "It is no wonder you are such a mover; your dad sure was. He was really active in a lot of areas."[24]

It was Melvin's fondest hope that Russell would one day join him in the automotive business, which was why Melvin had him work at the Ballard Motor Company on Saturdays and after school most days during his high school years. Russell worked in the parts department, on the grease rack, sanding fenders in the paint shop, and cleaning the building. Of the relationship between father and son, President James E. Faust, Second Counselor in the First Presidency, said, "Russ had the blessing and privilege of working side by side with his father day after day. I think, business-wise, his father was one of his heroes."[25]

Russell's involvement with his father's dealership was always a positive thing in his young life, and it helped to shape many of his future choices. Of course, there was that one time when his comfort and familiarity with his father's cars did not work out in his favor.

"I had been driving cars all around the dealership since I was twelve and could barely see over the steering wheel," President Ballard recalled years later. "So it didn't seem all that unusual when Mother asked me to drive her downtown. I never gave it a second thought. But I was only fourteen at the time, and the police officer who pulled me over thought that was inappropriate."

So did Judge Rulon Clark, who fined Russell's mother for allowing her fourteen-year-old son to drive.[26]

Thankfully, young Russell learned to think things through a little more quickly and a lot more carefully as he got older. Just before he started high school, he was with his family at the cabin in Lambs Canyon. As Melvin was cooking dinner over a hot coal stove, he began to experience the faintness, palpitations, and hallucinations of heat prostration. Grandmother Ballard repeatedly begged Russell to "Administer to him! Administer to him!" At age fifteen, Russell didn't hold the Melchizedek Priesthood, but his brother-in-law, Sterling M. Jensen, was there, and he was a returned missionary even though he had not been active in the Church for years. While everyone else seemed unsure of what to do, Russell took command of the situation.

"Place your hands on Dad's head," he told Sterling. "We'll use your priesthood, and I'll pray."

Russell pled with the Lord to bless his father. After the prayer, his father was taken to the car. Even though Russell was still not old enough to have a driver's license, he drove the car down the narrow canyon to the home of Dr. Eliot Snow, a distinguished Salt Lake physician and surgeon. Upon seeing Melvin's condition, the doctor sent Russell speeding to the nearest hospital. As it turned out, his father was fine once he received the needed medical attention.

By the time Russell began attending East High School, he was widely known and respected among his peers. His sister Ann said he was popular because he was "able to work with people. He was able to negotiate. I think he is a master negotiator. He had that trait from the beginning."[27]

President Ballard has many fond memories of high school and of his friends.[28] One was trying out for the football team. "That didn't last long," he said. "Pretty soon I figured out that I was neither fast enough nor big enough and, if I continued, I would soon be dead."[29] Church basketball, a formal basketball league started in 1908, was much more to his liking.

And then there was the day in chemistry class when he and his lab partner mixed ingredients in a test tube:

> My lab partner and I were in the laboratory and we thought we were following instructions from the teacher. He was having us mix some ingredients, and we thought we were doing the right thing. Then at the appropriate time he asked us to light the ingredients in the test tube and they would burn. And everybody's burned except ours. Ours exploded and the bottom end of the test tube was in one of those racks and it shot across the laboratory into the wall. I can still see Mr. Howells running down to us with his hands in the air, awfully upset, saying, "Boys, boys, what have you

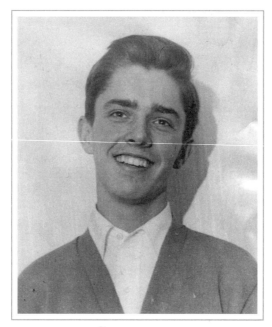

Russ as a teenager

done?" To this day, I don't know what we put into our test tube that was any different from all the rest of the kids in that class.[30]

It turned out he had much better aptitude for early-morning seminary, which started at 6:30 a.m. He really enjoyed studying the scriptures. Plus, nothing ever exploded in seminary.

One thing that surprised him a little was how much he loved singing in the a cappella choir, a musical group that performed without instrumental accompaniment.

"Lyle Bradford was the choir leader," President Ballard remembered. "I wasn't the best singer, but I was pretty good at keeping track of the music. I think they kept me in the choir because I was organized and could keep track of the music. We sang all over the place. We went to many different religious congregations in Salt Lake City in those days. And I made a lot of wonderful friends singing in the a cappella choir." One of the songs they sang was the American spiritual "Were

You There When They Crucified My Lord?" President Ballard recalled, "That song always brought tears to my eyes."[31]

In addition to his high school friends, Russell enjoyed the mentoring friendship of a great Aaronic Priesthood adviser: G. Homer Durham, a professor at the University of Utah, the first department chair of the university's political science department, and later a General Authority. "Homer came into my life at a very critical and important time," President Ballard said. "I was going through my teenage years, and while I didn't experience any major difficulties, it was a time in my life that I needed a special friend."[32] Of Russell, Homer said, "In the Aaronic Priesthood in the University Ward, his bright, shining countenance and handsome bearing, carried with the dignity of his ancestry, was already evident."[33]

Just before the start of his junior year, news came that sent most of the world into joyous celebration: the war was over. Germany surrendered to the Allied forces in May 1945, and then Japan surrendered three months later, in August 1945. "I remember people dancing in the streets, flags flying, parades—it was a grand moment," President Ballard said nearly seventy-five years later. "Both my father and I were greatly relieved that we weren't going to be drafted. And my friends and I talked about how, with the end of the war, more of us would have the opportunity to go on missions."[34] (The Church had agreed in 1942 not to call young men of draft age on missions.)

Russell was ordained a priest by Elder Joseph F. Merrill, an Apostle, on December 30, 1945, at age seventeen, the practice at the time. The next year was his senior year at East High, and he made the most of it. Russell didn't serve in every leadership position at the school, but just about. He was an officer in the a cappella choir; president of the East High Boosters Club, which supported students, faculty, and staff; a member of the Board of Control, a group of students who advised the school principal; a participant in student government; and president of the East High Latter-day Saint seminary.

To celebrate graduation, Russell helped plan a Dutch-oven cook-out in the canyon for his class. He also helped plan a banquet at the Newhouse Hotel, a twelve-story hotel built in 1912 on the southwest corner of 400 South and Main Street, to honor graduating seniors. Russell was among those being honored and was given a "special commendation" for leadership by the East High principal, Frank S. Allen. The guest speaker at their graduation was Elder Adam S. Bennion of the Quorum of the Twelve Apostles. "I do not remember the things that Elder Bennion said to us," said President Ballard, "but I do recall the wonderful spirit that was in attendance as he talked to the graduating seniors" of East High in 1946.[35]

With high school behind him and a bright future ahead, Russell's options seemed limitless. The University of Utah was practically in his neighborhood, and Russell enjoyed working with his father at the Ballard Motor Company. He could attend the university and work part-time for his father as a salesman. It seemed all laid out for him.

At the University of Utah, Russell pledged the Sigma Chi fraternity.[36] Founded in 1855 at Miami University in Ohio, Sigma Chi was one of the most prestigious and popular fraternities at the University of Utah.

As pledges, Russell and the other incoming freshmen were told to replant the front lawn at the fraternity house, located at 1395 East 100 South. The pledges reasoned the best way to ensure the lawn was up to standard was to take out all the old grass and lay down new sod. So, after talking about the project, they borrowed a truck from Russell's father and drove to Fairmont Park in Sugar House, where they cut out the squares of lawn needed for replanting. It was public property, they reasoned, and there was so much grass there. They were sure it would be okay.

They were wrong.

The next day, a police sergeant showed up at the Sigma Chi fraternity house. "That's a beautiful new lawn you have," he said, eyeing the newly sodded yard outside. Then he asked a direct question: "Did you steal that lawn from Fairmont Park?"

Suddenly the pledges were less certain of the decision that had seemed so clear the previous evening. They had never really thought of it as "stealing" until that moment. Sheepishly, they confessed that they had indeed "borrowed" the sod from the park. The police sergeant gruffly tasked the pledges with replanting the lawn in the park. Once they were finished, all was forgiven—except by their fraternity brothers, who still insisted that the lawn at the fraternity house be replanted.

Russell eventually passed the pledge requirements and was welcomed into Sigma Chi as a full-fledged fraternity member. He spent time with his fraternity brothers laughing, participating in school activities, and sometimes studying. It was all fun and part of being a young man in school at this time.

But something was missing in Russell's life—something important. And Russell knew it.

CHAPTER THREE

A MISSION TO ENGLAND

On November 30, 1947, Brother G. Homer Durham conferred upon Russell the Melchizedek Priesthood and ordained him to the office of elder. Russell was nineteen years old. He remembered fondly, "To have Homer be willing to ordain me an elder has always been a very special and choice experience in my life."[1] Suddenly that clear path of work and school that was laid out before him when he graduated from high school was obscured by a growing desire to serve a mission.

A huge part of that growth can be attributed to Russell's involvement in the Sigma Chi fraternity. "Going on a mission was always in the back of my mind as something I would like to do," he said. "But it became front of mind at Sigma Chi. There were about twenty of us who joined the fraternity that year, and we all decided that we were going on missions.

"After our missions, we organized a small gospel study group together, which met for another sixty years. We called it the Latter-day Sigs, and it became this really important, positive peer influence on all of us. The more time we spent together, the more committed all of us were to serving in the Church."[2]

Interestingly, a mission wasn't something that Russell really talked about with his parents. In fact, as he was meeting with his University Ward bishop, Lynn Richard, to fill out his mission papers, his parents were attending a Nash automobile dealers' convention in Chicago. His papers were filled out, submitted, and expedited while his parents were out of town so he could surprise them. Within two weeks of submission, Russell received a call to serve in the British Mission—the mission of his great-grandfathers Joseph F. Smith and Henry Ballard and his grandfather Hyrum Mack Smith. Later, Joseph F. and Hyrum Mack returned with their wives to the British Isles to serve as presidents of the mission.

When his parents returned home from the business trip in Chicago, Russell surprised them with an announcement: "I've been called to serve a mission in Great Britain!" His parents were startled, but fully supportive of the decision their son had made to serve a mission that would take him to the ancestral homeland of the Smiths, Bowmans, and Ballards.

A few days before Russell's missionary farewell, Church President George Albert Smith called Melvin. "I saw your father [Elder Melvin J. Ballard, who had died in 1939] in the dreams of the night; and he seemed to be disturbed about something," President Smith said. "I'm calling to ask if everybody is all right in your family." Melvin assured President Smith that his family was well and thanked him for his concern. President Smith then asked, "Is there anything at all that your father might be concerned about?" To this Melvin replied, "Well, the only thing that's happening is my son is going on a mission."[3] President Smith asked when and where the farewell would be held.

The missionary farewell for Elder M. Russell Ballard was held on Sunday, April 11, 1948, in the University Ward building in Salt Lake City. "You can imagine how surprised I was when President Smith came to my farewell and sat by me on the stand," he said.[4] President Smith presided and spoke at the farewell. Melvin Ballard was in the congregation—the first time Russell remembered his father ever attending a church meeting with him. Also in attendance was Elder Harold B. Lee of the Quorum of the Twelve, who had received a phone call from Grandmother Ballard requesting that he attend the farewell. Elder Lee wrote in his journal, "On the way home from [the] Springville Stake Conference yesterday I stopped at the University Ward where I went to the missionary farewell at the request of Sister Melvin J. Ballard, for her grandson, Melvin Russell Ballard. The family apparently were pleased that I went."[5] Elder Lee, who had enjoyed a long association with Elder Melvin J. Ballard in the great work of Church welfare in its early days, confided in the Ballard family that of all the men he knew, he most wanted to be like Melvin J. Ballard.

Of the presence of these venerable Church leaders at his farewell, Russell wrote:

> I was smart enough to realize that President George Albert Smith and Elder Harold B. Lee were not there because of M. Russell Ballard. They were there because of their deep love and affection for Melvin J. Ballard, my grandfather. That was an overwhelming tribute to Grandfather; but it was a humbling experience for me to have the President of the Church and a member of the Council of the Twelve come to see me off on my mission to England.[6]

As for the farewell itself, Russell noted, "I know that the spirit of the Lord was there, and also the spirit of my grandfathers. I learned that missionary work is profoundly important to our leaders on both sides of the veil. I was never so humble or thankful for my many blessings as I was that night."[7] He later wrote:

> At the end of the meeting, the prophet embraced me, and wished me well. I was touched by his kindness. Several months later I wrote to President Smith and among other things said, a bit brashly perhaps, "When you see my grandfathers, tell them

I'm doing the best I can." In reading President Smith's response I learned to expect the unexpected from the men the Lord has called to preside over His Church. He wrote: "I'll tell them—if I see them before you do." I wasn't exactly sure what he meant by that, so I was very careful to follow the mission rules.[8]

Russell was set apart for his mission by Elder Oscar A. Kirkham of the First Council of the Seventy (a group of seven general-level leaders that preceded the organization of the First Quorum of the Seventy under the direction of President Spencer W. Kimball in 1975). The words pronounced by Elder Kirkham were familiar to Russell, for many were written in his short but revelatory patriarchal blessing. Of the promises spoken by Elder Kirkham, Russell wrote, "I have the power blessed upon me to do a good work if I will remain righteous."[9]

Young Elder Ballard entered the mission home in Salt Lake City on Monday, April 12, 1948, just one day after his farewell. He resided with other newly called missionaries in Barrett Hall on the campus of the LDS Business College, located where the Church Office Building stands today. While there, he received instruction and encouragement from such apostolic leaders as Elders Joseph F. Merrill, Stephen L Richards, Harold B. Lee, Spencer W. Kimball, and Ezra Taft Benson.

After nine days of instruction, Elder Ballard and other missionaries assigned to Great Britain started their journey to England at the Salt Lake City Union Pacific Depot on the western edge of downtown Salt Lake City. At the station, Elder Ballard bid goodbye to his parents. "It was hard to kiss Mom and Dad goodbye," he wrote, "but they knew that I was embarking on a great experience."[10] He also bid farewell to several friends who had come to the station. The missionaries then boarded the train and stood on the caboose platform waving goodbye as the train roared out of sight.

Elder Ballard and his missionary companions spent three days on the train from Salt Lake City to New York. When the train stopped in New York City, the missionaries were conveyed to a hotel. The next day they went to the New York Harbor where they boarded the RMS *Queen Elizabeth,* the largest luxury passenger liner in the world at that time.[11] The six elders did not enjoy much luxury aboard ship, however. They shared one cabin for the five-day voyage from New York to Southampton. Although the voyage was mostly smooth sailing, the occasional swells and rough seas caused problems for all the elders except Elder Ballard and Elder Hugh West.[12]

Spending a Sunday on the high seas meant holding a worship service for the missionaries. Elder West recorded:

> We conducted our first Sunday services (May 2, 1948) as official missionaries. There were six missionaries in attendance. It being fast Sunday, we held a small testimonial meeting in which each elder bore his testimony. It was a very humble meeting and I believe the spirit of the Lord was with us. . . . Elder Russ Ballard took charge of this meeting. I was impressed with the ease with which he handled the group.[13]

The *Queen Elizabeth* docked at the port of Southampton at 10:30 p.m. on May 4, 1948. All passengers remained aboard ship until 10 a.m. the next day.

After disembarking, the missionaries traveled eighty miles northeast from Southampton to the British Mission headquarters, located at 149 Nightingale Lane in the heart of London. There they met their mission president, Selvoy J. Boyer, and his wife, Gladys. The Boyers were farmers from Springville, Utah.

President Boyer had the difficult task of reopening the British Mission following the end of World War II. English branches, like other European Church units, had been left without instruction and guidance during the war years. Naturally, without regular and direct contact from Church leaders in Salt Lake City, some had drifted from approved policies, procedures, and doctrine.

The most amazing aspect of the British branches was that they had

Young Elder Ballard around the time of his mission call

survived at all, considering the impact of total war in Europe. There had been no full-time missionaries since 1939. Many local priesthood holders had been sent to war, with some being killed and wounded and others becoming prisoners of war. The Church looked very different following the war than it had looked in the 1930s.

President Boyer needed missionaries—even the newly arriving missionaries—to be ready to work and prepared to lead the fledgling branches.

On their very first day in London, President Boyer expected the missionaries to preach the gospel of Jesus Christ. This experience took place where missionaries had proclaimed the gospel since the introduction of the message to that great land in the late 1830s: Hyde Park.

The missionaries were taken to Hyde Park Corner. Also called Speakers' Corner, the area had been established as a point of free speech and debate since 1872.

At this historic site, the young Elder Ballard began his preaching and teaching ministry.

Elder Ballard remembered the occasion:

After we had met with the president for a little while, I heard him say, "Let's take them to Hyde Park." We knew about street meetings. We had heard about that in the mission home. Never having participated in one and not knowing quite how a street meeting operated, we headed for Hyde Park. There were 15 missionaries. . . . I was standing next to President Boyer when he said, "We will only have time to hear from two of them." That gave me a great sense of confidence, recognizing that very likely I would not be one of the two. Then my name was called to be the second speaker, and I stepped up to the little stand there in Hyde Park to preach my first sermon.

As I started for the stand, President Boyer took hold of my arm. I will never forget what he said: "Teach the gospel." That was a new thought. I knew I was a missionary, set apart, but the reality of having to teach the gospel in that kind of a circumstance was somewhat frightening. I quickly got into my mind that I would teach the principle of baptism. And I said everything I knew about baptism in about forty-five seconds. My discourse was rather short and not very effective. As I came back off the stand, I thought to myself: "That will never happen to me again. I have a lot of work to do. I have a lot of learning to do. I have a lot of preparation to do in order to accomplish the purpose for which Heavenly Father has sent me to England."[14]

First Area

President Boyer assigned Elder Ballard to serve with Elder Keith E. Tibbitts, a hardworking missionary from Idaho Falls, Idaho.[15] They were to labor in Nottingham, a bustling city 128 miles north of London. At that time Nottingham was a tourist destination known for its lacemaking and bicycle industries. "As a boy I was a big fan of the 1938 Hollywood movie *The Adventures of Robin Hood,* with Errol Flynn and Olivia de Havilland," Elder Ballard recalled.

"I remember the first thing that happened when we came into

Nottingham," Elder Ballard said. "We put down our luggage, went to the Nottingham market square, and there we held a street meeting. We sang . . . we did the best we could. We gathered a little crowd about us. My sermon lasted about two minutes."[16]

On his first day of tracting door-to-door with Elder Tibbitts, Elder Ballard wrote, "I found myself becoming quite confused about things and people. I had to turn to God for the comfort and understanding that I needed."[17] Elder Tibbitts insisted that they keep tracting no matter the weather. This led Elder Ballard to wonder whether his companion had lost part of his sanity, but he soon found that in the most inclement weather people opened their doors and invited the missionaries to come in. After a week of knocking on doors in Nottingham, Elder Ballard wrote, "I know that the secret to our work is to forget ourselves and work as an instrument of God."[18]

The description in the following journal entry soon became the norm: "Tracting 6 hours, street meetings, and cottage meetings became the routine of each day with occasional branch meetings thrown in. We are becoming more and more convinced that our Father in Heaven must guide us to His children that He wants to come into His Church."[19]

Tracting, street meetings, and cottage meetings were staples of missionary work in England at the time. Street meetings were held with the missionaries standing on a busy street corner or market square singing hymns and preaching sermons. As people stopped to listen, the missionaries talked with them and invited them to attend regular church meetings or made appointments to teach them in their homes.

A cottage meeting consisted of a simple gospel lesson taught by the missionaries for a small group of individuals, often in an informal setting such as a member's or investigator's home.

In these settings, Elder Ballard began developing the skills that would become so important to him in his worldwide ministry as a General Authority.

On Sunday afternoon, May 16, 1948, Elder Ballard wrote: "I spent

Elder Ballard preaching at a street meeting in Nottingham Square, May 1949

the afternoon writing a letter to my folks. I said the things that I always wanted to say to my wonderful family. I had my first case of homesickness."[20] Everything about Nottingham was a far cry from his home in Salt Lake City.

Rationing of food, which had begun during World War II, continued in Britain following the end of the war in May 1945. Bread was the only food item readily available for purchase. Fresh produce was hard to find except for Brussels sprouts. Although not native to the British Isles, they were introduced in the nineteenth century and became popular at Christmas. However, because of the excellent climate condition, Brussels sprouts were popular and available in England before, during, and after the war.

President Ballard remembered, "Everywhere we went, these kind people offered what they had—and what they had were Brussels sprouts!" He continued, "I ate so many Brussels sprouts during my mission, I lost a taste for them. At ninety-two years of age, I still skip when the Brussels sprouts are passed around the dinner table!"[21]

Elder Ballard wrote short journal entries of his inconveniences with the continued rationing in the British Isles but detailed accounts of his missionary experiences, such as the entry of May 20, 1948:

> I had the most interesting experience that I have had since I arrived in the mission field today. The same man who was yesterday's heckler came back to the Nottingham Square with his Book of Mormon. He caused a great deal of trouble in our meeting and even held one of his own. He stated that the Mormons were evil devils and all the things that he could think of. After 1 hour and 45 minutes, he let us have our turn again. We answered in a friendly way and the crowd pulled for us, each and every one of them were on our side before we left. I know that it was the Spirit of the Lord. I know that we are the true church and that the Lord will defend us if we work for Him in righteousness. A perfect day![22]

During the month of May, Elder Ballard received a letter from his great-uncle John F. Bowman, a patriarch in Salt Lake City and the man who baptized him. The letter was filled with sage advice:

> Now you have the opportunity and responsibility again of proving your love for God, your loyalty and fidelity to our Lord and Savior Jesus Christ and His glorious cause and your love for your fellowmen in the greatest calling and most important and honorable one that can come to a young man, or to any one, for that matter. The chapters you will write in your book of life during the next two years will be the most glorious ones you will have the opportunity to write in many a moon, and you will do it if you will have no other objective than to do your utmost, in

humility and for the glory of God and the advancement of His work and the salvation of His children.

So my dear nephew, live up to the full measure of your glorious responsibility and you will find joy and satisfaction the like of which you didn't believe could be found in this confused world, and will lay a foundation from which you will never be moved.[23]

Elder Ballard did live up to his "glorious responsibility." When a speaker failed to attend sacrament meeting, Elder Ballard walked to the front of the congregation, opened the hymnal to "I Know That My Redeemer Lives," and spoke for twenty minutes about what the hymn meant to him and about the apostolic calling of his grandfathers, Hyrum Mack Smith and Melvin J. Ballard. Of that particular sacrament talk, Elder Ballard wrote, "I know the spirit of the Lord was with me and I know that my grandpa was close by."[24]

Confident of the Lord's Spirit guiding him and of the closeness of his apostolic progenitors, Elder Ballard thrust himself even more into his missionary labors. He quickened his pace to such an extent that on July 10, 1948, he was able to write:

> We retired at 11:00 and we were two tired Elders. We finished a hard week with 87 hours. We held 8 street meetings, 4 cottage meetings, 32 hours tracting, 12 hours individual study, 5 hours class study, 6 hours branch meetings, 5 hours travel, and 11 hours activity. We worked hard this week, but it actually is a very ordinary week since I have been in the field. I hope I can keep up this pace clear through my mission.[25]

A New Assignment

Sixteen days following that journal entry, Elder Ballard learned that he was being transferred to Hucknall, a market town nestled in the Trent Valley just seven miles northwest of Nottingham. The town was certainly not as imposing as Nottingham but was known for its knitting, coal mining, market square, and the St. Mary Magdalene parish church.

Elder Ballard was assigned to labor with Elder Thacker, a fun-loving, hardworking missionary. Just as their missionary labors were beginning, Elder Ballard received a letter from Elder Harold B. Lee, dated July 28, 1948:

> Your grandfather, through his noble ministry, endeared the name of *Ballard* to the membership of this Church. For a young man you have made a record worthy of his name and I feel confident that if you will continue the program you are now following as a missionary and be humble and prayerful you will grow and develop in the work of the Lord in a way that will delight the heart of not only your grandfather and your loved ones here but also your Heavenly Father whose son you are.[26]

The encouragement and assurance of the Lord's love from such great men as the patriarch, Brother Bowman, and Elder Lee served as an anchor for Elder Ballard as he ventured into the market square to share his testimony in word and in song. He was successful in his preaching, as were other missionaries in the British Isles. It is little wonder that President Boyer wrote in the *Millennial Star*, "Since the close of the late war [World War II], fully organized branches in Britain have increased in number from twenty-nine to seventy-one."[27]

As the work blossomed in the Hucknall countryside, Elder Ballard and Elder Thacker purchased a tandem bike. It was an unusual purchase—most missionaries just walked or took public transportation from place to place. But they believed that with a bike they could arrive faster to do more of the Lord's work. The first day they "rode it in a cloud burst for 4 miles. We were soaking wet, but we saved 5 pence (bus fare) so it was worth it."[28] Two days later they crashed the tandem into rosebushes.[29] The next day they parked the tandem and spoke in the market square. Elder Ballard wrote, "When we were singing for

Elders Ballard (left) and Thacker on their tandem bike

our first street meeting, a dog came up in front of us and started to howl. I started to laugh and so we went on to the speaking part of the meeting."[30]

These adventures and more were captured in verse:

"Two Mormon Elders"
—President Ted Wright of the Hucknall Branch

> *Did I ever tell the story*
> *Which now I'm telling you*
> *About two Mormon Elders*
> *Who came from Utah, too.*
>
> *One was dark and handsome,*
> *One was not a slacker,*
> *One was known as Ballard,*
> *And the other one was Thacker.*

To get around the country
They both disdained to walk,
So they bought themselves a tandem,
At speed, they were the talk.

Till a fellow in an auto
From the driving seat did hop
Cause they passed him doing fifty
And he thought his car had stopped.

At singing on the market
They really did do well,
And the people here in Hucknall
Said the harmony was swell.

Till a certain mongrel puppy
Looking lost and heavy jowled
Sat up upon its haunches
And howled and howled and howled.

. . .

Now, all you folks who live here
Where dogs can run so free,
When they litter up your doorstep
Now please don't make them flee.

And if you are so tempted
To give the dog a whacker,
Be sure it's not the dog
That's loved by Ballard and by Thacker.

Not everything was that merry for the young elders in Hucknall. On August 26, 1948, Elder Ballard wrote, "The roughest day tracting I have had since I came to the field. We had five doors slammed in succession, and I sure felt as if the world had come to an end."[31] It was not until two weeks later, on September 7, that he wrote:

We can now see some of the fruits of our labors. Today a gentleman came up to us and said, "Are you two Mormon elders?" We answered him, "Yes." He took one of our tracts and stated that he would contact the elders in Nottingham. He was a man who was really looking for the truth. He knew that none of the churches in England were the true church. He wanted to know about the LDS Church and the Book of Mormon.[32]

On another occasion, Elder Ballard and his companion were walking through the famous hedgerows in Hucknall. Elder Ballard had the distinct impression to go and visit Sister Hayes. "It was late," he said of the impression, "and we decided it was probably inappropriate to go visiting right then." So, first thing in the morning he and his companion knocked on the door of the Hayes home. Sister Hayes, with tears in her eyes, greeted them and said, "Elders, thank you for coming. I have been praying all night that you would come." She asked Elder Ballard and his companion to bless her daughter Kathleen, who was suffering from a high fever. "We did and immediately her fever broke," Elder Ballard said.[33]

And so, the experiences of his mission changed from day to day. Whether tracting in the rain, holding street meetings or cottage meetings, suffering from stomachaches, teaching Relief Society, or listening to a man rant and rave about nothing, Elder Ballard knew that these were experiences he would never have known if he had not chosen to serve a mission.

District President of the Nottingham District

President Boyer watched the young elder from Salt Lake City carefully and was impressed with Elder Ballard's dedication to the work. On February 25, 1949, President Boyer wrote to him:

This is to notify you that you have been appointed to preside over the Nottingham District in the British Mission of The Church of Jesus Christ of Latter-day Saints.

It is your duty to preach the Gospel, to administer the ordinances thereof that pertain to your holy calling as occasion may require, and to preside over all the interests of the work of the Lord within your jurisdiction, subject to the counsel and direction of the President of the Mission. . . .

It is your prime responsibility to see that the Elders under your direction attend faithfully to their duties. Visit each pair of Elders monthly or more often if felt necessary. . . . Finally, dear Brother, be humble, be vigilant and faithful in your labors, praying always that the Holy Spirit and the power of the Priesthood may attend your ministrations. Thus will the hearts of the people be open to receive your counsels and to supply your wants, and you will be made a Minister of Eternal life unto them.

Of his new assignment, Elder Ballard wrote, "I received the shock of my life today when President Selvoy J. Boyer made me District President of the Nottingham District" with responsibility for thirty-two missionaries and the branches in the district.[34] However, it was not in the busyness of being a district president that Elder Ballard received a convincing testimony of the restored gospel of Jesus Christ. It was in a quiet moment:

It had been a long day, not discouraging, but exhausting, filled with meetings and ministering that were associated with my assignment as a district president in Nottingham. The sun was about to set on another hectic Sunday in 1949. I had just concluded a successful street meeting with the other missionaries in the Nottingham District, during which we shared our message with passersby on Nottingham Square.

As I strolled along the Trent [riverbank], weary and yet happy and satisfied in the work, an overwhelming feeling of peace and understanding came over me. It was at that precise moment in time that I came to know that Jesus Christ knew me, that He loved me, and that He directed our missionary efforts in England and throughout the world. Of course I'd always believed those things. They were part of the testimony I had shared just a couple of hours earlier. But somehow in that instant of what I realized was pure revelation, my belief turned into knowledge. I didn't see any visions and I didn't hear any voices, but I could not have known of Christ's reality and divinity any more intensely had He stood before me and called out my name.

I had impressed upon my soul the fact that the Prophet Joseph Smith went into the grove near his home in Palmyra, New York, and there knelt and supplicated our Heavenly Father, wanting to know which of all the churches was true. The Father and the Son really did appear unto him, and the Father spoke to him, saying, "Joseph, this is my Beloved Son. Hear Him." That the Savior of the world, our Redeemer, our Lord, our God, our very best friend, spoke to that young prophet on that occasion became a reality to me.[35]

Of that quiet moment, President Ballard said, "My entire life has been shaped by that sweet and tender missionary experience. From that day to the present, every significant decision I have made has been influenced by my knowledge of the Savior and of the reality of the restoration of His gospel."[36]

Shortly after this life-shaping experience, Elder Ballard received a letter from his father that contained the testimony Elder Melvin J. Ballard had shared with the First Presidency and the Quorum of the Twelve Apostles some three decades earlier, in January 1919, in the Salt Lake Temple.

During his mission Elder Ballard heard of this experience but was unfamiliar with the details of the story, so he had written home to ask his father for the details. This is what his father sent him:

I [Melvin J. Ballard] received a wonderful manifestation and impression which has never left me. I was carried to this place [the Salt Lake Temple]—into this room. I saw myself here with you. I was told there was another privilege that was to be mine; and I was led into a room where I was informed I was to meet someone. As I entered the room I saw, seated on a raised platform, the most glorious being I have ever conceived of, and was taken forward to be introduced to Him. As I approached He smiled, calling my name, and stretched out His hands toward me. If I live to be a million years old I shall never forget that smile. He put His arms around me and kissed me, and He took me into His bosom, and He blessed me until my whole being was thrilled. As He finished I fell at His feet, and there saw the marks of the nails; and as I kissed them, with deep joy swelling through my whole being, I felt that I was in heaven indeed. The feeling that came to my heart then was: Oh! If I could live worthy, though it would require four-score years, so that in the end when I have finished I could go into His presence and receive the feeling that I then had in His presence, I would give everything that I am and ever hope to be!

I know—as I know that I live—that He lives. That is my testimony. . . . I esteem it the highest honor that could be given to a man, to be a special witness of the Lord Jesus Christ.[37]

As Elder Ballard began to read of the sacred experience of his grandfather Ballard, he excused himself from his companion and went upstairs to the bedroom to be alone as he read the rest of this remarkable account. Following his reading, Elder Ballard sat on his bed and wept as the Holy Spirit enveloped him and he received an unmistakable witness that the testimony of his grandfather was true.

"Perhaps the greatest blessing of my mission is the personal witness I received of the Restored Gospel of Jesus Christ," he said later. "Those sweet whispered assurances, buried deep in my heart through the power of the Holy Ghost, have moved and motivated me from that day to this. The Spirit spoke and confirmed truth to my soul. For me, that has made all the difference."[38]

Still, there was missionary work to be done in the Nottingham District, and Elder Ballard struggled with the question of how to increase the number of baptisms in the area. The answer he was seeking came in a wonderfully unexpected way: a chain letter.

Most of the Sigma Chi fraternity brothers at the University of Utah were by then serving missions in various parts of the world. They kept in contact by a circulated chain letter talking about their respective missionary experiences. One of these fraternity brothers, Preston Adams, was serving in the Northwestern States Mission, and he told the other Sigma Chi brothers about the Anderson plan, a step-by-step approach for sharing the Book of Mormon and the Restoration with illustrations and dialogue.

The Anderson plan had been created by Elder Richard Lloyd Anderson, a young missionary serving in the Northwestern States Mission at the time. After his mission president adopted it, the mission became the top-baptizing mission in the world.

The British Mission, like most of the other missions in the Church, did not have an organized plan for teaching or for contacting new people to teach. Most of Elder Ballard's time in Nottingham and Hucknall had been spent knocking on doors and handing out pamphlets on the Apostasy, the Restoration, and *Which Church Is Right?*

Decades later, President Ballard recalled, "Can you imagine? We knocked on the doors of these humble people's homes and handed them a tract on the Apostasy! What were we thinking? The woman who opened her door, whose husband was working long hours in the coal mine, must have thought we were crazy."

So the idea of a plan appealed to Elder Ballard's sense of order and organization. He quickly requested that Elder Adams send him a copy of the Anderson plan. Elder Adams agreed to send a copy if Elder

Ballard would send him a dollar. Elder Ballard has often remarked, "It took six weeks before the plan arrived."[39]

Elder Ballard and his companion immediately began using the Anderson plan in their teaching efforts. Their door approach was to show photographs of ancient ruins in the Old World and the New World. Instead of handing out pamphlets, they gave away copies of the Book of Mormon. Almost immediately, the size of their teaching pool of interested people increased.

Confident that the Anderson plan would increase the teaching pool for the thirty-two district missionaries, Elder Ballard asked President Boyer if he could share the plan with them. After receiving President Boyer's approval and implementing the plan, the Nottingham District became the leading district in the number of people being taught and in convert baptisms in the British Mission.

The sudden surge of success for the district over which he presided brought great joy to Elder Ballard. During the winter of 1949 he wrote: "What a great blessing I have as a Mormon elder."[40] Whether speaking in sacrament meetings, teaching a Book of Mormon Sunday School class, participating in a Cub Scout overnight campout, giving a lesson in Relief Society, directing a chorus, singing in a quartet, or organizing basketball or baseball leagues, he knew that his service was pleasing to God.[41]

Probably not coincidentally, his journal entries are more sporadic from this period of time on. Perhaps the April 28, 1949, entry has the best explanation as to why: "It has been three days since I wrote in this diary because I have been so darned busy. We will baptize 6 people on the 14th of May."[42] In addition to overseeing baptisms, he was expected to release branch presidents—some of whom didn't want to be released, and one who was old enough to be his father—to stand in for the father of a bride when the father couldn't make it to the wedding, to conduct funerals, and to dedicate graves.[43]

One day when he was working at the district office at 28 Loughboro

Road in Nottingham, Elder Ballard was visited by "a faithful little sister, 85 years old." Elder Ballard said, "I had never met her before. She was what we would call today 'numbered among the less active.' She handed me a small sack containing her tithing. She said to me, 'This is my tithing. I have sold a little piece of property. This belongs to the Lord. Please do not tell my family. My children would be furious if they knew that I was paying my tithing.'" Elder Ballard asked her, "How did you get here?" She indicated that she had come on the bus. When asked if she could be escorted home, she replied, "No, just help me get on the bus, and I will make my way home. I don't want my family to see me with one of the elders of the Church."[44]

As he passed his first-year benchmark in the mission field, Elder Ballard wrote:

> Boy, the time sure has flown. Before I know it I will be on my way home. My attitude towards life has changed a great deal because my understanding of the Gospel has increased by leaps and bounds during this past year in England. I am well and happy in the work, and I am fully prepared to work hard for the next year in trying to build up the Kingdom in this part of the world.[45]

Through his hard work he experienced some of the greatest joys he had ever known. On July 11, 1949, he baptized a Mr. Hannan and his son in the Trent River and wrote: "Today has been one of the happiest days of my life."[46]

His dedicated and tireless efforts also brought him some unusual and interesting experiences, like the time he was asked to speak to the Midland Cosmopolitan Debating Society in Nottingham.

"The last member of the Church to speak at the society was Elder John A. Widtsoe of the Quorum of the Twelve and who had been president of the European Mission from 1926 until 1932, so I considered this to be quite a coup for the Church," Elder Ballard said. "I picked up the telephone and called London, got President Boyer on the phone and said, 'I have worked out a wonderful thing for you. I have arranged for you to speak before the Midland Debating Society.' I was filled with enthusiasm and excitement because I thought this would open up doors of opportunity for us." But President Boyer didn't respond at all like Elder Ballard thought he would. The mission president listened to the young missionary's explanation and said simply: "Good luck, my boy."

Elder Ballard countered, "No, President, you do not understand. Let me take you through this again." He then restated the opportunity to speak before the debating society.

President Boyer said, "The Lord bless you, my boy," and then hung up the phone.[47]

The Sunday before the debate, missionaries in the Nottingham District gathered together "fasting and praying that the Lord somehow would take hold and help me as I represented the Church before the society," Elder Ballard said. On October 9, 1949, Elder Ballard stood on a platform in a large auditorium to address the seven hundred people in attendance at the debate. He was given thirty minutes to teach the basic tenets and beliefs of the Church and to explain the Restoration of the gospel of Jesus Christ. "I explained the apostasy, which necessitated a restoration," Elder Ballard recalled. "I explained how that occurred, including the restoration of the priesthood and the bringing forth of the Book of Mormon." When he finished, members of the debating society were invited to ask him questions or refute anything that he had said. Elder Ballard knew the answers to their questions before they finished asking them. He quoted scripture he had not memorized.[48] And in that setting, he learned much about the Spirit of the Lord that would bless his life for decades:

> Now I was barely 20 years of age. Although I knew more about the Church by this time than I did when I arrived in England, I want to bear testimony, and particularly to young people, that the Lord fulfills His promises. When we step forward

and do the very best that we know how, He has promised He would place into our mouths, at the very moment that we needed it, those things we need to say and to teach. I had never experienced the reality of the Comforter like I did on this occasion.[49]

Elder Ballard and the other missionaries present at the debate went back to the district office. "There we knelt and thanked our Heavenly Father for not abandoning us at a time of great need. We thanked Him for the privilege of witnessing the marvelous influence and power of the Holy Ghost in our lives."[50]

Counselor in the Mission Presidency

Although he had always been spiritually sensitive and astute, Elder Ballard's growth in spiritual stature during the first eighteen months of his mission was prodigious. In a letter from his father, Elder Ballard learned that Church President George Albert Smith had telephoned his father and told him of a temple meeting in which the First Presidency and the Quorum of the Twelve Apostles had approved the name of Melvin Russell Ballard Jr. as the new first counselor to President Selvoy J. Boyer of the British Mission. His father counseled him to "not allow this to go to my head and that I should remain humble and dutiful. He gave me some wonderful advice regarding this opportunity to serve as a counselor to President Boyer."[51] More than three weeks passed before President Boyer actually extended the call. Even though the young elder had been given some time to prepare himself, it was still incredibly humbling to him when that call finally came. Elder Ballard wrote: "I do not feel worthy of such a call, and I can hardly believe it is true. I hope and trust that the Lord will bless me to do my duty towards this calling."[52] Notice of his call appeared in the *Millennial Star* in December 1949:

President Selvoy J. Boyer of the British Mission recently announced the appointment of Elder Melvin Russell Ballard as first counselor in the Mission Presidency to fill the position made vacant by the return home this month of Elder Leland W. Rawson.

Elder Ballard has served eighteen months in the mission field and for the past nine months has directed the missionary activities in the Nottingham District. Much can be said about the fine work which Elder Ballard has done in the district. During his administration there have been thirty-four baptisms.

President Alma Sonne of the European Mission set Elder Ballard apart as first counselor in the Mission Presidency on November 12th [1949].[53]

Although he was a counselor in the mission presidency, Elder Ballard's residence continued to be in the Nottingham District. Attending mission presidency meetings, visiting the fourteen districts of the mission, and holding district conferences meant a lot of traveling for him. Whether it was meeting new missionaries as they disembarked from a ship in Southampton or meeting with missionaries in Wales, Elder Ballard's suitcase was always packed and ready to go.

One of the first and most powerful lessons Elder Ballard learned as he visited branches all around the mission—a lesson that would stay with him for the rest of his life and ministry—was the great faith, power, and strength of the women of the Church. "Many of the small branches were literally held together by the sisters," he said at the Preston England Temple dedication in 1998, adding that he "often found that it was the strength of a Relief Society president or a Primary president that kept these little branches going. Many of the priesthood holders had been off to war; many of them did not come back."[54]

Elder Ballard often accompanied President and Sister Boyer from London to Scotland and Ireland, and from there to far-flung areas in the British Isles. On one of their many train excursions to the seaport of Liverpool, he and the Boyers were seated in a dining car. Sister Boyer

Elder Ballard with President Selvoy J. Boyer (left) and President Stayner Richards (right)

asked a conductor, "Does this train stop in Liverpool?" They had a good laugh when the conductor replied, "It better, Ma'am, or there'll be a helluva splash."[55]

As Elder Ballard traveled with the Boyers, he learned much about President Boyer's no-nonsense approach and the order of the Church. At a Leicester Branch meeting, Elder Ballard closed the meeting by suggesting to the congregation that they had been fortunate to listen to the president, and on behalf of those assembled he expressed appreciation to the president for his instruction. Afterward President Boyer said to him, "If I need anybody to thank me for my talk, I will ask for it. You just get up and close the meeting."[56]

When Elder Ballard and President Boyer were meeting with a district president in Scotland, Elder Ballard saw President Boyer thump a missionary on the chest, look at him with his piercing blue-green eyes, and ask, "Have you been kissing your landlady?"[57] When the elder confessed that he had kissed his landlady once on the cheek, Elder Ballard was instructed to help the elder pack his bags and put him on the next train leaving for Wales. "President Boyer would look you in the eye and thump you in the chest with that crooked finger which had been hurt in a farm accident," said Elder Ballard, "and that was your interview. When his penetrating gaze locked with yours, you would just tell him everything you'd ever done in your whole life."[58]

Of his mission president, Elder Ballard wrote:

> My father was a great influence in my life, and next to him President Boyer influenced me the most to want to serve the Lord. In one of our conversations he said something I have never forgotten: "Brother Ballard, I do not have very much of this world's goods, but everything I have, I have placed on the altar in service." Then with that crooked finger of his, he thumped me in the chest, looked me in the eye, and said, "And I expect you to do exactly the same thing."[59]

As President Boyer's term as mission president came to a close, Elder Ballard accompanied him to the fourteen districts in the mission so he could bid his missionaries farewell. Clearly this was a tender, emotional time for the young elder, who was not only bidding farewell to a beloved leader but could also see the end of his own mission just a few months away. This reflective period of his mission is demonstrated in these words to his mother, written on January 1, 1950, as he contemplated her birthday: "A mother's birthday is a lot different when a son is 21 years old. Instead of thinking about the good food Mom can make and the swell cakes and ice cream she supplies you with and the neat and clean house she keeps, you see a pair of beautiful, clear, understanding eyes full of experience and good judgment. . . . I thank my Father in Heaven every morning and night for you. I ask all the choice blessings to fall upon you each day because I have finally come to a true realization of what my mother means to me."[60]

The new mission president, Stayner Richards (Elder Stephen L Richards's brother and future General Authority), and his wife, Jane Foote Taylor, arrived at the port of Southampton in February 1950. One of the first matters of mission business he wanted to attend to was to ask Elder Ballard to continue as his counselor, with the specific responsibility for teaching in the mission. And he wanted him to be closer; he asked Elder Ballard to move from Nottingham to the mission home in London so he could more easily travel with President and Sister Richards to district conferences. Elder Ballard wrote of his new president: "President Richards is a marvelous man, and I am learning to love and admire him a great deal."[61] As for Sister Richards, a former English teacher: "She worked me over more than once on when to use 'me' and when to use 'I' in speaking," recalled Elder Ballard.[62]

With a new president to introduce to the missionaries, Elder Ballard repeated in February 1950 his January journeys to all fourteen mission districts. It was interesting for Elder Ballard to observe first-hand the vastly different leadership styles of two great and effective mission presidents. For example, sometimes a missionary would be discouraged and think he ought to go home. President Richards would challenge the missionary to a game of horseshoes, saying, "If you can beat me, you can go home." He would even spot the elder 15 points in a game to 21, but the president was such a proficient horseshoe player that he would still win. If a missionary threw a ringer, the president could always place two on top of it. As far as President Ballard can remember, no one who accepted President Richards's horseshoe challenge ever won a game—or went home.

President Richards was also an avid golfer. One preparation day morning he invited Elder Ballard to go with him to Wimbledon, where the world-famous tennis tournament is held. Elder Ballard drove the only mission car, a 1937 Ford that had been driven more than 200,000 miles. Evidently, Elder Ballard was the only one brave enough to drive the car. Once at the famed site, they walked around and enjoyed the morning. When they got back in the car, President Richards said, "Now, let's go home this way," pointing to a different route on their map that led to a golf course. When they arrived at the course, Elder Ballard was surprised to learn that President Richards had somehow managed to slip his golf clubs into the boot (or trunk) of the old Ford when the young missionary wasn't looking. Elder Ballard was the caddy while the president played nine holes of golf.

Even though Elder Ballard was scheduled to go home in May of 1950, President Richards asked him to extend his service until September—and of course Elder Ballard, with the support of his parents, agreed. For the last few days of May and into June, Elder Ballard held meetings with the elders and was often seen preaching at street meetings and tracting door-to-door. He said: "I think of the hours that I spent tracting in England, knocking on doors. They would be too numerous to count. I did keep track of the number of street meetings I held during the two and one-half years that I had the privilege of serving in the British Isles. I was on street corners through England, Ireland, Scotland, and Wales speaking more than 740 times."[63]

As his mission would end in September, Elder Ballard asked President Richards for permission to go to Newbury, England, and visit the offices of the *Newbury Weekly News* to see the newspaper dated May 15, 1884, that had meant so much to the Ballard family. It was the newspaper given to the daughter of Henry Ballard by two unnamed strangers on May 18, 1884—the newspaper that had been printed three days earlier in England and contained epitaphs and genealogical data from headstones in Thatcham.

For Bishop Henry Ballard, this was a miracle. The Logan Temple had been dedicated on May 17, the day before the strangers arrived at his home. The newspaper provided Henry the names of friends and family members that he took to the temple in order to complete sacred vicarious work in their behalf.

Permission was granted. At the newspaper office, Elder Ballard "sought out the editor, inquiring as to whether or not he would be kind enough to let me go into the archives of the old newspapers. His name was Mr. Ashley Turner. After hearing my reason, he kindly consented and took me back into where all the old newspapers of the *Newbury Weekly News* were stored." In a back room Elder Ballard had the privilege of seeing for himself the May 15, 1884, newspaper: "I was permitted, although the papers were very brown with age, to take the copy of that paper out into the sunlight, where I took pictures."[64]

Elder Ballard then went with a "wonderful, older sister who was a master in genealogy, Ada Linton," to Thatcham, the birthplace of his great-grandfather Henry Ballard. "We found a little Church of England, the center of the activity at one time in the small community," he said. As Elder Ballard walked into the little village church, he experienced deep feelings, for it was in this church that his great-grandfather and other ancestors had worshipped. In the church cemetery, the very cemetery that inspired the article in the *Newbury Weekly News,* he heard Sister Linton exclaim, "Elder Ballard, Elder Ballard, come quick!" He thought that Sister Linton had met with some misfortune. "I came out of the church rather rapidly to find her on her hands and knees in the small churchyard with a wire brush, a wet rag-cloth, and a broom sweeping off the headstones. 'I think I have found them!' she said. 'Your great-great grandfather and grandmother, and their parents!'" He knelt down beside Sister Linton and carefully wrote down all the information on the headstones. "I remember getting my first lesson on the importance of being accurate in our genealogical pursuits. Sister Linton insisted that I write down as she read off of the headstone and then she made me repeat it to be certain that we had it correct."[65]

Of these two experiences, Elder Ballard wrote: "I was filled with the promise of the prophet Elijah. I had truly felt my heart being turned to the hearts of my fathers. I recall sending off [to home] airmail, the fastest way that I could, what I had discovered in this small church yard."[66]

Returning Home

About six weeks later, in late August 1950, Elder M. Russell Ballard was released from his mission and given permission to return home. President Richards presented him with a fly rod in appreciation for their association. Of this mission president, Elder Ballard wrote:

> Stayner Richards became another hero in my life. He was as kind and gentle and wonderful a man as you would ever meet. I have often said that he smiled so much in his lifetime that as he would sit at his desk working on something of a serious nature, his face would still appear to be smiling. He motivated us with love and trust.[67]

More recently, President Ballard said, "How fortunate I was to have two great mission presidents who influenced and taught me lessons that have blessed and served me in every assignment I've had in the Church."[68] Photographs of both presidents are prominently displayed on his office wall.

Before Elder Ballard departed from England, he wrote, "I did not have a great deal of success in bringing a lot of people into the Church as a missionary in England. I was able to baptize three families and participate in the conversion of others."[69] Yet for him, "My mission was the most important training period spiritually in my life. It was a foundation and gave me direction."[70]

Wondering if his labors were accepted by the Lord, on his journey home he stopped in New York, where he met a former companion, Sydney Nebecker. Together with Sydney's mother, they traveled to Palmyra in upstate New York. "I had never been to Palmyra prior to my mission, and so I was most anxious to be able to go there," Elder Ballard said. Early in the morning on a gray, overcast day, the two young elders walked into the Sacred Grove, the site of the First Vision in the spring of 1820.

Since there were few visitors in the Grove, they knelt, and each prayed aloud. They told the Lord that they had worked hard and had done their best as missionaries. They then said, "We come before Thee now as we are about to return home seeking to know if our labors have been acceptable." Just then, the clouds hovering over the Grove parted, and the sun shone down upon them. "For a brief moment," said Elder Ballard, "we saw the light shine down from the heavens on that gray day. It was significant to me that our Heavenly Father knew we were in the Grove and that we were offering this prayer." It was such a profound experience that Elder Ballard wrote, "Our prayers were answered. 'Yes, your labors have been acceptable.'"[71]

Having experienced such a heavenly affirmation, the elders happily continued their journey home. "I remember the night Russell came home," his sister Chaunie said. "He came home late and I was asleep and he came down and woke me up and I just thought that was wonderful to have him back."[72]

There were many family members and friends to see, but for Russell, one of the most meaningful was "Aunt Myrtle, the only surviving sibling of Melvin J. Ballard, [who] summoned me over to her home. As I walked into her home, Aunt Myrtle, great with age, stood up and came over and embraced me. She kissed me and said, 'You have found the missing key that we have been looking for all these years. Because of the work you did in the Thatcham cemetery, on your knees looking at a headstone . . . we can now proceed to do the marvelous work in the temple.'"[73]

Russell was privileged to be in a sealing room in the Salt Lake Temple and participate in the ordinance work for his ancestors. Of that sacred experience, he said: "I have to say that one of the great spiritual moments in my life was kneeling at the altar in the Salt Lake Temple taking part in the sacred sealing work for my family. . . . I came to know that if I did nothing more on my whole mission than this, I had had a great mission."[74]

CHAPTER FOUR

COURTSHIP AND MARRIAGE

Three days after he returned home from his mission, twenty-one-year-old Russ Ballard and a few friends attended the "Hello Day" dance at the University of Utah. The dance was an excuse for the friends to get together, share mission stories, and, if lucky, dance with some young women. It was a friend, Dick Harris, who first spotted a beautiful, blue-eyed blonde sophomore on the dance floor. He wanted Russ to meet her. Without Russ's encouragement, Dick tagged out the young man dancing with her and danced her over to where Russ was standing. Dick introduced Russ to Barbara Bowen and moved aside. "Barbara was vivacious and popular, so I got to dance with her for less than a minute before another young man tagged me out," President Ballard said years later. "That was just not acceptable to me. Having learned the importance of follow-up on my mission, I got her telephone number."[1]

Barbara Bowen

Of their first quick encounter, President Ballard often said: "The greatest day in my life was the day I met Barbara Bowen."[2] The moment was not lost on Barbara: "My first impression of Russ was 'What a handsome boy!' And he had this wonderful smile and beautiful brown eyes."[3]

The next day, Russ made that all-important phone call. The call revealed that Barbara was not just popular on the dance floor—her social calendar was full. A meeting after a university class and a date penciled in on the calendar for two weeks later were the only arrangements that fit her crowded schedule. "Thankfully, my mission taught me to be persistent even in the face of discouragement," recalled President Ballard.[4]

After a first date, Russ was ready for a second, a third, and so forth, but competition for Barbara's time was fierce, and he needed to wait his turn. Several young men were vying for her attention, including a missionary she was writing to while he served. "I have always been one who has enjoyed a challenge," President Ballard said.[5] He asked for the second date and took his place in the queue.

"I was smitten on the second date," he said. "She was not only beautiful but had a sparkling personality."[6] The thing that really impressed the returned missionary was how genuine and down-to-earth she was. "People liked her because she was easy to like," President Ballard said. "She was approachable and friendly to everyone. As a result, she had many friends, both young women and young men, who admired her depth and goodness."

Barbara was more cautious with her emotions: "I was impressed, but I wasn't looking for a serious relationship. I was eighteen and had three years of college in front of me."[7]

Barbara Bowen was the daughter of James Russell Bowen and Afton Wilkins. Her parents were good, honorable, hardworking people of modest means. She was born on January 5, 1932, in Salt Lake City. During her childhood and youth she lived with her parents and her sister, Joyce, in a duplex on Roberta Street in Salt Lake City, where she and Joyce shared a room.[8] Barbara had attended Lincoln Junior High and quickly became a leader among the students there. At South High

School she was a student-body officer for two years before being named class valedictorian. She was studying English at the university and was a member of the Chi Omega sorority. "As I look back at it, I was pretty audacious, thinking I could just step in ahead of these other young men who were interested in her," he said, chuckling, years later. "But at the time, it seemed like the most natural thing in the world. She and I belonged together. To me, it was that simple."[9]

Not that there wasn't anything else to occupy Russ's mind during those first weeks and months after his mission. University classes demanded his attention, and the Sigma Chi fraternity could not be ignored. Russ was dubbed "the bishop" and was expected to keep his fraternity friends in check.[10] There was also his work as a car salesman at Ballard Motor Company to fit in his schedule.

On one of his first days back at work, Russ met Thomas S. Monson. Of that meeting, President Monson recalled:

> I have known Elder M. Russell Ballard, whom I call "Russ," since I was a young advertising executive with the *Deseret News*. . . . In this capacity I was visiting one day with my good friend Melvin Ballard, proprietor of Ballard Motor Company in Salt Lake City, when he said to me, "Tom, I'd like you to meet my son, Russ. He's just returned from his mission to the British Isles." When Russ was introduced and we shook hands . . . he was enthusiastic about his service in Great Britain, said he had the most wonderful mission presidents in the world, and his enthusiasm for the gospel and sharing it just seemed to exude from him as though he were still in the mission field and was working on Melvin Ballard and me.[11]

With a myriad of thoughts swirling in his mind—his mission and commitment to the faith, university studies, the pull of friends (especially this intriguing and important new friend Barbara Bowen), and selecting a career path—Russ received an invitation from his great-uncle John F. Bowman, who was a patriarch, to receive a second

Russell in his twenties

patriarchal blessing. He felt that Russ's first blessing, though inspired, was not complete. On October 11, 1950, Russ was offered a patriarchal blessing by the same man who baptized him in the Salt Lake Tabernacle font. A portion of that blessing reads:

> Your great mission here upon the earth will be in preaching the gospel and working for the upbuilding of the kingdom of God, which you will accomplish with marked success. . . . You will be called, as you have been in the past, . . . [to] great positions of leadership and responsibility in the church, and will be looked upon by your associates as a man of God, and, your influence will always be one for good.[12]

Engagement

By winter of 1950 there was no question in Russ's mind that he loved Barbara and wanted to marry her. Every time he was with her, he became more convinced of it. And despite the still-sizable list of suitors who continued to pursue her, Barbara was becoming increasingly enamored of persistent, persuasive, and perfectly charming Russ Ballard—especially after the Christmas present he gave her.

"During my last trip to Edinburgh, Scotland, on my mission, I was walking along this street lined with shops selling these beautiful cashmere sweaters, a Scottish specialty," President Ballard said in 2020. "Suddenly I see this delicate pink sweater set, and I'm just drawn to it. I looked at it carefully—I even paid attention to the size. But then I asked myself, 'Who am I buying this for?' There was no one who I had in mind for it—I just knew I wanted to buy it."

When he got home and was unpacking from his mission, he showed the sweater set to his mother.

"What in the world are you going to do with this?" she asked.

Ever confident, Russ replied, "I'm going to find the girl who fits it and I'm going to marry her!"

So when Russ gave the pink sweater set to Barbara for Christmas 1950—a bold move, considering they weren't even dating steadily at the time ("you've got to be aggressive when you're fighting off the whole student body," he explained)—he wasn't at all surprised to see that it fit her perfectly.

"She looked absolutely stunning in it," he said. "Of course, she looked stunning in everything."[13]

Barbara loved the sweater set, and she was touched by the story of how and when he purchased it. She was growing to love Russ—no question about it. But she just wasn't sure the time was right for her to marry. "I felt that he knew where he was going," Barbara said. "He certainly was confident and knew what he wanted in life and how he was going to get there."[14] Although she loved and honored her father as a great and good man, he was not active in the Church, and so she was moved by Russ's devotion to the Lord and was as attracted to his sweet love of the gospel as she was to his dynamic personality. "I wanted to

Russell and Barbara when they were dating

marry someone who honored the priesthood and who would go to church with me, who would take our children to church," she said.[15]

There was so much good in Russ and in her growing relationship with him. The more time they spent together, the closer she felt to him. But she didn't know for sure that marriage to Russ was the right answer for her—at least not immediately. She was not yet twenty and was excited to continue with her schooling. She was popular, with many young men clamoring for her attention.

And then there was the matter of her mother.

It wasn't that Afton Bowen didn't like Russ. She liked him fine. But she felt Barbara was still too young to get married, and she made no secret of that fact. Russ saw Sister Bowen's perspective as an obstacle that needed to be conquered, and, as was his custom, he decided to confront this issue head-on. One day when Barbara wasn't home, Russ dropped in on Afton and spent an afternoon talking to her, answering her questions, getting to know her and her background, and helping her get to know him a little better. She was interested in the fact that Russ's parents were not active in the Church—that seemed to give them some common ground. After three hours of conversation, Russ emerged with great love and appreciation for Barbara's mother—and with more of an ally in the wooing of Barbara than he had before.

Still, the major obstacle that needed to be overcome was Barbara's own uncertainty in the matter. "I had already made my decision," President Ballard said. "I knew what I wanted to have happen here. And I believed it was the right thing for both Barbara and me. But it wasn't enough for me to know. Barbara needed to have her own witness of this—she had to know for herself that this was the right thing for her to do, independent of whatever prompting or revelation I had received."[16]

On many different occasions on his mission, Russ had seen miracles wrought through fasting and prayer. And so he suggested that he and Barbara take a weekend away from each other to devote to personal fasting and prayer for Barbara to receive an answer from heaven on the most important decision she would make in her life. Barbara agreed, and they spent a weekend apart, fasting and praying. When Russ arrived at the Bowen home on Sunday afternoon after their fast, Barbara burst through the front door, ran down the stairs, threw her arms around Russ, and told him she had her answer. She spoke of receiving a sure confirmation from the Lord that they were to be eternal companions. They were engaged on April 6, 1951.

Although President Ballard acknowledged the Lord's hand in their engagement, he often said that "the single greatest accomplishment of my life was convincing her that I was the only true and living returned missionary among all of those she was dating." He laughed aloud before adding, "Getting her to agree to marry me was the greatest sales job I ever did."[17]

During their engagement, Russ and Barbara decided to purchase a home. Of that experience, Russ wrote:

> We spent a long time looking all over the valley for a home
> we could afford and that would meet our needs. When we finally

found a house that looked perfect, I went to my father for counsel. He went with us and looked at the home we had chosen. It appeared that he was pleased with what he was seeing, but he didn't voice an opinion one way or the other. Finally, he asked me just one question: "Is it worth it?"

"It's worth it, Dad," I said. "Whatever it takes, it's worth it."

And you know what? Even though we had to scrimp a little at first, it was worth it.[18]

Russ borrowed $1,500 from his father for a down payment on the home at 1559 East 3010 South in the Mountair Acres area of Salt Lake. The price of the home was $15,750, and the monthly payment—including interest, taxes, and insurance—$67.50. Overall, the house was in a deteriorating condition and required both Russ and Barbara to work themselves "nearly to death" to make the place warm and comfortable for them to move into after they were married.[19]

The Military Stint

At the same time as Russ and Barbara were preparing for marriage, conflict in Korea was accelerating. What started as a series of border skirmishes became a full-fledged war when Communist-backed North Korea sent 75,000 soldiers across the 38th parallel into South Korea on June 25, 1950.

American leaders saw this as the front lines of the war against worldwide Communism, and they initiated and accelerated US involvement in the conflict. The possibility of being drafted to fight in the Korean War could not be ignored or set aside—by Russ or any other young man at the time.

Russ met with his cousin, Allen Acomb, who was the commanding officer of a military unit at Fort Douglas in Salt Lake City. The purpose of their meeting was to discuss Russ's best option: wait to see if he would be drafted and sent to Korea to fight in the bloody conflict, or join a military organization like the National Guard or Army Reserve and wait until the unit was sent to fight in Korea. Allen advised Russ to join the Army Reserve immediately.[20] Russ joined the 354th Quartermaster Corps and was assigned to the 361st General Depot Company. His basic military training was handled that summer at Camp Williams, located at the south end of the Salt Lake Valley.

At his first military summer camp in 1951, Private Russell Ballard was selected as one of two recruits to receive a commendation for outstanding performance in his training company. Due to the commendation, Private Ballard was assigned to be an "honor orderly" to Major General Hugh M. Milton, the executive officer for Reserve and ROTC Affairs of the Department of the Army, whenever he was in town. As an honor orderly, Russ was expected to keep General Milton's tent clean, shine his shoes, and complete any task the general assigned.

On one occasion, General Milton summoned Private Ballard to go with him to Temple Square in downtown Salt Lake City. While sitting with the general in the back seat of his command car, Russ took advantage of the opportunity to explain Brigham Young and the heroic pioneers who settled the Salt Lake Valley. Ever the missionary, Private Ballard made sure the general had a lesson on the Restoration of the gospel of Jesus Christ and gave him a copy of the Book of Mormon. In return, General Milton gave Russ a box of candy for Barbara.

"Everybody loved Barbara—even the general," President Ballard said. "She was easy to love."[21]

For Time and All Eternity

On August 28, 1951, following his first military summer camp at Camp Williams, twenty-two-year-old M. Russell Ballard and nineteen-year-old Barbara Bowen were married for time and all eternity in the Salt Lake Temple, with Elder Harold B. Lee officiating.[22]

Elder Lee gave the newlyweds wonderful counsel on loving and

Newlyweds Russ and Barbara Ballard outside the Salt Lake Temple

taking care of one another. He also explained that it was very important at the end of each day to kneel side by side and hold hands and take turns being voice in thanking the Lord for the blessings of that day. He challenged them to never lose sight of this, and promised them that if they did it faithfully, they would always stay together. The Ballards followed this practice diligently throughout their entire marriage, and it is a principle President Ballard has taught many times in his ministry, especially to couples whose marriages were in trouble.

Very few attended the sealing ceremony—no more than twelve. At this point, Russ's parents were returning to activity in the Church, and only his mother was able to attend the sealing. Barbara's parents were unable to be there. Years later, President Ballard said:

> I had worked very hard to get my father-in-law to go to church and finally worked it out of him and his wife to go to sacrament meeting with Barbara and me. A returned missionary was speaking, and he went on and on and on in his discourse. He wasn't really teaching the gospel of Christ quite like I was hoping

Cutting the wedding cake

he would. He was more talking about the various places he had served. It was past time for the meeting to be over and a little child started to cry and the mother took the child out. My father-in-law leaned over and said, "If I start to cry will you carry me out?" That was the last time I got him to church.[23]

Barbara's parents provided a lovely reception for the couple at the Church's Institute of Religion on University Street, next to the University of Utah. It was attended by many family members and friends. "I seem to remember a lot of very sad young men at the reception," President Ballard joked. "But I wasn't paying much attention. I couldn't keep my eyes off of my beautiful bride. She just radiated happiness. It was the beginning of a wonderful life together."[24]

Of their marriage, he has said, "It was the most important day of my life when we were married in the Salt Lake Temple. . . . I married the right woman. . . . I love deeply my wife, Barbara, who has been the light of my life from the day we were married."[25]

CHAPTER FIVE

STARTING A CAREER

T he newlyweds honeymooned in Sun Valley, Idaho, before moving into their "fixer-upper" home in the Cummings Ward of the Wilford Stake in Salt Lake. Soon Barbara was called to be Primary secretary and Russ was called to be the adviser to the Adult Aaronic Priesthood and given the specific assignment of fellowshipping twenty-seven adult men who had not attended worship services for years. It didn't take Russ and Barbara long to figure out that their assignments actually converged—many of the Adult Aaronic men were husbands to her Primary teachers. So they decided to hold some cottage meetings in their home, inviting the sisters to bring their husbands. During the cottage meetings, Russ taught the gospel using the Anderson plan, the same plan he had used so effectively on his mission in England.

Over the course of a year, with the help of their wives, twenty-one of these men came back into full Church activity. One—Boyd Nielson—became Russ's counselor in the bishopric; others later became bishops and temple ordinance workers.

The reactivation of these men taught Russ that reactivation is all about love—love for the Lord and love for the people to whom you are reaching out. Russ and Barbara became friends with these good people. They grew to care about them deeply, and it was in that loving, caring spirit that they were able to reach out to them one by one and help them understand that Heavenly Father loves them as His children, that He has a plan, that they are part of the plan, and that eternal life is worth everything.

While he was learning through experience how things work in God's kingdom, Russ was also learning about how things work in the world. One day, while performing his military duties, he was driving General Milton back to Camp Williams. As the two men were chatting amiably, the general suggested that Private Ballard consider becoming an army officer. Russ thought that sounded like a great idea—he had seen a huge difference between the life of an officer and that of an enlisted man. But he had never really given much thought to actually becoming an officer. The general instructed him to sign up for a correspondence course through which he could receive officer training.

Russ signed up, completed the training course, and reported back to General Milton. Soon he was summoned to appear before a board of review, which he was told would grill him on everything he needed to know about being an army officer. Russ was frankly concerned about it, and he did a lot of last-minute studying to prepare for the examination. By the time he appeared before the board of review he was filled with military information and heart-pounding anxiety, unsure of whether or not he was adequately prepared. But during the board of review he was asked only two questions: "Do you know General Hugh M. Milton?" and "How do you know him?" Evidently his answers were all the board members needed to hear. He was immediately commissioned a second lieutenant in the US Army Reserve.[1]

And that was that.

Thankfully, there were noncommissioned officers around to help keep the new army officer on his toes. As Lieutenant Ballard was learning his duties, he asked a tough old master sergeant what master sergeants do. He gruffly replied, "We take care of dumb second lieutenants like you."[2]

Between fulfilling his new army duties, fellowshipping new friends, attending the university, and working part-time as a salesman for his father, Russ knew that something had to give, especially since his hectic schedule left him precious little time to be with Barbara. "We drew together as we prayed together," he recalled, "but we wanted to also spend a little time together."[3] Unfortunately, life had become too crowded.

One item, however, could not be dropped from his daily to-do list: his regular visits with Grandmother Ballard. "I stopped to see her two or three times a week on the way home from work," President Ballard said. On one of those visits she said, "Bussy, when I die and get over on the other side, if I find out that this Church is not true I'm going to be damn mad!" She was just having fun with him, but Russ said, "Grandma, I don't think you need to worry about that. Grandpa will be there to make sure everything is okay."

He remembered: "One night she asked me to kneel by her bedside and ask the Lord to let her go to Grandfather. I tried to talk her out of such a thing, but she insisted. So, I knelt by her side, held her hand, and asked the Lord to release her from this world to rejoin Grandfather. I kissed Grandma after the prayer, and she died before dawn the next day, January 12, 1952."[4]

Her funeral was attended by many General Authorities. President J. Reuben Clark Jr. of the First Presidency and Elder Harold B. Lee spoke at the services.

Although Russ could now drive straight home from work, he still struggled to find enough time for all the things he was trying to do. He was concerned that by stretching himself so thin he would eventually begin to give inadequate attention to things that were most important to him. At last he concluded that something needed to be set aside, and that something was his university studies.

"When I was taking business courses from professors at the university, I realized that I was making more money than the teachers were making," President Ballard said. "I was, I guess, a fairly good salesman. I remember thinking: 'If I quit school and put full-time effort into sales I could really be financially secure. It seemed like a reasonable thought at the time. And so I didn't finish my last year of college. But I've regretted that decision my whole life."[5]

On another occasion, he told young adults:

> I don't think finishing my degree would have made a huge difference in my professional career, and I'm not aware of any opportunities that were denied me as a result of not holding a bachelor's degree. Then again, I don't know what opportunities might have come my way during the last year of my college program. But that isn't my point. I started school with the intention of completing a worthwhile objective, and I allowed myself to be deterred from accomplishing that worthy goal by not staying focused on what I was trying to do.[6]

Working full-time in his father's dealership had innumerable benefits, one of which was the many visits of Tom Monson. "Russ showed me how the new Nash could be made into a bed for fishermen and hunters and so forth. He knew I liked to do both," President Monson recalled. "So he and I were witnesses to the demonstration of making a bed out of the car. I said that's just what my aunt and uncle need. Sure enough she bought a blue Nash, which served her well for many years."[7]

Russ became such an able salesman that his father promoted him to sales manager and set up a compensation program designed especially for him. In the city directory of 1953, Melvin Ballard is listed as the president and manager of Ballard Motor Company located at 633 South Main in Salt Lake City. Listed directly below in the city directory is "Russ" Ballard as the new sales manager of used cars.[8]

His first month as sales manager, Russ made more money than his father thought he should. He also came to the attention of Frederick J. Bell, executive vice president of the National Automobile Dealers Association. Mr. Bell wrote in a December 7, 1953, letter, "Now if we can find a certain number of Russell Ballards in every state, I'll have no fears as to the future of our industry."[9]

As Russ's salary climbed, his father made adjustments to his individual compensation program that reduced the amount of money Russ could earn. "I understood completely why my father felt he needed to do that," President Ballard said. "There was no problem between us, no disagreement other than the fact that he didn't think I was worth as much as I thought I was worth." President Ballard laughed, then added: "So one day I went in to his office and said, 'Dad, I love you, but I think I can make more money somewhere else, so I'm going to go try.'"[10] With his father's blessing and best wishes, Russ left Ballard Motor Company in 1954 to strike out on his own.

He first joined Kay Stoker, a man he met at the Nash automobile dealership when he brought his car in to be serviced. Russ and Kay Stoker organized the Tatro Uranium Company—Kay as the largest stockholder and Russ as president. Although their search for uranium did not produce a profitable mine, other mining ventures were successful, including the Silver King Mines Company of Nevada (later known as the Alta Gold Company). Alta Gold and another company formed by Kay Stoker—La Teko Mining Company—traded on the NASDAQ. Shares in these companies produced a substantial profit until the price of precious metals dropped dramatically—gold dropped from $800 an ounce to less than $50 an ounce. Thankfully, Russ had pulled out of the company before the price of gold plummeted.[11]

By this point, Russ and Barbara were in their third year of marriage. Although they were financially solvent and had enjoyable assignments in their ward, they wanted children and were concerned that this didn't seem to be happening for them—especially since their married friends were all having children. A stanza in a poem by Russ's father reveals their concern:

They say roses are red
And violets are blue.
So listen and I'll tell you
A story that's true.
When Russ and Barbara
Decided to get married
No babies arrived and did this
Get them worried.[12]

After much discussion and prayer, Russ and Barbara requested a priesthood blessing from President Joseph Fielding Smith, Russell's great-uncle and President of the Quorum of the Twelve Apostles, in the fall of 1953. The blessing was pronounced, and Barbara was promised that she would yet be a mother. On September 13, 1954, Clark Russell Ballard was born, the first child of Russ and Barbara Ballard.

An Entrepreneur

With a baby in his arms and a loving and supportive wife at his side, Russ returned to the automobile industry. In 1955, in the midst of a decade of growth for the American economy, he opened his own automobile dealership, Russ Ballard Auto, Inc. He secured franchises and introduced the Volvo and the English-made Fords to Salt Lake customers. His business thrived from day one and set new records for car sales. Confident that they were catching the wave of prosperity that was sweeping across the country, Russ and Barbara moved from their small house in Mountair Acres to a more spacious home that Boyd Nielson built for them at 4020 Jupiter Drive in Holladay.[13] By the time boxes were put away and cupboards were lined with dishes, daughter Holly was on her way. She was born on December 6, 1955.

Soon after Holly joined the family, Russ and Barbara made a short trip to Los Angeles to meet with Herb Stayner, a Southern Californian who owned a business importing heavy-duty machinery in Santa Monica. The two men had met in Salt Lake City, and the meeting was impressive enough for Stayner to decide that he wanted the younger man to come join him in his business. "I wasn't looking for a job," President Ballard remembered decades later. "But I figured it wouldn't hurt to talk to him. And Barbara and I both liked the idea of a couple of days out of the Utah winter."[14]

Stayner made Russ a lucrative job offer—lucrative enough that Russ felt he and Barbara needed some time to talk about it, and to pray about it. On the drive home to Salt Lake, the couple weighed the pros and cons of the move for themselves and for their little family. They were pretty much undecided until they encountered a blinding snowstorm near the rural town of Nephi, Utah, about eighty-four miles from their home in Salt Lake City. The storm was frightening in its intensity and had them both offering prayers for their safety. After finally making it home, the Ballards were thinking that the storm had tipped the scales in favor of beautiful, warm, sun-drenched Southern California.

But the Lord had a different idea.

Second Counselor in a Bishopric

Russ and Barbara arrived home from California on a Saturday evening. Early the next morning the stake executive secretary called Russ and asked him to come to the stake president's office, where President G. Carlos Smith explained that due to the rapid growth in the Holladay area, the Holladay Sixth Ward was being divided, and the Holladay Seventh Ward was being created. President Smith then extended a call to Russ to be second counselor to Bishop William "Bill" S. Partridge of the new ward. Wayne Brown was called to be the first counselor. "What would have happened if I hadn't been able to get back to Salt Lake last night?" Russ asked. President Smith, who was also a distant cousin, chuckled and replied, "Well, we would have put you in the bishopric anyway."[15] When Russ returned home from the meeting and discussed the calling with Barbara, they both knew immediately that the move to California was off.

Before Russ could be sustained to the bishopric by members of the new Holladay Seventh Ward, Barbara's father died unexpectedly at age fifty.[16] His death was devastating to Barbara, her mother, and her sister, Joyce. But Russ was touched and inspired by Barbara's strength, and by how gracefully she comforted those around her who were mourning their loss—including Russ himself, who had great love for his father-in-law.

After a week filled with outpourings of sadness, emotion, faith, and love, twenty-seven-year-old M. Russell Ballard was ordained a high priest and set apart as a counselor to Bishop Partridge by Elder Clifford E. Young, an Assistant to the Quorum of the Twelve Apostles, on March 17, 1956.

Bishop Partridge put Russ to work right away—and in a brand-new ward there was much work to do. He was assigned to staff the Mutual Improvement Association (MIA)—the precursor of the Young Men's organization—and to oversee the establishment of a new Scout troop. He was fine with filling the MIA positions, but he was a little intimidated with the Scouting assignment. "I never had much to do with Scouting," he said years later. "I think I was a Tenderfoot, but I'm not 100 percent sure of that. And Brother Brown was an Eagle Scout. I thought he would be the more logical choice to organize the troop."[17] But Bishop Partridge assured Russ that he was up to the challenge, and so he "wore out the ward roster going over it and over it looking for a Scoutmaster."[18] In the spirit of fasting and prayer, he finally came up with the name of a man to be the new Scoutmaster.

"You can't call him," the bishop said when Russ presented the name to him. "He isn't active, and I believe he has a Word of Wisdom problem."[19] Russ explained to the bishop that the man was an Eagle Scout and knew how to organize a troop and make it work. Besides that, Russ reminded the bishop, he was the only man left in the ward who did not have a calling. The bishop agreed to go with Russ to issue the call.

"We went one evening, and the bishop knocked on the door," President Ballard later wrote of the experience. "This good man came to the door. The bishop said to him, 'We are the bishopric. We have come to visit with you, and Brother Ballard has something he would like to ask you.' With that, the bishop stepped back and pushed me forward."[20]

Russ hesitated a moment before saying, "I've been put in charge of the MIA. Part of the MIA is Scouting. We need you to be the Scoutmaster. Will you come to Church? Will you become active? We need you in this calling."[21]

The surprised man said that he would think it over. He then closed the door.

A few days later, Russ returned to the man's home. "Do you think I could really do it?" the man asked.

"I know you can," Russ said.

The man was sustained as the ward Scoutmaster. "The next Tuesday," President Ballard recalled, "he came in his Scout uniform with all the badges. He organized those boys into patrols. He knew the right names for everything. He could even tie the knots. We were off and running with a great Scout troop."

That is, until the Scoutmaster called Russ and said he needed to see him.

"I have to be released," the man said. "I didn't keep the promise I made to you. I went out and played golf with my brothers and I took a drink after I said I wouldn't. I am not worthy to be the Scoutmaster. You have to release me."

Russ looked him in the eye and said, "You can't give up. You can't quit. You can't let those boys down. You can't let your wife down. You can't let yourself down. You can't let the bishop down. You can't let me down. Most importantly, you can't let the Lord down. You have slipped one time. Just don't do it again. Next time you go to play golf and think you are going to be tempted, call me and I'll go with you."

Then he continued: "This good Scoutmaster made good on his commitment to never do it again. Soon he was sealed to his wife and children, and eventually, he became the bishop of that ward."[22]

The Ballard-Wade Partnership

The Scoutmaster was only one of a number of ward members with whom Russ established a quick and lasting connection. Another was Nate Wade. "The most important things in Russ's life were Church and family from day one," said Nate.[23] This was Nate's philosophy as well. They also had the automobile industry in common. At age sixteen Nate had "borrowed some money from his dad to buy a Ford Thunderbird Coupe. He shined it up and sold it a few days later at a nice profit."[24] At the time he and Russ met, Nate had recently discovered a fairly good market for buying used cars. He would purchase cars and drive them to Salt Lake City for resale. It was said of him, "If you were ever planning a road trip, Nate could tell you by memory what highway to take and when to buy gas."[25]

In 1956, Nate became part of Russ Ballard Auto, Inc.[26] They later changed the name to Ballard-Wade Auto and enjoyed many successes— all based on nothing more than shaking hands. As Russ explained, "It was a pleasure to be in business with someone like that where a hand-shake would finalize an agreement."[27] Ballard-Wade became a 50-50 partnership.

Nate's wife, Bonnie, observed, "They were like Abbott and Costello," the famous comedy team.[28] President Thomas S. Monson said, "Each had his own separate philosophy, but they made a great team. Each one supported the other, and they had a successful partnership."[29]

On more than one occasion Nate traveled long distances to buy cars. Several times Nate and Russ went to Detroit to buy cars and drive them back to Utah. Of one drive from Detroit to Salt Lake, President Ballard recalled:

> I think we were going through Rockville, Illinois, when Nate got pulled over and given a speeding ticket and taken to the justice of the peace. Nate went in and I was waiting in the car. He didn't come out and he didn't come out. Finally I went in and as I remember there was a $50 fine and it had to be paid in cash. It took all of Nate's change and everything I had. . . . Luckily we had credit cards we could [use to] make it the rest of the way back home.[30]

Russ applied their road adventures and the buying and selling of used cars to other situations in his life. In a chapter about the Church council system, President Ballard wrote:

> I learned to appreciate the sound and performance of a well-tuned engine. As far as I'm concerned, it's almost musical—from the gentle purring of an idling motor to the vibrant roar of a throttle fully open. And the power that sound represents is even more exciting. There's nothing quite like sitting behind the wheel of a fine automobile when all of the pistons are firing as they should and all of the assembled parts are pulling together.
>
> On the other hand, there's nothing more exasperating than a car that isn't functioning properly. No matter how beautifully it is painted or how comfortably it is furnished inside, a car with an engine that isn't fully functional is just a shell of unrealized potential. While it is possible for an automobile to run on only a few cylinders, it will never go as far or as fast, nor will the ride be as smooth and pleasant as when it is properly tuned. And when a few cylinders carry a load designed to be borne by more, the quality of performance deteriorates.[31]

As it turned out, selling used cars was not an ideal career path for Russ. He knew and understood the business, and he was good at it. But deep in his heart he knew he wasn't all about cars. That wasn't what excited him. He didn't even think much about cars. He was still apologizing nearly fifty years later to Barbara for the "need-to-be-repaired" used cars he brought home for her to drive. (The first brand-new car Barbara ever owned was given to her a few months before their fiftieth wedding anniversary.)

Russ was an entrepreneur. That was the thing that drove him—to create something, not with his hands, but with his heart and his brain and his creativity. And so he convinced Nate that they needed to branch out into other businesses. "We have invested together in various enterprises over the years, probably about ten different companies," said President Ballard.[32] "These were all interesting," said Nate. "They were all exciting—all new—we were just going to bat trying to hit a home run. Some investments were good and others . . . well, we didn't get out of [some] fast enough."[33]

In 1957, the Ballard-Wade partnership participated in organizing an airplane spraying business—Aerial Applicators, Inc.—with aircraft equipped to spray insecticides on forest lands and douse forest fires. This business was sold thirteen years later. Then there was the swimming pool company that sold and installed swimming pools lined with heavy vinyl. About fifty pools were sold and installed before the company was sold at a small profit. The Ballard-Wade partnership also owned and operated a foldaway trailer business. With so many people buying small cars like Volkswagens and Toyotas, foldaway trailers compensated for limited trunk space. That business was never profitable and eventually phased out. They also established a home-building business. Russ's father divided some of his farm acreage in Holladay into building lots. Russ built homes on some of the lots until all lots were sold.

The most outlandish business venture Russ and Nate found was the "safety suit," which was purported to be 100 percent fireproof. Russ traveled to Sweden, where the suits were manufactured, to see for himself how reliable and fireproof the suits really were. Convinced they were fireproof, he brought two suits back to Salt Lake City to show the mayor, fire chief, and other community leaders. As Russ and Nate demonstrated the reliability of the 100 percent fireproof suits to Salt Lake dignitaries at the Ballard-Wade dealership, the suits failed and caught on fire.

Edsel Dealer

Although the Ballard-Wade partnership got involved in a lot of different business ventures, the automobile business remained at the heart of their operation. But even in the car business, Russ was attracted to things that were new and different and a little entrepreneurial. In early 1957 he received a letter from L. Kouns, the western regional sales manager of the Ford Motor Company, inviting him to become Utah's first and only Edsel dealer.[34] Ford Motor Company had spent more than $200 million producing an automobile that carried the name of Edsel Ford, the father of Henry Ford II, who was then the president of Ford Motor Company and the grandson of Henry Ford Sr. "The sales promotion, anticipation, and excitement over the new Edsel were unbelievable," recalled President Ballard. "I was a young businessman and had all the power of the Ford Motor Company brought to bear on me to encourage me to become the Edsel dealer for Salt Lake City."

As he wrestled with the decision, he went to his father for advice. By this time, Melvin was easing his way out of the car business, but he still understood it as well as anyone Russ knew. "I said to my father, who was a great man in my life, 'Before I sign the franchise, I want to see the car,'" President Ballard said. "[After all,] it was a big decision, it involved a lot of money, a lot of commitment on my part." Ford personnel wanted his decision right away and thought by making arrangements for Russ and his father to fly to California to see the

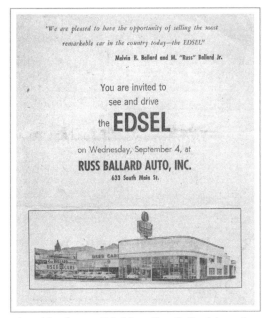

An ad for the new Edsel from Russ Ballard Auto, Inc.

An Edsel from the 1950s

Edsel models, they could seal the deal. The minute Russ saw the Edsel cars, he said he "had the distinct impression not to go ahead with the franchise."[35]

But "when I got away from the new car showing, the sales power of Ford Company started to work on me again. They assured me the car was going to be the greatest thing that ever came into the automobile industry," President Ballard recalled. There were eighteen different

Edsel models, featuring convertibles, two-door and four-door hard-tops, and station wagons. The list price—excluding federal, state, and local taxes—ranged from $2,300 to $3,489. Russ allowed himself to be persuaded, and he agreed to take the franchise. He rationalized that his father wanted to retire from the automobile industry and had given back the Nash franchise to Nash Motors. The Edsel franchise could be set up where Ballard Motor owned the dealership and where the used-car business would be operated under Nate Wade's leadership.[36]

"Everybody we knew who could afford one bought an Edsel because of Nate and Russ," said Bonnie Wade.[37] It was not long before they had the largest sales volume of any Edsel dealership in the country. Ford Motor Company invited Russ and Nate to come to Detroit and share with other dealers what they were doing to generate sales.

Despite the initial surge in sales, however, the Edsel was a dismal failure—"one of the most disastrous national marketing mistakes ever made in the United States."[38] Ford Motor Company lost more than $200 million, and Edsel dealers throughout the United States lost an estimated $100 million. Russ and Nate sold their Edsel franchise at a loss of $80,000. It took years for them to completely retire the debt and recover from the loss.

Somewhat philosophically, President Ballard looked back on this failure and said:

> I can think straight now when it comes to those kinds of decisions because of what I suffered. Perhaps we need to understand that failure is part of life. We are not going to be successful in everything we do, but from our failures we can learn the lessons that will cause us to become increasingly helpful to building the kingdom of God.[39]

Lessons learned from the Edsel automobile failure served him well. "If you are going to be an entrepreneur, an investor, you have to understand that there is risk," said President Ballard. "Sometimes . . . it takes years to recoup an investment and make a profit."[40] Through the ensuing years he became a very successful entrepreneur. Paul N. Davis, a longtime friend, banker, and stockbroker, said of him:

> Russ Ballard [has been] interested in men with new ideas and products that had a potential of being successful in the marketplace. His investments generally were all based on people. He has a gift in judging and believing in people and then being willing to invest in their ideas. Not all of the new ventures were winners, but overall, Russ was rewarded by his business acumen.[41]

No matter what business venture Russ bought or sold, the venture never took precedence over Barbara and their family or his Church calling. Those were always his highest priorities. And the most perplexing dilemmas he ever faced were when those two priorities seemed to come in conflict with each other. For example, on the very day his third child, Meleea, was born—April 6, 1957—he was expected to attend the groundbreaking of a new ward meetinghouse. Russ spent the morning hours in the hospital with Barbara and paced back and forth in the waiting room when she was wheeled on a bed to the delivery room. Their beautiful baby Meleea was born in time for Russ to spend some time with Barbara and the baby. When they were resting, he left the hospital to attend the groundbreaking ceremony for the new Holladay Seventh Ward meetinghouse.

Bishop of the Holladay Twelfth Ward

The construction of the new meetinghouse was evidence of the rapid growth of the Church in the Holladay area. Even though it was less than two years old, the Seventh Ward was bursting at the seams, and the stake presidency recommended to Church headquarters that the ward be divided. Twenty-nine-year-old M. Russell Ballard was called as the bishop of the newly created ward.

"It was frankly a little overwhelming to me," President Ballard recalled. "We were just finding our pace as a new ward (in the Seventh Ward). We were fully staffed and things were running smoothly. I felt like I was figuring out how to be a counselor in the bishopric, along with being a dad and a husband and running my business. And now this."[42]

Of course, it's possible that part of being overwhelmed may have had something to do with the fact Russ and Barbara's fourth child, Tamara, decided to be born on October 12, 1958—the very day Russ was to be ordained bishop of the new Holladay Twelfth Ward.[43] Early that morning they rushed to the hospital. Barbara was definitely in labor, but the baby seemed to be in no great hurry to be delivered. Barbara assured Russ that she and the doctors and nurses could handle the birth without him and that he really needed to go be ordained a bishop. Reluctantly, he left the hospital and arrived at the meetinghouse in time to be ordained and set apart by Elder Marion G. Romney of the Quorum of the Twelve Apostles. After the ordination was over, he shook hands with Elder Romney and others who were present—including President James E. Faust, who was then a counselor in the stake presidency and who would later become an Apostle and a member of the First Presidency—then hurried back to the hospital, arriving moments before Tamara was born.

Once Barbara and the baby were safely home and comfortable, Bishop Ballard threw himself into getting settled in with his new calling in his new ward. The Holladay Twelfth Ward consisted of 373 members, "with more than half of them, as I recall, under the age of twelve," wrote Bishop Ballard.[44]

During his six years as bishop, three men were called at different times to be his counselors—Clayton R. Williams, Glendon M. Whitmore, and Boyd N. Nielson (who had been one of his Adult Aaronic friends from the Cummings Ward). Of his counselors, Bishop Ballard said, "I am thankful that God sent to me counselors, two of

Bishop of the Holladay Twelfth Ward

whom had much to teach me. They were . . . considerably older than I and had experienced much more of life."[45]

As a young bishop, Russ truly valued the wisdom and understanding of those who were older and had more and different experiences in Church service. Indeed, throughout his life he seemed to draw special strength and energy from those who had traveled further down the path of life than he had. During one fast and testimony meeting, he listened intently as a much loved and respected patriarch bore his testimony and concluded by saying, "I pray that the Lord will see me safely dead, with my testimony burning brightly." After the meeting, Russ said to the patriarch, "Dear brother, if there is anyone in the Church who ought to be at peace as it pertains to being prepared to enter back into the presence of the Lord, surely it is you." The patriarch "took hold of my lapels and drew me up close," and said, "'My boy, not one of us is truly ready until we are safely dead with our testimonies burning brightly.'"[46]

M. Russell Ballard's sales acumen served him well as a bishop. For example, he promised seventeen deacons that if they achieved 100 percent attendance at sacrament and priesthood meetings for a year, he would take them to meet Church President David O. McKay. When they achieved the goal, President McKay's office staff got a telephone call. The staff member who answered the phone was singularly unimpressed. "If every bishop brought his deacons' quorum to meet the President of the Church," the staffer said, "the President would be shaking hands with deacons all day long." And then the person hung up.[47]

Not to be thwarted, Bishop Ballard wrote a personal letter to President McKay "explaining to him that one of his bishops—me—was in serious trouble." He outlined the issue and assured the prophet that he would never commit to such a promise again if he would rescue him this one time and meet with his deacons. To Bishop Ballard's delight, President McKay agreed. As the deacons sat in the north boardroom of the Church Administration Building, President McKay entered the room dressed in a white suit, having come directly from a meeting in the Salt Lake Temple. He greeted each boy personally and told them as a group that he wouldn't remember their names but if they met again they were to say they were one of "Bishop Ballard's 100 percenters."[48]

Another story is told of a young man who had fallen in love and was determined to marry his sweetheart instead of serving a mission. Heeding the promptings of the Spirit, Bishop Ballard told the young man that the Lord wanted him to serve a mission. The young man resisted. Bishop Ballard said, "The Lord is calling you on a mission." He then instructed the young man to fast and pray with his sweetheart and parents about the matter. The next Sunday the youth reported that he could not ignore a call from the Lord. He served an honorable mission and returned home to marry his sweetheart. "Years later he presided over one of the missions of the Church," President Ballard said.[49]

Of these experiences with youth and so many more, Bishop Ballard said: "I found that the most important principles to be taught to the youth are a love for the Lord, a love for the scriptures, and to be anchored to the doctrine. Where you teach the doctrine, testimonies are strengthened. That's the iron rod to see them through the tough times."[50]

Bishop Ballard was also influential in changing the lives of adult ward members. He told one man (the previously mentioned Scoutmaster) and his wife that it was time for them to be in the temple with their children. Bishop Ballard wrote:

> If I live to be a thousand years old, I'll never lose the vision of that good man and his dear wife kneeling at the altar. Henry D. Moyle performed the sealing. . . . When the children came in dressed in white and Brother Moyle lined them up according to age and had them take hold of hands and put their hands on top of their parents' hands, everyone in the room was in tears. When it was over the Scoutmaster's father put his arm around me and said, "Bishop, this is a good work. We thank you." I replied, "Well, it has been done by good people."[51]

Little children, too, received special attention from Bishop Ballard. When a Primary teacher brought an errant child to him, exclaiming, "Here's one of your flock, Bishop. Tend it!" the child and Bishop Ballard sat for a few minutes staring at each other. "We're going to work this out, and here's how we're going to do it," Bishop Ballard said to the child. "Every week before your class I want you to come and see me and let me know what you are going to do in class. We're going to have a chance to become really good friends."[52] And that was what happened. For the next couple of months, this little boy met with his bishop every week before his Primary class. They became good friends, and the boy's behavior improved.

Within the Walls of His Home

Such experiences as a bishop were satisfying and joyful—but nothing compared to the joy Russ found within the walls of his own home.

The Ballard family in the mid-1960s

Two more babies—Stacey, born December 30, 1960, and Brynn, born October 4, 1962—joined the Ballard family, bringing with them more love and more joy. President Ballard said, "To contemplate the miracle of birth, and to see a child born into mortality who had come so recently from the presence of our Father in Heaven" was his overwhelming joy. To him "the gift of new life brings a profound feeling of reverence. Welcoming each new little spirit into our family circle brings home again the incredible truth that God created the earth in all its magnificent glory, not as an end in itself, but for us His children. Indeed, we are His children, His offspring, and He is the Father of our spirits."[53]

Still, Russ found great joy—and sometimes bittersweet learning—in his continually expanding experience as a bishop. Late one cold, snowy winter evening, Bishop Ballard was leaving his office when he had a strong impression to visit an elderly widow in the ward. He glanced at his watch—it was 10 p.m. Too late to make such a visit, he thought. And besides, it was snowing. He decided to visit this good sister first thing in the morning rather than disturbing her at such a late hour. He drove home and went to bed but tossed and turned throughout the night. "When you get something like that on your mind, the Lord has a way of just stirring you all night long," Bishop Ballard said. "And that is exactly what happened."[54]

Early the next morning, he drove straight to the widow's home. "I arrived there about seven that morning," he recalled. Her daughter answered the door and tearfully said, "Oh, Bishop, thank you for coming. Mother passed away two hours ago." Bishop Ballard was devastated:

> I will never forget as long as I live the feelings of my heart. In fact, I wept. Who more than this dear widow deserved to have her bishop hold her hand, comfort her, perhaps give her a blessing prior to her passing? I missed that opportunity because I didn't act. I reasoned away this strong prompting from the Spirit. I committed that in the future I would be obedient to the promptings of the Spirit.[55]

Then there was the time when a single mother of a large family—a woman who was heavily in debt and had no prospects for employment—visited with him. When Bishop Ballard learned that the mother had a brother living in New York, he suggested the brother be made aware of their situation. "There's no reason to contact him," the mother said. "We haven't spoken in years. I can't go to him after all these years and say, 'Hi! Remember me? I'm your sister. Can you lend me some money?'"[56]

After counseling with the woman, Bishop Ballard was prompted to ask her permission to contact her brother. With her permission, he did contact the brother, and within three days her brother was helping put his sister's financial affairs in order. "I don't think I'll ever forget that tender moment of reunion between the sister and her brother after years of estrangement," said Bishop Ballard.[57]

The stake bishops' council, in which the bishops were asked to approve the annual stake welfare budget, was another learning experience for him. When President Smith called for a sustaining vote on the budget, two bishops refused to give their approval. "Why don't you brethren give the matter some thought and prayer," the stake president said. "We'll take another vote in our next meeting." At the next meeting the two bishops again voted no. "The way I see it," the stake president said, "either God is working through us or we are fallen leaders. That means that your choice here is simple: sustain us and this budget, or write a letter to the First Presidency and ask that we be released."[58] When the vote on the stake welfare budget was presented a third time, the two bishops voted in the affirmative.

Of all the experiences Russell had as a bishop, learning that blessings follow sacrifice was the most memorable. At a time when young families in his ward struggled to make ends meet, they were asked to contribute 50 percent of the money and labor needed to build a new meetinghouse, as was the Church practice at the time. Although their contributions and labor over a two-year period had been laudatory, they were $30,000 short in meeting their financial commitment.

At a priesthood meeting, Bishop Ballard was impressed to read the words of his grandfather Melvin J. Ballard as spoken before the First Presidency and the Quorum of the Twelve the day he was ordained an Apostle in the Salt Lake Temple. Bishop Ballard's reading of the account of his grandfather seeing in vision the Savior deeply moved the brethren of his stake. "There was hardly a dry eye," Nate Wade said.[59] Every man knew that with greater faith in the Lord Jesus Christ, the last $30,000 could be gathered. By eight o'clock Sunday evening, the ward clerk had written receipts for more than the needed $30,000. President Ballard said, "Sacrifice truly brought forth the blessings of heaven to the members of our ward. Never have I lived among people who were more united, more caring, more concerned for one another than these ward members were when making their greatest sacrifices."[60]

As Russ's years of service as the bishop of the Holladay Twelfth Ward were coming to a close, Barbara reflected on his service to the ward members:

> He took it so seriously and wanted to do it in a perfect way. He gave it everything he had. He had wonderful ideas and wasn't afraid to use them. He was humbly bold, you might say. He did a lot of wonderful things. He activated a lot of inactive men. I just think he was the quintessential bishop. He was especially tuned in to the youth. He made a big difference in many of their lives.[61]

When a release was extended to Bishop Ballard in 1964, it did not come with the relief he had expected. Russ wrote of his first experience sitting on the back row of the chapel:

> During the process of my sitting upon the stand . . . my wife had the back row. It was kind of her territory. She would come in and sit on that back row, and I was on the stand. I was so invigorated and exhilarated on the Sabbath Day doing the Lord's work, interviewing, visiting, and doing all those things that bishops do. I would come home at night, and my wife would be absolutely exhausted. Sunday was a hard day for her. She tried to explain what it was like to sit on that back row with those six children of ours. Then the day came that I was released. That was a moment of truth. . . .
>
> I was now sitting on the back row with the six children. Barbara was on the stand with a sisters' choir. . . .
>
> We had the opening song, the prayer, the sacrament. I was sitting with our six children. I have never been so busy in my whole life. I had the hand puppets going on both hands. That wasn't working too well. The Cheerios got away from me, and that was embarrassing. The coloring books didn't seem to entertain as well

as they should. I looked up and Barbara caught my eye and just smiled.

After struggling through the meeting, I started thinking, "Will it never end?" I proceeded to gather up all that stuff and the six children. As I walked into the foyer exhausted from the assignment, I understood!

Barbara later told me that she had never enjoyed a sacrament meeting as much as this one.[62]

CHAPTER SIX

YOUNG MAN
IN A HURRY

In 1964, Russ met Art Linkletter, a well-known radio and television personality. Linkletter was the host of a variety/talk program called *House Party* that ran for more than twenty years on national radio and television, as well as *People Are Funny,* a long-running radio and television game show. One of Linkletter's most lasting legacies was a lighthearted interview segment on *House Party* with children called "Kids Say the Darndest Things." By the 1960s Linkletter was branching out and was the owner and proprietor of the Art Linkletter School of Jazz, Tap and Ballet, with studios in Pomona and Claremont, California.

One of the things Linkletter shared with Russ when they met was his enthusiasm for the Valley Music Theater, a new theater-in-the-round that he and Bob Hope, among others, had been involved in establishing with great success in Woodland Hills, California. The intent of those who backed the theater was to provide good, wholesome, family-friendly entertainment featuring top-flight actors and entertainers, and Linkletter thought this kind of a theater would be successful in Utah. Russ was intrigued by the thought, and so Linkletter introduced

Art Linkletter and Russ Ballard became good friends

him to LeRoy Prinz, a Broadway choreographer and motion-picture producer and director who Linkletter felt could help bring the best entertainment to Utah.

Other than his brief experience as an actor during grade school, Russ didn't have an entertainment background. But he could see the business and cultural possibilities for the Salt Lake Valley. People—especially families—were always searching for good, decent, uplifting entertainment. He could envision huge crowds lining up to enjoy the work of talented Hollywood celebrities—many of them household names—without fear of being offended or having their values compromised. As Russ became more and more enthused with the idea of establishing something like the Valley Music Theater in the Salt Lake area, longtime friends and business associates were swept up in the tidal wave of his enthusiasm.

Emboldened by the success of the Valley Music Theater in California, Russ and Art decided to work together to build a theater-in-the-round in Utah called the Valley Music Hall. Of their collaboration,

Linkletter said, "We were good partners—Russ is a hardworking, generous, thoughtful, persistent, charismatic leader."[1] He later quipped that their partnership was more than a financial arrangement: "Russ has been trying to make a Mormon of me . . . and I am working on him to join the Baptist Church. But that's going nowhere, so we will rely on our friendship to get us through the next few years."[2]

The timing of such an innovative partnership and project couldn't have been better. Russ had recently been released as bishop of the Holladay Twelfth Ward and had the time and interest to devote to making the Valley Music Hall a reality. He was known and respected in the Salt Lake area as a successful entrepreneur, and investors trusted him—something that Russ never took lightly. By October 1964 the Valley Music Hall was incorporated and people began to purchase stock.

The site selected for the Valley Music Hall was 835 North 400 East in North Salt Lake, about ten miles north of Temple Square in Salt Lake City. The site was chosen because it was close to an interchange for Interstate 15, which would make the theater not only easily accessible but also incredibly visible to thousands of motorists each day. Due to the bold and innovative nature of the architectural plans—a large, round hall with a dome roof, only the third of its kind to be built in the United States—investors were certain that motorists would glance at the hall and wonder, "What's that building?"

The unique construction of the theater-in-the-round began on December 2, 1964. The intent was to build a concrete dome with no internal supporting columns in order to maintain clear sight lines for the entire theater. A large mound of earth was created, over which the steel and concrete dome would be formed. Thirty-two steel columns were placed around the dome that would—after the concrete in the dome had cured—be lifted into place with hydraulic lifts and locked into the columns. Although the construction process moved steadily forward without any obvious hitches, there was a moment of anxiety when the time finally came to lift the dome into place. The hydraulics were engaged, but the dome did not move. The large crowd of excited shareholders and construction teams who were there to see the dome lifted were deeply concerned. Would the Valley Music Hall be a failure before it even got off the ground—literally? But then a veteran contractor stepped up and said, "Turn it off and on—bounce it a little." The operators of the hydraulics bounced the huge dome a couple of times and broke it loose from the hardened material that was holding it down. The huge dome slowly began to rise, although the entire lifting process took more than two days.

As the construction process moved forward, so too did Russ's focus on finding funding for the building as well as for the productions it would house. After months of basically unimpeded construction and fundraising, there was shared optimism among investors that the Valley Music Hall would be a resounding success.

In the midst of this exciting professional time for Russ, there was also some excitement at home. Needing more room for their growing family, the Ballards moved from the Holladay area to 2611 East 1300 South in Salt Lake City.[3] The move meant more than a new and bigger house. There was also a new ward to attend—the Monument Park Thirteenth Ward—and there were new friends to meet and serve.

Even in his business life, things were happening for Russ other than just the Valley Music Hall—although it was pretty heady work, to be sure, to be meeting regularly with a governing board that included such Hollywood luminaries as Art Linkletter, Danny Thomas, Bob Cummings, Rhonda Fleming, and Bill Dossier (producer of the *Batman* TV series). But there were still other projects he was shepherding, including Ballard Wade Inc., with Nate primarily running the car business. One who knew Russ best during this period gave him an apt title: "Young Man in a Hurry."[4]

When the time finally came for the grand opening of the Valley Music Hall on July 19, 1965, it was a gala event attended by Hollywood celebrities and church and civic leaders.[5] Among their number was Elder Thomas S. Monson, who recalled, "There greeting everyone who came was Russ's father Melvin Ballard. He threw his arms around me and said, 'I am happy to see you come to Russ's latest endeavor.'"[6] Russ was heartily congratulated hundreds of times at the grand opening and on subsequent nights as guests expressed their thrill at attending high-caliber, clean, family entertainment presented in such a striking setting just a few miles from downtown Salt Lake City.

From theatrical productions such as *Camelot* to renowned artists such as Liberace, Tennessee Ernie Ford, Andy Williams with the Osmond Brothers, the Tijuana Brass, and Jack Benny, performances kept the Valley Music Hall filled with guests, including Church President David O. McKay and his wife, Emma. "They never missed a musical performance," President Ballard recalled.[7]

After attending many performances of Hollywood greats, Elder Monson wrote, "I enjoyed hearing Russ speak of the performers who came to the Valley Music Hall. I have never forgotten his description of Jack Benny, the comedian, for I have always been a fan of his":

> Russ said that when it was time for Mr. Benny to come on stage, Russ would go backstage to let him know how many minutes remained until curtain time. He said that Mr. Benny would usually look exhausted, but as soon as he got the word that he would soon be on stage, he was on his feet, with a smile on his face, and all ready to go before the public, like a true trooper and an excellent performer. Russ told me that as soon as Mr. Benny was through with his performance, he would go back to the dressing room and take a nap.[8]

No matter what the performance, Elder Monson observed that Russ was never too busy to notice the smallest need of a patron: "We took another couple with us. The wife was somewhat short in stature, and when she sat down her feet didn't touch the floor. Noticing this,

The Valley Music Hall

Russ promptly came forward with a small footstool on which she could put her feet so that she wouldn't be uncomfortable. This is just one small example of how attentive Russ Ballard has always been to the needs of others."[9]

With crowds packing the venue nightly, there seemed little reason to worry that the popularity of the Valley Music Hall would wane. The construction of the Salt Palace arena in downtown Salt Lake City in 1967 and the 1969 opening of the University of Utah Special Events Center were both welcomed. With performances attracting crowds, construction of these large, arena-like auditoriums was not expected to affect business. But in time it became clear that more venues competing to book the same popular entertainers would create increased costs and dip into profits more dramatically than anyone anticipated.

Bishop of the Monument Park Thirteenth Ward

Three years after the Valley Music Hall opened—and, more significantly, just four years after being released as a bishop of the Holladay Twelfth Ward—Russ was once again called to serve as a bishop, this time of the Monument Park Thirteenth Ward. He was set apart by Elder LeGrand Richards of the Quorum of the Twelve, who was a member of that ward. Elder Boyd K. Packer, also a member of the Twelve, later teased Russ that the real reason for his second term as bishop was because "he must have failed the first time so he was given a second chance to try to repair whatever damage he had done."[10]

One day while visiting with Elder Richards, Bishop Ballard asked him, "Elder Richards, if you were a bishop again, what would you do?"

The beloved Apostle replied, "Well, Brother Ballard, I'd take all of the books and the instructions and the manuals, and I'd put them off to the side, and I'd just go out and love the people. I'd put the round pegs in the round holes and the square pegs in the square holes, and I'd have everybody working."[11]

Bishop Ballard liked the advice and did just that. One of those he loved was Elder Richards. He often drove Elder Richards to his office in downtown Salt Lake. It was always a pleasure and an opportunity for Bishop Ballard to learn:

> One day we were coming off the hill down toward the Church Offices in a real snow blizzard. The snowflakes hitting the windshield were as big as dollars, and I was very busy trying to keep the car on the road. Brother Richards was sitting next to me singing, "Oh, What a Beautiful Morning."
>
> Then he said to me, "Brother Ballard, aren't those snowflakes beautiful?"
>
> I said, "Well, they are, Brother Richards, if they don't put us in the ditch." Then I asked him, "Brother Richards, how do you keep such a positive, upbeat, happy attitude? I would like you to tell me how you do this."
>
> "Oh," he said, "I never worry. I just do the very best I know how every day. I let the Lord do all the worrying. It is His Church. He can worry about it. I will just do the best I know how."[12]

Russell's second term as bishop lasted slightly more than a year, which was time enough to help prepare his counselor, who had also served as a counselor to another bishop, to serve as a bishop himself.[13]

Priests Quorum Adviser

A week or so after his release as bishop, Russ was called to serve as the priests quorum adviser. "That was quite an adjustment," he said. "Bishop one week and priests quorum adviser the next. I had to report to my former counselor, who was now my bishop and president of the priests quorum."[14] At a meeting of the Aaronic Priesthood committee, the bishop turned to Russ and said, "Brother Ballard, we want every priest in this ward active. I'll do all I can to help you, but it is your duty to get every one of them." The instruction had a very familiar ring to it, for it was the same instruction Russ had given the previous priests quorum leader a few weeks earlier.

One would logically conclude that his release from the bishopric would allow Russ to turn more of his attention to the Valley Music Hall, but his new Church assignment demanded his best effort and copious amounts of his time. There were thirty-two young men in the quorum, and many of them were not attending worship services or Church activities. Russ was determined to have a full quorum, and he tackled the problem head-on.

One of the less-active priests had a father who was not a member of the Church and a marginally active mother. The priest hadn't stepped inside a meetinghouse for six or seven years and was known as a "loner" and "friendless." As far as Russ was concerned, that was all the more reason to visit the young man early on Sunday mornings and bring him with him to church.

Another inactive priest required a different approach. "Why don't you take me for a ride in your Jeep?" Russ asked one day when he happened to catch the teenager at home. The young man's eyes lit up and he asked, "Where do you want to go?"

I replied, "I don't care, just anywhere you want to take me." Now if I could do it over again, I would have said, "Around the block five times." We got into the Jeep, strapped ourselves in, and he headed right for the hills. He knew how to drive that Jeep. That was the first and only time that I have ever been airborne in a four-wheel vehicle. I had eaten enough dust by the time we got back that I was determined not to lose this one. So I said to this boy, "I'll pick you up in the morning at 7:45 for priesthood meeting. You be ready." Then I left.[15]

The next day Russ went to the young man's home. The father was not pleased with the early-morning visit. When Russ asked him to tell his son that his ride to priesthood meeting had arrived, the father replied, "He's still in bed."[16] Russ asked where his bedroom was, and he went and awakened the boy himself. By about 8:20 a.m., the young man was ready to attend priesthood meeting. That was the beginning of a great relationship between a boy and his adviser. It wasn't long before the young man was serving a mission in Australia.

Father of Seven Children

Although miracles happened among those young men, and the goodness of their lives was a frequent topic of conversation in the Ballard home,[17] it was Russ's role as husband and father that gave him his greatest joy. Nothing, not even the adventures of his priests quorum, came close to the joy he felt being with Barbara and their six children.

Their seventh child and second son, Craig Bowen Ballard, was born on September 9, 1969. "It was a relief to be there when Craig was born," President Ballard recalled.[18] For the first time in all his years of being a "waiting room dad," the hospital staff encouraged Russ to put on a hospital gown and enter the delivery room with Barbara. After witnessing the miracle of the birth of his seventh child, Russ said:

I don't think I will ever forget the feeling I had when Craig was placed in my arms moments after his birth. I looked into his scrunched up little face, and I could not help wondering what this spirit son of God could tell us if only he could speak. To look into the face of a precious newborn child was to see etched in the tiny lines and creases the confluence of eternity with mortality.[19]

I don't know what families do who are not members of the Church as it relates to having a perspective of who we are within family relationships. Certainly fathers and mothers looking at little children that come into their families understand they are their children, and they love them. But without the gospel, they just simply cannot have the same perspective, the eternal perspective, of the destiny of these little ones as they come into their families. With the gospel, we have a different vision, a different view, a different concept of what life is all about and what families are all about.[20]

For Russ, these were joyous days—days that would continue from the time his children were young to today. Daughter Brynn has fond memories of her father's playfulness:

When I was very small I used to beg him to play horse with me. This is when he would bounce me on his knee and say, "This is the way the lady rides." I think I wore his knees out, but he would always play. He used to tickle us and get us laughing so hard that we would get whisker shaves. This is when he rubbed his cheeks against ours before he had shaved in the morning, and it would scratch and tickle at the same time. I loved it.[21]

Son Clark expresses gratitude for the guidance and patience given him by a loving father:

Thank you for your guidance when I have had difficult decisions to make, and for the teachings that have helped give me the knowledge and understanding that enabled me to make those decisions. Thank you for your patience with me throughout my life. . . . I'm glad to have the foundation that I do in the gospel and the values that you and Mom gave me as I was growing up.[22]

Of course, everything was not perfect in the Ballard household. Russ described family home evenings as "the only place I know of where confusion and chaos occurs with an opening and a closing prayer."[23] More than one child remembers it being "really fun to sit next to Dad to sing the hymns at family home evening, for when he tries to sing a song and doesn't know the words, he makes up new ones. It was just like listening to a foreign language."[24]

The childhood memories, with Russ and Barbara in the center, have lasted a lifetime. A favorite is jumping in the car and heading to the Lagoon amusement park in Farmington, Utah. Meleea recalls that her father "always wore a white shirt and tie! He was the only person there in a white shirt and tie. We knew everyone was staring at us, but we were kind of proud of him, so we didn't care. He would tend the little ones while the older ones and Mom went on the crazy rides. He didn't much care for the rides but was always willing to come with us. . . . He would even wait in lines if it's 'something the children really want to do' when everyone knew that patience wasn't his long suit."[25]

The family enjoyed vacations to Jackson Hole and the San Francisco Bay. The children all love the memory of their father driving a big motor home called "The Moose" through the streets of Chinatown with cars parked on both sides of the narrow streets. "We rode around those hills, all the skinny little streets and interesting alleyways, in this huge vehicle," Meleea recalls. "We were all so impressed with the driving skill and the courage that it took to do that. Timid is not a word that one would ever use to describe Dad!"[26]

But when it came to rearing the children so they could become happy, successful adults, Russ credited Barbara. She had a spirit of calmness when faced with traumatic, difficult family challenges. None of the children ever heard her voice raised in anger. Stacey said:

"Mother does not hold any college degrees or titles of this world, but what she has to offer is her wonderful example of a righteous woman. She has taught me what it means to be a daughter of God, to love the Lord and my family, and to serve faithfully."[27]

Russ wanted fathers and mothers everywhere to experience the joy he and Barbara had in their family. He shared this desire with Art Linkletter. "Russ and I, like most of the folks up there in Salt Lake City, consider that the family is the center of our lives," Linkletter said. "It is the thing that really counts after everything else is gone."[28]

Eventually, the children married, and President and Sister Ballard's family increased in size. As of March 2021, Russ and Barbara had forty-three grandchildren and ninety-eight great-grandchildren.

Family Achievement Institute

In addition to the Valley Music Hall, Russ and Linkletter founded the Family Achievement Institute (FAI). The purpose of the FAI was to develop and sell an interactive teaching product to assist families to be happier. Of the FAI, Russ wrote, "With my relationship to Art Linkletter and the difficulties of Valley Music Hall, we got the idea that we could take some of these personalities that we now had acquaintance with and develop a program on records that would teach basic family principles that would help fathers and mothers raise their children."[29]

Hollywood celebrities who had performed at or otherwise been associated with the Valley Music Hall participated in twenty recordings for the Family Achievement Institute. Danny Thomas, Dr. Norman Vincent Peale, and Olympic Champion Bob Richards willingly lent their voices to the recordings. Narrators—Art Linkletter, Pat Boone, and the former Miss America, Marilyn Van Derbur—carried the dialogue. Included with the recordings were printed materials to help families with day-to-day issues, and *Journey to Bethany*, a dramatization of the Savior's life backed by a Boston Philharmonic Orchestra soundtrack.

The packet produced and advertised by the Family Achievement Institute was dependent upon sales to distributors and the sale of the packet to individual customers. From the start, sales were sporadic. Perhaps the comment of Robert Pedersen, vice president of sales, best summed up the issue:

> We created a very attractive, relevant, credible product and a quality delivery system. We did our best to make it a fun, happy, and uplifting product for all families. But the market was not willing to spend approximately $300 to help strengthen the family. In hindsight, we were probably way ahead of ourselves in the market being ready to accept our products and advice.[30]

When it became clear that the Family Achievement Institute was not going to reach sales quotas or expectations, Art and Russ dropped the FAI and teamed up on another entrepreneurial project. This time it was a real-estate development in Mazatlán. Land development was a far cry from the Valley Music Hall and packets to help families, but it had financial potential. In seeking investors for the Mexico project, Linkletter approached billionaire D. K. Ludwig and others with large discretionary funds, such as James Kerr, president of the Avco Corporation. A few of the wealthy men expressed interest in the land deal in Mexico but wanted to see the real estate before investing. Russ was invited to join Linkletter and his wealthy friends on a corporate jet as they flew from Los Angeles to Mazatlán.

On the flight, Russ listened as one man spoke of purchasing an island and another talked of a recent $100 million acquisition. "D. K. Ludwig talked about purchasing this multimillion-dollar corporation and buying this multimillion-dollar organization and putting together another multimillion-dollar deal," President Ballard recalled. "Jim Kerr talked the same way about the big acquisitions his corporation had made."[31]

About thirty minutes outside of Mazatlán, the billionaire turned to Russ and asked, "What do you do, Mr. Ballard?" Not having anything to say that came close to buying an island or a multimillion-dollar acquisition, Russ replied, "After hearing what you have been talking about as it pertains to business, I don't do very much." He paused before telling the men, "I have a wife and a family of seven great children. I have a wonderful companion. We know where we came from before we were born. We know why we are here on earth and know where we can go if we are willing to follow the Lord Jesus Christ." When he returned home Russ said to Barbara:

> Honey, I have been with two multimillionaires and with a multibillionaire, but I was by far the richest man on that airplane because I was the only one who really understood the eternal purpose of life. I will take my wealth with me—my wife, my children, my friends. I will take with me the knowledge that I have earned. I hope that I can walk with head held high into the presence of God the Eternal Father and His Beloved Son, the Savior and Redeemer of the World, and feel comfortable and welcome to come into Their presence and spend the eternities with Them.[32]

Valley Music Hall Fire

At about two o'clock in the morning on September 14, 1970, Russ received a horrifying telephone call from George Condie, general manager of Valley Music Hall. There was a fire in the building—caused by an electrical short in the concession area—and it looked like the lobby of the hall was destroyed. Russ jumped in his car and drove to the theater, arriving to find firemen still fighting the flames. Although the fire had been contained to the lobby, the damage was estimated to be at least $150,000. Russ reported to the press that "the Valley Music Hall is fully insured and will be fully restored. There was some water damage to the walls over the main entrance to the theater from the lobby, but otherwise the theater portion is intact."[33]

The question was: now what? Because of increased competition in the marketplace and the rising cost of talent, the Valley Music Hall was no longer making a profit. It would be difficult to justify renovations for a facility that was losing money. Russ met with President N. Eldon Tanner of the First Presidency of the Church, who told Russ that the Church would be interested in buying the property and turning the Valley Music Hall into a regional center for use by the stakes in Davis County.[34] The idea was heartbreaking to Russ, who had poured so much of himself into making the theater a good business and a valuable asset to the community. But he felt immediately that it was the right thing to do. The sale of the Valley Music Hall to the Church moved forward, with all proceeds from the sale being used to satisfy the financial obligations of the Valley Music Hall Corporation.

In a letter written to President Tanner on April 15, 1971, Russ revealed his inner thoughts about the matter:

> Looking back over the last six years it seems to me in some ways like a nightmare when I think of all the effort we put forth to bring to our Valley the wonderful, clean entertainment that we presented, and then to have it ultimately fail to be accepted has been most disappointing.[35]

He also wrote:

> During the past several weeks I have really been evaluating my own personal life and past activities. . . . Thinking over the events of these years one basic principle has come to view very clearly to me and that is how easy it is to get involved in a project, and then how difficult it can become to honorably conclude the project.[36]

Clearly, Russ did not realize at the time of the sale just how beneficial the hall would be in the coming years to the Church. Elder Thomas S. Monson said:

> It became an ideal meeting place for priesthood leadership meetings, stake conferences, and other church meetings after it was remodeled and converted from a theater-in-the-round to a more conventional type of building. We wouldn't have had this building except for Russ Ballard and N. Eldon Tanner working things out so that the Church could purchase the facility and then make it available to the stakes in the general area.[37]

After a remodel, which added more seats to the hall, the regional center was dedicated in 1977 by Elder Mark E. Petersen of the Quorum of the Twelve Apostles. The center continues to be the location for conferences and special Church events in Davis County.

In 1989, the center was closed for remodeling once again. On February 3, 1991, the center was renamed the Bountiful Regional Center Performance and Event Venue, and it was rededicated. At the dedication, 1,600 people from Woods Cross, Bountiful, Centerville, and Farmington were in attendance. Elder M. Russell Ballard, now a member of the Quorum of the Twelve Apostles, said, "This building will serve the Lord. Twenty-two stakes can come here and worship the Lord and sing the songs of Zion."[38] President Gordon B. Hinckley, First Counselor in the First Presidency of the Church, offered the dedicatory prayer. In the prayer, President Hinckley said, "We thank thee for the faith of our fathers. . . . We thank thee, Father, for this beautiful structure . . . a place in which thy divine words shall be taught, a place where the peace of thy people will be strengthened, a place where testimony will be borne, and a place that will be filled with thy Holy Spirit as thy Saints gather here."[39]

With the Valley Music Hall sold, Russ turned his attention once more to the automotive industry, a career path that continued to link him with Nate Wade. Under Nate's direction, the partners secured the first Subaru dealership in Utah. The two great friends were excited about their acquisition, for Subaru was pioneering front-wheel-drive automobiles that were attractive to Utah buyers. During the first year, their Subaru dealership sold three or four cars each month. Sales increased in 1973, when a nationwide energy crunch led buyers to look for smaller, more economical cars. Through the years, Subaru sales have increased significantly.[40]

The Promise

In 1973, Russ and Haddon Salt, owner of the H. Salt food chain, boarded a twin-engine Aztec airplane in Salt Lake City to fly to the San Francisco area, where the H. Salt company headquarters were located. On that flight, Haddon—an Instrument Flight Rules trained pilot—was the pilot, and Russ was invited to sit in the copilot seat. Haddon landed the Aztec airplane at the Lake Tahoe airport to refuel and double-check weather reports. He found that it was a little cloudy, but not enough to stop them from completing the short flight to San Francisco.

As the plane approached the San Francisco Bay, however, the cloud cover became suddenly low and dense. Haddon tried to fly under the clouds so that he could see the ocean waters below and keep his visual bearings. As the clouds increased in density, Haddon lost all visibility. Russell recalled the panic of that moment and his promise to the Lord:

> When you fly into such clouds, you become totally disoriented. You lose your sense of forward motion, and it takes a few minutes for the pilot to orient himself from visual flying to instrument flying. At 180 miles an hour, you move a long distance in that few minutes and can get into serious trouble very quickly.
>
> At one point I knew the plane was upside down because the maps and everything that was over the visor was in my lap. The

only instrument I could read was the altimeter, and I could see that we were way too low at about 500 feet. My friend was near the point of panic as he tried to recall all that he had learned about instrument flying. All I could do was tell him to take a deep breath and get hold of himself. At the same time I was praying mightily because we were destined to either crash into the bay, into the bridge, a building, or the hillside. I kept saying to Haddon, "Get on the radio, get on the radio!"

It seemed an eternity before he finally made radio contact with Hamilton Air Force Base. All he could say was "I'm in trouble, help me." The air traffic controllers had us on their radar screen and immediately began to help. They told us where we were, how to straighten out the plane, and started to give instructions to guide us to safety.

The calm, reassuring voice on the other end of the radio helped Haddon regain confidence in what he was doing, and almost miraculously they were able to make an unscheduled landing at the air base. Of the experience, Russell concluded:

> At the peak of this crisis came a very tender moment as my entire life flashed through my mind. I thought of Barbara and our seven children, my parents, my business partners, the priests to whom I was the adviser, and many other things. I prayed fervently all through this crisis and made a commitment more deep and sincere than ever before in my life. As I prayed that Heavenly Father would bless my friend that he might regain control, I committed to Heavenly Father that if He would help us, I would place my life in His hands. I promised Him that I would be what He wanted me to be.[41]

It would not be long before he would come to understand what that promise truly meant.

CHAPTER SEVEN

PRESIDENT OF THE CANADA TORONTO MISSION

In 1973, Russ received a telephone call asking him to bring his wife and meet once again with President Tanner in his office in downtown Salt Lake. The purpose of the meeting, as Russ put it, was an "exploratory interview" to determine his willingness to serve the Lord full-time as a mission president. There was never any doubt that the response from both Russ and Barbara would be a wholehearted "yes." But President Tanner was aware of Russ's rich and varied business background, and he advised him to spend the next year putting his financial affairs in order so that he could accept the call.

That financial challenge was not an ordinary assignment, for forty-five-year-old M. Russell Ballard was not an ordinary businessman. He had investments in multiple enterprises. First and foremost was his long-standing partnership with Nate Wade. There were also significant business arrangements with George Condie as well as with his father. There was no question that Nate, George, and his father could capably manage the business and land investments—that was never the issue. But would they be willing to take over the business ventures for three years? It was no surprise to Russ that all three of these good men were equally supportive of Russ and Barbara's desire to serve a mission and willing to do whatever they needed to do, for as long as they needed to do it.

Russ didn't know it then, but when he and Barbara left for their mission, he was leaving his full-time professional business career behind him forever. For the rest of his life Russ would occasionally refer to himself as a "businessman-emeritus" and talk about how he sometimes misses "the satisfaction of working in the business world." But he knew in 1973—and still knows today—that the opportunity to serve the Lord trumps any investment project.[1] His advice, then and now, is, "Keep your financial affairs in order, but never become so involved in business that you feel unable to accept a Church calling."[2]

While Russ was working to prepare himself for full-time service, Elder Thomas S. Monson remembered talking to President Tanner about where Russ should serve:

> Brother Eldon Tanner talked to me about where I thought Russell Ballard would be a fine mission president. I said Russell Ballard would be an excellent mission president wherever he was sent. He probably would like to go to Great Britain, but President Tanner, you and I have an interest in Canada. With all the wonderful people that we left when we departed Canada I can't think of a man I would rather have over those people who are such dear friends [than] my friend Russ Ballard.[3]

In March 1974, Russ and Barbara were again seated across the desk from President Tanner. After speaking about their readiness to serve, President Tanner called Russ to serve as president of an English-speaking mission. But no specific mission assignment was mentioned.

The Mission Call

In April 1974, Russ just happened to be on the same airplane flight to Hawaii as Church President Spencer W. Kimball. While in flight, he teasingly asked the prophet where he and his family would be serving. "You'll get your letter," the President said with a twinkle in his eyes.[4] While Russ was still in Hawaii, the envelope with the much-anticipated letter arrived back at home. Over the telephone Russ implored Barbara to open the envelope. She pulled out the letter dated April 9, 1974, and read to him:

> We are pleased to extend to you a call to preside over the Canada Toronto Mission of The Church of Jesus Christ of Latter-day Saints to succeed President Roy R. Spackman. To Sister Ballard we extend a call to serve at your side as your companion in this important undertaking and as supervisor of the activities of the women and children in the mission.
>
> This assignment will bring to you the full responsibility for the supervision and conduct of the mission. . . . The corps of missionaries assigned to labor under your presidency will be reliant upon you for assignments to duty and for guidance and stimulation to put forth their best efforts. They are entrusted to your custody. To be close to them is an essential element in your leadership. They will deserve and need your understanding and sympathetic counsel.
>
> —Spencer W. Kimball, N. Eldon Tanner, and Marion G. Romney[5]

The call was exciting to Russ, and he was immediately grateful for it. He was well aware of the deep ties his Smith ancestors had to Toronto. In the spirit of prophecy, Elder Heber C. Kimball said to Elder Parley P. Pratt in 1836, "Go forth in the ministry, nothing doubting. . . . Thou shalt go to Upper Canada, even to the city of Toronto, the capital, and there thou shalt find a people prepared for the fulness of the gospel and they shall receive thee, and thou shalt organize the church among them."[6] Among those prepared to receive the gospel was Mary Fielding, the future wife of Hyrum Smith and Russ's great-great-grandmother.

Wanting to tell their children and parents about their call in a memorable way, Russ and Barbara reserved a private banquet room at the Five Alls, one of the nicest restaurants in Salt Lake City. "The children knew something was up, because we weren't eating at McDonald's," Russ said.[7] At the restaurant, Russ and Barbara announced the family mission call. "There was laughter, tears, and a sense of excitement" expressed by all.[8] Family members even raised their hands in a gesture of sustaining Barbara and him in the new assignment.

But his sister Chaunie remembers, "What mixed emotions I had, because that meant he was going away."[9] Her reaction expressed the tender feelings of other family members, for this kind of Church assignment turns lives upside down. Their home would be leased for three years, with no chance of an early return.[10] The Ballard children were expected to leave friends and familiar schools and join their parents in Canada. Clark was already preparing to serve a mission in Argentina, so he was not affected in the same way by the call. Meleea was running for a student-body office at East High School at the time, and Tammy was excited to start high school in the fall. Grandfather and Grandmother Ballard would need to step in and act as surrogate parents for children coming and going from Canada.

Of his mission call, Russ said, "When I was called to serve as president of the Canada Toronto Mission, I was overwhelmed by the exciting challenge that lay before me."[11]

As for Barbara, the call fulfilled a promise given in her patriarchal blessing of having the opportunity to serve a full-time mission. Barbara was set apart as a missionary by President Marion G. Romney, Second Counselor in the First Presidency. Russ was set apart as president of the Canada Toronto Mission by President Tanner, First Counselor in the First Presidency.

In preparation for their departure to Canada, the Ballards tried to learn everything they could about Toronto. They learned that the greater Toronto area had a population of five million people and was very cosmopolitan. Although photographs taken of the city in 1974 showed buildings covered in a coat of industrial soot, from what they read, the city was exciting. There was much to see, including the famous CN Tower, named after the Canadian National Railway company, which had built the communication tower. It was the tallest free-standing concrete structure in the world at the time. Other places of interest included the Toronto City Hall, the Nathan Phillips Square, and much more. Of course, the most important site for the Ballards was Black Creek, where Russell's great-great-grandmother and her brother and sister were baptized in 1836.

More important to the Ballards was information about the Canada Toronto Mission, one of 131 missions worldwide at the time.[12] They learned that at any given time many hundreds of miles would separate now-President Ballard from most of his missionaries, for the mission extended from the United States border near Detroit on the southwest to the province of Quebec on the east, and north to the North Pole. To reach all his missionaries would require a very long drive or airplane flights to Sudbury, Timmins, and Sault Ste. Marie. They also learned that the average complement of missionaries was 180 but could swell to 240. And the total number of Latter-day Saints living in Ontario was approximately 11,000.

On June 30, 1974, 720 people crowded into the Monument Park Thirteenth Ward to attend the Ballard family farewell. Among their number was President Tanner, who presided at the meeting. At the request of President Ballard, thirty-two members of his priests quorum sang "I Need Thee Every Hour."

"I am sure it was quite an effort to get us all to practice and sing," recalled Stan Poulsen, one of the priests.[13] As to their proficiency, President Tanner whispered to President Ballard, "They don't sing very well, but at least they are here."[14]

A New Mission President

In July 1974, the Ballards arrived at the Toronto International Airport. They were met by assistants Michael Glauser and James Anderson and driven to the mission home at 200 Main Street in South Brampton, Ontario. There the family was greeted by the outgoing mission president, Roy R. Spackman, and his wife, Donna Palmer Spackman. They were packed and ready to return to Cardston, Alberta, in western Canada, where President Spackman would resume his medical practice.

After they left, Barbara asked President Ballard if he was going to look that tired in three years.

A staff meeting was held the next morning at the mission office, at which the mission office staff informed the new president of their duties and explained their version of the needs and future plans for the mission. Mission presidency counselors Irving Wilson and Ralph Murffin—"two extraordinary men who were both mature priesthood leaders with a keen sense of the people and the history that is so important to Latter-day Saints in the Toronto area"—also met with the new president.[15] When President Ballard asked Irving Wilson how many people he had brought into the Church, his answer was "several hundred."[16]

President Ballard also met with news reporters. The *Toronto Sun* printed an article headlined, "Mormons Get New Leader," and the *Etobicoke Gazette* printed one titled, "New President Gave Up Profitable Auto Business to Lead Mormons." When a reporter asked President Ballard why anyone would leave friends and a good job in the United States to live in Toronto for three years, President Ballard said, "Well, it certainly isn't for the money." Then he told the reporter the reason for his move to Canada: "We believe the gospel has been restored and the Church is directed by a prophet today."[17] He explained

President and Sister Ballard with the missionaries of the Canada Toronto Mission

that he was called by a prophet to share news of the Restoration with the good people of Toronto.

At his first zone conference on July 16, 1974, President Ballard was very direct with the missionaries—not unlike his own first mission president, Selvoy J. Boyer. "I wanted to project a lot of love while letting them know that this was tough love and that we had a great work to do," President Ballard recalled.[18] He told the elders and sisters that there was nothing wrong with the gospel message; the problem was with the messengers. He promised that if the missionaries were obedient and worked hard, he could help them become better messengers and find greater success. At the end of the zone conference, Sister Ballard let the new president know that he was hard on them. As they drove to the next city, she said, "If you are going to be like that, I am not going to any more of these meetings with you."[19]

President Ballard quickly took a gentle but very direct approach to accomplish his goals. Sister Ballard helped create the cheerful mission motto, "A smile is the light in the window of your face that tells people that your heart is at home."[20]

At the end of President Ballard's first seven weeks in Canada, missionaries had reached new records—the missionaries had 2,500 referrals, and 500 copies of the Book of Mormon had been handed out to potential investigators. The exhibit "Ancient America Speaks," with an acrylic painting depicting the Resurrected Lord appearing to the Nephites in the Americas, was prominently displayed in the Canadian National Exhibition.[21] And President Ballard had held two rounds of zone conferences.

Of his new president, Elder Bradford J. Brower wrote:

> The Canada Toronto Mission is a geographically large mission, and when we would travel [President Ballard] always had us drive while he would sit in the back seat and work—dictating messages, reviewing talks, responding to missionary questions, and a dozen other tasks. He never, ever slowed down. . . .
>
> Once when we had just concluded a week-long, nonstop mission tour packed with meetings and long-distance travel, we finally pulled into the driveway at midnight. . . . He said, "Elders, you can sleep in tomorrow. You deserve it." We took his kind gesture to heart and didn't wake the following morning until around 8:00 a.m.
>
> At about 8:30 I received a phone call requiring President Ballard's attention. I was hesitant to call his home, thinking that at his age he must have been more tired than we were and would surely still be asleep. Reluctantly I called his home—only to find out that he had left his home three hours earlier to catch a flight for a district conference in the northern part of Ontario.[22]

As the missionaries were adjusting to their president's energetic leadership and high expectations, the Ballard children were trying to adjust to the Canadian schools. For five-year-old Craig, the adjustment was particularly difficult. He didn't want to go to school. President Ballard recalled:

> I was impressed to invite my son to come into my office and sit in what the missionaries called the "hot seat." He climbed up into the big, black chair, and I asked, "Son, how can I help you?" I shall never forget as long as I live the look of real concern on his

face. With his little chin quivering he said, "Daddy, I'm afraid." I understood, for I knew he had left behind several friends his same age, and so far he had found no one his age near the mission home. I said, "Craig, you have a friend that will always be with you. Let's kneel down together and ask Him to help you." We did, and Craig assigned me to say the prayer.

The Lord helped Craig find courage in this experience. Every morning, thereafter, we held our interview, and every morning I was assigned to pray. Then one morning, about two weeks later, there came no knock on my office door—no special father-and-son prayer. He had found his confidence and made some new friends, and I was the one that missed this very special experience each morning with my little boy.[23]

Daughters Meleea and Tammy were at the high school the day a crazed student gunned down a teacher and several students. When Meleea came home from school that day, she had blood on her clothes from holding a student who had been shot. These experiences and others pushed Barbara to say to President Ballard, "We've got to do more things with the family." He replied, "Yes, we sure do. We've got to do that." But missionary work had a way of crowding out family time. "Then one day I picked up my day planner and looked at it," President Ballard said. "There in the day planner was written the days we were going to do something with the children. Barbara wrote it right down there, and every one of those things she wrote down, we did. She wasn't demanding. But there were certain things that we did with the children, and she and I would have a date night."[24]

An Energetic Mission President

From his very first day in Canada, President Ballard found there was always something more that could be done to improve missionary labors. From September through December of 1974, he emphasized

"Strengthening the Church." He met with ward councils in the Toronto and Hamilton stakes to teach member missionary work, and he organized a missionary task force to visit the branches and help clerks locate "lost" members. In February 1975, he initiated a mission-wide fast so that the month of March would be the most successful proselyting month to date.

At the April zone conferences, President Ballard introduced the "Perfect Day" to improve the effectiveness of missionary work. To have a "perfect day" meant seven hours proselyting and one hour teaching. Then there was "Family Month," an initiative that received the Great Seal of Ontario and a proclamation from the lieutenant governor of the province of Ontario.[25]

This was followed by "Set a Date," an initiative in which members helped find someone to be baptized and then introduced them to the missionaries. His daughter Stacey took this initiative to heart. "Daddy, we have someone," she said. One of her friends at high school had said to her, "I've concluded that what makes you different must be your church, and I would like to know if I could go to church with you on Sunday."[26] The friend came to church and received permission from her parents to be taught the gospel of Jesus Christ by missionaries. She and her sister and brother were baptized.

Next President Ballard introduced "Commitment Meetings." Members and missionaries brought investigators to a fireside-type meeting to listen to President Ballard speak on such gospel topics as "The Apostasy and Restoration" and "The Purpose of Life." Afterward, President Ballard talked individually with investigators about their thoughts on baptism. He advised missionaries not to "tiptoe through the tulips," but to follow his example, being bold and forthright in teaching and committing investigators to join the Church.

At the conclusion of one Commitment Meeting, President Ballard spoke with an evangelical Christian couple who had been taught by the missionaries for five years but had never joined the Church. Yet they had a weekly standing appointment to feed the missionaries, which the missionaries loved because this woman was known to be an excellent cook.

The woman told President Ballard that she did not believe baptism was necessary. "Wait a minute," President Ballard said. "It doesn't matter what you think. It doesn't matter what I think. What matters is what the Lord taught about baptism." He turned to the scriptures and read in the book of Matthew of Jesus being baptized. He challenged the woman and her husband to get down on their knees that very night and ask Heavenly Father whether the missionaries were true representatives of the Lord Jesus Christ.

"Until you do that," President Ballard said, "the missionaries won't be able to visit you anymore." President Ballard could hear the missionaries groan behind him. Even though they hadn't made much progress with this couple over five years' worth of missionaries, they did enjoy those weekly meals.

That was on a Sunday night. At two in the morning the following Thursday, the woman telephoned the mission home and asked to speak with President Ballard. When the president pointed out that it was two o'clock in the morning, she said, "Yes, my husband and I know that! We figured the only way we could get even with you was to call you at this hour to invite you to come to our baptism. We did what you told us to do, and we now know that these missionaries truly are representatives of the Lord Jesus Christ, and we must be baptized by them."[27]

Then there was the time when his missionaries taught a family who were "poor, uneducated, and their personal appearance reflected a lack of appreciation or concern for normal hygiene and grooming. But they were among the honest in heart that we always pray for our missionaries to find," President Ballard said.

> When we learned that the family was going to be baptized, Sister Ballard and I attended the baptismal service. I happened to be standing next to the bishop of the ward when the family

arrived at the service. . . . The bishop's first impression was, to say the least, unimpressive. I thought I could feel the bishop's knees begin to buckle. I put my arms around this good bishop to give him my support—physically as well as spiritually. I felt prompted to say, "Bishop, isn't this wonderful?" He looked at me and smiled. I just couldn't tell if he was smiling because he agreed with me, or if he thought that I might be just another over-enthusiastic missionary.

The next Sunday I attended their ward sacrament meeting. I sat on the stand next to the bishop. The newly baptized family sat with their missionaries. They had come to church in Sunday attire that the missionaries had provided for them, and the light of the gospel literally shone in their faces. Alma describes this as "receiving [God's] image in your countenances" (see Alma 5:14). I leaned over to the bishop and said, "See, Bishop? We will make saints out of them!"[28]

With innovative programs that led to happiness in the lives of missionaries and converts alike, it was apparent to many that President Ballard lived close to the Spirit and looked to his missionaries to do the same. When a missionary telephoned and expressed feelings of homesickness, President Ballard called the missionary's zone leaders, told them there was a problem, and asked them to take care of it. When mission leaders reported a problem in their district, President Ballard often said, "You're the district leader. Get on your knees, ask the Lord to help you, and then you go solve it."[29]

As he pled with the Lord to bless and watch over his missionaries, President Ballard received impressions about individual missionaries. As he received such promptings, he telephoned the missionary and asked such direct questions that the missionary wondered how his president could have known. One elder wrote, "I'll be forever grateful for your help while on my mission, but I hope you've forgotten the details."[30]

For other missionaries, it was his sensitivity to the Spirit in medical emergencies that made a difference. After taking his assistant to the hospital for medical tests, President Ballard drove back to the mission office. Once seated in his office, he had the impression to return immediately to the hospital. He drove back to the hospital and found that his missionary was being prepped for surgery. President Ballard told the physician a second opinion was needed. The surgeon said the young man had internal bleeding, and without surgery he could die. President Ballard refused to allow the surgery to take place without a second opinion. The doctor was outraged, but President Ballard refused to relent. At the height of the confrontation, President Ballard told the missionary, "Put on your clothes, we're getting out of here." Assuming responsibility for the missionary, President Ballard took the elder back to the mission home and gave him a priesthood blessing. The elder then met with the mission doctor, who sent him to a specialist, and by the next morning all internal bleeding had stopped.

"I was by his side when I saw miracles I never dreamed I would see," said Elder Bradford J. Brower. "I witnessed as he cast out demons and healed the sick in most remarkable ways."[31]

It was not only missionaries and members who were impressed by the spiritual dimension of President Ballard, but also visiting Church leaders. Elder Boyd K. Packer of the Quorum of the Twelve wrote:

> When I returned home [from Canada], my wife was concerned because I was so tired. "Did you have a mission president that wouldn't listen to your instruction?" she asked.
>
> I replied, "No, just the opposite. I found a mission president who was so eager to learn and so desirous of obtaining instruction that I was drawn beyond what we ordinarily are able to do." . . .
>
> President Ballard is a man of great abilities, yet teachable. It is not unusual to find those who have very brilliant minds to at once lack humility and meekness. Not so with M. Russell Ballard. If I should choose a word to describe him, it would be *teachable*. It is a synonym for meekness.[32]

President Monson shared the same opinion of President Ballard: "He and his family fit right in with the people and in all of the activities of Eastern Canada. He serves with distinction, and the people love him. He has a way of working with all types: those of higher economic station and wealth as well as those of humble means."[33]

Takin' Care

This was clearly seen when President Ballard oversaw and arranged for the financing of a twenty-eight-minute film, *Takin' Care,* the title inspired by the popular rock song "Takin' Care of Business" by Latter-day Saint Canadian rock star Randy Bachman.

"We had to find some way to bring The Church of Jesus Christ of Latter-day Saints out of darkness and into the light in the great country of Canada," President Ballard said years later. "People just didn't know anything about us. I wanted to find some way to get their attention."

With the help of a Canadian Church member, Karl Konnry, the film was shot in 140 locations from the Atlantic to the Pacific coasts of Canada and featured prominent Canadian members sharing why they joined the Church of Jesus Christ and their joyous feelings about being baptized.[34]

Before the first viewing of *Takin' Care,* announcements of its upcoming premiere appeared in the *Toronto Star,* the *Globe and Mail,* the *Brampton Guardian,* and the *Financial Post.* The film was premiered on July 11, 1975, at the Etobicoke Olympium, a large, multiuse community center. Doors to the Olympium opened at 6:00 p.m., and crowds rushed into the building to find a seat before the 8:00 p.m. show began. The Toronto Stake center, across the street from the Olympium, was set up to accommodate the overflow crowd. Between the two facilities, approximately six thousand people attended the premiere event. President Tanner and Elder Monson were in attendance and participated in press interviews, as did President and Sister Ballard. Canadian members

Jack Armstrong, president and CEO of the Imperial Oil Company of Canada and president of the Canadian Council of the International Chamber of Commerce; Randy Bachman, composer of "Takin' Care of Business" and founder of the Bachman-Turner Overdrive and Guess Who rock music groups; and Diana Lynn MacDonald, 1974 Miss Teen Canada, also were interviewed.

"We had spent hours preparing for this premiere, trying to get everything just right," President Ballard said. "We practiced and practiced." But after President Tanner spoke to the overflow audience and they were ready to show the film, the projector malfunctioned. "This darn thing isn't working," President Ballard said loud enough for everyone to hear. President Tanner pretended to misunderstand him and replied, "I'm sorry, I have done the best I can."[35] The audience erupted in laughter.

President Monson later said of the event:

> When it came time for the film, the projector would not work. Here we were, with no means to show the film for which everyone had come. Russ did not panic. He simply said to President Tanner and me, "I am going to go get a projector out of one of the chapels. Until I get back, will you two please entertain the audience?" President Tanner spoke for a few minutes and then said, "I have to call on Brother Monson to take the rest of the time because I feel I have said all I need to say." Thus it became my duty to fill in the time until the projector was retrieved and assembled.[36]

Once President Ballard was back and the equipment was put in place, the film rolled on without a hitch, followed by applause and plaudits for all involved. "President Tanner and I were told to return to the mission home, where [President Ballard] would join us later. He had to say goodbye to a few people," recalled President Monson. "Unfortunately, no one gave us a key to the house, so when we arrived at the mission home, we just had to sit on the front porch, there were no chairs. We waited a while for Russ to come back and let us in the house."[37]

Although there was more than one mishap that night, *Takin' Care* was a big success. Approximately 5 percent of those who attended the premiere were baptized. This brought the number of baptisms in 1975 in the Canada Toronto Mission to 503. As for *Takin' Care,* it was shown thousands of times in missions throughout Canada. It was considered one of the most effective tools for helping Canadian members become actively involved in missionary work.

At about the same time as he was organizing and pushing *Takin' Care* along, President Ballard was also working with several prominent Latter-day Saints in Canada as well as religious leaders from other denominations to establish Family Unity Month in the province of Ontario. J. Bruce Smith, then president of the Toronto Stake, said that one of his stake members, Jack Armstrong, had "personal relationships with influential government officials, including Bill Davis, the Premier of Ontario," and that "President Ballard was alert to this fortunate situation."

"President Ballard was accustomed to thinking of and pursuing large initiatives," Smith said. Under President Ballard's direction, and taking advantage of Brother Armstrong's contacts, they were able to arrange a meeting with provincial leaders and a group of religious leaders that included President Ballard, the bishop of the Roman Catholic Diocese of Toronto, a Jewish rabbi, and senior officials from the United, Presbyterian, Anglican, and Baptist denominations. As a result of this very successful meeting, May 1975 was declared Family Unity Month in the province of Ontario, and subsequent declarations continued for several years thereafter.

"Responding to President Ballard's vision for publicizing Family Unity Month, our Church units throughout Ontario were encouraged to organize and facilitate local events that would attract members of the general public," Smith said. "A focus on our family home evening

Ballard family members in Canada. Left to right: Holly, Stacey, Brynn, President and Sister Ballard, Craig (in front), Meleea, and Tammy

program would provide the centerpiece of our outreach to members of the community. Church units would also seek opportunities to use local media to advertise their own events as well as generating awareness that Family Unity is to be celebrated in the month of May.

"We had many remarkable experiences through having the CEO of Imperial Oil as our media agent," Smith continued. "But even more important, we had the energy and creative mind of President Ballard generating the ideas and the enthusiasm to initiate Family Unity Month in Ontario, Canada."[38]

Projects like *Takin' Care* and Family Unity Month were successful and exciting, driven by a mission president who was anxious to do everything he possibly could to spread the good news of the restored gospel of Jesus Christ. But among all of his duties and activities as a mission president, they were the exception, not the rule. One tender story more closely illustrates his regular life and responsibilities among the missionaries and members of the Canada Toronto Mission. As he told it:

When I was a mission president in Toronto, we received a wonderful missionary couple who was sent to us in the middle of a very cold, snowy Canadian winter. I was impressed that this missionary couple ought to be sent to Kirkland Lake, Ontario, a place where we had tried to establish a branch of the Church for more than 100 years and had never been able to do it. They arrived in Toronto at our mission headquarters in their little Toyota. I interviewed them. The husband had been a stake patriarch for 18 years. The wife was the typical sweet and wonderful grandmother, complete with white hair, and scared to death. She said to me, "President, what do I do?"

"Well, Sister, repeat after me," and we recited the golden questions with each other.

Then I said, "Just looking at you with that angelic face you have, if you'll just smile at people and tell them who you are, and ask them if they would be interested in hearing about your message, I think great things are going to happen on your mission."

The next morning they left the mission home and drove up to North Bay, Ontario, where they overnighted with a missionary couple. They still had two hundred miles left to go, north.

"We thought you were angry with us when we were driving with drifts on the highway above the top of our car," they wrote in their first letter to the mission president. "We thought we were going to the end of the world."

I sent the zone leaders to be there when they arrived and to stay with them for a few days to get them oriented and started. I had previously asked them to find an apartment for this couple, instructing them to find something that they would be happy to have their father and mother stay in. The only mistake I made was that both of these missionaries had been out for over 18 months and they had become so indoctrinated in being missionaries that they had forgotten what it was like back home. So the apartment they picked out wasn't all that fancy, but they thought it was great. I also instructed the zone leaders to get a few provisions so that they would have something to eat when they arrived and something for breakfast the next morning. That was a mistake. I should have told them exactly what to get because after you are out 18 months, you think you could live forever on peanut butter and jelly sandwiches, because that is exactly what they bought.

So you can understand why, when the couple arrived, the first thing they wanted to do was to go to the store and get some provisions that made a little more sense. The next morning they went to the Dominion Grocery Store and obtained the items they needed, and went through the checkout and paid for what they had selected. The patriarch took the grocery sacks to the car and expected his wife to be right behind him. In 40-degree-below-zero weather, you don't stand around waiting for anyone too long. When she finally got to the car, she was smiling.

"Where in the world have you been?" the patriarch asked.

"Well, you got the groceries, but I got what we came for," she said. "I've got an appointment."

It seems that when she came through the check-out counter, she started talking to the checker.

"We're new here, this is our first day in Kirkland Lake," she said. "My husband and I are from Salt Lake City, Utah—a long way from home. We have come all this way to share with the people of Kirkland Lake, Ontario, a very precious message. It's a message of the Restoration of the gospel of Jesus Christ. Would you and your family be interested in hearing what we have come all this way to teach people?"

"Yes, I think my husband and I would like to know more about what you have to say," the checker said. And she made an appointment.

Then they got to worrying.

"Sweetheart, this is wonderful," the patriarch said. "But we don't know the discussions. What are we going to do?"

They were so nervous they went right to a phone booth and called me.

"My wife has gotten us an appointment, President, and we have to teach the gospel tonight," he said. "But we don't know the discussions." Bless his heart!

"Yes, but you know the gospel," I said. "Now tonight, you take the zone leaders with you, and you go bless that home, and you teach the gospel, and I have a feeling great things are going to happen because of your faithfulness."

They taught the discussion, and when they were finished, they said to Mr. and Mrs. Gild, "We have really appreciated being in your home. There has been a lovely spirit here. We'd like to come tomorrow night and teach you again. Who else would you like to invite to hear our message?"

To which Mr. Gild responded, "I think my brother, Don, and his wife would like to hear this."

The next night the zone leaders and my missionary couple were in that home teaching four people.

That one exposure by someone who had the Spirit, a grandmother, who was scared to death, who was relying on the Lord, who opened her mouth and explained who she was, that one invitation to hear about the Restoration, at last count has resulted in 19 convert baptisms. Those two brothers joined the Church and one became the branch president and the other became the elders quorum president. All because this wonderful grandmother did what she was called to do.[39]

As new missionaries continued to arrive in Toronto, President Ballard interviewed each one and got them up to speed as to mission expectations and innovations. At the conclusion of one such interview, the new elder said: "President, I am going to be the best missionary this mission has ever had. When I left Salt Lake City just a few hours ago, I kissed my father goodbye; and I have no assurance that I will ever see him again in mortality. In two days he will undergo a very serious operation. His chances of survival are less than 10 percent. All the way from Salt Lake City to Toronto, I have been praying and promising the Lord, and now I promise you, my mission president, if the Lord will just save my dad, I will be the greatest missionary this mission has ever had."[40]

The elder was assigned to Timmins, where the winter temperature hovers between thirty and forty degrees below zero when the wind chill is factored in. The elder's first night in Timmins, he and his senior companion had dinner in a member's home. After dinner, the young missionary stood up and said to his host, "We appreciate being invited to your home for dinner, but my companion and I have another appointment. May we be excused?" The senior companion knew that they had no other appointment. "I know," the young missionary said, "but if you would just go tracting with me I would appreciate it. You see, Elder, you need to help me save my dad."[41]

When that wonderful missionary completed his mission, he flew home on the same flight as President and Sister Ballard, who were returning to Salt Lake to attend general conference. At the Salt Lake International Airport, Russ and Barbara witnessed the joyful reunion as the dedicated missionary was swept up into the waiting arms of his father.

CHAPTER EIGHT

AN UNEXPECTED ASSIGNMENT

As April conference approached in 1976, President Ballard received a telephone call from President N. Eldon Tanner inviting him and Sister Ballard to attend general conference. President Tanner suggested that while in Salt Lake they come to his office for a short visit. Nothing more was said. "We never expected to receive a new call," President Ballard said.[1] However, the invitation was unusual, for mission presidents were seldom asked to leave their fields of labor. President and Sister Ballard concluded that they had either done something good or something really bad.

Maybe, President Ballard wondered, he should have gotten permission from someone to do that *Takin' Care* video?

The Ballards arrived in Salt Lake City on the evening of March 31. At 3:00 p.m. on April 1, they were seated across the desk from President Tanner in the Church Office Building.[2] President Tanner took them completely by surprise when he said, "President Kimball wants to see you."[3] They couldn't imagine what they had done to require a visit with the President of the Church. President Tanner walked across the hall with them to President Kimball's office.

With the First Presidency of the Church in 1976. Left to right: N. Eldon
Tanner, M. Russell Ballard, Spencer W. Kimball, Marion G. Romney

President Kimball invited them to sit down. He paused to look at them for a moment before saying, "We have invited you to come to conference to extend an invitation to you, Brother Ballard, to become a member of the First Quorum of the Seventy of the Church."[4] It was an earthshaking moment for President and Sister Ballard. President Ballard wondered if he was really worthy and capable of serving among the General Authorities of the Church.

Fifteen minutes later, they left President Kimball's office with President Tanner, who cautioned them to keep a low profile until the Saturday afternoon session of general conference. President and Sister Ballard watched the Saturday morning session on a television set at the home of his parents. They walked into the Tabernacle on Temple Square for the afternoon session, taking their seats as inconspicuously as possible. In that session, Elders Carlos E. Asay, John H. Groberg, and Jacob de Jager were also sustained as members of the First Quorum of the Seventy, along with Elder M. Russell Ballard. They were the second group called to the First Quorum of the Seventy, which had been organized six months earlier at the October general conference of 1975.[5]

From the time of that call until today, President Ballard has served more than forty-five years as a General Authority.

The four newly called members of the Seventy were invited to speak at the Saturday evening priesthood session in place of President Marion G. Romney, who had laryngitis. They were each told to take about three minutes to share their testimony. Elder Ballard was seated next to Elder Paul H. Dunn, a member of the First Council of the Seventy at the time. When Elder Dunn heard that Elder Ballard was to speak, he leaned over and said, "I want to tell you something about that pulpit up there. When you stand there, there's a little man who stands right next to you and puts cotton balls in your mouth."[6]

Forty-seven-year-old Elder Ballard shared the following message:

> As I contemplated the possibility of bearing my testimony tonight to you, my mind went back to many years ago when I was in the Aaronic Priesthood, and somehow I and one of my companions found ourselves over here by the stairs where we didn't belong, just prior to the beginning of the priesthood meeting. President George Albert Smith, in his kindly way, saw our plight, saw that we really had nowhere to go, and invited us to sit on these stairs by the pulpit. I sat there with my friend and watched the proceedings of that great priesthood session, never believing that I would ever again get that close to this pulpit.
>
> I remember that I said to my friend when we left the conference, "It sure would be nice to be a General Authority; then you would have one of those big red chairs to sit in."

I would like to say, my brethren, that I have been sitting in a big red chair for just a few minutes, and the greatest desire of my heart is that I will learn through my obedience and my service to become comfortable in that big red chair. I pray that the Lord will bless me that I might properly represent President Kimball, his counselors, the Council of the Twelve, and all my brethren of the General Authorities; that as they send me forth on whatever errand it might be, I might do the will and the bidding of the Lord.

I thank my wife, my seven children, my mother and father, for making this calling possible. I pledge my full support and loyalty to my brethren and to the Lord and ask for His peace and blessing to be with me as I grow in my assignment.

I have a great testimony of the gospel, for I know that it is true. I bring the greetings of the Saints in eastern Canada and all the missionaries there to all brethren of the priesthood around the world. I leave this testimony humbly, and in the worthy name of the Lord Jesus Christ, amen.[7]

The Return to Canada

After conference, Elder and Sister Ballard returned to Canada to complete the final fifteen months of their mission. "I will return to the mission a different person than when I left—sobered, awed, fully aware of my dependence on the Lord, and prayerful that I will fulfill my new calling in a way pleasing to Him," Elder Ballard said.[8]

The first Sunday back in Canada, Elder Ballard saw Brother Kenneth Shoesmith as he entered the Hamilton Second Ward meetinghouse. "Are you still here?" Elder Ballard asked. "I thought you would have lost your testimony this weekend." Brother Shoesmith smiled and replied, "I don't know why it took the brethren so long to call you."[9]

Knowing that it was not just three years that the Lord wanted his full-time service but until he turned age seventy, Elder Ballard wrote, "It seemed only prudent and fair that I would sell my interest in the property and the business to Nate Wade."[10] And so he left forever the entrepreneurial world with which he had been so enamored.

Although he was now a General Authority, Elder Ballard did not have many opportunities to interact with other General Authorities for the next fifteen months. However, on April 11, 1976, Elder Thomas S. Monson came to the area to organize the London Ontario Stake. Elder S. Dilworth Young, a member of the First Council of the Seventy, came to a stake conference held in the Toronto Stake center. About twenty minutes before the conference began, Elder Ballard recalled:

> Elder Young leaned over to me and said, "Do you sing like your grandfather?" [referring to my grandfather Elder Melvin J. Ballard]. I said, "No, sir." He said, "Well, that's too bad." I was scared to death that he was going to suggest that I sing in place of the choir. That would have ruined the whole process that morning.[11]

On May 7, 1976, the First Presidency, Elder Delbert L. Stapley of the Quorum of the Twelve Apostles, along with Elder O. Leslie Stone, a General Authority, and Elder M. Russell Ballard, held a solemn assembly for all priesthood leaders in eastern Canada. "I was given the assignment to be the chairman in planning for that solemn assembly," Elder Ballard said. "I had never been to one before, but they gave me careful instructions."[12]

Following the solemn assembly, Elder Ballard drove the First Presidency back to their hotel. "I have never driven more carefully in all my life than when I had the most precious cargo in this world in my car," Elder Ballard said. When they arrived at the hotel, the brethren bid Elder Ballard goodnight. Before leaving, however, Elder Ballard noticed that Arthur Haycock, President Kimball's secretary, was being detained at the front desk. "I asked him if I could take the key up to President Kimball so that he might get into his room. He appreciated my offering to do that and handed me the key. I took the elevator to the ninth floor and went down the hall." There President Ballard saw President Tanner and President Kimball standing in the doorway of President Tanner's room. As he approached them, he said:

> "President, here is your key. I thought I'd bring it up to you so you could get in and have a good night's rest."
>
> He thanked me for that in his loving way and then President Tanner took my arm and said, "Russ, how would you like to come in and have prayer with us?" I had never thought to ever have an opportunity to close the day with the First Presidency of the Church. We went into President Tanner's room with President Kimball; it was but a moment before President Romney and the other Brethren came in. I was overwhelmed. Tears welled up in my eyes as we knelt around that bed.
>
> I was kneeling next to President Tanner when President Kimball said, "Eldon, this is your room. Who would you like to have pray?" I think President Tanner sensed what was happening to me, for he said, "President, we would like you to pray." And then I heard a prophet pray. I learned a great lesson from that prayer. I felt the Spirit as I had never felt it before. When a prophet talks to God, close friends are speaking.
>
> In a short but sacred prayer, President Kimball said this, among other things: "And, Heavenly Father, we pray above everything else that the labors of this day have been acceptable unto Thee." That penetrated my heart like nothing else ever has on the principle of prayer. Here was a prophet of God pleading with the Lord that the efforts of that day had been acceptable unto Him! . . .
>
> I was nearly overcome with emotion. As we stood up each of them shook my hand. President Kimball took my hand last and he drew me up close and hugged me as only the prophet can. I'm a little taller than he was, and I looked down into his eyes and felt as though I was being interviewed again. Then he said, "Brother Ballard, I love you." I left the room. As I walked down the hallway

towards the elevator, I had borne to my soul a sure witness that I had just prayed with the prophet of God.[13]

From that point on, other than attending general conference in Salt Lake City, Elder Ballard was focused on missionary work in the Canada Toronto Mission. Once again, his innovative ideas were implemented, such as "August We Warm Up—September We Do It." Each missionary companionship was expected to keep mission rules: out of bed by 6:30 every morning, a minimum of one hour of companion study and one hour of individual study each day, and fifty hours teaching and tracting each week. The mission goal was one hundred baptisms in September. They had ninety-nine.

"On the first day of October we baptized four people," President Ballard remembered years later. "I was tempted to go ahead and count them so we could hit our goal. But I knew I was being watched by the mission office staff—and the Lord. So I let the ninety-nine stand. It still represented great work by our missionaries."[14]

At the October 1976 general conference, Elder Ballard was assigned to speak for thirteen minutes in the Sunday morning session. The Saturday before his talk, his missionaries sent him a telegram message—"Stand tall, think straight, and speak up"—counsel they often heard President Ballard give to them.[15] Although the Sunday morning session was not televised in eastern Canada and could not be seen by his missionaries, they united in fasting and prayer in his behalf. His talk, "The Making of a Missionary," became a classic.[16]

As the year 1976 drew to an end, Elder Ballard reported that the Canada Toronto Mission had baptized 723 converts. He praised stake presidents, bishops, and branch leaders and expressed "deep love for every missionary who is serving with us" for their diligence.[17] As for himself, there were always new goals to meet—some of them imposed by his missionaries.

When an elder telephoned and said, "President, guess what?" he replied, "I just can't guess, Elder, I've had so many surprises since I've been here that I won't even try."[18] The elder spoke of scheduling an appointment for him to speak in the School of Theology at the famous Toronto University. He was tempted to turn the tables on his missionary much as his first mission president, Selvoy J. Boyer, had turned the tables on him with the Midland Debating Society ("Good luck, my boy"). But Elder Ballard thought better of it and accepted the appointment.

The day of his scheduled speech, Elder Ballard was seated at a large table with thirty ministers who were anxious to grill him on the Church. Without hesitation, Elder Ballard spoke for forty-five minutes on the Restoration and doctrine of the Church of Jesus Christ. Questions followed:

> "Mr. Ballard, if you could just place the gold plates from which the Book of Mormon was translated on this table so all of us could handle them, then we would know what you are telling us is the truth," one minister said.
>
> "You are a minister and you know better than that," Elder Ballard replied. "You know that no truth has ever come into the heart of man except by the Holy Ghost. You could have the gold plates and you could hold them, and you would not know any more about whether this Church is true than before. Now, sir, have you read the Book of Mormon?"
>
> He answered, "No."
>
> "Don't you believe it would be wise to read the Book of Mormon, and then ponder and pray and ask God if the Book of Mormon is true? God answers the honest in heart by the confirmation of the truth through the Holy Ghost. Do you have any other questions?"
>
> He did not.[19]

Question after question was answered in the same masterful way, with President Ballard quoting scriptures, putting events in historical context, reviewing doctrine and authority of Christendom, and testifying of the Apostasy and the Restoration of priesthood authority. Each minister was given a copy of the Book of Mormon. Their names and addresses were collected so that missionaries could follow up with them if they had further questions.

Before Elder Ballard left Canada, he conducted one final round of zone, district, and stake conferences. Elder Ballard viewed these conferences as opportunities to express his love for the missionaries and the Lord. Missionaries, in turn, expressed their love for him.

In a mood for self-evaluation, President Ballard reviewed the progress and accomplishments made during the three years he had presided over the Canada Toronto Mission. There were now five stakes of the Church in Ontario, whereas when he began as president there were only two. Hundreds had been converted and baptized, and hundreds had been reactivated in the Church. More than five hundred missionaries had given service in preparation for the new stakes. The Ballard children had been accepted by classmates and had formed lasting friendships, with some of their friends accepting baptism. Daughter Brynn had been elected president of her school and named valedictorian. And for President Ballard, there was no question that serving in Canada was "one of the most refining periods of my life."[20]

Socials were held in various locations throughout the greater Toronto area to express appreciation to the Ballards and to bid them farewell. At the Halton Hills Ward, "The Ballad of the Ballards" was sung to the tune of "On Top of Old Smokey":

> *There once was a family, who lived in the West,*
> *With seven fine children, they truly were blessed.*
> *They grew strong and faithful, in ways of the Lord,*
> *So Heavenly Father brought them to our ward.*
> *Their call was demanding, yet special and fun,*
> *This dear mission family, just touched everyone.*
> *The dad was quite handsome, yet strict in his way,*
> *And once you had met him, you'd surely obey. . . .*

The wise words he'd tell you, all spoken in love,
He was a choice servant of Father above.
His dear wife was lovely, good-natured and sweet,
She kept their home peaceful, at 200 Main Street.
One son served a mission, then months passed away,
Now plans of his marriage, are well underway.
Two fine lovely daughters attend U. of U.,
Where many of the people are L.D.S. too.
The other three daughters grew well in our town,
Brought sunshine and laughter to all those around.
And Craig as their young son, so grown-up he'd be,
When wearing his name-tag, like a missionary.
The Ballards, we'll miss them, when shortly they'll be,
Arriving in Utah, in Salt Lake City.
And though they'll be gone soon, we never will part,
Of memories we cherish, down deep in our hearts.
We love you dear Ballards, but you must not stay,
The Lord has more blessings, for you underway.[21]

The Canada Toronto Mission history of June 22, 1977, simply reads:

Today is [President Ballard's] last official day as president of the Canada Toronto Mission. This mission has experienced great growth and expansion under the leadership of President Ballard. He has untiringly devoted himself to the cause of pushing forward the work of the Lord here in Ontario and there are many obvious results of his labours. He and his dear wife have been a great strength and aid to the many missionaries they presided over. Their family has been exemplary to the members of the Church living here in Ontario, and also to the many, many non-members they came in contact with.[22]

CHAPTER NINE

FIRST QUORUM OF
THE SEVENTY

In July 1977, the Ballard family returned to Salt Lake City. The renters moved out of their home and, for the most part, life with family and friends returned to a comfortable normalcy—other than for Elder Ballard. Although released as president of the Canada Toronto Mission, he had further assignments as a member of the First Quorum of the Seventy. He had served fifteen months in Upper Canada as a member of that quorum, but now that he was back in Salt Lake City there was more in store for him.

Two recent policy changes by the Quorum of the Twelve Apostles had expanded the responsibilities of the members of the Seventy. Under the leadership of Elder Franklin D. Richards of the First Council of the Seventy, the First Quorum of the Seventy was assigned to (1) direct ecclesiastical programs and departments at Church headquarters, and (2) supervise regions and stakes throughout the world. This meant Elder Ballard would be assigned to at least one department at Church headquarters and would also be supervising a geographical region somewhere in the world.

Aware of the policy change, Elder Ballard assumed he would have a minor assignment at Church headquarters until he was brought up to speed. He further assumed he would not be asked to uproot his family again so soon after they returned from Canada. He foresaw his family living in their home and himself standing on a road or a tarmac somewhere in the world, waiting for an airplane to lift off and take him home.

Managing Director of the Leadership Department

It was not surprising that before welcome-home festivities ended and suitcases and boxes were unpacked, forty-eight-year-old M. Russell Ballard was asked to meet with Elder Mark E. Petersen of the Quorum of the Twelve Apostles. After exchanging a few words about Canada, Elder Petersen suggested that Elder Ballard take a little time to rest— perhaps even take a vacation with his family. In the very next breath, Elder Petersen outlined the committees on which Elder Ballard would be serving. As Elder Ballard recalls, "I was up to my ears in alligators in Church assignments, even though Elder Petersen had said I should take some time off."[1]

Sitting on the couch or kicking back with popcorn in one hand and the television remote in the other wasn't his style anyway. As expected, Elder Ballard dove right into his committee assignments. "Russ has the ability to be what I would call a 'utility player,'" Elder Thomas S. Monson said. He went on to explain:

> The Salt Lake Bees years ago had a player to fill each position—catcher, pitcher, first base, second base, shortstop, third base, left field, center field, and right field—but they also had a man named Jack Hatchett who was the utility player. He could play any position on the team, including pitcher and catcher. So if a player got hurt, Jack Hatchett was the man who took his place. One night in Ogden, Jack Hatchett played one inning at each of the nine positions in baseball. This is the type of man Russ Ballard

The Ballard family in 1977. Clockwise from left: Craig, Holly, Tammy, Meleea, Brynn, Stacey, Clark, Sister Barbara Ballard, Elder Russell Ballard

exemplifies, and is. . . . He gives his heart and soul to the task and leaves his indelible image on that which is developed.[2]

Although committee work has an element of frustration, when Elder Ballard kept at the forefront of his mind his greatest desire, "to help the Saints," the work had its rewards.[3] Such was the case with his service on the Leadership Training Committee—a committee assigned to develop materials to assist in training priesthood leaders at the stake and ward levels throughout the world. As Elder Dean L. Larsen of the First Quorum of the Seventy observed the work of this committee, he wrote:

> Perhaps the greatest single challenge is to establish and maintain a system of Church government that is universal. . . . It is virtually impossible for those at Church headquarters who draft handbooks of policies and procedures to make provisions for every possible contingency that may arise in localized situations, where customs and personal relationships are so varied. When correct principles are understood by local leaders, however, it is often possible for them to resolve their problems in a way uniquely suited

to their special needs without violating the spirit of unity and common purpose that prevails throughout the Church.[4]

Elder Ballard was soon named managing director of the Leadership Department.

Supervisor of the
Southeastern United States

As for the geographic region he was to supervise, Elder Ballard was assigned to the Southeastern United States, which included the Southern United States, Caribbean islands, and small countries along the northern coast of South America. Beginning in August 1977, he presided at stake conferences, conducted leadership training meetings and mission presidents' seminars, and toured the missions in his area.

Passing through Salt Lake International Airport became a familiar ritual nearly every weekend as Elder Ballard left home on Friday afternoon and returned to Salt Lake on Monday. Living out of a suitcase was the norm.

After his first weekend in the South, Elder Ballard knew he loved the people. He found the Southerners he encountered to be gracious, and Southern hospitality was as warm and welcoming as its reputation. He also enjoyed the music, cuisines (except the boiled peanuts), and faith-and-family-focused culture in the South.

As he presided at stake conferences, leadership training meetings, and mission presidents' seminars, he observed: "I've noticed that stake congregations tend to reflect the attitudes and relationships of their leaders. Whenever I sense a spirit of loving brotherhood and cooperation among members of the stake presidency, that same spirit inevitably seems to permeate every stake meeting I attend. Unfortunately, the opposite is also true."[5]

His message to the Saints in Georgia, Florida, Arkansas, and South

Carolina was to love one another and share the gospel message with family and friends. David A. Bednar, who would later become a member of the Twelve, met with Elder Ballard as a member of the Fort Smith Arkansas Stake presidency. He recalled:

> I have always remembered how warm, gracious, inviting, engaging, and spiritually spontaneous Elder Ballard was as he met with the stake presidency. He did not come to our conference with a predetermined, standard, and "well worn" list of key points he wanted to emphasize. He clearly was in charge as the presiding officer, and he knew what he wanted to accomplish. But he also was interested in learning about our stake, in hearing about our successes and challenges, and in listening to us. . . . We did not feel "beat up" or burdened as a result of his training. Rather, we came away from our time with him edified, lifted, and wanting to do and be better. . . . He did not micromanage us or impose a rigid set of goals or expectations. Instead, he helped us become more effective in aligning our stake with prophetic priorities and in focusing upon the things that mattered the most. He was a wonderfully positive example of teaching correct principles so we could more effectively govern ourselves.[6]

Elder Neil L. Andersen of the Quorum of the Twelve wrote to Elder Ballard explaining his influence upon him when he came to Tampa, Florida, to call a new stake presidency:

> Being 32, it was the first time I had been in an interview schedule for the selection of a stake president. The new stake president, Lloyd Jones, recommended me as his first counselor and you extended the call. More importantly, in my brief interview with you, I told you, at your request, of my entrepreneurial ventures. You hesitated a moment and then wisely counseled me, "Remember Brother Andersen, sometimes another iron in the fire just means another hot handle that you must grab a hold of." It started me thinking, led me to more focused pursuits. Five years

later, I was called as a mission president, something I could not have easily accepted had I not disciplined my professional pursuits between my interview with Elder Ballard and my call as a mission president. He made a great difference in my life.[7]

On April 30, 1978, Elder Ballard presided over his first stake reorganization conference. He had participated in stake organizations in Canada, but on those occasions he had accompanied a member of the Quorum of the Twelve. This time he would be alone. "I was flying toward Florida when it hit me: I was going alone this time—just me and the Lord," Elder Ballard said. "I thought to myself: 'You better not pick a stake president just because you are impressed with him. You better pick the man the Lord has already called.'"[8]

Elder Ballard held scheduled interviews with several men who resided in what would be the Jacksonville Florida East Stake. Although each man was wonderful, it was not until Robert E. Bone walked through the door that Elder Ballard said, "How do I know you?" Brother Bone spoke of shaking his hand briefly at a youth conference a few years earlier. Yet to Elder Ballard, "He was as familiar to me as though he were my own brother."[9] Robert E. Bone was called to be president of the Jacksonville Florida East Stake.

The next morning at the stake conference, President Bone said:

> I was called at about 12:30 p.m. yesterday to be the stake president. Elder Ballard gave me permission to call my mother and father and tell them. I wasn't able to do it until about 6:00 p.m. My father is a stake patriarch and my mother a stake Relief Society president in another stake.
>
> My mother answered the telephone. I said, "Hello, Mother."
> She said, "Robert, you don't need to tell me. I already know."
> "You already know what, Mother?"
> "You've been called to be the stake president."
> "How did you know that? Who told you?"
> "I was standing at the sink," she said. "At about 12:30 an

impression came upon me that my son had just been called to be the stake president."

My father came on the phone. "Congratulations, my boy! As I was walking back from the store about 12:30, a voice came into my mind that you had been called to be the stake president."[10]

After returning to Salt Lake City in early May, Elder Ballard told Elder Howard W. Hunter of the Quorum of the Twelve the story President Bone had shared at conference. "Isn't it interesting?" Elder Hunter said. "The Lord expects us to keep our confidences completely, and yet He doesn't keep His very well. He oftentimes tells people what is going to happen before we even get there. But He puts us through the process; and by the power of the Spirit, His will is manifest."[11]

Managing Director of the Church Curriculum Department

Before catching a flight for his next round of conferences in the Southeast, Elder Ballard was released as managing director of the Leadership Department and named managing director of the Church Curriculum Department.[12] In his new administrative assignment, Elder Ballard was asked to formulate policy to govern the planning, writing, coordination, and implementation of Church curriculum. He was to be the editor of Church magazines and have oversight in the preparation of Church curriculum in addition to reviewing and evaluating the effectiveness of Church programs and activities.

Elder Ballard wondered how he could be managing director of the Church Curriculum Department and continue his service as the supervisor of the Southeast Area. Elder Monson knew the answer:

> [Elder Ballard] has the ability to delegate and yet to hold others accountable. I believe one element of his success in this regard is that he doesn't try to second guess those who help him on a

project. Rather than doing everything himself, he allows others to handle their assigned responsibilities and then to report to him and to keep him apprised of anything he needs to know. Thus, Russ is relieved of some of the strain of the detail that others less capable of delegating must endure.[13]

Under Elder Ballard's direction, the *Gospel Principles* manual was ready to be published. The manual was designed to be simple and basic enough for the developing areas of the Church. In addition, it was to be the curriculum for the Sunday School Gospel Essentials class, which was designed for new members, newly reactivated members, and investigators. "It took a mountain of courage to even think such a manual could be written," said Wayne Lynn, who had grown up as a farm boy in Wyoming and was the director of the Church Curriculum Department.

Brother Lynn and his staff wrote and rewrote *Gospel Principles* before submitting their materials to the Church Correlation Review Committee. The committee checked their work for doctrinal accuracy, general content, editing concerns, and other stringent criteria, then returned their submissions with red marks on nearly every page. Frustrated, but willing to press forward, Brother Lynn and his staff made the suggested revisions and submitted their materials again.

For Brother Lynn the most remembered day in that process was when he was sitting in the office of Elder Ballard:

> While I was visiting with Elder Ballard that afternoon, Elder Carlos Asay strolled over from his adjoining office. While we were talking he glanced down at my crossed legs and said, "Wayne, tell me about those boots."
>
> My wife had cautioned me against wearing them to the office. I knew they were not in harmony with the workplace. It's hard to change the ways of some old cowboys, and I had reasoned, "No one will notice them today." Both Elders Asay and Ballard chuckled. This old cowboy never wore boots to the office again.[14]

Several revisions later, and with the approval of the First Presidency, the *Gospel Principles* manual was published. Investigators, new converts, and longtime Church members have benefited from the manual over the years. A letter from Warsaw, Poland, suggests that *Gospel Principles* has also been a missionary tool:

> We received the book *Gospel Principles*. To me, a Catholic with some traditions, it was very shocking. The wisdom which I have found in the book impressed me very much, so much so, that I felt a desire to proclaim such wonderful truths among my closest circle of relatives. . . . *Gospel Principles* I call simply a pre-scription for living. We find there all the answers to questions how to live, so that we may be happy here, on the earth and later, in the spirit world. . . . We will soon be baptized, for which we want to offer heartfelt thanks to you, dear publishers of such a wonderful road sign as the *Gospel Principles*.[15]

Official Declaration 2

Although his committee responsibilities had escalated exponentially, Elder Ballard still traveled to the Southern states on a frequent basis. In May 1978, he went with Elder LeGrand Richards to Atlanta and helped organize the Atlanta Georgia Stake.[16] The next month he was in Baton Rouge, Louisiana, where convert baptisms in five stakes were on the rise.[17] But on June 8, 1978, he was in Salt Lake City. "I remember well one of the most remarkable meetings I have ever attended," said Elder Ballard. "It was on Thursday, June 8, 1978. All of the General Authorities met in the Salt Lake Temple. The First Presidency read to us a letter that would go to the world after our meeting":[18]

> He [the Lord] has heard our prayers, and by revelation has confirmed that the long-promised day has come when every faithful, worthy man in the Church may receive the holy priest-hood, with power to exercise its divine authority, and enjoy with

his loved ones every blessing that flows therefrom, including the blessings of the temple. Accordingly, all worthy male members of the Church may be ordained to the priesthood without regard for race or color.[19]

"The overwhelming spirit of the Lord was felt by everyone on this occasion," Elder Ballard continued, "and we all with grateful hearts knew that President Kimball had received this great message from our Heavenly Father. Tears flowed down my cheeks as I raised my hand to sustain this action."

The next morning, Elder Ballard telephoned President Richard Millett of the Florida Fort Lauderdale Mission.

> President Millett was in Puerto Rico with his counselor Frank Talley to hold a district conference. As I explained the content of the First Presidency letter, the mission presidency and their wives were overjoyed at the news, and from all of us tears of gratitude flowed that day. The brethren were authorized to proceed to interview and ordain worthy men to the holy priesthood and set them apart to serve in the various callings within the districts and the branches. The hand of the Lord is marvelous to observe as He directs His work here among men.[20]

Elder Ballard expressed his gratitude in an October 1978 general conference talk by speaking of the limitless opportunities now available to every child of God:

> It is possible, my brothers and sisters, that among the little ones in your homes and in your care are spirit children that were sent to you to be trained and prepared to fulfill callings as General Authorities, stake presidents, bishops, Relief Society or Primary presidents. In someone's home there is a little one sent from our Heavenly Father that someday will be called to sit in the seat where our great prophet now sits. Whoever is training our prophet of the future generations, please train him well.

Teach him to love the Lord, the scriptures, and his fellowmen as President Kimball loves us today.

I stand in awe when I consider the great confidence Heavenly Father has placed in you and me when he allows us the privilege of being the mortal fathers and mothers to his eternal spirit offspring. We must never forget that he has a vested interest in every one of us, and we must realize how important each human soul is in God's eternal plan.[21]

US President Jimmy Carter Speaks in the Salt Lake Tabernacle

Hoping to extend the gospel message to an ever greater audience, Elder Ballard began searching for ways to bring US President Jimmy Carter to Salt Lake City.[22] After eight months of tireless work by Elder Ballard and local Church leaders in Georgia, President Carter proclaimed the week of November 19, 1978, as National Family Week.[23] President Carter called "upon the American people to observe this week with appropriate thoughts and actions in their homes, and communities." He explained that "families are the building blocks of civilization. Our social and individual achievements, be they great or small, can generally be traced to early family influences. Family values are our most fundamental and lasting heritage."[24]

President Carter also said that he recognized "changing social patterns have threatened family stability. In today's increasingly complex world it is important to maintain the values and continuity of family life. All families are important, but the extended family, the foster family and the adoptive family play a special role by relieving the isolation of those who lack the comfort of a loving nuclear family."[25]

The National Family Week celebration culminated on November 27, 1978, when President Jimmy Carter spoke to an overflowing crowd in the Salt Lake Tabernacle. "I come here as president of a great country, and I tell you that our nation can say 'all is well,'" President Carter said, borrowing a well-known phrase from the Latter-day Saint hymn "Come, Come, Ye Saints."

"And even the American family can be characterized by the same phrase, 'all is well,'" he continued. "Because as was your early church in the minds and hearts of your own forefathers, so is our nation and the family so precious, so dear, so innately good and right and decent and strong, that challenges to us, to our nation, to the American family can successfully be withstood."[26]

President Carter personalized his talk by saying, "We have a large family, a close family, an exciting family, and one which has given one another great help and support and encouragement in times of difficulty or excitement or joy or achievement or sorrow. . . . There's nothing that gives me more pleasure, even as president of the United States, than to have [my wife] come to me in the evening, when I'm tired and concerned and worried, and put her arms around my neck and give me a kiss."[27]

Following his speech, President Jimmy Carter received the Family Unity Award. As for Elder Ballard, he treasured a letter from President Spencer W. Kimball that he saved in his personal journal: "While the memory of President Carter's visit is still fresh in our minds, we want you to know how much we appreciate the many hours you spent in helping to secure a Presidential visit to Salt Lake City to honor the American family."[28]

The Islands of Jamaica and the Dominican Republic Dedicated

The next time President Ballard returned to the Southeast, it was at the direction of President Kimball, who asked him to dedicate the Caribbean islands of Jamaica and the Dominican Republic for preaching the gospel of Jesus Christ.

In company with President Richard Millett of the Florida Fort Lauderdale Mission and his wife, Denna, as well as his counselor Frank Talley and his wife, Arleen, Elder Ballard flew on a twin-engine plane to Montego Bay, Jamaica, in early December 1978. The small group then traveled by car to Mandeville, where Elder Ballard met the Victor Nugent family and the Errol Tucker family, the only members of the Church in Jamaica. These two Jamaican families, six young missionaries, and those who had traveled with Elder Ballard to Jamaica met on December 5, 1978, at 6:30 a.m. under a large banyan tree in Brooks Park in Mandeville. Elder Ballard offered the dedicatory prayer:

> Heavenly Father, we dedicate this land unto thee and pray thy blessings to be poured down upon the people who live here in Jamaica, that the honest in heart, that the pure in heart, that those who love Thee and desire to know what they must do in order to qualify to come back into Thy holy presence might be sought out by the efforts of these great saints, who gather with us this morning, few in number. But may they be magnified, O Father, because of their faith and their love and their obedience unto Thee that they might be the catalyst around which a mighty Church might be built here in this land.[29]

At the conclusion of the dedicatory service, Elder Ballard set Victor Nugent apart as the branch president. Elder Ballard had the distinct impression that Errol Tucker should be ordained an elder and set apart as the elders quorum president in Jamaica. When Brother Tucker was asked who he would like to ordain him to the office of an elder and set him apart as president of the elders quorum, he said, "I want Brother Nugent to do it."[30] President Nugent set apart his elders quorum president as if he had been a bishop serving in the Church for many years.

From this small beginning, preaching the gospel of Jesus Christ has rolled forth on the island of Jamaica. In 2020, there were 6,668 Church members there, one stake with eighteen congregations (six wards and twelve branches), and one mission.

With Saints in the Dominican Republic in 1978

From Jamaica, Elder Ballard and his party flew to Punta Caucedo, located near Santo Domingo and Boca Chica in the Dominican Republic. On that island, Elder Ballard met John and Nancy Rappleye of Idaho Falls and Eddie and Mercedes Amparo of Guatemala. Elder Ballard learned that John Rappleye was living in the Dominican Republic on an international assignment with his company. John had initially turned down the position, but the night of the offer he and his wife could not sleep. Through prayer, they both knew the Lord needed them somewhere other than Idaho. The next day, John accepted a position in the Dominican Republic.

After hearing their story, Elder Ballard said, "Well, they [his company] didn't send you here. The Lord sent you here. Sit down and we'll set you apart as the president of the branch."[31] Eddie Amparo was set apart as president of the elders quorum in the Dominican Republic.

A small group of Saints and ten young missionaries gathered on

December 7, 1978, at 6:30 a.m. in the Park Paseo de los Indios at Santo Domingo. Elder Ballard offered the dedicatory prayer:

> And so, Heavenly Father, we dedicate this land unto Thee and now open it for missionary work and equally, Holy Father, we dedicate ourselves unto Thee, our very lives unto Thee that we might be found worthy, that we might ever be found doing Thy will and Thy bidding in the building of the kingdom of God here in this land of the Dominican Republic.[32]

From that small beginning in 1978, the Church has grown by leaps and bounds in the Dominican Republic. In 2020, there were 143,870 members, twenty-one stakes, 196 congregations (130 wards and 66 branches), three missions, and one temple.[33]

New Assignments from the First Presidency

Following the dedicatory services in the two Caribbean islands, Elder Ballard was released as the supervisor of the Southeast Area on January 1, 1979.[34] As a matter of policy and practice, General Authority assignments are routinely rotated among the Brethren. The First Presidency had three new assignments for him.

The first assignment was to succeed Elder James E. Faust as executive director of the Correlation Department. As news of his new assignment passed from one staff member to another, one brother said to Elder Ballard, "With your great talent for cutting through red tape and getting the job done, that department will be in excellent hands." Another said, "You have a tremendous ability to see through problems clearly, and to reach workable solutions and then get them implemented."[35]

His second assignment from the First Presidency was to serve a three-year term on the Salt Lake Chamber of Commerce (1979–1982).[36] "He knows the business community better than any of the brethren," said President Boyd K. Packer of the assignment. "He moves very freely, almost effortlessly in those circles, and in those circles he knows everybody."[37]

And the third First Presidency assignment was an invitation to serve on the board of directors of the Freedoms Foundation at Valley Forge, a nonprofit, nonpolitical organization dedicated to promoting America's heritage and values.[38] Elder Ballard was invited to take the place of Elder Monson, who had stepped down due to other commitments.

Reaching the One

In addition to his other assignments, Elder Ballard was to preside at stake conferences in the greater Salt Lake area when called on to do so. At one such conference held on November 4, 1979, he was handed an anonymous letter that read: "As you said at the opening of the 3:00 p.m. meeting, we were probably all disappointed when we found out that Elder Mark E. Petersen would not be our visitor, but you certainly had no reason to be apologetic. Your spirit, counsel, challenges, and testimony made this one of the greatest conferences I can remember attending."[39]

Another letter, received on December 13, 1979, simply read, "I love all the brethren, you know that. But there are some who are blessed with, and have learned to speak in a way that is understandable, strikes responsive chords, and kindles a desire in people to move forward. Such a gift is unique—such is your gift."[40]

His gift for helping people move forward was illustrated when the faith of a young man in his ward was shattered at the death of his beloved mother. "I gave her blessings," Elder Ballard said.

> Other General Authorities also gave her blessings. One of the blessings I gave was in the presence of her seventeen-year-old son. Another blessing was given to her when her son was eighteen.

A few days after the funeral service, I visited the father. I put my arm around him and asked, "What can I do to help?"

His response was direct and heartfelt: "Help my son to understand."

For days I tried to get in touch with this young man. I called his home about twenty times without success. I finally wrote him a letter and invited him to have lunch with me at the Church Administration Building.[41]

On the day Elder Ballard and the young man met for lunch, six Apostles came over to the table where he and Elder Ballard were seated. Two more Apostles shook the young man's hand as they were leaving the building. When they saw President Spencer W. Kimball walking through the back doors of 47 East South Temple, the young man asked, "Brother Ballard, does President Kimball ever see somebody like me?"[42]

Without hesitating, Elder Ballard decided to find out. He asked President Kimball's secretary if the prophet had time to meet with a young man who had recently lost his mother. For such a boy, President Kimball made time. As Elder Ballard and the young man walked into President Kimball's office, the prophet said, "My boy, your mother is all right."

"It was an extraordinary moment for my young friend and for me," Elder Ballard recalled. President Kimball gave the young man a hug and said, "When you return from your mission, you will understand more of what I am saying."[43] Until that moment, a mission hadn't been in the teenager's plans. But a few months later, Elder Ballard reported to President Kimball that their young friend had entered the Missionary Training Center.[44]

It had now been a year since passing through the Salt Lake International Airport had become nearly a weekly experience and living out of a suitcase had been the norm. In that year, Elder Ballard had spent most weekday nights at home with Barbara and their family, which now included his mother-in-law, Afton Wilkins Bowen, who lived with them for fifteen more years until her death in 1998.

He had attended ball games and had spent more than one afternoon at the Lagoon amusement park in Farmington. In so many ways, his life had returned to normal. Little did Elder Ballard know that this new, pleasant pace would soon end, or that he would again be seated across the desk from a member of the First Presidency and be asked to give even greater service to the Lord Jesus Christ.

CHAPTER TEN

PRESIDENCY OF
THE SEVENTY

On February 22, 1980, the First Presidency announced a change in the Presidency of the First Quorum of the Seventy. Four new presidents were called—Elder Carlos E. Asay as executive director of the Missionary Department, Elder M. Russell Ballard as executive director of the Curriculum Department, Elder Dean L. Larsen as executive director of the Priesthood Department, and Elder Royden G. Derrick as executive director of the Genealogical Department.[1] As one of the newly called presidents, Elder Ballard was set apart on March 14, 1980, by his longtime friend President N. Eldon Tanner.[2]

To the general membership of the Church, Elder Ballard's move from member of the Quorum of the Seventy to one of the seven Presidents of the Seventy may have seemed nothing more than a change of position within the quorum. To Elder Ballard, it was a meaningful opportunity to sit in meetings with senior Brethren and to give greater service on a larger global stage. Presidency meetings were "very interesting to me because of the vast experience of the senior Brethren and because of the extensive responsibilities members of the Presidency of the Seventy had as the executive directors of the various departments."[3] At these meetings he had many opportunities to share his concerns and successes in the Curriculum Department and, when called upon, to travel the world. Not only did far-off places like Bolivia, Peru, Israel, and Ethiopia become familiar to him, but Saints in these lands became close friends.

Nigeria

In 1980, Elder Ballard and Elder Derek Cuthbert of the First Quorum of the Seventy were assigned to travel to Nigeria in West Africa.[4] Since the end of the Nigerian civil war in 1970, Nigeria had experienced continued economic and political instability.

In Nigeria, the two brethren were introduced to Anthony Obinna, a schoolteacher and one of the first Latter-day Saints baptized in the country. Brother Obinna shared with them the remarkable story of how he came to know the truth of the restored gospel of Jesus Christ.

Brother Obinna said that one night he was shown in a dream an ornate building—the likes of which he had never seen before. He went back to sleep and had the same dream a second and a third time.

Soon thereafter, at an office in Lagos, Nigeria, Brother Obinna picked up an old copy of *Reader's Digest* magazine. As he casually thumbed through the tattered pages, he saw a photograph of the very building he had seen in his dreams: the Salt Lake Temple. Brother Obinna read the accompanying article and was filled with desire to know more about the Church. He wrote to Church headquarters, asking that information about the Church be sent to him. Not only did some literature arrive, but it was brought to him by some Latter-day Saint missionaries.[5] Before long, Brother Obinna was baptized, and soon he was set apart as the branch president of the Aboh Branch.

Brother Obinna was excited to show Elder Ballard and Elder Cuthbert a parcel of ground in Aboh covered with jungle foliage higher than a man's head. He explained that the tribal chief had given him the land to use in any way he saw fit. With great emotion he told of wanting to build a meetinghouse on the land. As Elder Ballard stood on that land, he felt something—something deep and profound—but said nothing about it at the time.

Toward evening, the two brethren retired for the night in a shared room. About four o'clock in the morning, Elder Ballard awoke Elder Cuthbert by saying: "Derek, how much courage do you have?"

"I have as much as you do," he answered. "Why in the world do you ask me that at this hour of the morning?"

"The Lord has prompted me that we ought to break ground for a chapel on the piece of land that we were shown today," Elder Ballard said.

"I don't think we should because we have no authorization; we have no clearance; we have no funds," Elder Cuthbert said. "What will the Brethren say when we go back and tell them that without any approval we broke ground and started a chapel in these far reaches of the country of Nigeria?"

Elder Ballard simply replied, "I don't know what they will say, but that is what the Lord wants us to do."[6]

A few hours later, Elder Ballard, Elder Cuthbert, and mission president Brian Espenshied were at the home of Brother Obinna asking him if he could clear the ground in two days so a groundbreaking ceremony could be held and construction for a meetinghouse started. To the credit of Brother Obinna and his friends, including a full-time missionary from the United States with extensive building construction experience, in two days about half an acre was cleared.

At six the following morning, more than a hundred people gathered on the half-acre parcel, most of whom were not members of the Church. At Elder Ballard's invitation, Brother Obinna conducted the meeting. When Elder Ballard asked him which hymn they would sing, Brother Obinna paused before saying, "Well, Brother Ballard, we really only know one song well enough to sing, and that is 'I Am a Child of God.'"⁷ Following the singing and a prayer, short talks were given by Elder Ballard, Elder Cuthbert, and Brother Obinna. Elder Ballard, with a Nigerian hoe in hand, then started digging the footings for the new meetinghouse along with Elder Cuthbert, President Espenshied, and Brother Obinna.

Elder Ballard returned to Salt Lake City, and Elder Cuthbert went back to England. "I asked for an appointment to meet with the Council of the Twelve," Elder Ballard said. "They invited me up to the fifth-floor boardroom, and I gave a report. I said, 'Incidentally, we broke ground on a building that we have no authorization for. Here's why we did it. Here were the impressions.' And the Brethren said, 'You did exactly the right thing.'"⁸

Without mentioning Brother Obinna or the Nigerian Saints by name, Elder Ballard said in his October 1980 general conference address:

> I realize that many of you are very conscious of the needs of others. I also know that you and I can do much more. Let us make the choice never to let a day pass without striving to touch the life of someone through our service! Then we can cherish and appreciate more the Savior's beautiful admonition: "Verily I say unto you, Inasmuch as ye have done it unto one of the least of these my brethren, ye have done it unto me."⁹

On the Lord's Errand

On a lighter note, in his October 1980 Brigham Young University devotional, Elder Ballard spoke of playing golf with the BYU golf team and watching as team members hit drive after drive three hundred yards—always straight down the fairway—while he kept pattering back and forth, in and out of the rough and the sand. One team member jokingly suggested that he hit the ball into the little hole in the center of the green, not into the sand to the side. "That was the longest eighteen holes I have ever played or ever expect to play," Elder Ballard said. "And I would suggest to President Holland [BYU president at the time] that anytime anybody on the faculty needs to be brought back to reality, have them play just a few holes with your great golf team."[10] His message to the students, including the golf team:

> Love the Lord. Get to know Him. Make Him your constant friend and companion. Counsel with Him. . . . I pray that you will be close enough to Him in your quest for your degree here that when you take your diploma and walk into life to establish your own family and your own set of circumstances, you will also take with you the most precious part of your education. It is far more precious, I believe, than anything you will learn in any laboratory or classroom. It is the testimony that Jesus is the Christ, the son of the living God—that He is the source of all light, that by His light we can walk fearlessly with heads held high, despite all kinds of obstacles.[11]

Among those who felt uplifted by the words of Elder Ballard was President Ezra Taft Benson, who was then President of the Quorum of the Twelve Apostles. He sent Elder Ballard a simple yet profound note: "Some human beings keep growing in spirit and in character. You are such a one."[12]

As the Church's senior leadership became more familiar with Elder Ballard's unique skills and capabilities, additional assignments came his way. In January 1981 the First Presidency invited him to serve on a committee chaired by President Tanner to consider organizational restructuring and other operations to ensure that Church organizations were consistent with scriptural teachings and revealed instruction.[13] After hours of discussions, the committee recommended to the First Presidency that three executive councils be organized: the Priesthood Executive Council, the Missionary Executive Council, and the Temple and Family History Executive Council.[14] Each council was to be chaired by a member of the First Presidency, with council members

The seven Presidents of the Seventy in 1981. Left to right, seated: Franklin D. Richards, J. Thomas Fyans, Neal A. Maxwell; standing: Carlos E. Asay, M. Russell Ballard, Dean L. Larsen, Royden G. Derrick

being drawn from the Quorum of the Twelve, the First Quorum of the Seventy, and the Presiding Bishopric. The committee also recommended that construction costs of Church-owned facilities, like ward meetinghouses, should come from general Church funds, with local units being responsible for utility and maintenance costs.

Outside of his service on the organizational restructuring committee and in the Curriculum Department, Elder Ballard was also expected to keep a rigorous travel schedule. In 1981, for example, he logged more than 50,000 miles as he traveled to meet with Church members in nine international countries. In Monterrey, Mexico, and Birmingham and Newcastle-under-Lyme, England, he presided over stake conferences. In Chile he divided a stake.

"I was sent by the Brethren to South America to divide a stake and choose new leadership for the new stake," Elder Ballard said.

My job was to seek to know the mind and will of the Lord in order to extend on His behalf the call to serve as stake president. It is an overwhelming responsibility. When I arrived at the stake to begin interviewing potential leaders, the current stake president told me that there were only three men who could possibly serve as the president. Through an interpreter I explained to the stake president that the procedure of the Church was that I would interview all of the priesthood leaders living within the new stake.[15]

There were thirty priesthood leaders to interview, and because they needed an interpreter, the interviews took longer than usual. "Late Saturday night, I had not yet found the person the Lord wanted to preside over this new stake," Elder Ballard said. As he reviewed the list of priesthood leaders, he discovered one brother who had not been interviewed. He learned that the brother was "home caring for his wife and three children, who were ill. It required sending someone out to the home of this brother, which was some distance away from where we were, to invite him to meet with me early Sunday morning."[16]

At seven o'clock on Sunday morning, that brother met with Elder Ballard and was extended the call to be the stake president.

I called this faithful brother to serve at 7:20 a.m. Sunday morning, knowing that the general session of the conference would begin at 10 a.m. It seemed almost impossible to me how he would ever select his counselors, organize his high council, and make other calls to leadership in such a short period of time. Expressing my concern that we were under such a terrible time constraint, this wonderful man smiled, reached into his shirt pocket, pulled out a piece of paper, and then said to me, "Brother Ballard, I am prepared. You see, I was told by the Spirit last night that I would be called to be the stake president. Here are my counselors; here are the men I would like to be on my high council; and here are the others to serve as leaders of the stake."[17]

The stake was organized, and leaders were sustained during the ten o'clock session of conference.

Following on the heels of Elder Ballard's journey to Chile were a planned return to England and then a stop in the Holy Land. Elder Ballard was escorted through biblical lands by David Galbraith, the first branch president in Jerusalem and later director of the BYU Jerusalem Center. At the Sea of Galilee, Brother Galbraith asked, "Have you ever seen a mustard seed?" Elder Ballard had not. Brother Galbraith pulled a pod down from a nearby plant, rubbed the pod in his hand, and blew away the chaff. In the palm of his hand were seeds the size of little pieces of black pepper. He looked at Elder Ballard and asked, "What did the Lord say about faith and mustard seeds?" Elder Ballard's mind went immediately to Matthew 17:20: "And Jesus said unto them, . . . Verily I say unto you, If ye have faith as a grain of mustard seed, ye shall say unto this mountain, Remove hence to yonder place; and it shall remove; and nothing shall be impossible unto you." Elder Ballard remarked: "I imagine the Lord was trying to teach that if we would just exercise even just a little more faith in Him and trust in Him we would be empowered to perform a mighty work among the people of the world who desperately need the gospel of Jesus Christ. We would see miracles."[18]

Elder Ballard did see many miracles as he testified of Christ in foreign lands. Whether in Saskatchewan, Canada, or Cochabamba, Bolivia, he bore witness of the love of God for each of His children. And he taught that God's children, in turn, show their love for the Lord by their faithful devotion to Him. When he returned home in December 1981, a letter from his daughter Stacey, who was at the Missionary Training Center (MTC) preparing to leave for her mission to Spain, was waiting for him:

I think I'm beginning to understand and catch a glimpse of what it's like to be a part of the building up of the kingdom of God and it's exciting. I know more about the importance of your calling and I love and respect you for your strength and testimony. . . . I wonder sometimes what I did in the pre-existence to be worthy to come to your family and be your daughter forever.[19]

The Passing of Melvin and Geraldine Ballard

As the year 1982 unfolded, there was more than one reason Elder Ballard needed to be at home. At age eighty-five, his father was facing huge health challenges and needed his son. Much had changed in Melvin's life besides his health. He was now an active and faithful high priest. Years before, as he and Geraldine were in the process of moving from their home on Butler Avenue into a home on Sunrise Avenue in Salt Lake, "the Lord put the bishop [Clarence Nelson] of their new ward [the Ensign Fourth Ward] in the same military unit I was in, and so the bishop and I got acquainted," Elder Ballard said. "He was a major and I was a lieutenant. I asked the bishop, 'When my folks move in, would you go visit them?' And that new bishop went and visited my parents the first day they moved into their new home and invited my father to become a counselor in the Sunday School presidency. That was the beginning of his full fellowship."[20] Melvin became a host on Temple Square and enjoyed many years of service as an ordinance worker and later as a sealer in the Salt Lake Temple.

But in 1982, as father and son sat together, Melvin expressed great apprehension, some discouragement, and a little bit of despondency, which was not at all like him.

I took hold of his hand and looked him in the eye, and said, "Father, do you really believe what you have been teaching all of your life?"

"You know I do," his father replied.

"Then I want you to do me a favor," I said.

"What is that?"

"Tell me about what it is going to be like when you go to the other side. Who do you think will greet you first?"[21]

Melvin spoke of his father, Elder Melvin J. Ballard, and of his mother. He talked about his brothers and sisters who had preceded him in death, and of his grandfather and grandmother Ballard. In the conversation that ensued, Elder Ballard saw excitement replace despondency and hope replace negativity as his father grew ever more anxious to get on with it and become busy once again in the great work of the kingdom of God in the spirit world. Elder Ballard counts it a "tremendous blessing to have held the hand of one whom you love, one who has drawn as close to you in mortality as anyone can, your father, and counsel together and bask in the light of Christ."[22]

Melvin R. Ballard died on December 22, 1982. Just ten months later, his widow, Geraldine Smith Ballard, joined him in the next life. During the months leading up to her death, Geraldine suffered from Alzheimer's disease. For weeks, she was unable to communicate. Yet, as Elder Ballard held her hand the last few minutes of her mortal life, she suddenly looked up from her bed and said, "Papa, Grandpapa!" Elder Ballard asked his mother if she saw her father, Hyrum Mack Smith, and her grandfather, Joseph F. Smith. His mother replied in a clear voice as she pointed upward, "Yes, right there."[23] Shortly after, she died.

Of Geraldine Ballard, the First Presidency—Spencer W. Kimball, Marion G. Romney, and Gordon B. Hinckley—wrote to Elder Ballard:

> Your mother was a living embodiment of the blessings of the gospel in her appearance and conduct, in the honor she always showed to her heritage and in the spiritual and cultural qualities of her life. She has set a high standard of conduct and achievement for you and your sisters and her grandchildren to follow, conduct worthy of a queen, which, indeed she is.[24]

Of his parents' passing, Elder Ballard wrote:

> While neither death was completely unexpected, it was still hard to say goodbye to both of my parents—especially just ten months apart. How grateful I was then—and am now—for the sweet assurance that God has a plan for us extending beyond the here and now, that our lives here have a great purpose and are an important preparation for what lies ahead. What a blessing it is to know that death is not an end.[25]

Blessing the One

Elder Ballard also knew that through the priesthood, those with special challenges could be blessed with greater health and happiness. In a testimony meeting of the First Quorum of the Seventy, Elder Ballard shared an experience he had in his home ward's sacrament meeting: "The daughter of a mission president, who is currently serving, bore her testimony about the tremendous difficulties that her older sister is undergoing in pregnancy, compounded with shingles that have moved into her eyes."[26]

While sitting at home that Sunday evening, the impression came to Elder Ballard that he needed to go and give this sister a blessing. So he asked Barbara to join him, which she always did without hesitation, and together they went to the home of the sick sister. When her husband opened the door, Elder Ballard explained their purpose in coming. The husband told them that his wife would not see anyone. "Will you tell her that we are here because the Lord has told us to come here and give her a blessing?" Elder Ballard said.[27] The husband invited the Ballards to sit down in the living room while he entreated his wife to come out of the bedroom and receive a priesthood blessing. In a few minutes, she came reluctantly into the living room. Her husband anointed her, and Elder Ballard pronounced a blessing.

As I sealed the anointing, words flowed and promises were made that were frightening. I even wanted to hold back, but it didn't seem right to hold back. I guess I was wondering about my own faith. The impression came to let her know that I was standing there, not only as her neighbor and as a member of this Quorum, but in proxy for her father who was serving as a mission president. When those words slipped from my lips and fell upon the head of his daughter, she, of course, wept. We were all weeping.[28]

That was on a Sunday night. On Wednesday, her doctor could not detect any serious problem with her pregnancy, and her shingles were clearing up. "Because of experiences like this that come into our lives on occasion," Elder Ballard testified, "it is easy for me to stand and bear testimony that I know that the Church is true and that I know that Jesus is the Christ and this is His work, and that our Heavenly Father is very close."[29]

Other sacred experiences followed. About six months before the death of Elder LeGrand Richards, one of his legs was amputated due to circulation problems. He was in great pain. As Elder Ballard was driving home from a stake conference and neared the intersection of Foothill Boulevard and 800 South, he received the impression, "Go see LeGrand Richards."[30]

Elder Ballard drove straight to the home of Elder Richards's daughter Nona and knocked on the door. When Nona came to the door, she said, "Oh, Brother Ballard, my daddy is something else!"

Elder Ballard replied, "Nona, the whole Church knows that your daddy is something else. Why did you say this?"

Nona replied, "Every time Daddy needs someone, the Lord sends someone to him."[31]

Elder Ballard asked Nona, "What am I here for?" Nona led him to her father's room, where "this great Apostle of the Lord lay in terrible pain." Elder Ballard said, "Elder Richards, it is Brother Ballard. Would you like me to give you a blessing?" Elder Richards nodded in agreement. Elder Ballard described placing his hands on the head of LeGrand Richards as a "spiritually refining experience." He then spoke these words: "LeGrand Richards, in the name of the Lord Jesus Christ, and by the authority of the holy priesthood vested in me, I lay my hands upon you to give you a blessing." Of the words that followed, Elder Ballard said: "I testify and witness that the heavens were literally opened to my mind, and the Lord spoke through me and blessed His servant. Before I concluded, Elder Richards was sleeping peacefully. As I left that sacred, special experience, I thanked the Lord for speaking to me at the red light on Foothill Boulevard and 800 South."[32]

Speaking of the event some years later, President Ballard said, "I have often wondered what would have happened had I not responded to that spiritual prompting to visit Brother Richards. It occurred to me that the Lord would have sent someone else—someone who was willing to listen and respond to bless His Apostle."[33]

Another example of the inspiration of the Lord occurred when Elder Ballard accompanied a newly called member of the Seventy to Pocatello, Idaho, for the purpose of selecting a stake president. The two Church leaders interviewed several worthy brethren before extending the call to a brother who had served in the previous stake presidency for about two years. After being sustained as the new stake president, the brother wrote to Elder Ballard:

> Elder Ballard, the day you were sustained as a member of the First Quorum of the Seventy and took your place on the rostrum in the Tabernacle, I was sitting in the congregation in the Tabernacle. A voice, as clear as any voice I have ever heard in my life, said to me, "Someday that man . . . will call you as a stake president." I have lived with that for all these years. When the notices came to us that the General Authority who was to come to the conference was not you, I went home to my wife and said, "You do not need to worry, dear, I am not going to be the stake

president." She said, "How do you know?" To which I replied, "Because Brother Ballard is not coming to conference."

Then three days before the conference, the stake president announced that you would be attending our conference. I went home and said, "I will be the stake president of the new stake after all." My wife said, "Why do you think that?" I told her that you were coming to our conference.[34]

Similarly, when Elder Ballard presided at the reorganization of the Franklin Tennessee Stake, the Spirit impressed him to call as stake president a thirty-seven-year-old attorney, D. Todd Christofferson, who would later be called to the Quorum of the Twelve. "Elder Ballard's attitude and expressions of confidence gave me a confidence that I otherwise would have lacked," Elder Christofferson said. "I have felt a closeness to him ever since."[35]

"He Is Willing to Welcome His Children Back"

During this period, Elder Ballard had a marvelous experience that taught him powerful lessons about the love of God for His children, wayward though some of them may be. He tells of receiving "an assignment from the First Presidency to interview a man who had been excommunicated from the Church for some behavior that required that kind of discipline."

This man lived out in the Midwest. He was in a hospital in a country town. It was difficult to get to him, and it required my leaving on Friday, overnighting in a hotel, and Saturday catching a small commuter plane to where he was. I was met by the regional representative at a small airport, and we drove for two hours into the country to the hospital. I was commissioned, under the direction of the President of the Church, to interview this man to determine whether or not it would be appropriate and pleasing to the Lord to restore unto him his priesthood and temple blessings.

When we walked into the hospital room, it was a scene that I did not anticipate. I knew he was very ill, but I did not realize that he was in the advanced stages of ALS, also known as Lou Gehrig's disease, a disease that had rendered him totally immobile, unable to speak. The only thing that he could move was his eyes. As I looked at the circumstance, I excused myself and asked his wife, the mother of his eight children, to step out into the hall with me. I said to her, "I am not sure how I proceed to interview your husband." Then came a beautiful experience. She said, "Brother Ballard, you ask him the questions, and I will tell you his answers. I have learned to read his eyes."

As I leaned over the hospital bed and looked at that dear man and asked him one or two questions, and then looked at his wife for his answers, I was satisfied that the time had come to restore his sacred blessings. I laid my hands on his head and said, "In the name of Jesus Christ and by the authority of the holy priesthood, I lay my hands upon your head, and I am authorized at the direction of the President of the Church to restore unto you the holy Melchizedek Priesthood." With which, he started to weep. "I am further authorized to restore unto you your calling as an elder in that priesthood with all of the rights and privileges appertaining thereto." Now he was weeping to where I could feel him shaking a little bit under my hands. "And the President of the Church authorizes the restoration of your endowment that you received when you entered the temple the first time, with all of its blessings appertaining thereto, and the sealing to your wife and your children."

A blessing flowed from the Lord to that good man. It was an emotional experience, which I think you can sense. Upon the conclusion of the blessing, I thought what a marvelous thing that God has provided for His children the privilege of repentance, and yet, how hard to walk such a difficult course as this brother had done.

We talked together—the stake president, who was there, and the regional representative, myself, and the man's wife. As we were about to leave the hospital room, I was impressed to say to the wife, "Would you like a blessing?"

"Oh, Brother Ballard, I would like a blessing. This has been so difficult," she said, "and I have not had a blessing for a long time."

We pulled up a chair and with the stake president and the regional representative on either side of me we laid our hands on her head to give her a priesthood blessing, a blessing of comfort and reassurance from our Heavenly Father. After calling her by name, for the first and only time in my ministry I had the experience of not being able to speak. I almost panicked. You ask yourself a lot of questions in a moment like that. Is there something wrong with me? Is there something wrong with her? Why can't I proceed to give this blessing? It seemed to me and also to the regional representative and the stake president as though it had been many minutes of silence, and yet it was, I am sure, less than a minute. Silence seems like a long time in a moment like that.

I took my hands off of her head and so did the regional representative and the stake president; and when I opened my eyes, I understood why we could not give the blessing. We moved the chair close to the bed. I asked this dear sister to lay her head on the bed by the side of her husband's hand. Then I reached down and picked up his hand that he could not pick up for himself and gently placed his hand on her head.

The regional representative and the stake president joined me. We placed our hands back upon her head, and this time a beautiful blessing flowed through us to this dear sister, who was so true, so faithful, so good, so righteous, so willing to forgive, so willing to receive under such desperate circumstances her family back in its celestial order again by the restoration of the blessings to her husband.

I learned, my brothers and sisters, on that occasion, like I may never learn again, the blessing it is to bear the priesthood of

God. I learned through that special experience that God loves His children. He does not want to see us make mistakes. He asks us to keep His commandments. He asks us to stay true to the covenants and commitments we make; but ever in His mercy and His love for His children, which abounds, He is willing to forgive. He is willing to welcome His children back. When I had that experience, I thought to have the priesthood and to lose it and then to have it again must be an experience that would cause any man to realize the great blessing of bearing the priesthood of God.[36]

Sharing the Gospel

In a letter dated August 23, 1984, Elder Ballard was released as executive director of the Curriculum Department and named managing director of the Missionary Department, serving under the supervision of Elders Boyd K. Packer, Bruce R. McConkie, and Dallin H. Oaks of the Quorum of the Twelve. Of Elder Ballard's new assignment, the president of Bonneville Media Communications wrote, "His deep personal involvement in strategic planning and creative development supports and demonstrates his stated belief in the power of the media and his grasp of the vision of the media role in communicating the gospel."[37]

Not only would media be enhanced by Elder Ballard's work in the Missionary Department, there would also be alterations in how the fundamental principles of missionary work were presented. Memorized discussions would change, but that would take time. The hymn "Called to Serve," suggested by Sister Donna Packer, would be introduced to all mission presidents throughout the world who gathered to Salt Lake for training meetings. But in the meantime, at the October 1984 general conference, Elder Ballard encouraged members to "write down a date in the near future on which you will have someone ready to be taught the gospel. Do not worry that you do not have someone already in mind. Let the Lord help you as you pray diligently for guidance. Fast and pray, seeking guidance and direction from our Heavenly Father."[38]

As managing director of the Missionary Department, Elder Ballard was asked to oversee the creation of sixty-second and ninety-second radio and television messages announcing that the gospel had been restored to the earth through the Prophet Joseph Smith and describing the Book of Mormon as "Another Testament of Jesus Christ." The assignment was clear, but making it happen was clouded with a wide variety of opinions as to what would be the best approach. When it appeared that every in-house effort to pull together a media spot had failed, Elder Ballard did not give up. He sought assistance from an outside agency. When the agency refused to help due to a possible conflict with Bonneville International, Elder Ballard did not throw in the towel or announce, "It can't be done."

He commissioned the outside agency to create a one-minute spot about the Book of Mormon, and he promised that he would personally handle any conflict that might arise. The media spot was an instant success. It began by showing the hands of a child, a youth, and an adult. This was followed by the image of a Bible and a narrator saying, "You know of His birth and of the stable, His ministry, death, and resurrection." The hands of Christ then appeared on the screen, and the narrator asked, "Is nothing more written of Him? Consider for a moment the glorious possibility there is more written of Jesus Christ." The Book of Mormon then appeared on the screen with the words, "The Book of Mormon is Another Testament of Jesus Christ." The narrator concluded by acknowledging to the listeners, "You have the Bible" before asking, "Do you have the other testament of Jesus Christ?" At the end of the media spot was a toll-free number to call for more information and a free copy of the Bible and/or the Book of Mormon.

In 1984, it was estimated that 259,943 cable viewers in Texas, Arizona, and Montana alone requested copies of the Bible and/or the Book of Mormon. Nearly 86,000 viewers asked for missionaries to visit them. One viewer reported:

I saw a commercial advertising a free Bible on TV. I called the number on the screen for my Bible, gave the information they needed, and waited. A few days later my doorbell rang and my new Bible had arrived. Not only did I get a new Bible but I also received the Book of Mormon free. These two books were given to me by two fantastic missionaries. They helped me overcome my alcoholism. I have been dry now almost a year and have joined the true Church of Jesus Christ. Life has never been so good. This all happened because of an ad for the free Bible and the missionaries who delivered the books.[39]

Ethiopia

As the year 1984 drew to a close, the world was becoming increasingly aware of a devastating famine that gripped Ethiopia and other parts of sub-Saharan Africa through 1985. In Ethiopia alone, the 1984–85 famine left as many as two million dead, four hundred thousand refugees outside the country, two and a half million displaced in the country, and nearly two hundred thousand orphans. Political revolution and civil strife exacerbated the situation and played a role in relief efforts.

President Gordon B. Hinckley, Second Counselor in the First Presidency at the time, observed, "Where there is stark hunger, regardless of the cause, I will not let political considerations dull my sense of mercy or thwart my responsibility to the sons and daughters of God, wherever they may be or whatever their circumstances."[40]

In a letter to priesthood leaders in the United States and Canada dated January 11, 1985, the First Presidency—Spencer W. Kimball, Marion G. Romney, and Gordon B. Hinckley—wrote:

> People throughout the world have been touched by the portrayal in the media of the plight of many thousands of starving people in Africa. There are others in similar circumstances in other areas. We have sent funds to assist those in need. We now feel that our people would like to participate more extensively in

the great humanitarian effort to assist those in Ethiopia, other areas of Africa, and perhaps in other parts of the world.

The First Presidency and the Council of the Twelve have accordingly determined that Sunday, January 27, should be designated as a special fast day. . . . All fast offering funds contributed on this day will be dedicated for the use of the victims of famine and other causes resulting in hunger and privation among people of Africa, and possibly in some other areas. They will be placed through agencies of unquestioned integrity.[41]

"President [Gordon B.] Hinckley called me into his office, after the membership of the Church was invited to have a special fast and to make a special contribution to help the starving people of Ethiopia," said Elder Ballard.[42] The fast offering donation on January 27, 1985, raised $6.4 million for famine relief. "The problem was how to administer the $6.4 million," Elder Ballard said. "Because I was the first contact for Africa, it was determined that I would be the one to travel with Glenn Pace, director of the Church Welfare Services Department at the time. We'd go to Ethiopia to determine what we ought to do with these funds."[43]

At the time, the Church did not have in place the infrastructure, a license, or the recognition needed to deliver goods to Ethiopia. President Hinckley told Brother Pace: "The First Presidency and Quorum of the Twelve will be praying for you and Elder Ballard, by name, that your mission will be successful."

Elder Ballard and Brother Pace left Salt Lake City in March 1985, transferring at the Dulles International Airport on March 11, 1985, to London and then on to the capital of Ethiopia, Addis Ababa. Dr. Joseph Kennedy, a leader of the Africare organization headquartered in Washington, DC, accompanied them to Ethiopia.[44] At the time, Africare was one of the most experienced and largest African-American-led nonprofit international development organizations focusing on development assistance to Africa.

Of their arrival in Ethiopia, Brother Pace wrote:

> We had less than two weeks to make some very important decisions. But first, I was ready to check into a [Hilton] hotel and freshen up—we had been traveling for more than twenty-four hours.
>
> I soon discovered Elder Ballard had other ideas. His first priority was to locate [the only known] member of the Church [Harry Hadlock]. . . . I grudgingly acquiesced, and we began our search by talking to people at the airport to see if they had heard of him. Much to my surprise, we found out he actually worked at an office in the airport, and within minutes someone brought him to us.
>
> We found out that he had been in Ethiopia for several months. His wife had not traveled with him because of the terrible conditions in the country, and he was very lonely. . . . Elder Ballard told him we would be holding a sacrament meeting the following Sunday and that we would love to come to his home for the meeting. Tears welled up in Brother Hadlock's eyes . . . as he said, "I have not partaken of the sacrament in months."[45]

"On Sunday," Elder Ballard wrote, "we went to Brother Hadlock's home and had the sacrament. . . . The only bread we had was a very dry cracker, but he broke it, I blessed it, Glenn blessed the water, and we passed the sacrament to the three of us and bore our testimonies and this dear brother just wept."[46]

According to Brother Pace, what happened next was quite extraordinary:

> At the close of the meeting, Elder Ballard offered a most sacred prayer and blessing on Ethiopia. . . . In his supplication to our Heavenly Father, Elder Ballard noted that we were the only Melchizedek Priesthood holders then in the country and that we were there on assignment from the First Presidency of the Church. He expressed gratitude to the members of the Church

who had contributed their means during the special fast and who had offered up individual and family prayers on behalf of the people of Ethiopia. Then, with as much power and boldness as I had ever witnessed, he called upon the power and authority of the holy Melchizedek Priesthood and commanded the elements to gather together to bring rain upon the land, thus to begin to relieve those who had been suffering for so many years. It hadn't rained in a year, and the prayer was offered on a clear and sunny Sunday morning.[47]

Meetings were then held with representatives of the Catholic Relief Services and Africare. It was agreed that the Church would work with these organizations in partnership on some relief endeavors. Elder Ballard and Brother Pace then returned to their hotel rooms that afternoon to rest and prepare for the journey of the coming week. In his room Brother Pace "heard a clap of thunder":

> I went to the patio just in time to see the beginning of a torrential downpour. People began to run out of their little huts and public buildings, looking up at the sky and reaching their arms toward the heavens. They were shouting and crying. The heavy downpour continued for some time. I was mesmerized as I watched the scene from the window. As the ground became saturated and began to puddle, children and adults alike began to frolic and splash on each other. They grabbed buckets and barrels to collect rain from the roofs. It was a celebration unlike any I've ever witnessed.
>
> As I stood at the window watching the scene unfold, my emotions turned from great joy to exquisite thanksgiving. I began to weep. I knew there were only two other people in the entire country who understood what had happened. Once I had gained control of my emotions, I went down the hall and knocked on Elder Ballard's door. When he came to the door, I could tell he had been overwhelmed in a like manner. We said a prayer of thanksgiving

and returned to the privacy of our own rooms and thoughts. From that day forward, wherever we traveled, it rained.[48]

"This was the first of several miracles we were to witness," Brother Pace wrote.

> One of our major objectives was to visit several of the camps to observe the distribution of food firsthand, so we could see how the infrastructure was working. Our first major obstacle came as we tried to obtain permits to travel into these areas. At that time Ethiopia was under Communist control, and movement from state to state was tightly restricted. . . . We were shocked and horrified to learn it would take at least ten days to obtain all of the documents we needed. . . . As we discussed the dilemma, we came to the mutual feeling that we had not come this far to have our mission fail. . . . We returned to the hotel, knelt in prayer, and literally asked the Lord for a miracle.[49]

Three days later permits were in hand and Joseph Kennedy had made arrangements for the brethren to fly on a Royal Air Force supply plane. "That plane was filled with supplies, and we just sat on the sides, right up against the wall of the plane, with all of these supplies around us," recalled Elder Ballard. "While we were airborne, I walked up into the cockpit where the pilot was, and it didn't look to me like we were more than fifteen hundred feet off the ground."[50]

After the plane landed, arrangements were made with the government for the brethren to be taken to feeding stations in a four-wheel-drive Land Rover. Elder Ballard said, "We wanted to get up to Mekelle, the location of one of the major feeding stations."[51] Mekelle had been set up to house 120,000 Ethiopians.

At Mekelle, the brethren saw some 30,000 Ethiopians outside the station waiting for their names to be placed on a list so they could go inside. As the scene of starvation, poverty, and sickness presented itself to Elder Ballard, he wrote:

Elder Ballard in Ethiopia

I've never been the same since that experience. . . . The understanding we have of the gospel, who the Savior is, the purpose of our existence, where we're attempting to go—really, it's an overwhelming blessing. And it hit me as I saw those little children starving, those mothers starving and trying to feed their babies with nothing for the babies to get from them, because they were so emaciated and malnourished. It was sobering. Any way you want to look at it, it was sobering.[52]

The men went to an area in the camp where those who "required intensive feeding and who are desperately ill" were being cared for. "The little children clung to our legs, grabbed hold of our arms and hands, just wanted to touch us," Elder Ballard said. "The parents who had sick children brought them to us, wanting us to do something. There were all kinds of open sores and diseases. It was really quite shocking. The reason they came to us is because they thought we were doctors."[53]

In the intensive care hospital they found "flies were all over the place. Two mothers and two children were on one cot." When they left the makeshift hospital, "the children again swarmed around with their sunken eyes and their thin little legs and arms," said Elder Ballard. "One man, I could not tell whether it was a father or a grandfather, holding a starving little child who was at risk, tried to give the child to us, begging us to take the child with us because the child's mother had died and he just simply didn't know what to do with this little baby."[54]

The men got back into the Land Rover and drove to another feeding and distribution station where between 20,000 and 30,000 Ethiopians were gathered. The children were crying, "Sister, Sister, Sister." Elder Ballard said, "This says an awful lot for the image and the understanding that people that are suffering have of the Catholic sisters who have rendered such great service through the Catholic Relief services." Elder Ballard expressed the hope, "Someday maybe the Church will be to the point where little children that are suffering will call, 'Elder, Elder.' I am sure this would be what our Father in Heaven would expect of us. . . .

"This, I believe, was by far the most heart-wrenching experience in my life," Elder Ballard said. "We saw thousands of human beings just sitting waiting for their turn to receive a 100-pound sack of wheat," their ration for the month. "It became abundantly apparent that the faith and prayers of all of the members of the Church have got to go to the heavens and the only relief is for rain to come."[55] Elder Ballard wrote in his journal:

> After driving about an hour we became very hungry. We had had lunches put up at the Hilton Hotel, so we pulled off to the side of the road where no one was to be found and got out our lunches, and by the time we had opened the box, we were surrounded by African children. This then became an impossibility because with those little children putting their hands out, rubbing their stomachs, and touching their lips, there was no way that I could eat anything, nor could Glenn. We each had two

sandwiches. I took my sandwiches and broke them into pieces and handed a piece to each of the children.[56]

Elder Ballard spoke of his Ethiopia experience at the priesthood session of general conference in April 1985:

> Just fifteen days ago, by assignment, I left for Addis Ababa, Ethiopia, which is approximately ten thousand miles from here. The world is very small in some ways. Had I been able to fly directly from Addis Ababa to Salt Lake City, it would have taken approximately nineteen hours. In many other ways, however, the world is very large. Billions of our Heavenly Father's children live upon the earth in all kinds of circumstances; the plight of those who are living in the drought-stricken areas of Africa is disastrous. Human suffering there is almost beyond description. I do not know all the reasons for the suffering. However, this most recent experience in my life has had a profound effect on me. I will never be the same.[57]

Nor was the Church. Within a year of Elder Ballard's return from Ethiopia, LDS Humanitarian Services was organized to provide benevolent Latter-day Saints—and the Church itself—with an appropriate vehicle through which they could provide aid and assistance to the poor and needy of the world, especially during times of crisis.

Speaking specifically of the life and ministry of Elder M. Russell Ballard, however, there is one additional—and most significant—way in which his life would "never be the same." During that same general conference, Elder Bruce R. McConkie had risen from his sickbed to share this memorable testimony of Jesus Christ:

> I am one of his witnesses, and in a coming day I shall feel the nail marks in his hands and in his feet and shall wet his feet with my tears. But I shall not know any better then than I know now that he is God's Almighty Son, that he is our Savior and

Redeemer, and that salvation comes in and through his atoning blood and in no other way.[58]

Elder McConkie died of cancer on April 19, 1985, about two weeks after giving his inspiring testimony.[59]

Elder Ballard mourned the loss of this beloved Apostle. He was not among those who speculated as to who would fill the vacancy in the Quorum of the Twelve that was created by the passing of Elder McConkie. He had much to do—the Missionary Department was undergoing a massive review; there were travel plans to keep and more than one stake president to call. His family was growing in number as his children married and had children of their own. Life for Elder Ballard was full, and he was content in the Lord's service.

CHAPTER ELEVEN

AN APOSTLE OF THE
LORD JESUS CHRIST

E arly Sunday morning, October 6, 1985, President Gordon B. Hinckley called Elder Ballard at home and asked if he was out of the shower yet and if he was planning on attending conference that morning. In the same jovial tone, he asked if Elder Ballard and Barbara could stop in to see him about nine o'clock before heading over to the Tabernacle to listen to *Music and the Spoken Word*, the longest continuous-running radio program in the United States, which was broadcast every Sunday morning, even on general conference weekends.

When Elder Ballard hung up the phone, he "started to prepare Barbara for the fact that we might be receiving an assignment to go overseas." He said to her, "You know, the members of the Seventy are being moved all over the world, and I just want you to know that when you get a call like this, it's very likely that President Hinckley wants to assign us to an overseas assignment." He confessed, "I was preparing her to be ready to go to Hong Kong, or to Latin America, or to Europe. I didn't want her to be too shocked when we were told that we were going someplace out of the country."[1]

As Russ and Barbara were driving toward President Hinckley's office, Russ "thought he would perhaps be called on to speak in conference, since one of the speakers was ill," Barbara said. "We were relaxed on the way to President Hinckley's office and discussed what Russ might talk about if called to speak."[2]

When the Ballards arrived at President Hinckley's office, he invited Elder Ballard to come in alone. President Hinckley explained that he had just come from President Spencer W. Kimball's apartment. He then said, "I am authorized to extend to you the invitation to serve as a member of the Quorum of the Twelve Apostles." Elder Ballard was shocked. "Immediately, I lost control of my emotions," he said. "Tears streamed from my eyes. To this day I am endeared to President Hinckley because he came around from his desk, took me in his arms, and wept with me."[3]

When Barbara was invited to enter the office, President Hinckley greeted her by saying, "*¿Cómo está?*" Because of his greeting, Barbara thought Russ had just been assigned to live in South America. After she was seated, President Hinckley said, "I've just extended a call, on behalf of President Kimball and the First Presidency and the Twelve, to Russ to become a member of the Quorum of the Twelve." Barbara later said, "I almost thought, please say that again, I don't know if I heard correctly. Russ looked at me with tears in his eyes. It was a sobering experience."[4]

The sustaining of General Authorities and General Officers of the Church took place that day at the Sunday afternoon session of general conference, two days before Elder Ballard's fifty-seventh birthday. When Elder Ballard took his seat as the newest member of the Quorum of the Twelve, he received hugs and congratulations from Elders Russell M. Nelson and Dallin H. Oaks, his immediate seniors in the Twelve. Observing the scene, President Ezra Taft Benson said, "We'll get our hugs later," referring to other members of the Quorum.[5]

Speaking at the Sunday afternoon session, Elder Ballard said:

*Elder M. Russell Ballard at the time of
his call to the Quorum of the Twelve*

My brothers and sisters, I am deeply humbled at the confidence of the Lord and my Brethren and pledge to you that I will do the very best I know how. The past nine and a half years, as I have been sent on errands for the Lord throughout the earth, have caused me to know that this Church is filled with righteous, good, dedicated men. Each of us obediently learns that we will come forth as we are called, to try to do the very best we can in our callings, whether it be home teacher, whether it be stake president, or whether it be General Authority.

I understand the source of the call. I have learned during the past nine and a half years that this is our Heavenly Father's church. The errands that I have been sent on to act in the name of the Lord enable me to witness to you today that I know, as I know that I stand before you, that Jesus is the Christ, that He lives. He is very close to this work and very close to all of us who are asked to perform the work throughout the earth in His name.

I would like also to bear witness that in my particular case the veil between here and the hereafter is rather thin. I acknowledge that it has been a great blessing in my life to be born of goodly parents, grandparents, and great-grandparents who have given everything they have been asked to give to the building of the kingdom of God upon the earth.

Now, my brothers and sisters, I would ask for an interest in your faith and prayers. I express my affection to my wife and my children, who sustain me in whatever the Lord might ask me to do. I am grateful for this abundant blessing and pray humbly that I might serve you, the membership of this Church, in a way that would be pleasing and acceptable unto our Heavenly Father, and ask this prayer humbly, in the name of Jesus Christ, amen.[6]

Four days later, on October 10, 1985, in the fourth-floor council room in the Salt Lake Temple, the First Presidency and the Apostles of the Lord Jesus Christ joined in a circle to ordain M. Russell Ballard a member of the Quorum of the Twelve Apostles. "I sat on a stool," recalled Elder Ballard. "President Kimball was also seated—he had his hands on my head but President Hinckley ordained and set me apart."[7]

Of President Hinckley's apostolic priesthood lineage, Elder Ballard wrote: "Gordon B. Hinckley . . . was ordained by David O. McKay, who was ordained by Joseph F. Smith, who was ordained by Brigham Young . . . who received his ordination from the Three Witnesses to the Book of Mormon . . . who were ordained by Joseph Smith and Oliver Cowdery, who were ordained by Peter, James, and John who were ordained under the hands of Jesus Christ."[8]

"I was given a blessing that is a great source of comfort and strength to me to this very day," President Ballard said. "I was then and am still now overwhelmed with this calling to serve as a special witness of the Lord."[9] In the blessing was an acknowledgment of his faithfulness and of his prophetic lineage:

> We commend you, Brother Ballard, on the goodness of your life; on your faithfulness in every call you have received

in the past. You come of a great heritage through the lineage of Hyrum Smith and the father of the Prophet Joseph Smith and of President Joseph F. Smith and of Elder Melvin J. Ballard of the Twelve; and we feel to say unto you we are confident that their voices have been heard in terms of your call to the apostleship and your membership in this quorum. You have a tremendous responsibility by reason of this birthright for much will be expected of you as one who comes of this birthright.[10]

Since that sacred blessing, Elder Ballard says he has had many occasions to ask the question, "Why me?"

"I'm still not sure I have a completely satisfying answer to that question," he said. "But I have come to the comforting knowledge that the Lord and my Brethren see in me something that I can do to help the work of the Lord continue to move forward in this calling."[11]

His son Craig acknowledges that when he was younger he asked a similar question: "Why my dad?"

I am the caboose of the family. When I was five my dad was a mission president. When I was eight, he was a member of the Seventy. When I was fifteen, he became an Apostle. My entire memories of my dad are of his being a Church leader. I didn't get it. Why couldn't my dad just be "Dad"? It wasn't until he took me to Tonga that I understood. When we arrived at the airport in Tonga there were a thousand people there to welcome him to the island. I finally got it and sustain him with all my heart.[12]

Responsibilities of an Apostle

As a special witness of Jesus Christ, Elder Ballard was called and ordained to testify of the living, loving reality of Jesus Christ—His life, His teachings, His Atonement, and the Restoration of His gospel and His Church through the Prophet Joseph Smith. He was to warn the people of dangers inherent in not keeping the commandments of God

The Quorum of the Twelve Apostles in 1985. Left to right, seated: Ezra Taft Benson, Howard W. Hunter; standing: Thomas S. Monson, Boyd K. Packer, Marvin J. Ashton, L. Tom Perry, David B. Haight, James E. Faust, Neal A. Maxwell, Russell M. Nelson, Dallin H. Oaks, M. Russell Ballard

and to speak in terms that could not be misunderstood. He was to preach the pure doctrine of Christ. His life was to be above reproach so that the Spirit of the Lord could convey to his mind and heart what the people of the world needed to hear to live closer to the Lord and be blessed.

In addition, Elder Ballard was expected to attend and participate in meetings of the Quorum of the Twelve. Elder Dallin H. Oaks has said of his comments in those meetings:

> He does not just see the narrow, he does not have a keyhole view of the Church or any part of its work. He has perspective and a broad view. And that is coupled with a courage to speak up. He is one of the few members of the Quorum of the Twelve that will speak out vigorously when others are afraid to say it. He will speak up. I have greatly appreciated that in him, and it has aided materially in our deliberations.[13]

As an Apostle, Elder Ballard would also speak in general conferences in April and October each year. "People ask, 'Is it hard to give a conference talk?'" Elder Ballard says. "My answer is 'No, it's not really hard to give a conference talk. But it is very hard to say something worthwhile, to say something meaningful, something that will change a life.'"[14]

He was also expected to be familiar with all aspects of Church councils and departments. Since service in Church departments is rotated from time to time, each Apostle has the opportunity to learn the purpose and function of all departments. Elder Ballard's first assignment as an Apostle was to serve on the Missionary Executive Council and on the Leadership Training Committee. His longest tenured assignment was on the Human Resources Committee (formerly Personnel Committee)—over nineteen years, from November 15, 1985 through January 13, 2005. This assignment and other administrative assignments have proven challenging—or, as Elder Ballard has said:

> I don't mind telling you that our task isn't always as easy as it may sound. With the rich diversity of languages, cultures, and environments that currently exists within the Church, all of our planning and preparation on a general level has to be both broad and narrow: broad enough to meet the varying needs of millions of members in dozens of different nations and narrow enough to reach the one.[15]

And last, but certainly not least, Elder Ballard was expected to be a "first contact" in a specific area in the world as directed by the First Presidency. First contact assignments, much like department assignments, rotate from time to time. Initially, Elder Ballard was assigned to be the first contact for South America. The assignment didn't mean just answering phone calls from mission presidents or stake presidents. It meant being away from home for long stretches of time conversing, comforting, and blessing the people in South America. Of course, Elder Ballard was home to attend important family events like sealing his children to their spouses in a holy temple, but the word *Apostle* means "one who is sent," and he was sent again and again.

First Contact for South America

Church membership in South America had grown exponentially since Elder Ballard's grandfather, Melvin J. Ballard, dedicated the continent for the preaching of the gospel in 1925. A year later, as Elder Melvin J. Ballard was preparing to return to Utah, he uttered these words of prophecy: "The work of the Lord will grow slowly for a time here just as an oak grows slowly from an acorn. It will not shoot up in a day as does the sunflower that grows quickly and then dies. But thousands will join the Church here. It will be divided into more than one mission and will be one of the strongest in the Church."

Sixty years later, with a new Elder Ballard in the Quorum of the Twelve Apostles, there were "30 missions, with 5,140 full-time missionaries, of which approximately 60 percent [were] natives of South America. One hundred eighty-six stakes covered the land, with 2,148 wards and branches dotting the countryside. [And there were] approximately 776,000 members of the Church."[16]

Within one month of being called to the Quorum of the Twelve, Elder Ballard was sent to Bolivia to begin a significant period of focused ministerial service filled with love and concern for the Saints in South America. "Each trip to South America is an emotional experience for me," Elder Ballard says. "It's hard to express what I feel as I see the marvelous results of the work that Elder Melvin J. Ballard helped to start. This makes me feel closer to my grandfather, and closer to the wonderful people of South America."[17]

On his first trip to Bolivia as an Apostle, Elder Ballard was driven to a regional conference in La Paz. Before the conference began, Elder Ballard and the other Church leaders who were traveling with him greeted one man whose shirt was a different color from about the chest

Greeting the Saints in Bolivia

up than it was from the chest down. Through an interpreter, Elder Ballard learned the man and his companions had come from a high plateau in the Andes Mountains called the Antiplano. They had walked six hours before catching a ride in the back of a truck for an additional two hours. During what had to have been an exhausting journey, the man had forded two rivers, with water coming up to his chest—hence the different coloration in his shirt. Elder Ballard asked if the man had eaten. He had not. When asked if he had any money, he replied, "No." The man then explained his reason for coming to the conference: "Brother Ballard, you are an Apostle of the Lord Jesus Christ. My companions and I would walk for weeks, if necessary, to come to hear from one of His Apostles what the Lord wants us to do."[18] Elder Ballard was humbled by the man's faith. The leaders saw that the man and his companions received food, shelter, and funds for the trip home.

While the group was traveling and holding meetings in Bolivia, they learned that the waters of Lake Titicaca, South America's largest lake, had been rising to crisis levels. Many people living near this lake, which straddles the border of Bolivia and Peru, had been flooded out—including a number of Church members.

"We went up into that country to meet with those people to try to encourage them and to try to bless their lives and let them know that we cared," Elder Ballard reported. "We stood there on a little piece of dry land and looked at the damage caused by the rising waters."

Before long, the other members of the traveling party returned to the vehicles in which they were traveling, anxious to be on their way to scheduled meetings. But Elder Ballard lingered on that piece of dry land, surveying the situation and pondering possible responses. As he stood there alone, he said he "had an impression come as powerfully as anything in my life: 'You are an Apostle; bless the land.'"

He asked those who were traveling with him to rejoin him on the dry piece of ground. "I do not know what the Lord has in mind, but I know that I am to pronounce a blessing on the land," he told them. "We joined in prayer, and in the name of the Lord Jesus Christ and by and through the holy apostleship which I had vested in me for less than a month, the power of God, the power of the Holy Ghost, spoke through me to command the lake to recede, that the land might be reclaimed to the people."

At the conclusion of the prayer there were tears in many eyes—including Elder Ballard's. But after the people had returned to the cars and resumed their travel, he said he started feeling doubts, asking himself incredulously, "What have I done?"

"When I got back to my room that night, I spent a good portion of the night on my knees pleading with the Lord to somehow honor that prayer," Elder Ballard said.

Within two weeks he received reports out of both Bolivia and Peru indicating that the water levels of Lake Titicaca had miraculously dropped by ten feet and that people were returning to their homes and tilling their land. "Hydrologists had no explanation for what happened," Elder Ballard said. "But those of us who were there knew and understood what had been done through the power of God."

In sharing this experience with a large group of missionaries, Elder Ballard said: "Now, you are not apostles, but you bear the priesthood. You sisters have been set apart by the priesthood. You have the power of God to do His will and to speak for Him if you are living worthy to receive it. You will know what to say, and you will know what not to say. You will know whom to bless and how to bless and how to teach and how to live and how to inspire—for you are servants of the Lord, Jesus Christ."[19]

Tough Questions

In 1987 Elder Ballard traveled to Brazil, where he encouraged the full-time missionaries to do the same thing he had been encouraging missionaries to do ever since he was a mission president in Canada: to "contact at least ten people every day in buses, supermarkets, and on streets, asking them individually or in groups if they'd like to learn about the Church." Mission President Demar Stanicia reported the lasting impact of Elder Ballard's message: "In the past five months, the missionaries contacted about 275,000 people and received the names of more than 10,000 people to teach. A substantial number of those who were taught have been baptized."[20]

While in Brazil, Elder Ballard also spoke to a fireside group of young adults. As he was speaking, he "noticed particularly a young sister who was sitting in a wheelchair, disabled . . . by multiple sclerosis."

> For some reason, I felt a bonding with her as I was teaching. That happens on occasion; spirit to spirit, you have a connection. At the conclusion of what I had to say, I went down and knelt on one knee and took hold of her hand so I could look her in the eye. Her head was hard to hold up. I had an interpreter because she spoke only Portuguese. And she said to me these words,

"Brother Ballard, why would God do this to me if He loves me? Why am I so ugly and so incapable of getting along in mortality?" Tough questions!

Then I looked at her face and into her eyes; and I said, "You know, as I look at you, I am impressed with how beautiful you are. I want you to understand that the real you is radiating a beautiful spirit. Don't you ever lose that. Don't curse God because of the challenges you have. Rather, let this wonderful spirit, captured inside this crippled body, soar. Let it touch as many lives as you know how to possibly do as you experience mortality. That glorious day will come when you will be relieved from this challenge in mortality; and I promise you in the name of the Lord that if you will work on the inner self, the real you, that you will have a sense of accomplishment, a sense of peace, a sense of joy that will be eternal in its nature."

I shall never forget . . . as she looked back at me and said, "Do you really think I am beautiful?" And I replied, "Absolutely."[21]

The experience prompted Elder Ballard to ponder and study some significant questions: Why do we have challenges? Why do we have trials? Why do we have to suffer? Why do we have difficulties in life? In his study he came upon some powerful words from an earlier Apostle, Elder Orson F. Whitney:

No pain that we suffer, no trial that we experience is wasted. It ministers to our education, to the development of such qualities as patience, faith, fortitude, and humility. All that we suffer and all that we endure, especially when we endure it patiently, builds up our characters, purifies our hearts, expands our souls, and makes us more tender and charitable, more worthy to be called the children of God . . . and it is through sorrow and suffering, toil and tribulation, that we gain the education that we come here to acquire and which will make us more like our Father and Mother in heaven.[22]

Elder Ballard was well equipped to answer difficult questions about life's trials. Some months earlier, Jay M. Todd, managing editor of the Church's *Ensign* magazine, visited Elder Ballard to invite him to prepare an article on a very sensitive subject—suicide. Elder Ballard, like many people, knew people who had taken their own lives, had spoken at their funerals, and had spent time consoling those left behind.

The article, "Suicide: Some Things We Know, and Some We Do Not," published in October 1987, was a landmark statement on the subject. (It was later published by Deseret Book as a small paperback.) Many souls were healed by the article because it offered hope and invited people to not judge others. In it, Elder Ballard stated:

> I believe the Lord will consider each case separately and judge the circumstances of each individual. . . . I have sincerely sought direction from our Father in Heaven to help me understand the nature of suicide. And I have come to know, as well as anything else that I know from God, that these people have a place in the kingdom of our Father, and it is not one of darkness or despair, but one where they can receive comfort and experience serenity.

The Church Continues to Grow

In early 1988, Elder Ballard was in Lima, Peru, to preside over what the *Church News* called "one of the largest and most ambitious stake divisions in the history of the Church." In a twenty-eight-hour period, fourteen new stake presidencies were called, seven new stakes were created, and six separate stake conferences were held involving some 10,500 Church members. With Elders Charles A. Didier, Angel Abrea, and Derek A. Cuthbert of the Seventy impressively overseeing the logistics, arrangements were made for Elder Ballard to speak at all six conferences. "Even in a Church where multiplication by division is commonplace," the *Church News* reported, "this equation was

Presiding over the creation of seven new stakes in Lima, Peru

staggering: Take 11 stakes in Lima, Peru, divide them to become 18 stakes, and do it all in one weekend."[23]

Such an arduous schedule was not without hiccups. A general power outage hit the Palao Stake Center five minutes before the scheduled start time of the final conference session. When notified of the power outage, Elder Ballard said, "We'd better start praying."[24] The lights came back on three minutes later, and the conference went on uninterrupted. His message at that conference was a call for more missionaries from Peru and a mission fund in every ward. He told the Saints: "The day is not far away when your sons and daughters will be leaving to study other languages and to teach people on other continents. This work is just beginning. Many more thousands, and even hundreds of thousands, will join the Church."[25]

On another occasion in Lima, Elder Ballard was with President Hinckley. "After conducting a multiregional conference with nine stakes in the city of Lima, we went to the Lima Peru Temple," Elder Ballard said. "When we arrived at the temple, we found a large number of Saints out in front." They were from the Huancayo Stake in the Peruvian Andes Mountains, about 11,000 feet above sea level. Of their number, 210 had received their own endowments and 26 families had been sealed for eternity. They had just come from the multiregional conference to board buses for their return home, only to find that the bus drivers refused to take them back to Huancayo due to a nationwide bus strike.

It was at this point that Elder Ballard and President Hinckley arrived at the temple. Elder Ballard said to President Hinckley, "Let's go out and shake hands with the Saints from Huancayo."

"As we did, I lost sight of him," Elder Ballard said. "They just mobbed President Hinckley, and I thought, 'Oh, what have I done? How will I ever explain to President Benson that I have lost one of his counselors?' But he finally emerged, and we finished shaking hands with those faithful, devoted Saints from Peru."

When Church members in Lima learned these good souls had no transportation, they came to the temple and gathered up the Huancayo Saints and took them into their homes. Two days later, they were taken to a train station and returned home. Said Elder Ballard: "They were all happy."[26]

May 26, 1989, was a day of heartbreak and pain. The stunning, sobering word came out of Bolivia that two Latter-day Saint missionaries—Elder Todd Ray Wilson and Elder Jeffrey Brent Ball, both from Utah—had been shot and killed in front of their living quarters by men characterized as enemies of the Church of Jesus Christ. As soon as he heard about the tragedy, Elder Ballard flew immediately to Bolivia to meet with all the missionaries in the area, then returned to Utah to offer what comfort he could to the families of the slain elders. At the October 1989 general conference, he said:

> I was saddened, as I know you were, at the news that two faithful missionaries . . . lost their lives in Bolivia. The deaths of these two righteous young men while they were in the service of the Lord caused the entire Church membership to mourn. We grieve also for other missionaries who have died from illness or accident since the first of the year.

Our sorrow at the loss of any faithful missionary can be tempered by this declaration from the Lord himself: "And whoso layeth down his life in my cause, for my name's sake, shall find it again, even life eternal" (D&C 98:13). To all parents, family members, and friends of missionaries who have lost their lives while in the service of the Master, we extend to you our love, gratitude, and prayers for comfort and peace.[27]

"A Blessing for This Land"

Less than a year after the tragedy in Bolivia, that country and its neighbors were again suffering from drought. At a meeting of regional representatives, stake presidents, and mission presidents from Peru, Bolivia, and Venezuela, Elder Ballard asked that May 20, 1990, be designated as a special day of fasting for all members of the Church in the area, that they might seek the Lord's blessings on the land for rain, electricity, and other basic needs, and also that they might choose wisely those national political leaders who would best govern them. On that very date, there was a downpour in the city of Ayacucho, Peru, even though the month of May is not the rainy season in that part of the country. Streets were flooded like rivers. Rain even fell in Lima, which is highly unusual.[28] A mission president in Bolivia reported:

It began raining lightly in La Paz late Sunday evening, and has rained hard for four days straight since the conference. We fasted yesterday in gratitude as well as petition for more rain. The much-needed moisture has begun to relieve the drought in La Paz. . . . The fact that it rained these past days has been a great testimony to the people of the power of the priesthood of God in bringing about righteous purposes.[29]

Before Elder Ballard returned to the United States, he spoke to the temple ordinance workers in Lima. "The temple president always wants to have the Brethren, when they can, talk to the faithful, wonderful

Saints, who come to the temple to carry on that sacred work," Elder Ballard reported during his traditional Christmas message in his home ward later that year. "I think of one dear sister in her late sixties, who arises at 3 a.m. and walks several hours to be able to arrive at the Lima Temple in time to carry on her duty and responsibility."[30]

Elder Ballard went on to share a special experience that occurred while he was speaking to the temple workers in Lima:

> A very unusual thing occurred on this occasion. Bolivia, Peru, and parts of Colombia had been suffering a very serious drought. Though the farmers were able to get their seed into the ground, they were concerned there would be no crops by virtue of the fact that there was no water. That was weighing heavily on me because I had visited with some of the stake presidents and had been among some of the Saints, and could see their struggle. It was on my mind, and I was concerned.
>
> As I was standing in the temple annex building speaking to the temple workers, I said, "The Lord has prompted me that we join in prayer. If you will join me, He has a blessing for this land." Unknown to me, one of the sisters who was there knew shorthand, and transcribed the prayer. In that prayer I said, "Now, Father, with all of our hearts, we plead with thee to send the rains to this parched earth, which has undergone several seasons of drought. Bless the ground that the seeds therein might produce food for the people. May the rains fill their wells, reservoirs, lakes, and streams with water to sustain life among these, Thy children."[31]

Shortly after Elder Ballard returned home from this South American visit, he received several letters from stake presidents and other leaders in Bolivia and Peru about the heavy rainfall. A regional representative in Bolivia wrote, "Even though some hoped for rain only from the point of view of an agricultural interest, the rain and snow helped cities like Sucre, Cochabamba, Potosi, and La Paz and others, to fill their reservoirs with water, to supply the cities with the vital necessities."[32] A stake president from Cochabamba, Bolivia, reported, "On Thursday, May 24, a very heavy rain fell. The commentaries about the snow on radio and television said there hadn't been that much snow in Cochabamba during the past 50 years."[33]

Elder Ballard's joy at their news was tempered a few months later when he received word that two native Peruvian missionaries had been killed in Peru on the outskirts of Huancayo. Within the week he was on an airplane traveling with Elders Angel Abrea and Charles Didier to Trujillo and Arequipa to meet with the families of the deceased missionaries. The father of one elder had been baptized just eight months earlier. He said, "Brother Ballard, we look forward to January when we can go to the Lima Temple and be sealed for time and for all eternity and have our faithful son sealed to us." His wife spoke of a night vision in which her son appeared and said, "Mother, don't weep for me. I am all right. I am busy doing the work of the Lord."[34]

Effective December 1, 1990, Elder Ballard was released as first contact for South America. Although he received many notes of gratitude for his service, one letter from a stake executive secretary was probably his favorite because it so clearly reflected the humility of these wonderful people and his relationship to them:

> You might think it silly but it made an impression on me—that one of the Lord's Apostles was willing to sit in the backseat of the car to give me, an executive secretary, the front seat. I know that may seem like a trivial thing, but I was humbled by that and it will be something I will always remember.[35]

CHAPTER TWELVE

THE WORK GOES FORWARD

Although his ministry in South America was important to Elder Ballard during the first five years of his apostleship, there were also other assignments and opportunities that captured his attention during that period of time—and at least one personal, painful challenge to get through.

On October 27–29, 1986, Elder Ballard attended the Denver Colorado Temple dedication, speaking at three dedicatory sessions and leading the Hosanna Shout in two others—all while enduring severe back pain.[1] He tried to ignore the pain but could not. When his airplane landed at the Salt Lake International Airport, he drove straight home and went to bed—which set off alarms for Barbara because this was so unlike him. She reached out to their friend and neighbor Jon Huntsman, who contacted Dr. Bruce F. Sorensen and brought him to Elder Ballard's bedside. Despite his patient's protests, Dr. Sorensen ordered an ambulance, and Elder Ballard was conveyed to the LDS Hospital for a CT scan of his back. During the scan, the head of radiology walked in and instructed the technician to keep scanning down Elder Ballard's spine farther than had been ordered. As a result of this additional scanning, a cyst on his left kidney was revealed. About a liter of fluid was drained from the cyst, which was large enough that the pressure from it pressing against his spine probably accounted for the back pain.

But there were more complications. The day after the procedure on the cyst, the urologist telephoned Elder Ballard and explained that their tests indicated the fluid drained from the cyst was benign, but it had calcification in it, which sometimes indicates cancer, and an exploratory surgery was necessary. Elder Ballard again called Jon Huntsman and told him of the diagnosis, asking him to come over to his house and give him a blessing. The next Sunday, the family gathered at the Ballards' home in the spirit of fasting. They knelt together as the oldest daughter, Holly, offered a prayer.[2] That evening, Paul Clayton, Brad Brower, and Hal Murdock, three of the Ballard sons-in-law, gave Elder Ballard another blessing.

The next morning, Elder Ballard entered the LDS Hospital, and shortly thereafter Elder Boyd K. Packer came into his room, followed by the surgeon. Together they gave him a third priesthood blessing, after which Elder Packer and Elder Ballard gave the surgeon a blessing that he would receive inspiration and guidance as he did the work he was trained to do. During the procedure, the surgeon found in Elder Ballard's left kidney what he said was the smallest malignant tumor that he had ever encountered in his thirty years of practice. They removed the kidney, and no other procedures were required.

Within days of his hospital release, President Howard W. Hunter called Jon Huntsman and said, "We need to take Russ out for some yogurt." This was a tradition among the friends—whenever one of them had health issues, the other two took him out for yogurt at their favorite frozen yogurt shop.[3] The two friends picked him up, and "the three of us enjoyed our frozen yogurt together."[4]

Less than two months later, Elder Ballard was in the British Isles celebrating the sesquicentennial anniversary of the first Latter-day

Saint missionaries on that continent.[5] Thankfully, he experienced no health challenges on the trip, although there was another kind of irritating discomfort: Elder Ballard's suit bag didn't arrive with the rest of his luggage. And so for the first few events of the sesquicentennial celebration—including the dedication of a plaque at Loughbrickland to honor the first Latter-day Saint baptisms in Ireland, which was presided over by Elder Marvin J. Ashton—he had to stand alongside the other Church leaders, who were all dressed in suits, wearing slacks and a sports jacket. He felt a little uncomfortable and out of place—especially when he attended a formal dinner held at the luxurious Culloden Hotel in Belfast.[6] But toward the end of the evening he forgot all about his own discomfort when he noticed a rather distressed stake president who had been handed the sizable bill for the hotel festivities and was clearly unsure what to do with it.

"I couldn't help but chuckle," President Ballard said, looking back on the moment. "The entire event had been wonderfully planned and perfectly executed—except nobody told this dear stake president what to do with the bill. In that moment I decided there were probably worse things than not having the right suit to wear to a fancy dinner—like having a hotel official standing next to you expecting to be paid a significant amount of money, and you having no idea where that money is coming from."

Elder Ballard quietly inserted himself into the discussion and handled the situation—much to the relief of the frazzled stake president. And no one said anything about his sports jacket.[7]

Elder Ballard returned to Salt Lake City long enough to meet with doctors and learn that all health indicators pointed to a complete recovery from the removal of his kidney. After speaking on missionary work at the October general conference, he had no qualms about returning to a vigorous travel schedule. He flew from Salt Lake to Toronto with Elder Thomas S. Monson for the groundbreaking of the Toronto Canada Temple on October 10, 1987, and then returned home to

catch up on a few assignments at Church headquarters before heading
out on his next journey.

Helping a Brother

As it turned out, there could not have been a better time for him to
spend some time in Utah—not because of his Church assignment, but
because of a family crisis for his dear friends the Huntsmans.

Jon Huntsman wrote:

> In order to foster a family atmosphere at the [Huntsman in-
> dustrial] plants, we usually took some of our children with us
> on the Christmas circuit. We had most of them with us on the
> 1987 tour. Following the Christmas party at the Chesapeake,
> Virginia, facility, Karen [his wife] and I flew to Belpre, Ohio, on
> December 8. Our sixteen-year-old son James and eighteen-year-
> old son Paul had to get back to their high school classes, so they
> boarded a commercial flight for Salt Lake City. They arrived in
> Utah around 5:00 p.m. and headed home. Paul had a recreation-
> league basketball game that night and left the house. James was
> scheduled for a tutoring session in math, after which he planned
> to stop at his girlfriend's home.
>
> Around 6:30 p.m., after the winter sun had set, James climbed
> into his Jeep Wagoneer, slipped the key into the ignition, and tried
> to start it. The engine wouldn't turn over, which was not surpris-
> ing since it had been sitting in the cold for a week. Suddenly the
> driver's door flew open and an assailant in a ski mask rushed at
> James. Before he could react, James was handcuffed, his eyes cov-
> ered with a strip of duct tape, and he was shoved into the pas-
> senger side of the front seat. His attacker got behind the wheel
> and turned the ignition key, but the car wouldn't start for him,
> either. He yanked James from the vehicle and led him down a trail
> through our wooded backyard to a side street where a car waited.
> James was placed in the back seat and whisked off into the night.[8]

About 9 p.m., Paul Huntsman had returned to the home and received a phone call. A "menacing voice" asked to speak to Jon Huntsman. When Paul explained that his father was on a business trip, the caller said, "I've got James. If I don't speak to your dad by tomorrow, the next time you see James he will be in little pieces. If you tell the police or anyone, I'll kill him."[9] Paul called his father, and Jon Huntsman called the FBI.

When Elder Ballard and Barbara learned what had happened, they immediately stepped forward to help. "The center for all of the activity with the family, the press, the FBI was at Elder Ballard's home," said Ronald A. Rasband, then president and chief executive officer of Huntsman Chemical, who was traveling with the Huntsman family. "This was pleasing to Jon [Huntsman] and he knew that his interests would be well represented by Elder and Sister Ballard until we could return home."[10] Shortly before midnight, several FBI agents gathered in the Ballard home. When the Huntsmans arrived in Salt Lake at three in the morning, they drove straight to the Ballard home, having no idea that they passed within five hundred yards of the seedy motel where James was being held, pushed to the bathroom floor and cuffed to the sink's drainpipe.

"It was late, late that night, perhaps even into the wee hours of Wednesday morning," recalled Elder Rasband. "I was privileged to join as Elder Ballard gave Jon a blessing in his home." In the blessing Jon was promised that he "would be wise, make proper decisions, and be guided by the Holy Ghost" in his attempts to recover his son. In the meantime, FBI agents formed several two-man teams on twelve-hour shifts and moved about the city.

A kidnapper called at 7:28 a.m. on December 9. Through the technical tracking devices of the FBI, they knew the kidnapper was calling from a pay phone outside a grocery store on Salt Lake City's west side, and they scrambled agents to the location. The kidnapper demanded a ransom of $1,000,000—$100,000 of it in used $100 bills. He said that

Good friends M. Russell Ballard and Jon Huntsman

if he didn't get the money, James would die. Jon Huntsman told the caller, "I will pay nothing until I know James is unharmed." About a half hour later the kidnapper returned to the phone with James so that he could assure his father that he was okay. FBI agents Alan Jacobsen and Cal Clegg, who happened to have been some of James's Young Men advisers in their ward, confronted the kidnapper. Agent Jacobsen was stabbed in the chest during the altercation (he later fully recovered), but Agent Clegg was able to subdue the kidnapper and free James.

Huntsman was profoundly grateful for the way Elder and Sister Ballard immediately stepped up to provide support and comfort, even opening their home as a staging area for law enforcement and media. "The meaning of real friendship," Huntsman said, "is when your friend is in trouble, you're in trouble too." Of Elder Ballard, he wrote, "Russ Ballard was and is like a brother to me in every respect."[11]

Elder Ballard agreed. "My parents didn't give me a brother, but God gave me one in Jon Huntsman."

Such experiences, traumatic though they may have been, kept Elder Ballard anchored in his belief that family and friends are among life's greatest treasures. And as busy and hectic as his apostolic schedule may have been, there was always time to be a husband, a father, and a friend. He tells a story that illustrates that point:

> Our son, Craig, was a good missionary in Japan. He had lived with us in the mission field in Canada, so he knew what good missionaries do, and he worked very hard to be that kind of missionary. But one day I got this letter from him: "Dear Dad, I'm working as hard as I know how. I'm getting up a half hour earlier than required. I'm studying; I've got the language down pretty well. But, Dad, we're not baptizing anybody. It's hard to find somebody to teach here in Japan. What am I doing wrong?"
>
> He was writing to his father, who is a member of the Council of the Twelve and a member of the Missionary Executive Council of the Church. I guess he thought I would be able to write some magical formula to help him be successful. As I pondered his concern, these were the promptings that came from the Lord for me to answer him:
>
> "Dear Craig, All you need to be sure of is that before you retire every night you can get down on your knees and report in prayer to your Heavenly Father that you have done the very best you knew how to do that day. If you can honestly say that in your prayer at the close of every day, I want you to know that so far as I am concerned, you are a great missionary."[12]

Southeast Asia and Japan

After Elder Ballard spent some time taking care of matters on the home front, it was time for him to set off on another international journey—this time with Jon Huntsman and Ronald Rasband in tow. Along with US Senator Jake Garn (Utah), they traveled to Singapore, where Elder Ballard encouraged Jon and the senator to meet with Prime Minister Lee Kuan Yew because the prime minister had said he would not meet with a Church representative. Prior to the meeting, the four men privately knelt in prayer, and Elder Ballard pled with the Lord for His Spirit to accompany Jon and Senator Garn so that the prime minister might see the value and wisdom of allowing missionaries to work in Singapore. During the meeting, the two men discussed with the prime minister a notification sent to the Church that Singapore would no longer permit missionaries from English-speaking countries to labor in their country. After a cordial discussion about the importance of families to the Church and the prime minister's concern over the decline in the number of children in Singapore, Yew said: "We need more Mormon missionaries. We have great respect for your faith. I will have our country change our rules immediately so that your missionaries from anywhere in the world can teach your Church doctrine in this country."[13]

They made many other stops in Asia, including in Hiroshima, Japan. Teruyuki Asada was in the congregation there and later said: "He blessed our ward so that more people would start coming to church and more converts would be made. He also blessed that from those converts many would go out on missions. I am the first missionary leaving since his special blessing upon our ward."[14]

At a Thailand district conference, Ronald Rasband was not surprised at the "excitement and thrill of the Saints as they had come from all over Thailand to hear an Apostle speak."[15] In a crowded marketplace in Bangkok, where tourists are expected to negotiate downward from the vendors' prices, Ron negotiated with a vendor for a fake Rolex watch in behalf of Elder Ballard:

> This poor little girl kept cutting the price, and cutting the price, and cutting the price. Eventually, I got it to a very low price and I was feeling quite pleased with what I had done in getting this watch for Elder Ballard. And as Elder Ballard got out his wallet to pay the poor girl for the watch that I had negotiated the price downward, he . . . paid her the original price. I was taught by Elder Ballard that getting the lowest price is not always the most important thing.[16]

In Taiwan, Elder Ballard expressed concern that there was a strong cadre of missionaries but few convert baptisms:

> As I worked with the missionaries, I found that they were not talking to everybody that they met during the day. I taught the missionaries to open their mouths and talk to everybody that they met. At the conclusion of the training the assistants took us back to the hotel. Knowing that they had not had anything to eat since early in the day, I invited them to come into the hotel and have a bowl of soup with us. We sat down at the table, and a handsome young man about twenty-six years of age came to take our order. He went around the table, took the order from all of us without one word being said to him about who we were or what we were doing in Taiwan. When the waiter left, I said, "All right, Elders, talk to him."
>
> They asked, "Who?"
>
> I said, "The waiter."
>
> "You mean now?"
>
> "Yes, now. Talk to him about the gospel."
>
> That was a tough spot for a missionary to be in with a member of the Twelve making such a request. They looked at each other and realized with me sitting there they had very little alternative but to talk to him. The waiter came back, and the assistants

engaged him in a discussion. At the conclusion of the dinner, the assistants had his name and address, with an appointment to teach him the first discussion the next day at 3 p.m. As we left, they commented, "Elder Ballard, it really does work, doesn't it?"[17]

In Taipei, Taiwan, Elder Ballard saw two Utah businessmen, Scott Waterson and Gary Stevenson, standing in a hotel lobby trying to find the address of a meetinghouse so they could attend church. Gary recalled:

> We were startled to hear a voice behind us saying "Hello, Elders, where are you headed today?" We turned to see the newly called Apostle, Elder M. Russell Ballard, reaching out his hand to greet us. He told us that we would find no one in their regular meetinghouse that day, as he was conducting a regional conference in an arena large enough to accommodate Saints from throughout Taiwan. He arranged seats for us at the arena and expressed interest in learning of our business endeavors, our families, and our devotion to the gospel. Remarkably, his interest in us didn't stop in that hotel lobby or the assembly hall in Taipei, Taiwan.[18]

From that encounter began a long-lasting friendship with these two young men, who later founded the ICON Health & Fitness company. Both also served as mission presidents in Asia.

Dedicating Countries and Temples

As an Apostle, Elder Ballard was learning that there was no such thing as settling into a routine. Around every corner, it seemed, was a new experience, a new adventure, a new opportunity to serve the Lord's children. In early 1990, for example, he and Elder Charles Didier—along with approximately 108 missionaries, members, and investigators—met in Port of Spain for the dedication of the Republic of Trinidad and Tobago for the preaching of the gospel. In the dedicatory prayer, Elder Ballard pled with the Lord to "stay the influence of the

Elder Ballard in Suriname

evil one that he may not have power over the honest in heart that dwell here upon this land." He blessed the people that as they came in contact with the missionaries and the members of the Church, they would be nurtured by the Spirit and accepting of the saving doctrine and ordinances of the Church. He also invoked a blessing upon government leaders that they would provide fair and stable leadership and grant the clearances and permissions necessary for the progress of the Church.[19]

The next day, Elder Ballard, again in company with Elder Didier, offered a dedicatory prayer in Georgetown, Guyana. This was followed by dedicatory prayers in Paramaribo, Suriname, and in Kourou, French Guiana, on February 27.[20]

Just a few months later, Elder Ballard was back in Toronto to attend the dedicatory ceremonies of the Toronto Canada Temple. He hosted Lord Thompson of Fleet as well as a group of local clergy for a tour of the temple. One clergyman took him aside after the tour and said, "I have felt the Spirit of the Lord twice in my life abundantly: once as I stood at the open tomb in the Holy Land and the second time as I stood in the celestial room of this temple. I have never felt anything like this except on these two occasions." Elder Ballard replied: "That is Heavenly Father and the power of the Holy Ghost witnessing to your heart and to your mind that our message is true, that these temples are in fact houses of the Lord. His Spirit dwells here. The work of eternal salvation for our Father's children is undertaken in this holy house." The clergyman shook hands with Elder Ballard as if "we had been friends for many, many years."[21]

Elder Ballard was the first speaker in the fourth dedicatory session of the Toronto Canada Temple, led the Hosanna Shout in the fifth dedicatory session, and read the dedicatory prayer in the seventh session. He is most remembered for saying on that occasion, "When temples are dedicated, I have a feeling that those on the other side of the veil that helped to establish the Church in the temple district are allowed to look in upon the proceedings of the dedication of the temple."[22]

Although the dedication of the Toronto Canada Temple was dear to his heart, it was the dedication ceremonies at the Las Vegas Nevada Temple some months earlier that brought him to the attention of Bruce L. Olsen, managing director of the Church Public Affairs Department. Elder Ballard led a group of city dignitaries through the temple, giving brief explanations and sharing his testimony of temple work. He did so with such ease that Brother Olsen wrote to the First Presidency:

> I believe the press and the important people attending could not have received a better introduction to the Church nor the temple. Many people in Nevada have benefitted from seeing and coming to know Elder Ballard personally. Many understand as never before that we are a Christian Church and that the leaders of the Church are warm, caring individuals with a powerful message.[23]

Perhaps it was not a coincidence when, in late 1990, Elder Ballard was assigned by the First Presidency to serve on the Public Affairs Committee, with Neal A. Maxwell of the Quorum of the Twelve as chairman.

Energetic, bold, forthright, fearless, transparent, and *honest* were a few words used by the Public Affairs staff to describe Elder Ballard's service. They saw him as a man of action who works tirelessly to bring the Church out of obscurity. There was plenty of evidence to support such claims.[24] Elder Ballard saw that Church books and videos were placed in thousands of public libraries as well as university libraries throughout the United States, Canada, and Great Britain. He pushed for a change in the official Church logo so that it was clearer, it was easier to read, and it placed special emphasis on the Savior's name. He oversaw the placement of a Church DVD in an issue of the *Ensign* magazine and encouraged members to give the DVD as a Christmas gift to friends of other faiths. The film *Legacy,* shown daily in the Joseph Smith Memorial Building in Salt Lake City, was also under Elder Ballard's administrative umbrella. And the musical *Savior of the World,* which was then presented every year during the Christmas and Easter seasons at the Conference Center Theater in Salt Lake City, also had his input.[25]

First Contact for the United Kingdom

One leader Elder Ballard was assigned to supervise in his new role as first contact for the United Kingdom was Elder Jeffrey R. Holland of the Seventy, who was presiding over the Europe North Area and residing in Solihull, England. Elder Holland did not know Elder Ballard except by reputation and was somewhat anxious about his upcoming visit and their subsequent relationship. Apprehension led Elder Holland to pray.

> I just needed to know that I could do what he wanted me to do, that I could do what was right and succeed as a new General Authority. There came into my mind and into my heart a burst of revelation as powerful in its own way as any I have ever had. For almost literally the words were spoken, perilously close to audibly, "Russell Ballard will become one of your warmest and best friends for the rest of your life." . . . This ranks among the great personal

spiritual experiences of my life. . . . Looking back as a member of the Quorum of the Twelve, it has wonderfully prophetic meaning for me now. That impression has been literally fulfilled tenfold, one hundredfold.[26]

Elder Ballard stayed with the Hollands for only a short time, but it was long enough to create a fun memory for a young boy. "Our youngest son was delighted when Elder Ballard would be caught in our house between the bedroom and the bathroom in his pajamas," Elder Holland recalled. "One of my son's greatest delights was to see a member of the Twelve flitting about in his pajamas."[27]

Among all his meetings with the Saints in the British Isles during this visit, Elder Ballard said the one that had the most impact on him personally was not a scheduled meeting at all. Rather, it was a brief but powerful impromptu conversation that took place between him and a stake Relief Society president who was busily preparing refreshments for the evening when he walked into the stake center.

"I took occasion to visit with her privately to thank her for her faithful service," Elder Ballard said. "While we were talking, I asked her how she was feeling about her calling in the Church."

"Elder Ballard," she said, her voice edged with exasperation, "will the brethren in leadership positions ever understand that the sisters want to make a contribution to the real issues facing the Church and its members?"

As you might expect, I was a little surprised at her answer and the palpable frustration that clearly had prompted it. So I asked her to elaborate.

"Sometimes I feel like the hired help at the council table," she said. "I'm there to serve, but not to contribute. When they talk about ways to accomplish the mission of the Church, my opinion is never sought. And when they refer to the decisions of stake leaders, they never acknowledge me as a leader who can make a contribution to the spiritual growth and development of stake members. Sometimes they even talk about ways to meet the needs of the sisters in our stake without even inviting me to participate. I'm given assignments, and I do what I'm told. But I never feel that I am asked to counsel. And I was wondering: Is that the way it's supposed to work?"[28]

The sincerity and truth of her question "resonated within me," Elder Ballard said. "I talked with the auxiliary leaders and listened to my daughters. I counseled with my wife, Barbara."[29] He concluded it was time to make changes. The role of women in the Church needed to be appreciated more.

Sheri Dew, who worked with Elder Ballard on a variety of projects through the years, said, "Elder Ballard was one of the early proponents of the importance of women's voices in councils, whether it be a family council, a ward council, or a stake council. He wrote an important book, *Counseling with Our Councils* (1997), that has significantly influenced how councils, and the voices of women who sit on those councils, are viewed in the Church today."[30]

As the year 1990 was drawing to a close, Elder Ballard was asked to turn on the festive lights at both the Salt Lake Temple grounds and the Washington DC Temple grounds.[31] Ambassadors to the United States and other members of the diplomatic community came together on November 21, 1990, to witness the light display on the Washington DC Temple grounds. Among their number was the Soviet Ambassador to the United States, Yuri Dubinin. Thirty-five children from the Soviet Embassy School's choir accompanied him. This was the first time the children performed in the Washington, DC, area outside the Soviet community. Following the program, Elder Ballard invited them to sit in front of the Christus statue. "Christ said we must become like little children," he remarked. "Perhaps if we turned the world over to the children for one month each year, all our problems would meet with peaceful solutions."[32]

CHAPTER THIRTEEN

THE FAMILY,
THE COUNTRY,
THE WORLD

It is said that the Prophet Joseph Smith was occasionally criticized for the time he spent roughhousing and playing with the children of Nauvoo. To answer the criticism, Joseph told a parable about a prophet and a hunter—clearly explaining his own philosophy about the relationship of play to work. As the story goes, a certain prophet sat under a tree "amusing himself in some way." Along came a hunter and reproved him. The prophet asked the hunter if he always kept his hunting bow strung up.

"Oh no," said he.

"Why not?"

"Because it would lose its elasticity."

"It is just so with my mind," stated the prophet; "I do not want it strung up all the time."[1]

If you were to ask Elder Ballard around 1991 what he did to "unstring his bow," his immediate answer would have been: "Spend time with Barbara and my family." That was always his greatest joy. Nothing could refresh and revitalize his soul like the precious moments he enjoyed with Barbara, their children, and the ever-growing number of grandchildren. Beyond that, he felt himself drawn to his extended family: his sisters and their families, as well as the extended Ballard and Smith families. He had always treasured and tried to honor his noble ancestors. And occasionally he found the time and opportunity to do something about it.

Elder Ballard's work to forge relationships in the extended Joseph Smith Sr. family continued to bear fruit. As a result of the growing trust between Elder Ballard and President Wallace B. Smith of the Reorganized Church of Jesus Christ of Latter Day Saints (Community of Christ), an extraordinary event was able to take place—this time in Kirtland, Ohio. In November 1993, Elder Ballard was assigned to preside over area training meetings in Kirtland for stake presidents, mission presidents, and temple presidents in the North America Northeast Area.[2] As plans for the meetings were being formulated, it occurred to Elder Ballard to approach his distant cousin to ask a special favor:

> "Cousin, I'd like to use the Kirtland Temple. Would you let me use the Kirtland Temple for two hours as part of the training that we want to do with the stake presidents, mission presidents, and other priesthood leaders that I'm responsible for here in the eastern part of the United States? Would you give me permission to hold such a meeting in the Kirtland Temple?" He had to ponder that for a few minutes, and then he said, "Yes, I think that would be all right." Then I said, "Not only the meeting, but permission to pass the sacrament." He pondered for another moment and then gave permission to do that.[3]

And so a special sacrament meeting was held on November 6, 1993, in the Kirtland Temple in conjunction with the training meetings.[4] This was the first sacrament meeting held there since the Saints left the area 160 years earlier.

Ralph W. Hardy Jr., president of the Washington DC Stake, wrote of this sacred event:

The Saturday morning training meeting proceeded until a little past ten o'clock. . . . Elder Ballard stood up and, to our surprise, announced that the training meeting was over. He asked all those in attendance to gather up their belongings and board the busses waiting outside to take them 800 yards up the hill to the Kirtland Temple to hold a sacrament meeting.

Collectively, our hearts almost stopped. We stood up in silence, gathered our things, and filed into the waiting busses. Except for the growling motor of the bus, there was complete silence as we tried to take in what was about to happen at the Kirtland Temple at the top of the hill. We were aware that we were going to be eyewitnesses at another important moment in Church history, and that we would be joined in this experience by Elder M. Russell Ballard, our teacher, fellow servant, and an Apostle of the Lord Jesus Christ.

After the sacrament was blessed and passed by the General Authorities, Elder Ballard called on the other Brethren present to bear their testimonies . . . of the Savior's mission, the Restoration of the gospel through the Prophet Joseph Smith, and what had occurred in the very room where we sat.

The concluding and principal speaker was Elder Ballard. As the presiding officer of the Church in this service . . . Elder Ballard . . . recounted in considerable detail the miraculous history of the construction of the Kirtland Temple, the great sacrifice of the poverty-stricken Latter-day Saints (too poor, except for a handful, to even be listed on the county tax rolls) and the efforts of his great-great-grandfather, Hyrum Smith, to fulfill the special commission given him by his brother, the Prophet Joseph Smith, to superintend and complete the Lord's Holy House.

As Elder Ballard spoke in direct and earnest tones, we, his brethren, wept—our "hearts . . . swollen with joy, unto the gushing out of many tears, because of the great goodness of God" (3 Nephi 4:33).[5]

Allen R. Walters, manager of the Kirtland Temple property and a member of the Reorganized Church of Jesus Christ of Latter Day Saints, had no such feelings:

> I was becoming more and more agitated at their service . . . and ready to leave. Before I could walk out my chest got tight and my breathing got very difficult. I thought I was having a heart attack. At this point it became very evident to me that I was not being Christian, and I prayed silently, "Oh Lord please forgive me and don't let me die." For lack of a better term what happened next was a spiritual spanking, being loved and chastised at the same time. I heard an audible message, turned to see if anyone else was hearing anything, which it appeared they were not. The message was: "Allen, this is not your temple. This is *my* temple. These are also *my* saints, and this is appropriate use of this sacred place."[6]

At the conclusion of the meeting, Walters found Elder Ballard and said to him, "I want to apologize."

"For what?" Elder Ballard asked.

He said, "As I stood here and listened to you bless the sacrament, I heard a voice that said, 'This is not your temple. This is *my* temple.' I want to apologize."[7]

The two men embraced, and in that moment more than a century and a half of religious animus seemed to melt away in the pleasant warmth of shared faith and Christian love.

Less than a year later, in June 1994, Elder Ballard was again at a location of special historical significance to Latter-day Saints in general and to the Smith family specifically, joining President Howard W. Hunter and President Gordon B. Hinckley in Carthage, Illinois, for a sesquicentennial remembrance of the martyrdom of the Prophet Joseph Smith and his brother Hyrum. As Elder Ballard stood in Carthage Jail, the very place where a barbaric act of religious bigotry took the lives of prophets who were also his forebears, he felt an inexplicable sense of peace. He said:

As a great-great-grandson of Hyrum Smith, it is impossible for me to consider the traumatic events that took place here 150 years ago tomorrow and not be deeply touched in a personal, emotional way. And as a dedicated believer in the great and eternal principles for which Hyrum and his younger brother Joseph gave their lives, I am in awe of their courageous faith and inspired by the testimony of truth they sealed here with their blood.

There is a sweet and peaceful feeling here today, and that is just as it should be. These were men of peace, brothers who were bound by their love of God as well as their love for each other. . . . "In life they were not divided, and in death they were not separated!" (D&C 135:7).[8]

US Presidents and the Congressional Record

In addition to participating in events at locations significant to Church history, Elder Ballard also represented the Church on the national and international stage. In early 1992, Elder Ballard joined Beverly Campbell, the Church's public affairs director for Washington, DC, in representing the Church at the National Prayer Breakfast and the dedication of the interdenominational chapel at Camp David, located in the wooded hills of Catoctin Mountain Park about sixty-two miles northwest of Washington, DC. Guests from all fifty states and more than 120 countries gathered for the occasion, representing a wide diversity of ethnic, cultural, religious, and political backgrounds. The events were hosted by US President George H. W. Bush and his wife, Barbara Bush. US Vice President Dan Quayle and his wife, Marilyn, also attended.

As President Bush was about to address the attendees, a child started to cry. His mother took him out. President Bush began his speech by saying, "Wouldn't you know that my grandson would tear up this whole meeting?" He then read from his prepared remarks before saying, "Let us pray that peoples everywhere will discover the simple

Shaking hands with US President George H. W. Bush

joy of praying to God; and let the people of this nation remember that it was conceived under God."⁹

After President Bush's remarks, a reception was held. "President Bush was standing by himself, and I went over and visited with him," recalled Elder Ballard. "I talked to him I guess for ten or fifteen minutes, and nobody else was bothering him. Then all of a sudden we heard somebody giving out instructions, and it was Barbara Bush telling everybody where to get their plates and what line to follow to get their food." President Bush laughed and said, "The Silver Fox is running the operation."¹⁰

Inspired by what he saw and felt among so many of the nation's political and religious leaders, Elder Ballard began to ponder the role of religion in a free society. It's no wonder, then, that he chose that topic when he was asked to speak at the Provo, Utah, Freedom Festival devotional in July of that same year. Representative John T. Doolittle (R-Calif.) commended his address, "Religion in a Free Society," on the floor of the US House of Representatives, saying, "I believe that Elder Ballard raises an extremely valid point: a simple constitutional prohibition of a State-sponsored church has evolved into court-ordered bans against the slightest mention of God in the public square."[11] The speech was also awarded a George Washington Medal of Honor for excellence in public communication by the Freedom Foundation at Valley Forge.[12] In part, Elder Ballard said:

> The Founding Fathers very likely were aware of the experiences of Roger Williams and others when they wrote in the First Amendment that the government cannot impede the free exercise of religion. They wrote that the church and the state were to be separate, independent entities, not to eliminate morality and God's law but to make sure that the power of government could never be used to silence religious expression or to persecute religious practice. I quote George Washington: "If I could have entertained the slightest apprehension that the Constitution, framed in the convention where I had the honor to preside, might possibly endanger the religious rights of any ecclesiastical society, certainly I would never have placed my signature to it" (*Maxims of Washington,* New York: D. Appleton and Company, 1894, 370–371).
>
> What would Washington have thought if he could have foreseen our day? Would he have signed the document? I believe he would have been troubled to see a time when citizens are forbidden to pray in public meetings; when people claim that "you can't legislate morality," as if any law ever passed did not have at its heart some notion of right and wrong; when churches are called intruders when they speak out against public policy that is contrary to the commandments of God; when many people reject the correcting influence of churches if it infringes on daily living; when religion is accepted as a social organization but not as an integral part of national culture; when people bristle if churches speak in any forum except from the pulpit.
>
> As M. J. Sobran recently wrote, "A religious conviction is now a second-class conviction, expected to step deferentially to the

With US President Bill Clinton

back of the secular bus, and not to get uppity about it" (*Human Life Review,* Summer 1978, 58–59).

Organized religion finds itself increasingly on the defensive. Not only are people questioning the right of the church—any church—to be involved in matters of public policy, but some are even beginning to wonder whether the church is entitled to exert any kind of meaningful influence in people's lives. As one churchgoer recently said on a radio talk show, "I think the world of my minister—as long as he doesn't try to tell me how to live my life."[13]

The First Presidency subsequently assigned Elder Ballard to join Senator Orrin Hatch in representing the Church as President Bill Clinton signed the Religious Freedom Restoration Act of 1993. Of that signing, Elder Ballard said: "This is the most historic piece of legislation dealing with religious freedom in our lifetime. It preserves the right of every American to freely worship his God or her God. . . . This legislation implements into federal law the same vital principle embodied in our Church's 11th Article of Faith."[14] Elder Ballard shook hands with President Clinton and met with US Vice President Al Gore on that occasion.[15]

Despite all the honors and extraordinary experiences he was having as an Apostle of the Lord Jesus Christ and a representative of His Church, Elder Ballard never lost sight of life's greatest and most valued treasures. Just before Christmas in 1992, a surgical procedure forced him to the apostolic sidelines for a short time. Because of the surgery, he said, "my daughter Holly invited us out to her home for our annual family Christmas party.

"The family had a reclining chair for Grandpa to sit in," Elder Ballard continued. "As I sat among my family with no work to do, I had time to look at my children and grandchildren. I was overwhelmed because of the bounteous blessings Barbara and I enjoy. My emotions welled up within me as I contemplated the great gift of life, the great gift of family, the great gift of grandchildren who are being raised in the Church by faithful fathers and mothers who love their Heavenly Father. What more could one ask for than a family that wants to be together forever! I thought to myself, what a glorious gift. Whether or not I am worthy of all this, I am not sure. But this I can tell you, I am so deeply grateful that I will strive with all of my strength to be worthy of Barbara, of our seven children, and our thirty-three grandchildren."[16]

Sharing Vision at Home and Abroad

Elder Ballard soon had a golden opportunity to share his testimony of the great blessing of family with two leaders from another faith group who came to Salt Lake City looking for answers to some of the challenges they were facing in their church. He recalled:

> I was assigned, along with then Bishop Robert D. Hales, to host these two fine men. They had come to Salt Lake City because they had a great concern within their own church that the

attendance was falling off, and they were anxious and worried about the loss of activity among their members. They concluded that perhaps the reason they were having some of their challenges was that they were not focused as well as they ought to be on the family. So, they surveyed literally the world and concluded that the organization on the earth that best understood the family was The Church of Jesus Christ of Latter-day Saints. They came here to gather materials and to be instructed and to see what they could learn that they could put to work within their own church.

We were delighted to meet them early in the morning, and then we had them visit all the various departments of the Church that had anything to do with the family. By evening time, when we hosted them at a dinner on the tenth floor of the Joseph Smith Memorial Building, they had gathered up so much material that they had to have it shipped back to the Midwest. They couldn't carry all the manuals, all the videotapes, and all the TV spots and other things that we have done and said about the importance of family life.

At the conclusion of the dinner, one of these fine gentlemen said to me: "Mr. Ballard, we cannot thank you enough for your courtesy and all that you have shared with us. We are very anxious about taking these things back now and trying to implement them into the activities of our church."

I assured him that it was our honor that we were able to share with him some of the materials that we had, and then I said: "I would be less than honest, though, if I did not tell you one thing. Those materials will never work for you like they work for us."

Whereupon he said, "Oh? Why is that?"

I said, "Because your concept of the family is very, very different from our concept of the family."

I asked him, "Do you perform marriages?" When he responded that he did, that both of them did, I said, "Do you still have language something like this in the marriage ceremony—that you marry a husband to a wife until death do they part?"

"Yes, we do have that language in our marriage ceremony."

"Then, in effect, when you marry a couple you also make a pronouncement of divorce at death. Not so in The Church of Jesus Christ of Latter-day Saints."

We were where we could see the temple. I pointed to the temple and I said to them, "In that temple across the street those who have the authority of the priesthood of God that has been restored through the Prophet Joseph Smith by John the Baptist and Peter, James, and John, the Aaronic and Melchizedek Priesthoods, by that authority when one marries in the house of the Lord they are married for time and for all eternity. They are sealed or bound together by the same priesthood binding power that our Savior gave to Peter and the apostles of old. Therefore, the family in The Church of Jesus Christ of Latter-day Saints is different in concept from a family in any other organization. When a man is bound to his wife, sealed by the power of the holy priesthood for time and all eternity, and children are born under that covenant, then a family can be together forever. Therefore, a father and a mother, if they are thinking straight, in The Church of Jesus Christ of Latter-day Saints, would always respect and love, cherish and nurture, watch out for one another; and they would always recognize that children who come into that bond or that marriage are precious spirits, sons and daughters of God. Stewardship as parents is one of the most cherished and responsible obligations we have in mortality."

My friend said, "That's a beautiful thought, a beautiful doctrine."

I said, "Well, you can have it. You just have to be baptized by the authority of the holy priesthood which we bear." They left without any question of our position—that of being the restored Church of Jesus Christ here upon the earth.[17]

That same position—that The Church of Jesus Christ of Latter-day Saints is the restored Church of Jesus Christ upon the earth—was also made abundantly clear a few months later when Elder Ballard was sent to Lithuania, a former Soviet bloc nation in Europe's Baltic States, to dedicate that nation for the preaching of the gospel. On May 20, 1993, in Vilnius, Lithuania, before a few members of the Church, Elder Ballard offered the dedicatory prayer and asked the Lord to "bless the people that they may put aside tradition and the past, and have the vision of the future, which vision will prosper the land and lift this people to receive all the blessings that thou would have in store for them."[18]

Our Search for Happiness

For many years, Elder Ballard had been asking the Missionary Department and Deseret Book to prepare a book that would explain in simple terms the message of the Restoration. He thought it should be something like LeGrand Richards's *A Marvelous Work and a Wonder*, but short and clear and simple enough to be completely read in a flight from Salt Lake City to Chicago. After repeated requests, representatives from the Missionary Department and Deseret Book gathered in his office and said, "Why don't you write the book?" Sheri Dew, who was then the executive vice president of publishing at Deseret Book, recalled, "He wanted to write a book presenting the Restoration of the gospel and the blessings of living the principles of the gospel in a simple and concise way."[19] In 1993, Elder Ballard published *Our Search for Happiness*, although he wondered if anyone would be interested in anything he wrote. He need not have worried. "His book defied every normal bell curve," Sheri said. "It sold well over a million copies. Its influence has been quite unique in the Latter-day Saint publishing industry."[20]

Elder Ballard was unimpressed by the numbers. He wasn't interested in whatever notoriety might come from writing a bestseller. What drove him to write it, and what consumed him during the laborious editing process, was the sincere hope that it might do someone some good and bring people closer to Jesus Christ and His Church. So he was thrilled when the letters started coming in.

One said: "A friend gave me your book and made me promise to read every word. I took it with me on a recent trip. The first night I figured I'd read a chapter in the bathtub. Hours later, I climbed out of the tub, cold and wrinkled, but changed forever."[21]

Another reader said: "I asked a friend if he knew any Mormons in Salt Lake. . . . He laughed and said he was a Mormon, and gave me your book. I read it from cover to cover that night and again the next night. The second night, when I closed the book I said out loud, 'At last I have come home.'" Yet another reader, a dairyman, wrote, "I still read frequently your book *Our Search for Happiness*. This has given me a great testimony. My favorite heifer is named 'Happiness,' and this year's baby I called 'Ballard.'"[22]

"This is why we did this," he said as he showed a visitor to his office the latest collection of correspondence from grateful readers. "I just wanted people to understand who we are, what we believe, and why we believe it. If it's doing that, even to a small degree, then it was worth it."[23]

That desire and that influence extended well beyond the pages of *Our Search for Happiness*. Wherever he went, Elder Ballard looked for opportunities to share the truth of the restored gospel of Jesus Christ. In September 1994, for example, he attended the Orlando Florida Temple open house, aware that there had been a certain amount of opposition to the location of the temple, spearheaded by two women who lived in the neighborhood. It was no small surprise to local Church leaders that these two women appeared at the open house. Elder Ballard greeted them warmly and later said of that moment:

> I was standing at the doorway as these neighbors came in, and you could almost feel the chill as the women walked past me into the temple. I had the privilege of taking them through the temple. We went to the various rooms, and I explained to them that this is our best effort to try to teach our people the importance of life

and the principal objectives of mortality, looking on into eternity. . . . At the conclusion of that experience, I walked back out with the neighbors, and the one lady who had been the most vocal stood in the foyer of the Orlando Temple, took hold of my hand, and wept. Tears streamed down her cheeks as she said, "I had no idea. I didn't understand. Please forgive me." The next morning, the second day of the open house, a large basket of flowers was delivered to the temple. The card simply read, "Thank you, with love, your neighbors."[24]

Media Interactions

After nearly ten years as an Apostle—with nearly half of those years spent working with the Public Affairs Department—Elder Ballard was growing more and more comfortable representing the Church and its teachings in front of the media. "I don't look at the media as the enemy," he once told members of the Public Affairs staff. "Nor do I look at them as our friends. They are simply professionals doing their job. When I speak to them, I believe it is my job to simply tell the truth as simply and directly and accurately as I can, and trust that they will be fair with what they do with that."[25]

Because he was always so willing to interact with the media and did so comfortably and effectively, Elder Ballard was called upon to represent the Church in many media interviews. When a request came for someone to talk about Church doctrine and policies on the cable-television program *Perspectives: Faith in Our Times* (produced by United Methodist Communications and hosted by Dr. Richard Nesmith, a professor of sociology and religion in the School of Theology at Boston University), Elder Ballard was both willing and anxious to accept the assignment.[26] During the interview he discussed a wide range of topics, from the divinity of Jesus Christ to the role of Joseph Smith to the Restoration to missionary work to the different roles of men and women within the Church and society. Response to his straightforward remarks was positive.

Of course, not every media interview went smoothly. In 1994, Ted Koppel, a famous newscaster on ABC, was making a documentary on The Church of Jesus Christ of Latter-day Saints. Koppel planned to air the documentary on *Nightline,* an ABC television show viewed by millions of people. Koppel's television crew taped a series of interviews with a number of different people in New York City, Los Angeles, the Philippines, and Salt Lake City for what they termed a "balanced documentary." Included among the people they interviewed were a number of dissenters and disaffected Church members, and they wanted a response from a General Officer of the Church. Elder Ballard stepped forward.

Plans were underway for Elder Ballard to be at the local ABC affiliate in Salt Lake City while Ted Koppel would be at the ABC studio in Washington, DC. Elder Ballard felt uneasy about the arrangement and asked if Koppel and his staff would consider filming the interview at the Washington DC Temple Visitors' Center. They agreed.

For the interview on September 7, 1994, cameras were set up so that the Washington DC Temple was the background whenever the focus was on Elder Ballard. The background for Ted Koppel was the *Christus* statue. Koppel came a few minutes early for the interview and watched with Elder Ballard a short film about temples. Koppel was very warm and cordial, and Elder Ballard thought they had a good rapport. However, as soon as the red light on the camera came on, Koppel became quite different.

> "Mr. Ballard, it seems that the Mormon Church receives revelation when it is politically expedient," Koppel said. "For example, you received the revelation on polygamy when the government of the United States was taking severe action against your church. And you received revelation on the priesthood in the midst of the

civil rights issue. My question is, when will you have a revelation on homosexuality?"

First question! I thought, "What happened to that nice guy?" I have to tell you that through that interview, I was hanging on to the ropes. And the Lord blessed me because the nature of this interview was very difficult. Well, they interviewed me for about 45–50 minutes, out of which they used five or six. I don't think I embarrassed the Church. I could have done better. If I could redo it now knowing what I know now, I could have done better. But that interview, I think, had a tremendous impact on the Brethren, helping them feel that we could in fact take on the national press.[27]

Although Elder Ballard felt he could have done better, he handled Koppel's biting questions with poise and calm. The documentary aired on national television in late October 1994. Of Elder Ballard's participation in the documentary, the Washington Advisory Group to Public Affairs wrote, "It is our view that Elder Ballard did a superior job representing the senior, apostolic leadership of the Church. [His] . . . quick, confident answers and pleasing countenance evidenced obvious sincerity and conviction."[28] The Public Affairs staff at Church headquarters wrote, "Elder Ballard's talent to speak clearly and forthrightly has made him one of the most requested interviews among the Church leadership. He is simply unafraid of any question and unbowed by any interviewer. No one does it better!"[29]

As comfortable and at ease as he was standing as a witness of Jesus Christ and His Church before millions of people at a time through his media interviews, Elder Ballard continued to cherish opportunities to minister "one by one," as the Savior had done.[30] At around the same time as the interview with Ted Koppel, he and Barbara participated in a fireside in Idaho Falls. "A wonderful family there knew that I was coming, and they asked if I would meet with their daughter, and consider giving her a blessing," Elder Ballard said. "I agreed to do that. This girl, seventeen years of age, had cancer. She had been in and out of remission over several years, and now it had flared up again. The family members were converts to the Church.

"As we went into the Relief Society room and sat with this beautiful family," he continued, "the father said, 'Brother Ballard, we understand the gospel. We understand that our Heavenly Father is in control. We love our daughter. We would like to keep her with us but nevertheless, we understand that she belongs to Him.'

"Then that beautiful girl, whom I shall never forget as long as I live, with her bright brown eyes, looked at me and said, 'Brother Ballard, I am not afraid to die. I would like to live. I have so much I would like to do, but if Heavenly Father wants me to come to Him, I understand. Please bless me that the will of my Heavenly Father will be fulfilled in my behalf.'"

Together with her father, Elder Ballard gave the young woman a blessing of comfort. "The Spirit was there—powerfully," he said. "The room was filled with an almost tangible feeling of love and peace." As Elder and Sister Ballard walked back to their car, he said, "Sweetheart, what do people do who don't have the gospel? How blessed is that little girl to have a father and a mother who have taught her and brought her peace and brought her confidence and assurance that life is an eternal process, not just an earthly one?"

The young woman passed away about a month after that experience, but Elder Ballard said, "She left a legacy and an impression on me that shall never die. She was the epitome to me of gospel teaching, and she got it primarily from her father and her mother in her home, at their teaching, at their beckoning."[31]

Bypass Surgery

Beginning on June 15, 1995, and extending into the twenty-first century, Elder Ballard was assigned to be the first contact in the Twelve for the Utah area. The assignment meant driving in a car instead of waiting for an airplane to lift off the tarmac. It meant more nights at home with Barbara and fewer nights staying in the homes of members or in hotel rooms.

It also meant more opportunities to spend time with friends, like the evening in late July when Elder Ballard and Barbara went to Deer Valley with Nate and Bonnie Wade. It was intended as an evening of peaceful relaxation, and it started out that way. But as Elder Ballard walked up a small hill, he felt a burning sensation in his throat. It was serious enough that he made an appointment with Dr. Robert E. Fowles the next day. As a result of his appointment with Dr. Fowles, Elder Ballard was sent to the LDS Hospital in Salt Lake City to have an angiogram, an imaging test that looks at the arteries that supply blood to the heart. Dr. Fowles reviewed the angiogram results with him and told him that although his heart muscle was strong, bypass surgery was needed to correct five arterial blockages. And the doctor said the surgery needed to happen immediately—that day.

Within hours he was sitting in his room at the LDS Hospital speaking to Dr. Donald Doty, a respected cardiovascular surgeon. After explaining the complexity of the surgical procedure, the doctor suggested that Elder Ballard gather his family. When Dr. Doty returned a few hours later, he asked, "Have you arranged to have your family gathered around you?" Elder Ballard replied, "Well, no, I really haven't." Dr. Doty looked at him sternly. "Elder Ballard, gather your family around you—now. You will be going into surgery at six o'clock tonight."[32]

Before his family arrived at the hospital, Elder Ballard thought about what he would say to them:

> It is interesting what goes through a person's mind. . . . Things come into focus quickly when you are at such a moment in your life. Family became my top priority. I had deep thoughts about Barbara and each of our children, about their companions, about our grandchildren and about what I had done as a father and a

grandfather. A lot of weaknesses came into my mind, and I started thinking to myself, "Heavenly Father, if I have a little more time I have some things I need to do better."[33]

As the children gathered around his bedside, Elder Ballard instructed them that if he did not survive the surgery, they were to take care of their mother and to take care of each other. As his daughter Tammy recalled:

> They had given him some Valium, so he was a little bit loopy. But even as they were wheeling him to the elevator to go to surgery, he was telling us what we needed to do to be happy: "Love the Lord, love each other, go to church, and pay your tithing." He kept repeating it. As the elevator doors closed you could still hear him—"Love the Lord." We all looked at each other and started to laugh. Even in his "loopiness," things were black and white, no gray areas for Dad. Either you are doing what the Lord wants you to do and you are happy or you are not and bringing sadness into your soul.[34]

Upon hearing of the surgery, Elder Ballard's longtime friend and fellow Apostle Russell M. Nelson came immediately to the hospital. Prior to his call to full-time Church service, Elder Nelson had been a world-renowned heart surgeon and a colleague of Dr. Doty. He asked the doctor if he could observe the operation, which he knew, based on his own experience, would be complex. Thankfully, the surgery was a complete success. "Elder Russell M. Nelson was at my left elbow for the entire procedure," Dr. Doty wrote. "It was a good operation and will serve [Elder Ballard] well for a long time."[35]

His recovery was remarkable. Stephen M. Studdert, a friend who worked with Elder Ballard on several projects through the years, visited him in the cardiac intensive care unit. "There he lay in bed wired to numerous monitoring machines and obviously in physical discomfort, yet on the telephone talking to someone about priesthood matters that needed attention."[36]

The third day after surgery, Elder Ballard was talking about going home. His condition had been upgraded to satisfactory, and, with the help of Jon Huntsman, he had moved from intensive care to a private room. "I told the attendant who was pushing the wheelchair that I would take over," Huntsman said. "Elder Ballard has never traveled so fast in his life as we rounded corners and went down the hall at full speed."[37] Dr. Doty wrote, "I agreed that he could go home on the fifth day, which was Sunday. I went in to discharge him about 10:00 a.m. but he was already gone. He talked the resident into letting him go, packed up, and left."[38]

When Elder Ballard arrived home that Sunday, his children met him at the house. As a family they partook of the sacrament together. Elder Ballard's emotions were very tender on that occasion. His daughter Tammy said:

> Dad just looked at all of us and said, "You know that I know the Savior lives." As tears streamed down his cheeks, Mother got up and put her arms around him. It was just the sweetest sight. He told us not to ever take the sacrament for granted. Dad said, "Every day of your life be so thankful for what the Savior has done for us. I cannot comprehend the pain that He has suffered. I am not worthy."[39]

Hundreds of phone calls and letters from well-wishers expressed concern and support for Elder Ballard. Art Linkletter wrote:

> As the newly elected president of the Board of Trustees of UCLA's Center on Aging, I am available for all kinds of advice on living better, longer. So if you need advice about anything in life not already covered by the Book of Mormon, I stand ready and willing to provide it. . . . Meanwhile, remember Yogi Berra's sage advice: "When you come to a fork in the road, take it!"[40]

Wallace B. Smith, president of the Reorganized Church of Jesus Christ of Latter Day Saints, wrote, "We will all be thinking of you and praying that you will be richly blessed as you recover your strength."[41] A word of advice was given by President Thomas S. Monson: "The only counsel I would give Russ Ballard is that we want you with us for an awfully long time. Don't try to do it all too quickly to the detriment of your own health."[42]

Ten days after the surgery, Elder Ballard attended the meeting of the Quorum of the Twelve in the Church Administration Building. "What are you doing here?" he was asked by both President Packer and Elder Nelson. "I'm here to protect my one-twelfth interest!" Elder Ballard replied. As soon as the meeting was over, he was kindly but firmly ushered to the parking lot and told to go home and stay there for a few more days.

He was, however, able to make it back to quorum meetings soon enough to be able to continue his full participation in the process of creating "The Family: A Proclamation to the World."

"We had been talking about this for a number of months," he said during an interview on the subject in 2020.

"As we looked around the world, we were seeing different groups of people who were trying to define what marriage is, and what a family is. And we thought, 'Look, we're The Church of Jesus Christ. We're the only true and living Church on the face of the earth. We have the scriptures. We have living prophets, seers and revelators. If anyone is going to define marriage and family, it ought to be us.'"[43]

For several months the members of the Quorum of the Twelve Apostles discussed the language of the proclamation. They went through several drafts until they were all comfortable with what they had created. "It took a lot of deliberation, and a lot of prayer," Elder Ballard acknowledged. "It was carefully reviewed. We could all see that this was so important."

At last the members of the Quorum of the Twelve felt the document was ready to submit to the First Presidency for their approval. The First Presidency studied and re-reviewed the proclamation until the entire group—the First Presidency and the Quorum of the Twelve Apostles—unanimously felt it was ready for President Hinckley to present it for the first time at the General Women's Meeting on September 23, 1995.

One of only a handful of official Church proclamations signed by both the First Presidency and the Quorum of the Twelve Apostles, "The Family: A Proclamation to the World" solemnly declares that "marriage between a man and a woman is ordained of God and that the family is central to the Creator's plan for the eternal destiny of His children." It speaks clearly and succinctly about the different but equally significant roles that men and women play in the creation and management of a family, and concludes by warning that "the disintegration of the family will bring upon individuals, communities, and nations the calamities foretold by ancient and modern prophets."[44]

"It was an incredible thing to be there as the Spirit moved on all of these prophets and apostles together," Elder Ballard said. "I know that the mind and will of the Lord regarding His precious children and their families was manifest through His servants in that proclamation to the world, and that the principles and positions of the proclamation have informed and guided many of the decisions we have made from that time until this."[45]

CHAPTER FOURTEEN

CELEBRATING HISTORY

W hen Utah became the forty-fifth state in the United States in 1896, parades, speeches, rallies, dances, and choir performances celebrated the event. An enormous forty-five-star flag was hung over the ceiling of the Salt Lake Tabernacle for the Statehood Day ceremonies. A hundred years later, could any less be expected in the way of celebrations and festivities? Utah Governor Norman H. Bangerter thought the statehood centennial should be a major celebration, and so did the Utah State Legislature. In anticipation of the hundredth anniversary of Utah's statehood, the Utah Legislature created the Utah Statehood Centennial Commission. Governor Bangerter asked Stephen M. Studdert to be chairman of the commission, which included twenty-five Utah citizens, most having treasured pioneer ancestry and all having a love of Utah's unique history. As first contact for Utah, Elder Ballard was appointed by the First Presidency to represent the Church on the commission.[1] The governor was pleased with his appointment and wrote to him, "Your experience and abilities will be invaluable as we prepare for our centennial celebration."[2]

The charge given the commission was to commemorate Utah's centennial on a national and state scale, and to honor Utah's founding pioneers of many faiths, cultures, and languages who came from all over the world and endured extraordinary hardships in settling the western deserts and mountain valleys. Many of the courageous founding pioneers participated in the largest exodus for religious liberty in United States history. Celebrations, historical research, sporting and cultural activities, and performances were planned in every Utah community, regardless of population.

It would be difficult to imagine anyone more enthusiastic about celebrating Utah's pioneering past than M. Russell Ballard. With pioneer forebears on both sides of his family tree, he embraced the Utah centennial celebration with all his heart and soul. On January 2, 1996, he and Barbara were in Fillmore dusting off their dance moves at the Governor's Grand Ball. The next day they traveled aboard the Centennial Train from Cedar City to Salt Lake City. When a *KSL News* reporter asked Elder Ballard, "What do you think the pioneers would have thought of all of Utah today?" Elder Ballard replied, "Pioneers of yesteryear looking upon this celebration would be smiling to see what has been accomplished, to see what we have in this great state and the cities of Utah."[3] On January 4, Elder Ballard was seated with Utah dignitaries in the Salt Lake Tabernacle for the gala statehood celebration in which President Gordon B. Hinckley said:

> Today we begin a new century building on the solid foundation laid by those who have gone before. . . . They planned wisely and built well. This remarkable edifice in which we meet is an example of their work. . . .
>
> As we move into another century we must resolve to live together in a society of men and women of diverse backgrounds, interests, and cultures. We must live with respect and tolerance and understanding for one another. We can and should retain our individuality and respect [the individuality] of others, while

nurturing together a great society dedicated to the blessing of all who reside here.[4]

With so many festive events throughout Utah, it is probably no coincidence that 1996 was a record year for international visitors coming to the state. From the moment they stepped off airplanes at the Salt Lake International Airport, visitors were made aware through centennial art displays that it was a great year to be in Utah. Some 83 ambassadors, 520 religious leaders, 92 business leaders, and 148 educators visited the state to join in one of dozens of festivities underway. Elder Ballard was at the forefront, hosting presidents, ambassadors, congressmen, and other guests when invited to do so by the First Presidency.

But of all the commission's activities and responsibilities, none captured Elder Ballard's heart like Governor Bangerter's request that they consider the possibility of refurbishing and revitalizing Pioneer Trail State Park. Situated on a 450-acre plot of land on Sunnyside Avenue right at the base of Emigration Canyon, the park featured the *This Is the Place* monument created by Mahonri M. Young, a grandson of Brigham Young, which had been unveiled at the pioneer centennial celebrations in 1947. It also included an obelisk that had been placed by the Young Men's Mutual Improvement Association in July 1921 to mark the spot where Brigham Young had said, "This is the right place. Drive on." And then there was the matter of the neglected Brigham Young forest farmhouse, moved to the park in 1973 to make way for a new interstate freeway, and seven rustic pioneer cabins.

Although Pioneer Trail State Park was a fine facility, Elder Ballard was among those who thought it could be transformed into something quite special. And so he went to work with the Utah Statehood Centennial Commission to adopt the park as its Living Legacy Project, with the construction of a visitors' center next to the *This Is the Place* monument, as well as other additions and improvements.[5] Today, This is the Place Heritage Park is a bustling attraction, with historic cabins and buildings, shops, trains, demonstrations, a Native American village, meeting and reception facilities, and a gift shop.

Elder Ballard participated with President Hinckley, the First Presidency, and the Quorum of the Twelve in the dedication of This Is the Place Heritage Park and the new visitors' center in the park. Stephen Studdert recalled, "Elder Ballard, himself a dignitary, was busy scurrying around to ensure that the prophet was shaded from the extreme direct heat, that he was comfortable, and that he was not being inappropriately burdened by the demands of the occasion."[6] Elder Ballard also joined President Hinckley in dedicating the *Journey's End* monument in the park to honor the handcart pioneers.

"Utah's pioneer history has always been important to me," Elder Ballard said. "I draw strength from the courage of these great men and women, and inspiration from their faith. I am so pleased that the Utah Statehood Centennial Commission was able to find ways to protect and preserve our pioneering legacy at This Is the Place Heritage Park so that future generations of Utahns can see and hear and experience this significant element of our state's remarkable history."[7]

Pioneer Sesquicentennial Celebrations

As plans for Utah's statehood centennial celebration were beginning to come together, Elder Ballard was asked to update the First Presidency on the planned events. After listening to Elder Ballard's characteristically detailed report, President Hinckley said, "Well, since you're representing us on the Centennial Commission, you might as well be the chairman of the Church sesquicentennial celebration."[8] The sesquicentennial to which President Hinckley referred was the 150th anniversary of the day Brigham Young's vanguard pioneer company entered the Salt Lake Valley—July 24, 1847. By coincidence, the sesquicentennial would fall just one year after the Utah statehood centennial. Although there was a certain dovetailing symmetry to the two anniversaries, the thought of pulling together two such landmark events within a year of each other was daunting—even to someone with Elder Ballard's background and experience.

But an assignment is an assignment, and Elder Ballard approached this one with energy, enthusiasm, and deep appreciation for the anniversary that was being celebrated. Although none of his beloved forebears were members of that vanguard pioneer company, the sesquicentennial was intended to honor *all* of the Church's pioneers—not just those who arrived in 1847. The celebration would eventually involve hundreds of thousands of Church members giving some three million hours of community service. It would also include:

- A wagon train and handcarts that traveled from Winter Quarters to the Salt Lake Valley;
- A handcart built in Siberia that traveled across the missions of Eastern Europe and was flown to the United States for the final leg of its journey down Emigration Canyon to This Is the Place Heritage Park;
- Symposia, musicals, and presentations on the theme "Faith in Every Footstep";
- A two-night grand spectacular honoring the courageous pioneers from every era that would be staged in BYU's Cougar Stadium (now LaVell Edwards Stadium) in Provo, Utah, to an audience of more than 60,000 people each night.

Clearly, there was much to do and precious little time to make all the necessary arrangements.

"We had a tremendous committee pulling everything together," President Ballard said. "This was not a one-man band by any means."[9] Committee members included, among others, Elder Jeffrey R. Holland, Elder Joe J. Christensen, Elder Robert L. Backman, Ruth L. Shumway, Jayne B. Malan, Glen M. Leonard, Richard E. Turley Jr., Ronald A. Rasband, and Dwan J. Young.

*Logo developed for the
pioneer sesquicentennial*

On a visit to New York in January 1997, President Boyd K. Packer and Elder Ballard had lunch with the editorial board of the *New York Times.* Publisher Arthur Sulzberger Jr. and eighteen of his editors, including Peter Jennings—the television anchorman for ABC's daily *World News Tonight*—attended the luncheon, and these journalists had questions for the two Apostles. President Packer disarmed them by saying, "We need to set some ground rules, and the ground rules are, I will answer all the easy questions and Elder Ballard will answer all the hard questions. And I will decide which ones are easy and which ones are hard."[10] Among the questions President Packer sent Elder Ballard's way were those about the sesquicentennial celebration and the transition over time from a Utah-based Church to an international denomination.

Similar questions were asked by journalists around the world. There seemed to be a great fascination with the Church's pioneering past and its foundational impact on the modern Church. Elder Ballard, as chairman of the sesquicentennial committee, and Elder Robert L. Backman, as vice chairman, had many opportunities to speak with the media about the faith of the pioneers and the theme of the sesquicentennial celebrations, "Faith in Every Footstep." In his April 1997 general conference talk, Elder Ballard spoke of the sesquicentennial:

For the Utah pioneers of 1847, their faith was grounded in principle. They left their homes, their temple, and in some cases their families, in search of a place of refuge where they could worship without fear of persecution. There was little that they could carry with them in the way of provisions and material possessions, but each wagon and handcart was heavily laden with faith—faith in God, faith in the Restoration of His Church through the Prophet Joseph Smith, and faith that God knew where they were going and that He would see them through. . . .

We are all bound together—19th and 20th century pioneers and more—in our great journey to follow the Lord Jesus Christ and to allow His atoning sacrifice to work its miracle in our lives. While we all can appreciate the footsteps of faith walked by Joseph Smith and his followers from Palmyra to Carthage Jail and across the Great Plains, we should ever stand in reverential awe as we contemplate the path trod by the Master. His faithful footsteps to Gethsemane and to Calvary rescued all of us and opened the way for us to return to our heavenly home.[11]

Reporters from all over the world requested copies of his talk. There was daily coverage in local papers from Nebraska to Utah and significant exposure in the *New York Times,* the *Wall Street Journal, USA Today,* and television broadcasts such as *Good Morning America, ABC World News Tonight,* and the *Today Show.*

Although there were many celebratory events for the media to cover—such as the play *Barefoot to Zion,* portraying early General Authority and historian B. H. Roberts and the epic journey to the Salt Lake Valley, presented at the Bountiful Regional Center; the sesquicentennial concert in Abravanel Hall in Salt Lake City; a pioneer exhibit at the Smithsonian Institution in Washington, DC; the *Trail of Hope* documentary shown on PBS stations; and the worldwide day of service—the event that captured the most media coverage was the journey of a modern-day wagon train, including real handcarts, from Winter Quarters to Salt Lake City.

*Elder and Sister Ballard join Elder and Sister Holland
to welcome the sesquicentennial wagon train*

Elder Ballard saw the wagon train off on the first leg of its journey from Winter Quarters and met it at several stops along the way:

> I had the impression that those early pioneers survived because they had a simple faith. . . . The faith that built this Church was the faith of the simple people, many of whom were uneducated. Some of them could not read or spell. But they knew deep in their hearts that Joseph Smith was a Prophet to whom God the Father and His Son Jesus Christ had appeared, and they knew this was the work of God established here upon the earth in this last dispensation of time.[12]

Following the wagon train were thousands of Church members and friends. A few of them followed the entire distance of 1,100 miles. Some travelers spent a week or so on the trail, while others walked for a single day. Sore muscles, sunburns, rope burns, and blistered feet were all part of the sesquicentennial trek experience. Those who joined in pulling the wagons up Big Mountain discovered it to be an incredibly strenuous task, which was then followed by an equally difficult descent. Television cameras took footage of the end-over-end crash of a runaway wagon descending the mountain (thankfully, the animals involved escaped injury, while the driver of the wagon suffered only a broken wrist).

On the morning of July 22, 1997, Elder Ballard and Stephen Studdert stood at the top of East Canyon, the first point where the weary travelers caught a glimpse of the Salt Lake Valley:

> We watched as first came the handcarts pulled by tired and weary men and women, girls and boys. . . . No one spoke, there was no laughter. This was a tender moment. . . . On their heels came the wagons carrying remarkable modern pioneers. . . . As they passed by Elder Ballard, those modern handcart and wagon pioneers knew this was an Apostle standing by the road. Yet none spoke; the moment was too private. Some nodded to Elder Ballard, some softly waved, some merely smiled. And Elder Ballard stood there silent, erect, and weeping.[13]

Two days later, those pulling handcarts and driving wagons or just walking beside them entered the Salt Lake Valley to the cheering applause of more than 50,000 spectators. Among the spectators were members of the First Presidency and the entire Quorum of the Twelve, who sat on the stand below the *This Is the Place* monument. "Tears were streaming down President Hinckley's cheeks, and some of the other brethren . . . well, we all lost it. That is the spirit we cannot lose," said Elder Ballard.[14] Studdert wrote: "They had survived trials and struggles and hardship, and they were safely home."[15]

The culminating event of the sesquicentennial celebration was the two-night spectacular presented outdoors in the BYU football stadium. More than sixty thousand spectators filled the stadium for each performance featuring a cast of thousands, including the Mormon Tabernacle

Choir and the Mormon Youth Chorus and Symphony. President Gordon B. Hinckley, hand in hand with a grandchild, opened the evening by walking across the stadium field to his seat. He was followed by his counselors, Thomas S. Monson and James E. Faust. The finale of the program was the appearance of several thousand missionaries from the Missionary Training Center walking into the stadium exuberantly singing "Called to Serve" while waving flags from the countries to which they were bound. There was a sustained standing ovation from a surprised and tearful audience. Although Elder Ballard was aware of the plan and knew what was coming, when the missionaries entered the stadium he was simply overcome by the faith-filled power of the moment.

Elder Ballard and Elder Backman received hundreds of letters congratulating them and the sesquicentennial committee on the celebratory events. Clifford Wallace, the senior judge of the Ninth Circuit Court in San Diego, California, wrote: "I confess that, as a convert to the Church and a lifelong resident of California, I have treated the July 24 celebration as a Utah event with little relevance to me. This year has changed all of that. You have done a splendid job in not only assisting us in understanding the sacrifice and the commitment of the pioneers, but making us feel a part of it."[16]

Elder Earl C. Tingey wrote, "The spirit of the Sesquicentennial has absolutely captivated the entire Church. I have never seen anything like it in all my experience."[17] President Gordon B. Hinckley wrote, "July was a month of significant events which will be remembered for many years to come. You and your associates have done a remarkable work. We are all grateful to you."[18]

Added Elder Holland: "I really believe, Russ, that you are the only man in the Church who could have handled this so skillfully and so successfully. It's been a privilege to tag along and to enjoy the ride."[19]

CHAPTER FIFTEEN

A PROBLEM SOLVER

A s Elder Jeffrey R. Holland suggested in his post-sesquicentennial note, Elder Ballard is a man of unique talent when it comes to taking on challenges and getting things done. Some might call him a problem solver, a brilliant tactician, or a gifted strategist. But Elder Richard J. Maynes said it has more to do with vision: "Elder Ballard has an ability to see afar."[1]

Barbara's mother, Afton Bowen, for example, was living alone following the death of her husband. Since she had never learned how to drive, she often found herself alone and isolated. But Elder Ballard came up with the perfect solution: "We will just build you a house on the back of our home." For the last fifteen years of her life, that was where she lived.[2] At Sister Bowen's funeral on May 23, 1998, Elder Ballard spoke of his wonderful association with her:

> It has been an interesting experience living with these two women [Barbara and her mother] for the past fifteen years. We would sit at the table sometimes, and they would start to giggle, which would go into uncontrollable laughter. I never did know what they were laughing about. They never clued me in as to what

*Afton Wilkins Bowen, mother of
Sister Barbara Ballard*

was going on. I just simply sat there and grinned. . . . I would try
to encourage her to eat her vegetables. As she got a little older,
she would respond, "If you live as old as I am, then you can tell
me what I should eat. In the meantime, I shall enjoy scones and
Coca-Cola."[3]

Following the funeral, President James E. Faust wrote a note to
Elder Ballard, saying, "Russ, your constant support of Barbara and
Grandmother Afton Bowen was one of the most noble things you have
accomplished in your life."[4]

Less than a year later, Elder Ballard had to figure out how to deal
with some new, more personal problems when he was diagnosed with
prostate cancer. "I figured I could either use this as an excuse to quit,
or I could just push on through it," he said. "I decided I was having too much fun to quit, so I might just as well push on through."[5]
Elder Ballard underwent radiation treatment. He knew there would be

good days and bad days following the treatment and planned accordingly. He was in his office at Church headquarters every day—he never missed a day of apostolic service. Observing the rigorous pace Elder Ballard set for himself and concerned that he wasn't getting the needed rest, President Boyd K. Packer telephoned Nate Wade and told him to "take good care of Elder Ballard and make sure he relaxes."[6]

That trial, fortunately, had a happy conclusion. Not so with a tragedy the family faced at the beginning of 2004, when Elder and Sister Ballard's grandson Nathan was killed in an airplane crash. Nathan had served in the Russian-speaking Baltic Mission and had recently been sealed to his sweetheart, Jennifer.

In 2016, Elder Ballard prepared a short blog article, "What My Grandson's Death Taught Me about Christ's Love," for the Church's website:

> Three months after I officiated at his eternal marriage to his sweetheart, Jennifer, this accident took his life. Nathan's being taken so suddenly from our mortal presence turned each of our hearts and minds to the Atonement of the Lord Jesus Christ.
>
> While it is impossible for me to put into words the full meaning of the Atonement of Christ, I pray that I can explain what His Atonement means to me and our family and what it might also mean to you and yours.
>
> The Savior's precious birth, life, Atonement in the Garden of Gethsemane, suffering on the cross, burial in Joseph's tomb, and glorious Resurrection all became a renewed reality for us. The Savior's Resurrection assures all of us that someday we too will follow Him and experience our own resurrection.
>
> What peace, what comfort this great gift is which comes through the loving grace of Jesus Christ, the Savior and Redeemer of all mankind. Because of Him we know we can be with Nathan again.

Chairman of the Church Board of Education Executive Committee

In 1999, Elder Ballard was assigned by the First Presidency to be the chairman of the executive committee of the Church Board of Education. In that capacity, he and Henry B. Eyring of the Quorum of the Twelve met with administrators and faculty in small settings at Brigham Young University. As Elder Ballard met with the athletic faculty, he said, "Not only do winning teams bring attention to the university and the Church, but athletes who live Church standards have a great influence on young people."[7] At the conclusion of his remarks, Elder Ballard asked if the faculty was getting all the support they needed. Legendary football coach LaVell Edwards spoke up. He told Elder Ballard the faculty needed additional office space and an indoor practice field plus other training facilities. Coach Edwards explained that the existing office complex had been built nearly fifty years ago, when the number of intercollegiate teams was seven or eight and the number of athletes was about two hundred. In 1999, the intercollegiate teams exceeded twenty and the number of athletes had more than tripled.

Other coaches agreed with Coach Edwards. So did BYU President Merrill J. Bateman. But the university was already reaching out to all of its supporters and donors to raise money to build the new Joseph F. Smith Building, which would house the two largest colleges on campus: the College of Family, Home, and Social Sciences and the College of Humanities. To try to raise money to build an expensive new athletic facility at the same time was beyond the vision of many BYU officials. But not Elder Ballard and President Bateman. They both strongly supported raising funds for a state-of-the-art indoor practice facility and a new student athlete building with individual office space for coaches, exercise and training rooms, and meeting rooms for the teams. They went to work and were able to raise the $50 million needed for the new athletic facilities entirely from private donations without adversely impacting the flow of fundraising for the Joseph F. Smith Building.

"Without Elder Ballard's vision, drive and personal commitment, it would have been impossible," remarked President Bateman.[8] As for Elder Ballard, he thought that his father, Melvin Ballard, who secured the funding for the first BYU football uniforms, might have had something to do with it too.[9]

"We both attended the University of Utah, at least for a time," Elder Ballard joked, "but somehow we keep showing up to help support BYU athletics."[10]

The Living Christ

The practical business of Elder Ballard's assignments never eclipsed his primary responsibility as a special apostolic witness of the Lord Jesus Christ. On January 1, 2000, "The Living Christ: The Testimony of the Apostles, The Church of Jesus Christ of Latter-day Saints" was presented to the world.[11] In this declaration, the Apostles stated:

> As we commemorate the birth of Jesus Christ two millennia ago, we offer our testimony of the reality of His matchless life and the infinite virtue of His great atoning sacrifice. None other has had so profound an influence upon all who have lived and will yet live upon the earth. He was the Great Jehovah of the Old Testament, the Messiah of the New. . . . We bear testimony, as His duly ordained Apostles—that Jesus is the Living Christ, the immortal Son of God. He is the great King Immanuel, who stands today on the right hand of His Father. He is the light, the life, and the hope of the world. His way is the path that leads to happiness in this life and eternal life in the world to come. God be thanked for the matchless gift of His divine Son.[12]

A few months later, in the month of April, each Apostle recorded his personal witness of Jesus Christ on video. Elder Ballard was filmed standing in front of a mural depicting the Savior instructing His Apostles to *Go unto All the World*.[13] Elder Ballard's testimony affirms that Apostles today have accountability to the Savior to share the gospel:

> When the Savior originally charged His Apostles, "Go ye into all the world" (Mark 16:15), His Church was very small, with members scattered in the geographic region now known as the Middle East. His dynamic Apostles, like Peter, James, John, and Paul, traveling mostly by foot or by ship, did everything they could to keep the little flock together.
>
> But the distance and the lack of communication made their work very difficult. They themselves knew that the future would bring "a falling away" from the teachings of the gospel (2 Thessalonians 2:3); they also knew that eventually there would come to the world a restoration of the fulness of the gospel of Jesus Christ. I testify that the Restoration of the gospel was accomplished, beginning with the appearance of Heavenly Father and the Lord Jesus Christ to the Prophet Joseph Smith in the spring of 1820.
>
> Since that glorious day, more than ninety men have been called to serve as Apostles with the same commission as the Apostles of old, to teach all nations that Jesus is the Christ, the Son of God our Eternal Father. Today, our labors are greatly enhanced by jet airplanes and remarkable technology that stretch the reach of our ministry to the furthest parts of the world. Since 1830, over 750,000 full-time missionaries have served in the world, teaching and testifying of Christ in over 100 languages and in 137 nations and territories.[14]
>
> I testify to you that it is the will of our Father in Heaven, through His Beloved Son, the Lord Jesus Christ, that this mighty work moves forward. It is by Him and through Him that our missionaries bear humble and sincere testimony. I'm a witness of that. I came to know for myself the truth of this work and of the Savior's divinity while serving as a full-time missionary in

Dedicating the land of Moldova

England 50 years ago. I know it more surely today, through experiences too numerous and too sacred to discuss.

This is His gospel. He stands at the head—holy, divine, supreme, full of power, majesty, grace, and truth. He lived for us, and He died for us, because He loves us. I love Him more deeply and powerfully than I can find words to express. He is my Lord, my Savior, my Redeemer, and my friend. I know that Jesus Christ is the Son of God our Eternal Father. He lives and directs His Church today through His prophet and His Apostles. His great work will continue to roll forth until it fills the whole earth. This is my testimony in the name of the Lord Jesus Christ, amen.[15]

Dedicating Moldova

A wonderful example of the gospel rolling forth into more obscure areas of the world occurred in 2001, when Elder M. Russell Ballard and Elder Ronald A. Rasband of the Seventy were assigned by the First Presidency to dedicate Moldova (formerly part of the Soviet Union) for the preaching of the gospel. At that time the total Church membership in Moldova was 174.[16] Members attending the dedication fit in a minibus. On May 16, they were driven to a hilltop overlooking the city of Chisinau. There Elder Ballard offered a prayer of dedication.

"This was during my first year as a General Authority, and so this was an extraordinary experience for me," Elder Rasband said during a 2020 interview. "I was so touched and inspired by the language Elder Ballard used, how clearly he stated the authority by which he performed the dedication, and the apostolic blessing he left on the land. It was truly remarkable."[17]

In his dedicatory prayer, Elder Ballard said, "By the power of the holy apostleship, I turn the keys and open the way more widely to the teaching and the reception of the gospel. . . .

"Thou knowest, Father, that many of Thy children live under extreme and difficult circumstances," Elder Ballard continued. "May they know that through the blessings of freedom and the knowledge of the gospel, they now have the power to make their own choices as it pertains to their spiritual lives."[18]

The "turning of the keys" of which Elder Ballard spoke seemed to have almost immediate impact. A devotional was held for which Moldovan members were asked to invite their friends and neighbors to hear the two General Authorities speak. "When we arrived at the building for the devotional, the crowd was huge," Elder Rasband said. "People were sitting on window ledges and in the aisles and on the floor. The interest was just immense."

Elder Rasband spoke about the Great Apostasy, and then Elder Ballard taught about the Restoration. "There's nobody who can speak with such power and authority on the Restoration as President Ballard," Elder Rasband said. "The feeling there was one of the strongest manifestations of the Spirit I've ever felt—especially among the nonmembers who were present. After the meeting I told Elder Ballard that if we could do what John Benbow did we could have baptized thirty people that night."[19]

Elder Ballard asked Elder Rasband to follow up with the missionaries who taught people who had attended the devotional. "To the best of my memory," Elder Rasband said, "there were twelve baptisms over the next thirty days. It was remarkable. In his prayer, Elder Ballard asked the Lord to bless Moldova with the gospel, and He did."[20]

Alliance for Unity Committee

Meanwhile, on the home front, Elder Ballard received another kind of assignment outside of his official quorum responsibilities. According to Salt Lake City's *Deseret News,* the Alliance for Unity Committee was "the brainchild of two political opposites—industrialist Jon Huntsman Sr. and Salt Lake Mayor Rocky Anderson" through which they "brought together community leaders from many faiths, ethnic backgrounds and community interests" to address the "troubling divisions that are keeping [Utah] from obtaining its full potential."[21]

It was no surprise that Elder Ballard was Huntsman's first choice to serve on the Alliance. Other members included two prominent bank presidents, a representative from the *Salt Lake Tribune* and a representative from the Church-owned *Deseret News,* the University of Utah president, bishops from the Catholic and Episcopal churches, the leader of an African-American congregation in Salt Lake, a representative of the Jewish faith, and representatives from the Latino and Asian-American communities. It was a diverse and dynamic group, with the potential for heated discussion on almost any issue.

The Alliance actually started meeting a few months before the tragic events of September 11, 2001, but those events underscored the pressing need for kindness, compassion, understanding, and cooperation among people of varying backgrounds and perspectives.

"It was a morning like other Tuesday mornings, filled with meetings and conversations and things to think about," President Ballard remembered of 9/11. "Then somebody—I don't remember who—came into the office area and said, 'There's something terrible going on in New York.' It was so stunning and we were all confused as to what exactly was happening. A horrible accident? An act of terrorism? A declaration of war?"

As the day unfolded, he found himself worrying about the safety and security of the missionaries and the members of the Church throughout the world. He asked himself, "What's going to happen next? And what are we going to do about it?" It occurred to him that the Church's participation in the Alliance for Unity Committee was as good a place as any to begin working through many of the differences that divide us as individuals, as communities, and as nations.[22]

"We . . . are concerned that acceptance of diversity in Utah today is not of the scope or at the level it ought to be," Alliance members wrote in a statement issued a week after 9/11. "We ask Utahns of every background to cast a broader look at diversity and to nurture a deeper respect for our differences. It is only when we respect differences that we can be united in a healthy community."[23]

Elder Ballard spoke of the Alliance for Unity Committee in his general conference talk in October 2001, just one month after 9/11:

> We are all neighbors and should love, esteem, respect, and serve one another despite our deepest differences—including religious, political, and cultural differences. . . . In our communities we can and must work together in an atmosphere of courtesy, respect, and civility. Here in Utah, a group of concerned citizens formed the Alliance for Unity. This effort has been endorsed by our Church as well as other churches and organizations. One of its purposes is "to seek to build a community where differing viewpoints are acknowledged and valued." Perhaps there has never been a more important time for neighbors all around the world to stand together for the common good of one another.[24]

Within a few months the world saw a compelling example of how people from different backgrounds can "stand together for the

Elder Ballard (upper right) looks on as Elder Neal A. Maxwell and President Gordon B. Hinckley participate in the torch relay for the 2002 Olympic Winter Games

common good of one another," as Salt Lake City hosted the Games of the 2002 Winter Olympics. Following as they did so closely after the horrifying uncertainty of 9/11, the Salt Lake City Olympics had the potential to be filled with tension and shrouded in fear. But the entire community came together in the Olympic spirit of *Citius, Altius, Fortius*—"Faster, Higher, Stronger"—to stage an Olympics that was internationally noted for its friendliness and openness. The venues were staffed by thousands of volunteers, many of whom were able to speak to attendees and athletes in their own languages.

"There aren't many places in the world where you can find so many people who can speak so many different languages so fluently as you can find here in the Salt Lake area among all our returned missionaries," Elder Ballard said. "It was a real opportunity for all of us here in Utah—everyone, regardless of their faith or background or political persuasion—to come together in a meaningful way to let the world know that they are all welcome here."

As far as attending events was concerned, Elder Ballard watched most of the Games on TV. "Why go out and be cold when you can see everything better from a warm, comfortable seat at home?" he said, chuckling.[25]

Honored for a Life of Service

Elder Ballard served in so many capacities in the community that it is no surprise he would receive recognitions from a variety of sources. On September 25, 2002, Elder Ballard received the Helping Hands Award from the Utah Youth Village, a nonprofit organization founded in 1969 to bring about positive changes in the lives of troubled youth. At that time, the Utah Youth Village served more than 3,000 young people annually. Elder Ballard was presented the award for his unwavering support of the children of Utah.

About seven months later he was awarded an honorary degree, Doctor of Christian Service, from Brigham Young University.[26] In conferring the degree upon him, BYU President Merrill J. Bateman said, "In recognition of the love he manifests for his Elder Brother Jesus Christ and for all his brothers and sisters, Brigham Young University is pleased to confer upon Elder M. Russell Ballard, member of the Quorum of the Twelve Apostles, the degree of Doctor of Christian Service, *honoris causa.*"[27]

On November 13, 2003, Elder Ballard received the People of Vision Award from the Friends for Sight Organization, whose purpose is to screen children for sight-threatening conditions and provide treatment to prevent blindness. The cover of the evening's program read, "Congratulations for seeing and understanding the needs of others, and making a difference in our community." In paying tribute to him on that occasion, President James E. Faust said, "What has made Elder Ballard a person of vision is his foresightedness. He is able to look ahead and separate the wheat from the chaff."[28]

With these honors and awards that started coming his way, Elder

Elder and Sister Ballard celebrated their
fiftieth wedding anniversary in 2001

Ballard was characteristically unimpressed. But he was overjoyed about an award given to Barbara: the 2002 BYU–Idaho Exemplary Woman of the Year. Introducing her at the award ceremony was then-BYU–Idaho President David A. Bednar:

> Sister Ballard readily admits that her family has always been and continues to be her top priority. She loves being a wife and mother and has found fulfillment in these important roles. Her children describe her as being a calm, patient person. None of them can remember her losing her temper and yelling at them— not once. She has the ability to see the humor in all things, and she can laugh at herself, a trait that her husband and children find to be most delightful. Having at one point been a mother of six children, the oldest of whom was eight, and before long a mother

of seven children, it is no wonder that when asked about hobbies she responds, "Whatever my children were doing at the time."[29]

Barbara accepted the honor and expressed gratitude for being the mother of seven beautiful children and for sharing in many ways her husband's extraordinary calling:

> It is tempting to me to rave about the wonderful qualities of this man, but if I did, you would all say, "Well, she is rather prejudiced." So I won't do that. I will just say Elder Ballard is just barely imperfect enough to keep him from being translated, and for that I am grateful. He has a delightful sense of humor which does not always come through when he is speaking seriously about gospel subjects. He is a wonderful, delightful person to know. He is an outstanding father and a terrific husband. He loves the Lord and has devoted his life to serving Him. It is such a privilege and honor to be married to a member of the Council of the Twelve. I do not take it lightly. I am grateful for that every day. Those are wonderful, wonderful men. All of the General Authorities, leaders of the Church, are wonderful men, but I am happy to say my favorite member of the Council of the Twelve is Elder Ballard.[30]

Preach My Gospel

By mid-2002, Elder Ballard was no stranger to the Missionary Department. Before his call to the Twelve, in addition to his service as president of the Canada Toronto Mission, he had served as the executive director of that department, as president of the International Mission (with Elders Jack H. Goaslind and John K. Carmack as counselors), and as a member of the Missionary Executive Council. On August 15, 2002, he was assigned to be chairman of the Missionary Executive Council.[31] The First Presidency were well aware that macular degeneration had destroyed his left eye, and he had lost all vision in that eye. "If I close my right eye, no one is there. I have to keep the right eye open to see anything," he said.[32] Nevertheless, Elder Ballard was asked to take on this new assignment, with very specific instructions from President Gordon B. Hinckley:

1. Missionaries need to be freed up from what he called "wooden" presentations; they must be able to teach in their own words.
2. The spirituality and commitment of our missionaries need to be raised to new levels.
3. We must stop baptizing people before they are ready. Retention of converts must be an essential part of the conversion process.
4. Standards for missionary service need to be raised.[33]

Elder Ballard moved into action, building on work previously done by Elders Dallin H. Oaks and Jeffrey R. Holland, his predecessors in this assignment. Elder Oaks said of Elder Ballard, "He is a 'real pusher' in the best sense of the word. He has a knack for pushing hard without offending. . . . He knows how to delegate, to give direction, and free up people to work on a job. He is the kind of person you want to put in charge if you want to have the job done."[34]

The first thing he did as chairman of the Missionary Executive Council was to ask staff members in the Missionary Department in Salt Lake and at the Missionary Training Center in Provo to take a hard look at effective ways to improve the preaching of the gospel. Richard Heaton, administrative director of the Provo Missionary Training Center, said:

> We were young new employees and Elder Ballard believed in us and asked us to do important things without written instructions or timetable. When he asked me, "What do you think?" I knew he wanted to know. We put together a team of young employees, each with something to contribute and a commitment to work. There is nobody that can light a fire under me like Elder Ballard. He connects me with God and invites me to do God's work.[35]

As the committee worked on the first three directives outlined by President Hinckley, Elder Ballard's talk at the priesthood session of general conference in October 2002 squarely and directly addressed the fourth:

> Please understand this: the bar that is the standard for missionary service is being raised. While it is true that you can repent of sins, you may or you may not qualify to serve. It is far better to keep yourselves clean and pure and valiant. We expect you to have an understanding and a solid testimony of the restored gospel of Jesus Christ. We expect you to work hard. We expect you to be covenant makers and covenant keepers. We expect you to be missionaries to match our glorious message.[36]

President Hinckley endorsed Elder Ballard's remarks in his address: "Elder Ballard has spoken to you concerning missionaries. I wish to endorse what he said. I hope that our young men, and our young women, will rise to the challenge he has set forth. We must raise the bar on the worthiness and qualifications of those who go into the world as ambassadors of the Lord Jesus Christ."[37]

Neither Elder Ballard nor President Hinckley mentioned that missionary discussions were under review. It was not until the first worldwide leadership training satellite broadcast on January 11, 2003, that President Hinckley said: "The question now rises as to how the missionaries shall teach those who are willing to listen. For many years now we have had a standard set of missionary lessons. Great good has come of this. . . . But unfortunately this method, in all too many cases, has resulted in a memorized presentation, lacking in Spirit and in personal conviction."[38]

On the heels of his address, the Church published *Teaching by the Spirit: Guidelines for MTC Teachers and Supervisors*. This was the first step toward creating a manual that provided "doctrinal summaries to be studied rather than discussion scripts to be memorized."[39] On June 12,

2003, the First Presidency and Quorum of the Twelve approved pulling together the missionary curriculum into a single manual, with the invaluable support of Elder Quentin L. Cook of the Seventy, executive director of the Missionary Department, as well as other assigned General Authorities.[40] This was a major step toward what would eventually become the *Preach My Gospel* missionary curriculum. As the committee worked on the manual, chapter numbers and order evolved. Eventually draft copies were printed in full color, and these copies were circulated and reviewed before *Preach My Gospel* was ready for testing.

From March to May of 2004, fourteen missions—from Japan Fukuoka to Mexico Puebla, and from England Manchester to California Anaheim—were asked to field test *Preach My Gospel* and determine if (1) each chapter was simple and easy to use, (2) missionaries applied the principles presented in *Preach My Gospel* in their study and proselyting efforts, and (3) anything had been overlooked. When the results came in, it was back to the drawing board for the writers.

When a final draft of *Preach My Gospel* was ready for review, Elder Ballard sent copies to General Authorities and lay members. He and Elder Cook saw that copies were given to all members of the Twelve, including Elder Oaks, who was serving as Area President in the Philippines, and Elder Holland, who was the Area President in Chile.

Elder Ballard and Elder Cook delivered President Boyd K. Packer's copy to him personally. As President Packer thumbed through the colorful manual, he asked, "Are you preparing the people for the King James Version of the Bible or a comic book?"

There was a long pause before Elder Ballard said, "President, we will do what you want and go back to a black-and-white manual, but if the missionaries don't take the manual out of the cellophane, don't be surprised."[41]

Elder Cook recalls, "We left a copy of *Preach My Gospel* with President Packer and waited for his decision. As we waited, Elder Ballard sent school textbooks to President Packer that had full-color pages. A while later, I received a phone call from President Packer telling me to get Elder Ballard to stop sending him textbooks—'I get the picture.'" He signed off on the manual.[42]

Next up: getting the approval of the First Presidency. Elder Ballard recalled:

> I was concerned and worried about how that would happen, but one Sunday morning I realized that all three members of the First Presidency were at home. So I called President Hinckley that Sunday morning and said, "President, can I come and see you?" I went to his apartment, laid out the rough draft, explained what it was, showed him what we had done, how we reduced almost seven hundred pages down to two hundred plus pages, and he thought that was fine. Then I took it to President Faust, who lived in the same building as President Hinckley. He accepted it and said, "Well, I'll look it over." I took Barbara with me to President Monson's home Sunday evening. We went out in the backyard and checked all the birds, he showed me where the pigeons were, and he shared a lot of that love he has for birds. Then we went into his home, sat down, and he said, "Now, Russ, what is it that you want?"[43]

President Monson tells the rest of the story: "Russell showed up at my house one Sunday night with the preliminary transcript of *Preach My Gospel.* He said, 'We'd like it tomorrow with your corrections.' I said, 'You might as well take it home then, because I don't read that way.' Russell, who had been my friend since 1950, said, 'Well, take two days, then.'"[44]

Feedback from President Monson and others was overwhelmingly positive, along with suggestions for refining the manual.

Once *Preach My Gospel* had been thoroughly vetted, publication preparation began. Elder Ballard telephoned Richard Heaton at the Missionary Training Center and asked, "Can you have *Preach My Gospel* ready by August?" Then, "Can you have it ready by mid-July?"

Then, "Can it be ready by July 1?" And finally, "How about having it ready by mid-June?" To meet the mid-June deadline, Heaton recalls: "The staff housed at the Missionary Training Center worked 24/7. For three weeks I daily drove from Provo to Salt Lake City with a section of the manuscript for Elder Ballard and Elder Cook to review. I then returned to the MTC with their revisions for the night shift to work on. We made the mid-June deadline."[45]

More miracles followed. Elder Ballard said:

> We learned that there was no paper available on which to print *Preach My Gospel* for at least two or three months. . . . We prayed about that in the Missionary Executive Council, and two days later the representative of a paper company called and said, "We've had a cancellation of an order" for the exact paper that we needed to print *Preach My Gospel* on. And the same thing happened with the ink. . . . I have a witness and testimony that the preparation of that document, *Preach My Gospel,* was led not by the Missionary Executive Council but by the Lord Jesus Christ. We had miracle after miracle, inspiration and revelation pour down upon us, because it was really unheard of to take a document of that significance from conception to the field in about fourteen months. I don't know that there's ever been anything else done that quickly before.[46]

Preach My Gospel was given to missionaries in the fall of 2004. Translations into various languages were made available as soon as they came off the press. On October 15, 2004, mission presidents, assistants, and zone leaders in 338 missions worldwide gathered via satellite broadcast to be trained on how to use *Preach My Gospel.* President Hinckley said at the broadcast:

> When I was on a mission seventy years ago, we had no proselyting program. Missionaries would decide each morning on what tract they would use for the day and then go out and knock on

doors. Remarkably enough, investigators were found and taught. Years later, when I had responsibility for the missionary program under the direction of the members of the Twelve, the first unified plan was introduced and used. The effects were wonderful. But the plan through the years grew into a procedure where memorization was the principal endeavor. The lessons were given in a rote manner from memory. Missionaries were prone to rely more on their memories than on the Spirit of the Lord.[47]

On November 6, 2004, *Preach My Gospel* was introduced to the membership of the Church in a *Church News* article.[48] This marked the first time missionary lessons were made available to the Church membership.

Of Elder Ballard's service as chairman of the Missionary Executive Council, Elder Richard G. Scott said, "I know there has been great input by a lot of people in the development of *Preach My Gospel,* but the one who has been the driving engine, the power behind getting it accomplished, is Elder Ballard."[49] Elder L. Tom Perry said, "You almost had to run to keep up with him because of the energy and enthusiasm he brought into missionary work. He is just a tireless advocate of carrying the gospel to the world—and I emphasize *tireless.*"[50] Elder Neil L. Andersen wrote, "What a marvelous example of modern revelation and the Lord using the talents of Elder M. Russell Ballard."[51] And Elder Quentin L. Cook said, "There is no General Authority of his generation who has been more intensely involved in missionary work. . . . Elder Ballard has been at the forefront of presenting the gospel to our Father in Heaven's children throughout his adult life. I do not believe that *Preach My Gospel* could have been brought forth without his inspired guidance."[52]

CHAPTER SIXTEEN

IN DEFENSE
OF TRUTH

t age seventy-seven, Elder Ballard began his third decade as a
member of the Quorum of the Twelve Apostles. Lingering
feelings of being young in the quorum had long since
passed, but the weight of his apostolic responsibilities had not. At a
time when most men pause to recall "the good old days," Elder Ballard
had little time for a rearview look at life. Such backward reflections
didn't suit him well, anyway. A round of golf was much more to his
liking—but not a daily dose. He said, "I'm a horrible golfer. I don't go
out to get a score. I go out for the fresh air and to be with good friends
and have some laughs."[1]

Good laughs come to him in all sizes. "Brother Ballard, can I tell
you a story about my five-year-old son?" a sister asked. Of course, he
was delighted to hear it. "After a stake conference in which you spoke,
my little boy wanted to speak with his grandfather. I dialed his number
on my phone and handed the telephone to my son. 'Grandpa, Grandpa,
guess what happened to me today? I got to hear an old fossil speak.'"[2]

Elder Ballard loved that story and shared it widely. Sometimes, he
said, he even felt like an "old fossil."

On January 20, 2006, Elder Ballard had double knee-replacement surgery, the most painful of all his physical trials to date. His recovery from the surgical procedure was difficult. Barbara, their children, and his sisters, Ann and Chaunie, took turns being his caregivers. Of caring for her brother, Chaunie said, "It is one of my most treasured memories of recent times. . . . It was just being there and feeling the spirit in the home."[3] There were many well-wishers and get-well cards, including a letter from US Senator Orrin G. Hatch (Utah): "I just heard about your operations. You are in my prayers."[4]

Buoyed by so many prayers and the support and tender care of his loving family, Elder Ballard pushed through the excruciating pain of rehabilitation:

> There were these machines that had been attached to my bed to help me rehabilitate my knees, and I really hated them. I especially hated that my children had to help me use those machines, which was difficult for all of us. After I had been home two days, I asked the doctor when I could get rid of the machines. He said, "As soon as you can ride that stationary bike," which was in the room. The greatest physical test I've ever had is climbing out of bed when no one was around and trying to get to that bike using canes. There was just so much pain. At first, I couldn't make my legs go forward. But I was determined I was going to get rid of those machines so the kids didn't have to do that for me anymore. Finally I got my knees to go forward. I was sweating and grunting and there were tears in my eyes. But I made it to the bike. So I told the doctor the next day I could ride the bike. The doctor said, "No you can't." And I said, "I'll show you." I got on and showed him. It was so painful. But the doctor saw it and kept his promise. The machines should have been there for a week—they were there for two days.
>
> That pain that I experienced was the worst physical pain I've ever felt in my life. Bypass surgery was a piece of cake compared to double knee replacement. I kept thinking, Jesus felt every bit of

this in the Atonement. All this—multiplied by billions! I almost couldn't handle the pain—and that was just MY pain. It is fully beyond my comprehension how He could bear my pain and suffering plus that of everyone else who ever lived. It was the greatest object lesson on the Atonement I ever experienced—and it is one that I hope to never experience again![5]

When at last he was able to return to his office in the Church Administration Building, Elder Ballard felt an overwhelming desire to get back to work. Perhaps that had something to do with some of his office decor: small bronze representations of the Prophet Joseph Smith, his brother Hyrum, and Hyrum's son Joseph F. Smith. Elder Ballard said, "As I look at the faces of these mighty prophets, I think I hear them say, 'Russell, get going! Do more! Work a little harder while you still have time.'"[6]

In Harm's Way

At a reunion of Canada Toronto missionaries in October 2006, Elder Ballard learned that one of his missionaries, Steve J. Merrill, a US Air Force lieutenant colonel and chaplain, was being deployed for six months to Ali Al Saleem, Kuwait. The Gulf War, code-named Operation Desert Shield, ended in 1991, yet tension in the region never did. By March 2003, Kuwait had become a springboard for the US-led invasion of Iraq. Knowing something of the political unrest in the Middle East region, Elder Ballard asked Colonel Merrill, "Is there anything I can do for you?" The colonel jokingly replied, "Yes, President, you can come and visit me!" They both laughed, and Colonel Merrill never thought about it again until a few months later, when he received an email from the Church Military Relations office informing him that Elder Ballard wanted to come to Kuwait to see him and the other Latter-day Saint servicemen and women who were deployed there. He reread the email and smiled—yes, that seemed like something his beloved mission president would do. Then he took note of the dates—Elder Ballard would be there during the evening hours on February 27, just five weeks away.

"I was an air force chaplain embedded in an army operation answering to an Army Command Chaplain Section that had their own unique set of procedures," Colonel Merrill wrote of the event. "I fired back an email to Salt Lake that my chaplain assistants, Master Sergeant Ben Trevino and Staff Sergeant Tom Tipton (not members of the Church), would make it happen. But even as I sent the email I felt we would need a miracle."

Master Sergeant Trevino contacted the command office at Camp Arifjan and was told the process would require at least six months for the paperwork and clearances to be completed. He was also informed that even after all that, their office would almost certainly deny the recommendation for a civilian church leader to come into the theater of operations. "I followed up with a phone call and was given the same story," Colonel Merrill said. "I prayed for a miracle and began the paperwork process despite the doom and gloom attitude we encountered."[7]

The miracle began to unfold when Colonel Merrill spoke with the wing commander at the Ali Al Saleem Air Force Base, about five miles away from his camp. The commander assured him, "Don't worry about any paperwork, Steve. Let's make it happen!" Colonel Merrill let the commander know that the Army Chaplain Office would challenge his decision. To this the commander replied, "I don't work for the army and they can't tell me what to do on my base. Press on, Chaplain!"

On the evening of February 27, 2007, Elder Ballard, Jon Huntsman, and Peter Huntsman (Elder Ballard's son-in-law and son of Jon Huntsman) arrived at the air force base in Ali Al Saleem in a motorcade accompanied by Brother Mathew H. Tueller, acting ambassador and a high councilor in the Arabian Peninsula Stake. "Elder Ballard came up to me and gave me a big hug! I will never forget that feeling of

With members of the military in Kuwait

being embraced by my former mission president and now an Apostle of the Lord," said Colonel Merrill. "I thanked him for remembering my request that he come and visit me. And then I noticed how weary he looked from the long and demanding trip, and I said, 'President, you look exhausted.' He replied, 'What time is it? Where are we? And what time zone are we in?'"[8]

Elder Ballard and Jon Huntsman went with Colonel Merrill into the small chapel on the base to welcome some seventy-five Church members, including army, navy, and air force personnel as well as contractors and civilian employees assigned to six separate camps in Kuwait. Elder Ballard remembered US Army Brigadier General Keith Lee Thurgood arriving late to the meeting after all chairs in the small chapel were full. Military personnel offered him their chairs, but the general refused and sat on the floor.

Colonel Merrill conducted the fireside. "Elder Ballard turned to me and asked if I was going to introduce him," Colonel Merrill said. "I replied, 'President, they know who you are! That's why they came!' We both chuckled, and I asked him what he'd like me to say. Elder Ballard jokingly said, 'Tell them what a great mission president I was!'"

> I proceeded to tell everyone he is the greatest leader I have ever served under and that no military leader I had served with came close to him.[9] I testified that he was an Apostle of the Savior

Jesus Christ just as sure as Peter, James and John were. I witnessed that Elder Ballard had taught me how to be a priesthood leader as a young man.

When Elder Ballard stood on his feet and began speaking as an Apostle, I saw a physical change in his countenance and his voice. Suddenly this travel-weary champion of salvation had energy and spoke with great power in his voice. He told the military personnel that when the First Presidency and Quorum of the Twelve met in the Salt Lake Temple every Thursday, they always prayed for military members and their families. He stated that without men and women like us, the United States would not be the great country that it is. He asked us to take every opportunity to share what we knew to be true and that our greatest sermon would be the way we live our lives. He told us that since he was the first modern day Apostle to visit Kuwait, he would close with prayer and invoke a blessing on each of us. Elder Ballard asked our Heavenly Father to look down from his throne upon our gathering and touch our hearts with the Spirit. He blessed the leaders of the region to rise and find solutions to the present conflict. He pleaded on our behalf and asked the Lord to accept our service in protecting the United States of America, the home base of Church operations throughout the world. He asked the Lord to watch over and protect us and our families, and that, if the world grew more chaotic, we would individually have peace in our hearts.[10]

At the conclusion of the meeting, Elder Ballard went to the rear door of the chapel and shook everyone's hand and looked them in the eye and said, "The Lord bless you." The Spirit was so strong that many remarked that they experienced "a holy feeling, as if we had just spent the day in the temple."[11] Colonel Merrill said, "To the men and women who serve in the military, far away from home and loved ones, the affirmation we received from an Apostle of the Lord was monumental."[12] In honor of Elder Ballard's visit to the Ali Al Saleem Air Force Base, he received a United States flag that had flown over Iraq in support of Operation Iraqi Freedom.

From Kuwait, Elder Ballard and the Huntsmans[13] flew to Dubai, the capital city of the United Arab Emirates, so that Elder Ballard could speak to members of the Arabian Peninsula Stake. This was the first time an Apostle had been in Dubai since 1983, when Elder Boyd K. Packer came to organize the stake. Elder Ballard spoke to 398 members who represented 30 percent of a stake membership that covered eight countries. His message: "Know you are loved, live the gospel, and influence those around you for the better."[14]

Leaving Dubai, the party traveled to Germany and then to Milan, Italy, where Elder Ballard spoke at a member/missionary fireside.

On his return to the States, Elder Ballard remarked: "I am humbled to have been with many members . . . particularly those who wear their country's uniform and are away from their families. When you stand in front of those who are willing to put their lives on the line in order to defend our freedoms and our way of life, you have to stand in awe."[15] As for complaints about health, long plane rides, poor accommodations, or unsavory food, he had none.

Another Canadian Missionary

"The telephone rang one day in my office," Elder Ballard said. "When I answered it, a fine young man, whom I had known since my days in Canada as a mission president, said, 'President, I need to come and visit with you. I have a serious problem.'" Elder Ballard set a time the following day for his missionary to meet with him in his office. That night Elder Ballard thought, "Oh, his marriage must be in difficulty." He was hoping that was not the case because he had performed his sealing to a beautiful young woman, and together they were now parents of three charming children. Elder Ballard added, "In the mind of a mission president, you continue to worry about the missionaries who served with you."[16]

When the young man arrived at Elder Ballard's office the next day, he was embraced and invited to sit down near the desk. Concerned for his obviously distraught former missionary, Elder Ballard asked: "Elder, how can I help you? What is the matter?"

"President, I am in trouble. I think I am losing my testimony of the gospel."

Elder Ballard was stunned. "Oh, Elder," he said, "how could that possibly be?"

"For the first time in my life I have been reading some of the literature that the enemies of the Church have produced," he said. "I have a lot of questions that I have never had before, and I am concerned. I am worried about my feelings for the Church."

"Have you talked to your bishop?" I asked.

"Yes, I have."

"What did your bishop say?"

"He patted me on the shoulder and said, 'Just don't read that literature and don't bother with it and you will be all right.' That didn't really help."

The young man had questions about his faith and wanted answers. Elder Ballard asked that he write down his questions and come back in two weeks for the answers. Before the missionary left his office, Elder Ballard asked, "Elder, how long has it been since you have read from the Book of Mormon?"

The elder confessed, "It has been a long time."

So Elder Ballard challenged him: "You have given me an assignment. It is only fair that I give you one. You read one hour from the Book of Mormon each day until you come back for your answers." The young man accepted the challenge.

When his missionary came for his second appointment, Elder Ballard was waiting for him along with well-known Latter-day Saint historian and scholar Daniel Ludlow, to whom Elder Ballard had given the missionary's list of questions. But before any questions were addressed, the missionary said with tears in his eyes, "President, I am not sure we need this meeting."

"Why is that, Elder?" Elder Ballard asked.

"I have kept my promise," he said. "I have read from the Book of Mormon, and, President, I know Joseph Smith is a prophet of God. I know the Book of Mormon is true. I am not worried about my questions anymore."

"How grateful I am, Elder, that you kept your promise," I said. "But Brother Ludlow and I spent time on your questions so you are going to get the answers to your questions anyway."[17]

In sharing this story with young adults at a BYU–Idaho fireside some years later, Elder Ballard said, "We've got to be so solidly anchored in our testimonies of the gospel of Jesus Christ that, regardless of what may come next, we will not waffle; we will stand firm in our belief; we won't question the doctrines that are part of our belief."[18]

Chairman of the Public Affairs Committee

In August 2007, Elder Ballard returned to the Public Affairs Committee of the Church, this time as its chairman. Reflecting on that assignment, President Ballard said: "I have to say it's even more intense than running the Missionary Department because the world seems to be unraveling. People have the misconception that Public Affairs is only about community service, like Helping Hands or service projects. Public Affairs does all of that, but there is also a constant need to deal with daily issues involving the Church in the media, social media, and other public-facing platforms."[19]

Elder Ballard continued: "There are problems that surface in the world, and whatever happens that affects the Church comes to Public

Affairs. The media asks, 'What is the Church going to do on this or that?'"[20]

Many of the questions that come to the Church now, and the misunderstandings people have about who we are, are difficult to understand. As active members of the Church we cannot comprehend that anybody would question whether or not we are Christian. And yet, when we meet with media representatives nearly always one of the first questions asked is "Are Mormons Christians?"

This misunderstanding is centered on the [popular Christian] belief in the Nicene Creed. The Nicene Creed basically is very confusing as to who God our Father is, the Lord Jesus Christ is, and who the Holy Ghost is. When we explain our belief of who our Heavenly Father is, who the Lord Jesus Christ is, and who the Holy Ghost is as revealed through the Prophet Joseph Smith, it is interesting to watch the wonderment that comes into their eyes. . . .

It intrigues them when we say, "You know, we just don't believe that the Lord Jesus Christ was praying to Himself. He often prayed to His Heavenly Father for guidance and told us to do the same thing." We explain that our Heavenly Father is a glorified God, a resurrected being, and that the Lord Jesus Christ is His Beloved Son, His firstborn son in the spirit, and His Only Begotten Son in the flesh. They are distinct and separate individuals. The Holy Ghost is a teacher who enlightens our minds. He is a personage of spirit but still distinct and separate from the Father and the Son. I'm not sure they [the media] comprehend everything we tell them. But they often express that they felt a good spirit.[21]

As to his leadership style as chairman of the Public Affairs Committee, Elder Ballard said, "I'm an advocate that we will be ahead if we stay on the offense, be more active in calling the press if they have misinformation. As former Public Affairs chairman Neal A. Maxwell used to say, we don't let them have any free slam dunks as they have in the past."[22]

When *Big Love,* a drama about a fictionalized polygamous family in Utah, appeared on HBO television, it was unsettling to many Latter-day Saints—especially the show's mocking and vulgar references to "very sacred parts of the temple ceremony."[23] Elder Ballard was not about to back away from this fight. In a Brigham Young University commencement address, he talked about *Big Love* and said, "We maintained dignity but at the same time made it clear that this was in very poor taste."[24]

In late 2007, President Gordon B. Hinckley assigned Elder Ballard and Elder Quentin L. Cook to visit media in the eastern United States. According to Elder Cook:

> President Hinckley had become concerned that with Governor Mitt Romney [a former stake president] running for president there was a lot of reportage of the Church, but a lot of it was incorrect. . . . They were asking the opinions of everybody but members of the Church. We were assigned to go back, and we went to 14—actually more, because we got some in the West—but 14 in the East, editorial boards and newspapers and television outlets.[25]

In thinking about his media visits, Elder Ballard told Elder Cook, "I want to give them a three- to five-minute Restoration lesson in every one of these meetings. I don't know when I'll do it. I don't know when I'll get a chance, but if we're going to tell or ask them to talk to us about our doctrine, don't they have to have a little exposure to what that doctrine is?"[26]

As the two Church leaders ventured east, they found media personnel were quite receptive to their message. "We kind of put them back on their heels," Elder Cook said. "But you don't keep them back on their heels for long." Editors at the *Boston Globe,* the *Washington Post,* and the *Wall Street Journal* threw out "some pretty tough questions, and Elder Ballard would pick his spot, and then he would come in and give that three- to five-minute lesson." In those few minutes "something very powerful happened. Suddenly, we weren't politicians. We weren't connected with a candidate. We were leaders of a church, the restored Church of Jesus Christ. Suddenly, they had a different view of us."[27]

Of all their interviews, including the one with Charlie Rose, famed news broadcaster and journalist, and Laureen Green, the religion editor at Fox, it was an interview with the Al Jazeera Media Network that proved most memorable. And probably the most spontaneous. In fact, originally there was no scheduled interview with Al Jazeera.

"We were in the car going back to the hotel after some other interviews when a consultant mentioned Al Jazeera," President Ballard recalled. "I said, 'Wait, tell me about that.'"

The consultant informed him that while Al Jazeera had started as an Arabic news TV channel, it had since become a global news network with 80 bureaus around the world and millions of viewers on television and the internet, with specialty television channels in multiple languages.

"I said to Elder Ballard, 'No, let's not go to Al Jazeera. We've got enough on our shoulders without going to Al Jazeera,'" Elder Cook recalled. "But Elder Ballard asked our consultant, 'How many people will hear this if we have the interview?' The consultant replied, 'Millions will hear it because it will be translated into Arabic.' Elder Ballard said, 'We'll do it.' He saw it as an opportunity to tell millions of viewers in the Arab world about Jesus Christ and the Restoration of the gospel."[28]

And so they went in unannounced. "We just knocked on the door," Elder Ballard said, "and we told them who we were and asked if they wanted to talk to us."[29]

It turned out that they did. Elder Ballard was interviewed by bureau chief Abderrahim-al-Rahim Fuqara, who also hosts one of the Al Jezeera news programs. A portion of the translation of the interview reads:

> **Abderrahim-al-Rahim Fuqara:** I'm very happy to welcome here to our studio Melvin Russell Ballard, one of the leaders of the church of Christ and a member of that which is known by

followers of the Mormon religion as the Quorum of the Twelve Apostles. . . . Regarding Jesus Christ, you say that Jesus Christ visited America after His Crucifixion. Can you explain this to us?

Elder Ballard: We believe that after the Resurrection, Jesus Christ came and visited those that were living in North America. As He Himself said in the New Testament: 'I have a flock not of the flock of Jerusalem, and I will visit them.' He did in fact visit them, and this is the history recorded and found in our book, the Book of Mormon, with the rest of the message and teachings of Jesus Christ. We accept the Book of Mormon as another witness of the life of Jesus Christ, His priesthood, His doctrine, and His teachings.

Abderrahim-al-Rahim Fuqara: Do you find it unusual that Mormons were subject to persecution in the history of the United States?

Elder Ballard: Whenever you comment on the matter of religion and faith there will always be those who reject and stand in opposition to that which others believe to be the truth. . . . But today we don't feel persecuted, but we do feel misunderstood. . . . Thank you for this opportunity to clarify for all our doctrine, which is centered around the life, teachings, and priesthood of Jesus Christ, who we believe is the Savior of the World.[30]

"It was a difficult and yet interesting interview, maybe the most challenging interview I've ever done, with all of the translating and interpreting back and forth," President Ballard said years later. "You're not just dealing with different languages, which is always tricky, but you're also speaking from the perspective of two very different cultures. Sometimes what you think you said comes across differently in the language and cultural translation. But I think it was worth the effort. I just hope we did some good."[31]

*With President Dieter F. Uchtdorf in Washington, DC,
for President Barack Obama's inauguration*

Presidential Inauguration

When Barack Obama won the United States presidential election in 2008, Elder and Sister Ballard were invited to accompany President and Sister Uchtdorf to his inauguration in Washington, DC, on January 20, 2009, as well as the National Prayer Service at the Washington National Cathedral the next day. "It was *cold*. Oh, it was cold," Elder Ballard recalled of being in the nation's capital for the inauguration.[32] President Uchtdorf wrote:

These were some of the coldest winter days Harriet and I had spent in an outside setting ever. We had to walk long distances amid huge crowds, bundled up in everything we brought to D.C. President Ballard always kept a happy and dignified demeanor, perfectly representing the Church and his sacred call as an Apostle. He was kind and helpful to strangers and friends we bumped into, and confident and radiant with all in high positions, regardless of their or his own political leaning. It was a wonderful experience to see M. Russell Ballard living the public life of an Apostle of the Lord with distinction.[33]

Following the celebratory services, Elder Ballard reported: "I left Washington, DC, with a feeling that the people of America are going to unite behind this new president and his administration and that we need to pray for him. We need to exercise our prayers and help him accomplish the great objectives that he has set."[34]

Within a few years it became clear that President Obama would be challenged in his run for a second term by Mitt Romney, former governor of Massachusetts and a lifelong member of the Church. Romney's father, George W. Romney, a former governor of Michigan, also ran for the same office in 1968.

"Can you imagine the number of questions that surfaced about the Church with a good, faithful Latter-day Saint, a former stake president, running for the highest office in the country?" asked Elder Ballard. "It became evident that the media just plain misunderstood who we are and what we believe. They had all of the old wives' tales and questions about obscure historical fiction that have been promulgated since the nineteenth century."[35]

He continued:

We held a lot of meetings with the media during the time Mitt Romney was running for president. The press was defining who we are based on comments from those not of our faith. You remember those days when [politician and minister Mike] Huckabee, along with other things, said that the Mormons believe that Jesus and the devil are brothers. Well, they are! The world doesn't understand that unless they have the Restoration.

Preparing to throw the first pitch at Dodger Stadium

They don't understand our spiritual relationship as sons and daughters of God our Eternal Father.

The media writers do not have the least degree of understanding of our premortal life. There are not very many people in the world who understand where we came from, the real purpose why we are here, and where we hope to go. I was really stunned, to be honest with you, at how very spiritually ignorant the world is.[36]

When Elder Ballard and Elder Quentin L. Cook met with an editor of the *Cleveland Plain Dealer*, they were asked, "Is it true that the Mormon church is not Christian? And why do people say you're not Christian?" Elder Ballard replied, "That is a real puzzle to us, because the name of the Church is The Church of Jesus Christ of Latter-day Saints." Another question was, "Why is the Mormon church so secretive and such a closed society?" Elder Ballard replied, "We have nineteen thousand chapels, with fifty-three thousand missionaries inviting people to those chapels to worship with us. So it's ridiculous for people to claim that The Church of Jesus Christ of Latter-day Saints is a closed society."[37]

Much publicity followed about the Church—some negative and some positive, such as when Elder Ballard was featured wearing a Los Angeles Dodgers baseball shirt while throwing the ceremonial first pitch at the fifteenth annual Mormon night at Dodger Stadium.[38]

Looking back on his time overseeing Public Affairs and leading the charge in defense of the truth of the gospel of Jesus Christ, he said:

> This is *not* an easy work. I've said publicly that I would not do this work for money. If you were to offer me a big salary to do what we're called upon to do, I wouldn't do it. But to do it for the Lord, it's the greatest privilege that ever could be imagined, to be called as a witness of His name and His Church throughout the earth. You do that because you know Him. You know what His desires are and what the Atonement's all about. . . .
>
> After serving as a General Authority for over three decades, you see a lot of situations, you meet a lot of different people and you see people with great gifts and skills. You wonder to yourself, how in the world did I ever end up here? Because you see all the power and strength that's out there in others.[39]

Noting the great truths that Elder Ballard defends, Elder Jeffrey R. Holland wrote, "The 'kids' in the Quorum are honored to walk in your footsteps."[40]

CHAPTER SEVENTEEN

TO ALL THE WORLD

I n his first landmark address after he became President of the Church, President Spencer W. Kimball shared with Church leaders throughout the world a glimpse of his vision for taking the gospel to all the world, as the Savior commanded.[1]

"That was really a remarkable talk," President Ballard said some forty-six years later.[2] "It impacted me tremendously then, as I was in the process of preparing to take my family with me to Canada to preside over the mission in Toronto. And it has impacted me through the years since then. He talked about 'using all the latest inventions and equipment and paraphernalia already developed and that which will follow,' and he asked: 'Can you see that perhaps the day may come when the world will be converted and covered?'"[3]

Although Elder Ballard had traveled hundreds of thousands of miles to testify of Jesus Christ in large auditoriums and humble, small settings, as the world moved deeper into the twenty-first century he became more convinced that technology could advance the work of the Lord as never before—and it could do so on a more global scale. He could see the day of which President Kimball had prophetically spoken, and he knew that the answer for reaching people in the four corners of the earth was intricately linked to modern technology.

As he looked around him, he could see that even among some of the world's poorest and most underprivileged people, there is still access to technology. At the other end of the economic spectrum, technology reaches people living in gated neighborhoods and secured high-rise buildings where missionaries do not have access. Elder Ballard also knew that even if people were not ready to listen to missionaries teach about the restored gospel of Jesus Christ, many of them would listen to quality messages portraying honesty, integrity, the importance of family, and being a good neighbor. Such people would not be found waiting in long lines at movie theaters to see films featuring extreme violence, intimacy outside of marriage, or unethical choices. They would be found searching for uplifting programming on television and on their computers but not knowing where to find it.

In a way, Elder Ballard reasoned, this idea was a lot like his efforts to bring family entertainment to the Salt Lake Valley in the 1960s. It also reminded him of his father, who had the vision of the day when Church members would gather in their places of worship to hear from the President of the Church via the wireless radio station—the earliest incarnation of KSL Radio—that he was building of wood and tin on top of the old Deseret News building.[4]

But the technology of the twenty-first century was beyond anything he or his father had ever dreamed of. Like many of his generation, he had a hard time keeping up with all of the latest technological advances. But he had a knack for finding people who *did* understand cutting-edge technology and could help him learn how it could be harnessed to advance the work of the Lord.

One such learning opportunity occurred in 2005, when he was asked to accompany President Gordon B. Hinckley to Sharon, Vermont, to the birthplace of the Prophet Joseph Smith. There they

*With President Gordon B. Hinckley at
the monument in Sharon, Vermont*

would speak at a special fireside to commemorate the Prophet's two-hundredth birthday.

"This remarkable monument to [Joseph Smith] here in Sharon, Vermont, was dedicated one hundred years ago by my great-grandfather President Joseph F. Smith," Elder Ballard said. "On that occasion, my grandfather Hyrum Mack Smith challenged the good citizens of Vermont that it would do them no harm to read the numerous tracts and books with prayerful hearts. 'On the contrary,' he said. 'It will do you good.' I echo the same challenge today to all people everywhere in this world."[5]

Although only a small number of people were physically present at the commemorative fireside, the proceedings were translated into 81 languages and broadcast to 161 countries by satellite and worldwide via internet. Following the broadcast, Elder David A. Bednar of the Quorum of the Twelve wrote to Elder Ballard, "I suspect Peter and Paul are envious in the spirit world as they observe the opportunities we have today to reach out to so many people all at once gathered in various locations all over the world."[6]

Elder Ballard agreed that those ancient Apostles might be envious, and the thought made him smile. But the experience in Vermont got him thinking more than ever about the possibilities of modern technology and how it might be used to reach out to the billions of people around the world who *hadn't* seen the fireside, and who had no knowledge of Jesus Christ, the Prophet Joseph Smith, or what it meant for them that the gospel had been restored to the earth.

BYUtv

The more Elder Ballard thought about the potential of technology in building the kingdom of God on the earth, the more it permeated his personal ministry. One can see it in this 2007 personal journal entry by Derek Marquis, with whom Elder Ballard worked closely in the visionary evolution of BYUtv:

> Elder Ballard is an amazing man who knows how to cut to the heart of the issue. My testimony of living prophets and modern-day revelation has truly blossomed as I've had the opportunity to be taught by him. He has repeatedly shared with us that Heavenly Father has put into our hands the technologies that have resulted in BYU Television and we will be held accountable if we do not use them to build the kingdom of God. He said there is great urgency to "do it now" and not procrastinate the opportunities before us.[7]

According to Marquis, Elder Ballard was intimately involved in bringing a whole new sense of purpose and direction to BYUtv, constantly emphasizing that there should be no wavering from the course of action he had outlined to them: to reach a worldwide audience.[8]

In order to fully appreciate Elder Ballard's unique contribution to this evolutionary process, one must understand a little of the history of television at BYU.

In 1946, Brigham Young University students launched an experimental radio station—KBYU-AM 660—transmitted to Amanda Knight and Allen Residence Halls on the Provo campus. It was a start, and the students were ecstatic, but in reality, the transmission was not auspicious or newsworthy. A few years later, student Owen S. Rich wanted to extend KBYU-AM 660 beyond the campus residence halls to residents in the city of Provo. He believed a radio signal could be transmitted citywide via Provo electric power lines, and he pitched his idea to city officials. In 1948, officials agreed to let him try. Rich said, "We gathered together a group of bright young physics and electrical engineering students and we figured out a method to couple a transmitter into the power line without burning down the studio. Then we threw the switch, and our broadcast covered the whole city of Provo." Campus news, a campus variety show, a quiz show, athletic events, and a program titled *Music of the Masters* were transmitted, to the delight of Provo residents. "We hung a big sign in front of the Butler Hut [a military surplus tin shack where KBYU-AM was housed]—'The Student Voice of BYU.'"[9]

It was not until 1960 that the Federal Communications Commission (FCC) gave KBYU radio the go-ahead to broadcast on an FM frequency. BYU President Ernest L. Wilkinson wanted more: a sister television station to go with KBYU-FM. Following President Wilkinson's lead, construction of the KBYU-TV station began, and programs were up and running by November 1965 on channel 11 over-the-air television broadcast frequency.[10] The KBYU channel was limited in reach by virtue of its FCC license to broadcast only in Utah. As the station migrated into a Public Broadcasting Service (PBS) member station, channel programming skewed the audience to children and senior citizens.

That changed in 1999. John Reim, managing director and CEO of BYU Broadcasting (1993–2006), became aware of a law requiring satellite television distributors to "set aside" 4 percent of their bandwidth to transmit noncommercial educational television channels. (The 4 percent bandwidth allocation was referred to as "FCC's Public Interest Set-Aside Requirement.") Wanting to expand the station's reach, and hoping the law might favor programs stemming from KBYU-TV during the Christmas holidays of 1999, Reim said, "There was no one around at the university to ask if writing an application to try to secure a channel nationally on the Dish Network was a good idea or not. So we applied."

Within days, Reim received a telephone call from the director of business and educational television for EchoStar, a worldwide provider of satellite communication solutions and the owner and operator of the satellite fleet for Dish Network and other customers. "Congratulations, you've been selected. When would you like to be on?" When Reim suggested BYU could be ready in four months, there was a long pause and a second phone call before he was told, "I'm awfully sorry, but the FCC is really pushing us. If you can't get a signal to Cheyenne within four days, the deal is off."[11]

"I remember this scene like it was yesterday," Reim said. "I had this gang of people—managers, engineers—in my office and said, 'Okay, can we pull this off?' And to a person—with one or two possible exceptions . . . everyone said, 'Well, let's do this!'"[12] Four days later at the appointed deadline, which was twelve p.m. Mountain Time, the senior staff of BYU Broadcasting stood in the master control operations room of KBYU-TV in the Harris Fine Arts Center looking at a television monitor as "up came a logo that said, 'You're Watching BYU Television.'"

The first program broadcast was a BYU devotional given by President Gordon B. Hinckley on November 30, 1999, in which he said:

> As we close this great and remarkable century, I stand in awe of the blessings we have. I have now lived through 90 years of this century. When I think of the wonders that have come to pass in my lifetime—more than during all the rest of human history together—I stand in reverence and gratitude. . . . You and I are a part of the miracle and wonder of this great cause and kingdom that is sweeping over the earth blessing the lives of people wherever it reaches. How profoundly thankful I feel.[13]

"It was very quiet for a control room," Reim said, "and that was the beginning."[14]

BYU Television—branded as BYUtv in 2000—soon had a small cluster of cable systems in the western United States airing the channel. With the tagline "Keeping You Connected," the implication was the channel would provide a connecting link for members of the Church living outside of Utah to the Church and BYU. Devotionals, forums, roundtable scripture discussions, and addresses from general conference were the typical programs offered. Viewership over the first five years, as tracked by the Nielsen Television Ratings Service, was small enough so as to be "not measurable."[15] Yet anecdotal measurement suggested viewer satisfaction was high.

It would take a series of miracles to move BYUtv from "not measurable" to becoming a recognized international network. Miracles included a domino effect that led 600 cable systems in the United States to pick up BYUtv. Another miracle, even more impressive, began with a simple telephone call from Elder Spencer J. Condie of the Seventy in 2004 to Derek A. Marquis at BYU Broadcasting. The purpose of Elder Condie's call was to explain to Marquis that permission had been secured from the cable company in American Samoa to add BYUtv to their cable lineup. Elder Condie asked Marquis to work directly with the cable operator to make that happen. He passed along contact information and then hung up the phone.

Marquis contacted BYU President Cecil O. Samuelson and excitedly explained to him that this international opportunity in American Samoa could be a catalyst for other international distribution points. President Samuelson reminded Marquis that BYUtv did not have a source of funding and that perhaps he could contact local members in Samoa for funds. But he cautioned him to be careful not to "get ahead of the Brethren."[16]

By October 2004, Marquis had faced one stumbling block after another in his attempt to establish an international outreach for BYUtv. When he met Rex Maughan, a former missionary to Samoa, things began to change. Marquis outlined for Maughan the opportunity BYUtv had to expand to an international viewership in Samoa if they could raise as much as $10,000 to $15,000 for satellite equipment and installation. Before Maughan was willing to donate the requested funds, he told Marquis that he wanted to speak with his close friends H. Burke Peterson, an emeritus General Authority, and Elder M. Russell Ballard.

Rex and Ruth Maughan's meeting with Elder Ballard was life-changing—both for them and for BYUtv.

"Elder Ballard shared with me that maybe one day BYUtv could be the technology that would in essence be the voice of the Lord to all the world," said Maughan. "I was excited to be part of something so meaningful. This was the beginning of a love affair with BYUtv for Ruth and me." As for his wife, Ruth, she was regularly heard to explain to those who asked or would listen, "This is not about us. It has never been about us. It is about the vision that Elder Ballard laid out that this channel could be the voice of the Lord to all the world."[17] Rex Maughan stated, "None have made a greater contribution to the development of positive media that is blessing lives around the world than Elder M. Russell Ballard," and he set up a full-tuition scholarship for a student working in BYU Broadcasting in the names of M. Russell Ballard and his wife, Barbara.[18]

Marquis was named the interim managing director and CEO of BYU Broadcasting in 2006, replacing John Reim. Under his guidance, BYUtv moved forward. From American Samoa, Samoa, Brazil, and Peru, it began to broadcast internationally with the help of donors like the Maughans and many others who shared Elder Ballard's vision that media would bless individuals and families worldwide.

Elder Ballard invited Marquis to meet with him, Elder Dieter F. Uchtdorf, Elder Quentin L. Cook, Elder Richard J. Maynes, BYU President Samuelson, a few key producers from the Missionary Department, and managing directors from other departments to discuss the future of BYUtv. The December 6 meeting was opened with prayer, followed by Elder Ballard talking about "public faces" that represent The Church of Jesus Christ of Latter-day Saints—missionaries, temples, the Mormon Tabernacle Choir, and Church pageants. Elder Ballard spoke of a new public face with the potential to reach a larger audience of Heavenly Father's children than perhaps all of the other public faces of the Church combined: BYUtv.[19]

Those in attendance concurred that there was much programming on the BYUtv channel that was good and a blessing to members of the Church in the United States and selected international areas. Plaudits aside, Elder Ballard turned the discussion to some of the concerns about BYUtv that were perceived at Church headquarters:

1. BYUtv lacked a programming and production strategy to capture the attention of those who surf channels.
2. Break elements (referred to as *interstitials*) between BYUtv programs were lacking in quality. There was no consistency in audio levels, color palettes, font types, or font sizes.
3. There did not appear to be a specific strategy in place as to what would air on any particular day or night. Viewers

found it difficult to tune in at a regular time to see a favorite
program or a genre of programs.

4. BYUtv was focusing its programming on members of the
Church. The channel was unintentionally excluding those
the channel most needed to reach—good people of all faiths
or no faith at all.

5. BYUtv was not attracting Heavenly Father's elect who shared
similar values but "who are only kept from the truth because
they know not where to find it" (Doctrine and Covenants
123:12).[20]

Elder Ballard did not try to soften the critique. Instead, he made
this prophetic promise:

If BYUtv provided programming that blessed families and
programming that those of other faiths would want to watch,
such as documentaries, movies, music, dance, comedies, and variety programming that lift the soul and do not detract from the
Spirit, more hearts would be softened, myths about the Church
would be dispelled, and Heavenly Father's elect would be prepared when the missionaries knock on their doors or when friends
or neighbors invite them to learn about the Church. If done correctly, viewers would respond in even greater numbers by saying,
"I have been watching your television channel, and you're not as
strange as I used to think. Yes, I'd like to learn more."[21]

Elder Ballard continued the discussion, referring to "When the
World Will Be Converted," President Kimball's 1974 speech that had
had such an impact on him:

President Kimball believed that there would come the day
when everybody in the high mountains east of Lima, Peru, or in
Ecuador, or in the Andes would have a device on which to receive
the message of the Restoration in their own tongue. He was talking about how everyone ought to have a little transistor radio they

could put up to their ear and hear the word of the gospel in their own tongue. President Kimball's got to be smiling when he sees people with their cell phones. I've always felt that if that's what President Kimball saw, then *we* ought to see it. We're in a day when the gospel can cover all the face of the earth.[22]

Elder Ballard also spoke of Philo T. Farnsworth, a gifted Latter-day Saint inventor credited with inventing television in 1927. Elder Ballard went on to say that nobody in the room knew exactly what the BYUtv channel would ultimately become, but that he felt impressed to say that at that moment in time, they were chasing the wrong audience. In his view, the channel had been launched to connect members of the Church to the truths they hold sacred, but chasing such an audience was like preaching to the choir. He reminded those present that the injunction of the Lord was to take the gospel to every nation, kindred, tongue, and people, and he said that if BYUtv could create content that would be entertaining, interesting, and a blessing to good people of all faiths, it would still be a blessing to Church members. He encouraged BYU Broadcasting to move with haste to get things in place so that they could take the Lord's message to all the world. After informing the group that he had asked Elder Maynes to work with Derek Marquis and the staff at BYU Broadcasting to oversee the process of redefining the BYUtv channel so that it could help dispel myths, soften hearts, and prepare viewers to ultimately receive the message of the gospel, the meeting was adjourned.

"It felt for many in the room as though Elder Ballard had received and was receiving revelation as he instructed the group," Marquis wrote in his journal.[23]

As he oversaw the reconstruction and reconfiguration of BYUtv's vision and mission, Elder Ballard also saw the need to create a new state-of-the-art physical facility on the BYU campus to serve as its home. He and Elder Maynes were able to share their vision for a new building with the board of trustees of Brigham Young University, which included the First Presidency, members of the Quorum of the Twelve Apostles, and General Officers of the Church. The board approved a $50 million fundraising initiative for a new facility for BYU Broadcasting, to be built immediately north of the Monte L. Bean Life Science Museum.

On May 7, 2009, Elder Ballard presided at the groundbreaking ceremony for the new building. In explaining the need for the facility, he said:

> My vision and my feeling is that this broadcasting effort from Brigham Young University has the potential of being the voice that will be heard around the world, that will be the voice of the Lord, that will take head-on the contest that is going on in the world between good and evil. Lucifer has had far too much freedom on this issue of his influence in the media. . . . This is a great time for the Church and for BYU to let the Lord's voice . . . be heard around the world.[24]

Two years later, speaking at the building's dedication, Elder Ballard said: "I think that building is going to be a center of telling the whole world what is good, and the gospel is good. The honest in heart, and there are millions and millions of them, are seeking and looking for something that's decent and nice and faith-promoting and spiritually enriching, and that's what they are going to find if they find BYUtv."[25]

Eventually Elder Ballard's administrative assignments were changed, and he was no longer directly responsible for BYUtv. But Marquis and others continued to refer to what everyone at BYU Broadcasting called "the vision of Elder M. Russell Ballard." They viewed him as the man who took BYUtv from where it was, an obscure television channel created to keep members of the Church connected, to a worldwide television service that reaches tens of millions of Heavenly Father's children around the globe.

CHAPTER EIGHTEEN

ANXIOUSLY ENGAGED
IN A GOOD CAUSE

M en," the Savior explained to Joseph Smith, "should be anxiously engaged in a good cause."[1] As a senior member of
the Quorum of the Twelve Apostles, Elder Ballard was
nothing if not anxiously engaged in good causes. Although he recognized that "time flies, pretty fast, especially when you get older" and occasionally found himself wondering why he was still on this side of the
veil, he clearly knew the answer: "The Lord doesn't want me over there
yet. I've had all kinds of surgeries and health issues over the years, yet
I'm still up, and I can still carry on a full day here."[2] Even in his eight-
ies, a full day for Elder Ballard was a day at the office attending meetings and preparing talks, or boarding an airplane to travel the world to
testify of the Lord Jesus Christ and the love of our Heavenly Father for
each of His children.

Still, Elder Ballard was driven by what he has always believed
about himself: "I can do more." With that constant motivation, he
shepherded projects of great worth while keeping up with a relentless
calendar of assignments.

Elder Ballard's love of and reverence for the pioneers drove his involvement in such local, civic projects as helping to revitalize This Is the Place Heritage Park and the Days of '47 Rodeo. As he put it:

> I feel very strongly about the youth of this Church not losing an appreciation for our forefathers, who gave everything to accept the gospel, to support the Prophet Joseph Smith and Hyrum to carry the gospel out to these valleys and to establish it and then to carry the gospel out into the world from here. If we lose that, we have lost something that's irreplaceable. I worry about the youth who are so hooked up into social media that they're losing sight of who they are and the price the pioneers paid for them.[3]

Those who worked on these initiatives acknowledged the vital role Elder Ballard played in bringing people together and inspiring them with his vision. There were other things to be accomplished, though, that would operate on a more global scale.

JustServe

As he prepared his general conference address for April 2011, Elder Ballard felt impressed to focus on one of the simplest, most fundamental doctrines of the gospel of Jesus Christ:

> It is only when we love God and Christ with all of our hearts, souls, and minds that we are able to share this love with our neighbors through acts of kindness and service—the way that the Savior would love and serve all of us if He were among us today.
>
> When this pure love of Christ—or charity—envelops us, we think, feel, and act more like Heavenly Father and Jesus would think, feel, and act. Our motivation and heartfelt desire are like unto that of the Savior. . . . [This love] is an active love. It is not manifest through large and heroic deeds but rather through simple acts of kindness and service.

According to Elder Ballard, loving and serving our brothers and sisters is not only a foundational gospel doctrine, but it is also critical to our ability to fulfill our sacred responsibility to share the gospel with "every nation, kindred, tongue and people":

> The future growth of the Church will not happen through just knocking on strangers' doors. It will happen when the members, along with our missionaries, filled with the love of God and Christ discern needs and respond to those needs in the spirit of charitable service. When we do this . . . the honest in heart will feel our sincerity and our love. Many will want to know more about us. Then and only then will the Church expand to fill all of the earth. This cannot be accomplished by missionaries alone, but requires the interest and service of every member.[4]

With these thoughts swirling in his mind as well as his heart, the concept of full-time missionaries using a portion of their time giving service in the community became a major point of discussion between Elder Ballard and Elder Richard Maynes as they worked together in the Missionary Department. At the time, Elder Ballard was serving as chairman of the Missionary Executive Council and was concerned that typical missionaries had too much downtime when they weren't studying, teaching, or engaged in finding investigators—especially during the afternoon hours. Mission presidents likewise expressed their concern about how to keep missionaries productive in the afternoon. Elder Ballard believed that missionaries would thrive—and people would feel their great spirit—during those hours by serving in soup kitchens, at neighborhood parks trimming trees, or putting together hygiene kits for the homeless. Could it be that by serving in the community, missionaries could better shine their light for all the world to see?[5]

Elder Ballard was intrigued by this concept—missionaries serving in their respective communities without any missionary motive other than to just do good. Yet finding service opportunities was difficult, and missionaries who were new to the communities in which they served had no idea where to look. The idea of a service website for the world surfaced. There were many variables to consider, such as who would manage and administer projects on the site and who would interface with community leaders. Although most people who were familiar with the idea believed it had real merit, the logistics were daunting, and the concept found its way to the back shelf among projects under consideration.

It moved back to the front shelf in 2011, when Elder Ballard and Elder Maynes expanded the service discussion to include making service opportunities easily accessible to members of the Church and nonmembers alike. They foresaw the day when members—including missionaries—would serve alongside other service-oriented people in their respective communities at food banks, hospitals, care centers, and endless other possibilities. They believed each member and missionary could make a difference in their part of the world, and a website focused on bringing people together with projects would make it easy to do so.[6] Through the website the Church could offer a simple solution to help people bless the lives of those in their communities who were in need.

This was the foundation upon which JustServe.org was built. Not only did technology need to be in place, but there also needed to be a clear and consistent message of what JustServe.org would be—and, perhaps even more important, what it would *not* be. JustServe was not to be a proselyting tool, have a political agenda, or be a specific advocacy focus. Likewise, JustServe was not to have a profit motive or even a fundraising component.[7] JustServe.org was to have only one simple, clear, unmistakable objective: service to neighbors.[8]

"Imagine what good we can do in the world if we all join together, united as followers of Christ, anxiously and busily responding to the needs of others and serving those around us," Elder Ballard said. "What would be the cumulative effect of millions of small, compassionate acts performed daily because of our heartfelt Christian love for others? Over time this would have a transformative effect upon all of our Heavenly Father's children through the extension of His love to them through us."[9]

With many details yet to be hammered out, Elder Ballard was anxious to see if a JustServe website could put missionaries, Church members, and nonmembers in a position to relieve suffering, care for the poor and needy, and enhance the quality of life in a community. JustServe could also have the secondary benefit of becoming a vehicle to build bridges with community and faith leaders, improve the public perception of the Church and its members, improve missionary productivity, and perhaps even rescue less-active members.

To test these theories, the First Presidency authorized the creation of a JustServe beta website, and the California San Jose Mission was selected as the location for the pilot program. Senior missionaries William and Sidney Price, seasoned in missionary work and public affairs, were asked to help roll out the JustServe initiative in California. At their first meeting with Elder Maynes, Elder and Sister Price were asked to help develop an organizational structure through which anyone who wanted to serve others could easily find a way to engage in community service. They were told "to try whatever is necessary until we come up with a website model that works, and build upon that success until you find a pattern for community service we can test in other missions."[10]

From day one in San Jose, Elder and Sister Price were met with enthusiasm for the idea. Members in the eleven stakes in the California San Jose Mission embraced JustServe and often said to Elder Price, "I wish JustServe had been available when I was a missionary." Rob Davis, a counselor in the mission presidency and a former chief of police in San Jose, arranged for the Prices to meet with city officials. "When he went with us, every door opened," Sister Price said. Some civic and religious leaders in the community were excited about JustServe, although there were a few skeptics, of course, who wanted nothing to do with the Church even when they were assured that JustServe was not a proselyting tool.[11] There was also the issue of unexpected glitches within the website that delayed the posting of projects. Tech-savvy members in San Jose were the first to critique the website.[12] Their suggestions pushed computer software designers at Church headquarters to create a sophisticated electronic bulletin board of service opportunities that could handle content in any language. The Church technicians also found ways to enhance graphics and layout on the opening pages, and to upgrade the site with search capabilities and filtering.

Elder and Sister Price reported, "There was an undercurrent of happiness and success that began to surface as the pilot project continued."[13] Church leaders and community leaders were starting to work together to consider the needs of the community.[14] Missionaries reported being happier when participating in meaningful projects posted on JustServe, and they had three times more contact with nonmembers when engaged in community service. Missionaries also reported a higher level of personal fulfillment and improved physical and emotional well-being. Dr. Dennis Lange, who performed medical service to missionaries in the California San Jose Mission, reported:

> When I first began to do this service, there were so many missionaries going for doctor visits. . . . Most of the medical issues were really mental health problems. Before the JustServe program there were many missionaries that complained of homesickness, insomnia, depression, sadness and there were several that complained about their companionships. Since JustServe was implemented, those complaints are greatly diminished. The number of missionaries that need to see me has fallen.[15]

Before JustServe became the gold standard on the internet for matching volunteers and volunteer opportunities, the pilot initiative of JustServe was expanded to the Colorado Denver Mission and the Texas Dallas Mission in 2013. The rollout of the JustServe resource in these missions was dramatically different from the rollout in San Jose—there were approved guidelines and an effective organization model in place. Priesthood leaders were quick to adopt the JustServe guidelines and find best practices for their stakes' respective circumstances.[16]

From this point on, Elder and Sister Price reported "receiving phone calls daily from Church public affairs leaders who are meeting for the first time with other faith groups, nonprofits, and city and county representatives."[17] When Jon Anderson, president of the Powder Springs Georgia Stake, was first introduced to JustServe, he was skeptical: "I saw it as simply one more program to manage." As he learned more about JustServe, he realized that working together on service projects was "not a mandate or a duty." He registered and discovered, "As everyone reaches out to help people in need, we create a spirit of love and cooperation that transcends differences and connects us. Members of the community work side by side with people they would not have otherwise met. When they do, they build mutual understanding and we all become a little more like Jesus Christ."[18]

By the end of 2013 there were more than 114,000 registered volunteers on JustServe.org and 19,402 projects posted by such humanitarian organizations as the Salvation Army, the American Red Cross, Boys & Girls Clubs, American Cancer Society, United Way, and Habitat for Humanity, as well as lesser-known organizations like Friends of the Marsh Creek Watershed and cda.cares (California Dental Association Foundation). Between 2012 and 2018, 370,000 volunteers had registered on JustServe.org or the JustServe mobile app, and nearly 58,000 projects had been completed. On a typical day, two hundred projects were added to the website. When a BYUtv JustServe documentary was shown between sessions of general conference in April 2017, 50,000 new visitors viewed the site and 13,000 registered. Elder and Sister Price conclude, "When we exceed one million volunteers we will likely be the largest army of community volunteers in the nation."[19]

Elder Ballard believes that JustServe will eventually be a household word in mission fields across the nation and around the world. He also foresees JustServe.org as a bridge to connect Latter-day Saints with those of other faiths (or no faith) with no motive other than to work together to serve and bless the lives of those in their communities who are in need. Major League Baseball's San Diego Padres baseball team adopted JustServe.[20] Nicholls State University in Thibodaux, Louisiana, uses JustServe.org to communicate volunteerism needs for service projects, such as coastal restoration and tree planting. North Carolina state government posts a JustServe link on its volunteerism website. One volunteer wrote:

> I attended an informal community meeting where a promi-nent nonprofit leader bemoaned the fact that there were very few nonprofits in the area. He claimed there were less than 10 in the entire city. I opened up JustServe in the app and typed in the zip code. Instantly 55 separate posts showed up within five miles of the city. I raised my hand and showed the speaker the JustServe posts, each from separate and distinct nonprofit agencies. . . . That day, everyone who attended that meeting, about 50 people, registered on JustServe.[21]

"We may not solve world hunger immediately," said Elder Ballard, "but we're convinced that by serving with each other in our local com-munities, we're paving the way for much broader changes. Our indi-vidual efforts don't need to be huge—a little bit of change here, a few hours there—but even small efforts quickly add up to make a real dif-ference."[22] As Elder Ballard and Elder Maynes have watched the growth of JustServe spread across the nation and to foreign lands, they marvel at the limitless possibilities for neighbors to be neighborly and to reach beyond themselves to better their communities.[23]

While Elder Ballard was thrilled to see the growth of JustServe, he wondered if there weren't more that he could have done. His mind went to an experience in November 2015 when he was on assignment in Europe. His itinerary included stops at three Syrian refugee camps: Messe Berlin Refugee Camp, Lesbos Greece Refugee Camp, and Skopje Macedonia Refugee Camp.

"It's overwhelming to see the magnitude of the number of refugees," Elder Ballard said. "I have seen a lot of photographs, heard a lot of reports, but it's different to walk through the camps and see the faces."[24] In Lesbos, Elder Ballard watched refugees coming across the sea in dinghies:

> It was criminal what some of those bandits, as I would call them, were charging refugees for unsafe ways to take them to safety. They were taking most of the resources from refugees who made their way from Syria and Pakistan, and from Iraq and Iran, and from other places to Turkey, trying to get out of harm's way. They would put refugees in rubber rafts that were not seaworthy. They put far more people in the rafts than was safe, oftentimes at night. The wind would come up, and it would swamp the dinghy. Men and women and children all drowned in the Aegean Sea.
>
> We went into those camps and tried to understand the depth of the problem. You see a lot of wonderful people from the Mideast. Some of them have lost everything they had, if they were from Syria and other places where their homes were bombed. So they were refugees. They were just trying to get someplace where they could take care of their families and find a future.[25]

A poignant moment for Elder Ballard was seeing a Syrian woman and her three children reach camp still wet from their voyage. Volunteers in the camp handed out little rolls of Oreo cookies wrapped in plastic cylinders to the arriving children.

"Amer, a nine- or ten-year-old little boy, the son of the Syrian woman, opened a cylinder of cookies near me," Elder Ballard said, "and presented me with one of his cookies. 'No! No! No! These are for you,' I told the boy. 'The Lord loves you.' I put my arm around him and gave him a hug, but he would not move. He would not budge until I took

With Elder and Sister Patrick Kearon in the Lesbos Refugee Camp.
Amer is on the far left with the soccer ball

Elder Ballard keeps this cookie as a reminder
of his experience with Syrian refugees

the first Oreo cookie in the cylinder. I took the cookie and then started thinking, *I'm going to figure out how to get this cookie back to Salt Lake so that I will never ever forget those brown eyes of that little boy who insisted that I have the first cookie.*"[26]

When Elder Ballard returned to Salt Lake City, his secretary preserved the cookie in a small plastic cube. Every day thereafter, as Elder Ballard glances at that cookie in his office, he commits anew to remember the poor[27] and to love and serve them "through acts of kindness and service—the way that the Savior would love and serve all of us if He were among us today."[28]

The Passing of President Thomas S. Monson

By 2017, there were many additional causes that had captured the attention of Elder Ballard, but there was a deeply personal concern that could not be ignored. In May 2017, the Church announced that President Thomas S. Monson was no longer attending regular meetings and that his health was failing. He missed general conference in October, which was uncharacteristic of him. President Monson never regained his health. He died peacefully on January 2, 2018, at age ninety, of causes incident to age. "I knew President Monson longer than any of the brethren," Elder Ballard said. "I first met Tom Monson in September 1950 when he worked for the *Deseret News* in the classified ad division. He would pick up the ads from automobile dealers like my father."[29]

Through the passing years Tom Monson and Russ Ballard became the best of friends. Elder Ballard said of President Monson, "He was a brilliant, powerful servant of the Lord. He was dedicated to the service of the Lord and lived his life following closely the promptings of the Spirit. He served for fifty-four years as a General Authority."[30] But as for his passing, Elder Ballard said, "It was good that he could be released and go on and do some more things in the great world of the

With President Thomas S. Monson

spirits of the dead."³¹ After a public viewing at the Conference Center in downtown Salt Lake City, thousands attended President Monson's funeral on January 12, 2018, which was translated into many languages and broadcast across the globe. Elder Ballard offered the opening prayer.

With the passing of his dear friend, eighty-nine-year-old Elder Ballard was suddenly the third most senior Apostle in the Quorum of the Twelve Apostles, behind only President Russell M. Nelson and Elder Dallin H. Oaks, two men whom he loved and with whom he had served for many years. The order of the Church was clear: President Nelson would succeed President Monson as President of the Church. Beyond that—who knew? Even after thirty-three years of service in the Quorum of the Twelve, Elder Ballard only knew that an exciting new chapter was about to begin—for the Church, and for himself.

CHAPTER NINETEEN

ACTING PRESIDENT OF THE QUORUM OF THE TWELVE

O n Sunday, January 14, 2018, Elder Ballard stood in a circle with all of the Apostles in the upper room of the Salt Lake Temple as President Dallin H. Oaks ordained and set apart the senior Apostle, Russell M. Nelson, as the seventeenth President of The Church of Jesus Christ of Latter-day Saints. This was the fifth time that Elder Ballard had had this sacred privilege:

> I was ordained an Apostle in 1985. The hands of President Spencer W. Kimball were placed on my head along with all the other Apostles. About a month after my ordination to the apostleship, I was privileged to stand in the circle when Ezra Taft Benson was ordained President of the Church. President Benson had a great regard for my grandfather, Melvin J. Ballard, and often spoke of hearing Grandfather give one of his last sermons in Washington, D.C., when he was stake president there. The second time I stood in a sacred circle, my neighbor and dear friend Howard W. Hunter was ordained President. I often went to President Hunter's home to visit him and sometimes helped him get in and out of a wheelchair, and in and out of the car. Then there was Gordon B. Hinckley. He absolutely loved the Prophet

Enjoying a moment with President Russell M. Nelson

Joseph Smith, Joseph F. Smith, and the Restoration. I learned from him if you were not feeling well, you didn't tell him. He never stopped, so those of us in the Twelve never stopped either. We just kept going.[1] The fourth to be ordained President was my close friend Thomas S. Monson. To him, visiting the widow and the downtrodden were never just sentiments, they were actions.[2]

Being in the Salt Lake Temple with President Nelson as he officially became President of the Church was one of the choice experiences of Elder Ballard's life:

I've known of Russell Nelson from his days at East High School—he was a legend at the school. When he was the General President of the Sunday School, he came to Toronto and visited our mission. I have been blessed to sit in the Quorum of the Twelve with him for thirty-three years. He comes to the office of President with a background of being able to see what the needs are and to articulate them. We've got a president who's not afraid to see the issues, discuss them with the Brethren, and ponder and pray about the decision. When he has confirmation from the Lord, he's not afraid to move on it. He feels an urgency to get things done.[3]

Following the ordination and setting apart of President Nelson, Elders Dallin H. Oaks and Henry B. Eyring were set apart as his first and second counselors, respectively.[4] As second in seniority among the Apostles, President Oaks was also set apart as President of the Quorum of the Twelve Apostles. Because the responsibilities of being a member of the First Presidency are so weighty and time-consuming, the order of the Church is that the next in seniority in the Twelve—in this case, Elder Ballard—is set apart as Acting President of the Quorum of the Twelve Apostles.[5] The blessing pronounced upon now-President Ballard by President Nelson was that he would "be able to lead this group of inspired and noble men, mobilizing them in coming up with solutions to the many challenges that we have and that we face in the future." He was told, "You are a strong man. You are a faithful man and you are of the chosen lineage—the lineage of those who were chosen to restore the doctrine and priesthood authority in these latter days." He was blessed with "longevity, vigor of mind and body and health that will allow you to serve as long as the Lord needs you here."[6]

Two days after that sacred event, President Ballard received a note from Elder Jeffrey R. Holland, who occupies the chair next to him in the Quorum:

> You have all my love and support—lock, stock and barrel. We are your brothers and we are committed to your success and your leadership. This will be an exciting time in the Quorum of the Twelve with your unique ability to get things done, the straight-thinking you inherited from your grandfather, and the uncompromised testimony you have of the Prophet Joseph Smith and the work of the Restoration. All of that promises an exhilarating era ahead, and it is an era I am thrilled to watch unfold standing at your side. I await your counsel and look forward to every moment ahead.[7]

At a solemn assembly during the first session of the 188th Annual General Conference on March 31, 2018, President Russell M. Nelson and the members of the First Presidency were sustained. "In an orderly way we have now begun a new chapter in our Church history," President Ballard said. "By sustaining President Nelson, we stood as witnesses before God and acknowledged that he is President Monson's rightful successor. With our raised hands we promised to hearken unto his voice as he receives direction from the Lord."[8]

Also sustained at that conference were two new members of the Twelve: Gerrit W. Gong and Ulisses Soares. "I've known both of them very well," President Ballard said. "Gerrit is brilliant—a Rhodes Scholar, PhD, an educator. Ulisses knows five languages. He is beloved in Brazil and in many other parts of the world."[9] President Ballard affectionately refers to Elder Gong and Elder Soares as "my boys" because they were the first Apostles he was privileged to train.

"You don't sit down and say, 'Now here's what you do,'" President Ballard said of training the new Apostles. "They know what to do because they've been General Authorities.[10] Some of the best training I've done is when I've put my arm around a brother and said, 'You might want to consider this.' Never, not once, have I ever had a General Authority say anything other than, 'Thank you.'"[11] Elder Gong recalled being invited to visit with President Ballard: "He kindly welcomed and encouraged me, gave me indispensable counsel about my call and our quorum, and said his door was always open—and it always is."[12] Elder Soares recalled:

> President Ballard called me into his office to welcome me and to offer some guidance in this new, sacred calling. . . . I started telling him how much I felt unqualified for this calling. He said, "Well, the Lord called you. You can do this. Stop thinking about yourself and start thinking about the things you will have to do and the Lord will bless you with the strength and capacity that you need." When I heard that counsel, I felt confident that I can

learn and progress through this wonderful calling and responsibility to testify of the Savior Jesus Christ to the world.[13]

Responsibilities as Acting President of the Twelve

"The alarm goes off in the morning and I say, 'Well, I'm still here. I guess I better get up,'" said President Ballard.[14] In referring to himself and other members of his quorum, he said, "We all have aches and pains, but it doesn't do you any good to complain. So you might as well just keep going."[15]

"Keep going" to him means starting the day by eating whatever he wants. President Ballard noted, "At my age we are allowed to do this." After breakfast he leaves his apartment and walks through the tunnel under State Street to the Church Administration Building (CAB). President Ballard generally arrives early at his office to begin the day, a lifelong habit.[16]

As quickly as possible after his setting apart, President Ballard moved to the office of the (Acting) President of the Quorum of the Twelve on the second floor of the CAB. His new office is connected to a series of offices and a meeting room reserved for Quorum of the Twelve committees and quorum meetings. The offices nearby are reserved for his personal administrative assistant, the secretary and assistant secretary to the Quorum of the Twelve, and others who work under President Ballard's direction.

President Ballard observed, "There is a significant difference between being a member of the Twelve and functioning as President of the quorum." Additionally, "many of the questions that members of the Twelve or Seventy have end up in my office. I find myself all day long answering questions and giving directions and learning how to do the things that matter most."[17]

Of his days in the office, he said:

Working at his desk in the Church Administration Building

This is a busy place. This is kind of a control center for the Quorum of the Twelve and the Seventy. Whatever is going on in the world or in the departments, where somebody needs to come in and say, "I'd like to run something by you," this is it. It's kind of like a doctor's office. They're just in and out all day. When I get home at night, I pray and say, "Heavenly Father, I answered a lot of questions today. I sure hope they were good answers. If they're not, please make them good."[18]

President Ballard is keenly aware that "this is the Lord's Church and his major responsibility is to be sure we are in tune with how He would want us to carry out His kingdom."[19] He receives directions from the First Presidency, and at their behest he serves as chairman of the Leadership and Planning Committee and the Assignment Committee. "This is important," he said. "We have a couple of brethren that work full-time to determine, for example, which stake conferences, area leadership meetings, area priesthood conferences, and mission president seminars need assignments and which of the Brethren are available to fulfill those assignments. Committee members offer suggestions and give approval, when appropriate, or disapproval if necessary." These assignments are sent under his signature. As to his own assignments,

"I haven't worried about my own. I just do what I can do and work to strengthen the Church the best I can."[20]

His assignment to preside over weekly meetings of the Quorum of the Twelve rests heavily upon his mind. President Ballard explains:

> My way of getting the quorum to do our duty for the First Presidency is to see that everything we take to them has been discussed with everybody's point of view, then we crystallize and prepare the best we can so whatever we send forward has been thought through carefully and is worthy of the Presidency's time. That's our duty and responsibility. The council system of leadership is what I've done all my life—a team effort. Leaders have to be good listeners. The council system is working . . . we talk with each other, we counsel with each other, and consequently we make good decisions.[21]

Of his leadership in quorum meetings, his brethren have much to say. Elder Holland writes:

> From the vantage point of sitting next to him in the Quorum of the Twelve, I can bear personal witness of President Ballard's skill and courtesy in leading that strong body of men. He is very organized. He is very decisive. He is always knowledgeable about the issue at hand, including whatever staff work needs to be assigned and gathered prior to the meeting. He is very capable in all the traditional skills of leadership. But above and beyond that, he is wonderfully courteous, which not every leader in industry, government, education, or the Church might be. He unfailingly says "thank you" for virtually anything anyone in our quorum does. And he is a great listener. That is one of the lessons I have learned from him as much as any other. . . . He wants to make sure that everyone in our circle is heard and that no one is excluded intentionally or unintentionally.[22]

Elder Dieter F. Uchtdorf echoes Elder Holland's sentiments and says, "President Ballard brought a thoughtfulness and an openness into the discussions. . . . He is always inclusive, knows how to listen, and is gifted in applying the important over the urgent. The Lord has placed him at the right time in the right spot."[23]

Elder Neil L. Andersen sees "President Ballard leading the way the Savior Himself leads. He guides the Twelve, encourages each to speak and to respond to others. He understands that unity comes as we pray, teach, discuss, and ponder together."[24] Elder D. Todd Christofferson writes, "He is constantly thinking about the big picture and about what actions need to be taken and what initiatives need to be put in place now to be prepared for the future. He feels keenly that a good discussion is not an end in itself and that things are not finished until some concrete decision or action is agreed upon. Then he follows up."[25]

Elder Christofferson knew, long before he sustained President Ballard as his quorum president, the importance he placed on not being finished until a concrete decision is made:

> When I was serving in the presidency of the Mexico South Area (1994–1997), then-Elder Ballard came to visit. One of our meetings was a training for stake presidencies at the Mexico City Temple complex. He assigned me to train the leaders about the stake high council. I gave what I thought was a thorough presentation about how high councils are organized and how they function vis-à-vis the stake presidency. I sat down fairly pleased with myself, but Elder Ballard turned to me and said, "You did a good job explaining what the high council is, but you didn't talk about what a high council is supposed to accomplish. Get up again and tell them what high councilors do." He was kind but direct, and I have always remembered the lesson taught me: organizations exist for a purpose, to accomplish something, and that I should never be content just to put in place or teach about structure or organization without focusing on outcomes.[26]

Elder Ronald A. Rasband said, "President Ballard brings people together and gets things done—he is the best leader of a council I have ever known."[27] Elder Dale G. Renlund added, "President Ballard is not 'acting' in the role of leader. He has assumed the full mantle of the responsibilities of leadership. He is able to seamlessly work with President Nelson, President Oaks, and President Eyring."[28]

The Name of the Church

One of the important tasks assigned to the Quorum of the Twelve under President Ballard's leadership had its impetus in a trip he took with President Nelson to Church history sites in Missouri and Illinois. On their trip, the two Church leaders visited with President Stephen M. Veazey and his counselors of the Community of Christ Church, formerly known as the Reorganized Church of Jesus Christ of Latter Day Saints, in Independence, Missouri. They also participated in endowment sessions at the Kansas City Missouri Temple and the Nauvoo Illinois Temple. They visited Liberty Jail, the Far West temple site, the valley of Adam-ondi-Ahman, and historic sites in Nauvoo. And as they traveled, they talked.

"In spite of it being a short trip, we were not rushed," President Ballard said. "We had time to have an in-depth discussion on the name of the Church and why we needed to give attention to the proper name, the name given by the Savior Himself—The Church of Jesus Christ of Latter-day Saints. If there was ever a time in the history of the world when the name of Jesus Christ needs to be connected every way and everywhere to His church and kingdom on the earth, it is today. The world is pushing His name, and even our Heavenly Father's name, out of the public square."[29]

The day after the two Church leaders returned to Salt Lake City, May 10, 2018, President Nelson sent a heartfelt letter to members of the Quorum of the Twelve Apostles in which he said:

I am distressed by the egregious error that has evolved regarding the name of The Church of Jesus Christ of Latter-day Saints. Weighing heavily upon my mind is the gap between that name, as revealed by the Lord, and the nicknames by which the Church is called, such as "Mormon Church" or the "LDS Church." We are erroneously known as "Mormons." We have also tolerated use of the term "Mormonism" as a substitute for the "restored gospel of Jesus Christ." I know the Lord is not pleased with these practices. . . .

We will be held accountable for this error in nomenclature. While we have no control over what other people may call us, we cannot call ourselves by any other than the name as prescribed by the Lord: The Church of Jesus Christ of Latter-day Saints. . . .

I would like to ask the Quorum of the Twelve Apostles to devise a comprehensive plan to correct this error. It will require a protracted and focused effort. The expense may be great but the Lord will provide both the spiritual and temporal means for us to comply with His commandments. Thank you for your thoughtful consideration of this great concern.

President Nelson had beautifully articulated the very concern President Ballard had addressed in general conference in October 2011:

Because the full name of the Church is so important, I echo the revelations from the scriptures, the First Presidency's instructions in letters of 1982 and 2001, and the words of other Apostles who have encouraged the members of the Church to uphold and teach the world that the Church is known by the name of the Lord Jesus Christ. This is the name by which the Lord will call us at the last day. It is the name by which His Church will be distinguished from all others.[30]

During that talk, Elder Ballard discussed all nine words of the official name of the Church to explain why each is important and how together they serve "as a descriptive overview of what the Church is."

And so he fully embraced President Nelson's vision for reemphasizing the correct and full name of the Church, and he accepted the challenge to "correct this error."

So did the other members of the Quorum of the Twelve Apostles. President Ballard said: "We saw this as an opportunity to reenthrone the sacred name of Jesus Christ as the head of our Church, both among our members as well as among the people of the world. In our minds, if ever there was a time when the Savior needed to be heralded to the world, it is today."[31]

Working with the various Church departments and organizations for which they had oversight, members of the Twelve began identifying everything that would need to be changed or adjusted, from the names of Church websites to the names of various media outreach platforms to the most beloved and iconic representative of the Church, the Mormon Tabernacle Choir.

"You just really have no idea what a tremendous undertaking this was, to do all that internally," President Ballard said. "But even in the middle of identifying and responding to all of the challenges, there was this overwhelming feeling of joy in knowing we were doing what the Savior would have us do—what the Savior had commanded us to do when He said, 'Thus shall my church be called in the last days, even The Church of Jesus Christ of Latter-day Saints.'[32] As President Nelson said, we weren't rebranding—we were reaffirming and reemphasizing the original brand, which had been designated by the Lord Himself."[33]

President Ballard was pleased to note that Church members responded well to the prophet's challenge to make it clear they are members of The Church of Jesus Christ of Latter-day Saints—not the Mormon Church. "They have been wonderful about this," he said. "They are really trying."

But, he added, "the media and most of the rest of the world still see us as Mormons. It's probably going to take a while to get that ship completely turned around. But we'll get there. We have to. The Lord expects this of us."[34]

From Houston to New Zealand and Beyond

As he was settling into his assignment as Acting President of the Quorum of the Twelve Apostles, the First Presidency asked President Ballard to do something he had never done before: dedicate a temple. Although he had participated in dozens of temple dedications through the years, this was the first time he had been asked to represent the First Presidency as the presiding authority at such a gathering.

In August 2017, Hurricane Harvey, a Category 4 hurricane, made landfall in Texas and Louisiana, causing catastrophic flooding and becoming the wettest tropical cyclone in US history. In the Houston area alone, thousands of homes were flooded with filthy water, displacing an estimated 30,000 residents. The beautiful Houston Texas Temple, nestled among trees about twenty-five miles from the heart of downtown Houston, was not immune from floodwaters. On August 26 the temple was breached by a nearby river that flooded the main floor, basement, and temple annex with more than a foot of water. A photograph posted on Facebook showed a young man kayaking to the entrance of the temple.

The Houston Texas Temple was closed for repairs for seven months. Due to the extensive nature of those repairs, the First Presidency decided the temple needed to be rededicated. It would be a sacred but simple dedication—no open house, cultural celebrations, or broadcasts to meetinghouses in the temple district. President Ballard was asked by the First Presidency to rededicate the Houston Texas Temple on April 22, 2018, which was almost exactly eighteen years after the original Houston Texas Temple dedication by President Gordon B. Hinckley.[35]

President Ballard conducted the dedicatory session and reminded those present of the damage caused by the catastrophic Hurricane

Harvey.[36] In the dedicatory prayer, President Ballard asked Heavenly Father "for protection over Thy temple that Thy sacred work for the living and for the deceased may continue from this day forward. May Thy children come here often to make covenants and receive ordinances for themselves and for their kindred dead. . . . And now as Thy servant, acting in the authority of the everlasting priesthood and in the name of Jesus Christ, we consecrate and rededicate to Thee and to Thy Beloved Son this, the Houston Texas Temple of The Church of Jesus Christ of Latter-day Saints."[37]

Not long afterward, in May 2018, President Ballard, Elder Gary E. Stevenson, and Elder Carl B. Cook of the Presidency of the Seventy were in New Zealand and Australia on assignment. "I observed President Ballard as we arrived late at a distant airport after a long day of traveling," said Elder Stevenson.

At age 89, President Ballard, exhausted, had every reason to sit back, relax and rest as we shuttled 20 minutes to the hotel. However, as soon as he entered the van, he struck up a conversation with the driver. It was such a normal and natural conversation. Decades of age difference notwithstanding, he quickly bonded with this young shuttle driver. Before we reached our destination, the driver knew about modern-day apostles and prophets and the great plan of happiness, and provided President Ballard with contact information about himself and his immigrant family as well as his brother and his family.[38]

The prearranged schedule in New Zealand and Australia was demanding—leadership conferences in two different countries on the same day plus meetings with missionaries. Despite a full schedule, when President Ballard learned there was internet access to all the Pacific Islands, he said, on Friday morning, May 18: "Let's have a family home evening Sunday night, and we'll talk to everybody. We'll talk to Church members scattered far away that we won't have a chance to see on this trip." The brethren asked, "What are we going to say?

Who's going to do what?" President Ballard replied, "Why don't we let the Lord tell us what's going to happen."[39]

The unscripted family home evening was webcast via Facebook Live from Sydney, Australia, on May 20, with two members of the Twelve, a member of the Seventy, and the Area Presidency and their wives participating. "This was the first time in the history of the Church we've ever done something like this," President Ballard said. "We were able to reach via internet more members of the Church during this family home evening meeting than I ever have in any leadership conference. We were broadcast into living rooms of hundreds, maybe thousands of our members in the Pacific region."[40] President Ballard shared a message about ministering in the home. He encouraged families to pray and reminded them, "Perfection is a process. It is not an event. There is no point in time when we say, 'Ah hah, now I'm perfect!'"[41] As to his feelings about the unscripted broadcast, President Ballard said, "It was fabulous. Everybody talked about what families are facing."[42]

He liked it so much he decided to do it again three months later when he traveled to Brazil in August 2018 with Elder Ulisses Soares. After speaking at leadership conferences and missionary meetings in Sao Paulo and Rio de Janeiro, the two Apostles held a Sunday night family home evening broadcast via Facebook Live and talked to Saints all over Brazil in a family setting. President Ballard said, "Here we were with a brand-new Brazilian Apostle and his wife, with a great opportunity for him to speak to all of his fellow countrymen through the internet. Like the broadcast that originated from Sydney, Australia, it was fabulous."[43]

The Passing of Barbara Bowen Ballard

As joyfully energized as President Ballard was by the work he was doing among his brethren of the Quorum of the Twelve Apostles and among Church members around the world, there was one constant, nagging heartache: Barbara's health was declining. The love of his life was struggling, and there wasn't much he could do about it except care for her to the best of his ability. Her physical health had reached the point where she was unable to do much of anything outside the walls of their home, and her memory of people, places, and events was fading.

On numerous occasions in private and in public, President Ballard spoke of his love for Barbara. At the Preston Temple dedication in June 1998 he said, "There is no one in this world more precious than my eternal companion, the mother of my children, grandmother of my grandchildren. We pay tribute to you, Barbara, particularly today, as we sit here in the celestial room as your family."[44]

At a General Authority Wives' Luncheon in May 2016, he spoke of Barbara being at his side "in many places in the world, while at the same time shepherding our very large family."

> She has attended hundreds of firesides, missionary meetings, conferences, funerals, weddings, and special meetings, to name just a few. She is filled with love for everyone and her countenance and smile reaches the hearts of all those she meets. Speaking is not her favorite thing to do, but sharing the love of Heavenly Father and the Savior of the World comes naturally to her, and people are blessed by her presence. . . . I married the right daughter of God. Without the help and direction of Barbara our family relationships would not have been as happy and fulfilling as they are. Barbara is a treasure to our family forever.[45]

In turn, Barbara occasionally spoke of what it was like to be married to a General Authority:

> As a young girl, I didn't actually realize I was setting values. As I looked around and spent time with friends and family, I knew that I wanted to marry someone who honored the priesthood and who would go to church with me, who would take our children to church, and this is what has happened. I look at him today and

The Ballard family in 2008

think, "Well, I can't complain about his being gone too much because I kind of asked for it." So here we sit together once in a while as we have that opportunity, and I am grateful for that.[46]

Barbara maintained her health until her later years, when stenosis of the spine led to back surgery. The corrective surgery, the placing of two rods and eight screws in her spine, left her in terrible pain. Compounding her health challenge was the onset of Alzheimer's, which for seven years became progressively worse. "My dad moved heaven and earth to get her every help available, but nothing worked," said daughter Stacey. "It was a heartbreaking illness."[47]

On May 2, 2018, President Ballard wrote to his family:

> The past two years have been perhaps the most difficult years for your Mother/Grandmother and me. . . . It is heartbreaking to watch your Mother suffer relentless pain in her back ever since her battle with stenosis and the subsequent surgery. . . . Now we face the reality that her memory of the past, and particularly of the present, has become progressively dim. . . . We do not know

what she feels and captures in her heart when we hold her hand and talk to her.[48]

Many who enter the dark tunnel of memory loss get upset, worried, more anxious, and more easily perturbed. But Barbara never became angry. Her native cheery disposition and ready smile was always what everyone saw, even if she did not remember who they were when they visited. She appreciated anyone who had a kind word to say. One neighbor remembered saying "I love you" as she left Sister Ballard. "Barbara would smile, look into my eyes, hold my hand, and say, 'I love you too. I really do!'"[49]

Toward the end of her life, President Ballard said, "Barbara knew my voice, but sometimes she would not know what my name was, or her children. She couldn't carry on a conversation. She would say two or three words, and then she would not be able to finish. It was as difficult on me as it was her because when your sweetheart is suffering, you suffer with her."[50]

When asked how he handled connections with Barbara on those days he was away from Salt Lake City, President Ballard explained that he called her every night to see how she was doing. "Would she know if you didn't call?" he was asked by a friend. "Probably not," he said, "but I would know. I would know that I had missed hearing the voice of my eternal companion whom I love more than life itself."[51]

When he was home in Salt Lake City, President Ballard spoke of sitting "next to her when I came home from the office during the last few months of her life, to hold her hand as we watched the endings of some of her favorite musicals—over and over again because Alzheimer's would not allow her to remember that she had seen them just the afternoon before. Memories of those special hand-holding sessions are now very, very precious to me."[52]

Barbara Bowen Ballard died on Monday, October 1, 2018, at her home in Salt Lake City surrounded by her family. She was eighty-six years old.

Sister Barbara Bowen Ballard

"Her death has been a tremendous adjustment after sixty-seven years of being companions," President Ballard said. "But you have to adjust that in your mind and realize it is what it is. You can't change it. It is a terrible loss—a big void in my life. We had a great life together. Barbara was one of the most Christlike, gentle, loving people that anybody would ever meet in mortality. When I would go to a conference, she would sit on the stand and smile at the people, and I'm not sure they even knew I was there."[53]

Sympathy cards and letters expressing love for him and for Barbara arrived soon after her passing. Kathy Andersen, wife of Elder Neil L. Andersen, wrote:

> During the first few months after Neil's call to the Twelve, I asked Barbara, "Sister Ballard, could you give me any advice on what I should do?" Without a moment's hesitation, she looked

at me, smiled, and said, "Enjoy every minute of it." . . . This was not the advice that I had expected. I was thinking of advice such as work hard, do your best, study the scriptures. . . . I cannot tell you how many hundreds of times her words have echoed in my mind. The Lord knew what I needed to hear.[54]

Elder Uchtdorf noted, "Sister Barbara Ballard was always a beautiful and supportive companion to you. She not only had a beautiful smile but also a radiance of goodness that did not need long and deep talks to impress."[55]

Her children had more to say. Daughter Tammy Brower recalled sitting next to her mother when her father spoke at the Missionary Training Center in June 2012: "The best part of the evening was watching her watch him. She just glowed. They adored each other. They were complete partners. We never got away with pitting mom against dad or vice versa. They were always on the same page—a perfect example of companions."[56] Son-in-law Paul Clayton said, "Barbara could temper the drive of Dad. On family vacations he wanted to go from one place to another. Barbara would say, 'That's a great idea, but first give us time to catch up with you.' Together, they were the definition of teamwork."[57] Daughter Brynn Huntsman said, "I often wondered how Mother could give and give of herself, without ever once complaining about all the demands on her. Dad was a consistent source of strength and wisdom as I grew up—always the gentleman toward Mom. It doesn't get any better than that. I lived a fairy-tale life having both as parents."[58]

As Barbara surely would have wanted, President Ballard attended and spoke at the general conference held on October 6–7, 2018—less than a week after Barbara's death. He began his talk on "The Vision of the Redemption of the Dead" by saying, "My brothers and sisters, my talk was prepared some time before the passing of my dear wife, Barbara. My family and I thank you for your love and your outreach of kindness. I pray the Lord will bless me as I speak to you this morning."

He concluded his message with, "How grateful I am to know where my precious Barbara is and that we will be together again, with our family, for all eternity."[59]

A year later, at the October 2019 general conference, President Ballard said:

> As the days have turned into weeks, then months, and now a year since Barbara's passing, I find myself more fully appreciating this scripture: "Thou shalt live together in love, insomuch that thou shalt weep for the loss of them that die" [D&C 42:45]. . . . I have learned in a very real way what it means to "weep for the loss" of those we love. Oh, how I love and miss her! . . . She was, in a word, magnificent—as a wife, as a mother, as a friend, as a neighbor, and as a daughter of God. . . . But here I am, in two days 91 years old, and I'm still wondering, . . . "Am I doing everything I need to do to be able to hold her hand once again?" . . . I certainly married right. Of that there can be no doubt.[60]

CHAPTER TWENTY

AT HOME AND ABROAD

I n 2019, it was announced that all three members of the First
Presidency and the entire Quorum of the Twelve Apostles would be
traveling to Italy for the Rome Italy Temple dedication. This would
be the first time in the history of the Church of Jesus Christ that the
entire First Presidency and the Twelve would be together in the ancient
city of Rome, where the ancient Apostles Peter and Paul both preached
the gospel and died martyrs' deaths.

The announcement was electrifying.

While many of the Church's other temple visitors' centers have
replicas of the *Christus* statue, the Rome facility features replicas of all
thirteen of Bertel Thorvaldsen's original works—with Paul replacing
Judas Iscariot among the twelve Apostles—as found in the Church of
Our Lady in Copenhagen, Denmark.

During this momentous dedication celebration, the First
Presidency and Quorum of the Twelve stood dressed in white before
the statues for a historic photograph. Additionally, as special witnesses
to the world of the divinity of Jesus Christ, the First Presidency and the
Quorum of the Twelve Apostles shared their testimony of the Savior

The First Presidency and Quorum of the Twelve in Rome

by recording excerpts from the document "The Living Christ: The Testimony of the Apostles," originally released in 2000.

This was significant, as only five of the original signers of the document were still alive: President Nelson, President Oaks, President Eyring, President Ballard, and Elder Holland. Now, all fifteen living Apostles testified again of the Savior.

Of the photographs taken before and after the temple dedication, there was one that has special significance for President Ballard: a picture of President Nelson and Pope Francis embracing each other in the Vatican. President Ballard was most likely more aware than almost anyone else of what had been required to make that moment happen.

Throughout his life, people of all faiths have called President Ballard "friend."[1] One of his dearest friends is the Most Reverend John C. Wester, archbishop of Santa Fe and the former bishop of the Catholic diocese in Salt Lake City.

"The two of us played golf a couple of times every year until he moved to Santa Fe," President Ballard said. "I told him he's got to come back to Salt Lake so we can finish our tournament. Many times, I've said to him, 'John, you'd make a wonderful stake president.' He thinks that's hilarious. But he's never told me that I'd make a good priest, because I wouldn't."[2]

When Bishop Wester was installed as archbishop of Santa Fe, President Ballard and businessman Ellis Ivory were there to offer their love and support. "Toward the end of the ceremony, John acknowledged publicly that Ellis and I were there—he called us 'his friends from Salt Lake City,'" President Ballard recalled. "When we went up to shake hands with him, John threw his arms around us."[3]

President Ballard also attended the ceremony in Salt Lake City when Bishop Oscar Solis was installed as the new bishop of the Catholic diocese there. When Robbie George, a celebrated Catholic scholar, gave the April 2015 BYU commencement speech, Elder Ballard was seated on the stand.[4] When His Eminence Cardinal Donald Wuerl, archbishop of Washington, DC, received a Marriott School of Management Award in June 2018, President Ballard publicly expressed gratitude to the cardinal for his commitment to religious freedom.[5] A photographer captured a shot of them walking arm in arm.[6]

Because of the close personal relationships he had established with so many good people from different faith groups, it was only natural for President Ballard to reach out to Archbishop Wester in 2017 when he learned he was traveling to Europe.

"I'm going back to Rome again," he said, "and I'd like to meet with the highest-ranking cardinal in the Vatican. Can you get me an appointment?"

"I didn't know what I was asking," President Ballard admitted, "but, to his credit, and bless his heart, John called back and said, 'I've got you an appointment with Cardinal Pietro Parolin, the secretary of state for the Vatican. He's the number-two man to the Pope.'"[7]

In October 2017, Elder Ballard, Elder L. Whitney Clayton of the Seventy, and the European Area Presidency walked into Vatican City

Meeting Pope Francis in Rome

and, for a brief moment, acted the part of tourists gazing at the exqui-
site artwork that adorns the Vatican halls. "We were in the heart of it,"
President Ballard said.

> We walked and walked and finally got to the cardinal's area
> where he was going to meet with us. We thought we would have a
> ten-minute get-acquainted kind of a thing, but he sat down with
> us. . . . We were there an hour and ten minutes. . . . We talked
> about everything you can talk about: concerns about the world
> and about the Christian faith. We talked about youth, social me-
> dia, the lack of interest in religion that is creeping in, seculariza-
> tion. . . . It was a very warm and cordial experience for us.[8]

Meeting Cardinal Parolin was an important precursor to the 2019
meeting of President Nelson and Pope Francis. Largely because that
meeting had been so pleasant and worthwhile for everyone involved,
when President Ballard went back to his contacts to suggest a meeting
with President Nelson and the Pope while the prophet was in Rome to

dedicate the new temple, the idea was well received and the arrangements were made without a great deal of difficulty or concern.[9]

As that historic meeting began, "President Nelson greeted Pope Francis by speaking to him in Spanish," recalled President Ballard.

> When President Nelson spoke about Argentina, the native country of Pope Francis, and told him that my grandfather actually started our work in Buenos Aires in 1925, the Pope perked right up. We talked about religious freedom, social media and its impact upon our youth, and the lack of a moral compass in society. We told him of our missionary efforts and showed him a photograph of the Rome Italy Temple. About thirty-five minutes later, we shook hands with him and embraced. The embrace of the President of The Church of Jesus Christ of Latter-day Saints and the Pope of the Holy Roman Apostolic Church was a wonderful moment.[10]

It was a trip filled with wonderful moments. For example, on March 9, President Ballard joined President Nelson and other leaders in speaking at a youth devotional that was broadcast to all units in the Rome Italy Temple district. Elder Ballard's grandson, Elder James Ballard Huntsman, who was serving at the time as an assistant to the Italy Rome mission president, translated for him. Afterward President Ballard said proudly: "He never missed a beat."[11]

On March 10, 2019, the first of seven dedicatory sessions for the Rome Italy Temple was held. President Nelson offered the dedicatory prayer at each session and said:

> In this ancient and great city that has stood since biblical times—in this historic nation of Italy—we acknowledge the ministry of two of Thy Son's early Apostles, Peter and Paul, who once blessed this land with their labors. May the influence of their abiding testimony of Jesus Christ continue to be felt among the vital values of this great country. We express gratitude for the

feelings of faith in and service to Jesus Christ that have long established this area as a bastion of Christianity. . . .

We thank Thee that Thou hast called Apostles in these latter days to bear special witness of the name of Jesus Christ throughout the world. We pray for Thy blessings to be upon them as they teach and testify of Thy Son and His gospel. We are grateful that all living Apostles are participating in these dedicatory services.[12]

After Rome

The dedication of the Rome Italy Temple, President Nelson said, was "a hinge point in the history of the Church.

"Things are going to move forward at an accelerated pace," he continued. "The Church is going to have an unprecedented future, unparalleled. We're just building up to what's ahead now."[13]

That certainly looked to be true for President Ballard. Within weeks of the historical and remarkable experience in Rome, he was in India, participating in a New Delhi Stake conference and an India Delhi Mission meeting. From there he went to Hong Kong, Taiwan, and Thailand for similar meetings. "Years ago, it would have taken months to reach these faraway places," said President Ballard. "Riding horses or driving a Model T Ford that you had to crank would never do now as the Lord hastens His work. My brethren and I are in a hurry. We can't be casual about our responsibility to bless God's children."[14]

On September 29, President Ballard helped introduce the Church's new Children and Youth Program on a worldwide broadcast. On that broadcast, he said: "It is going to be the most exciting youth and children program ever used in the Church. Wish I were younger to be a part of the program. If someone had helped me . . . I would have turned out better."[15] In October he gave his seventy-fourth conference address, celebrated his ninety-first birthday, and then headed to North Carolina to rededicate the Raleigh North Carolina Temple, which had been closed for a year and a half for extensive renovations.

As President Ballard was exiting the temple following the rededication service, a reporter stopped him and asked how he managed to keep up with such a vigorous schedule at his age. "I can't complain because President Nelson is 95—he's four years older than I am," President Ballard replied. "I feel honored that the Lord has allowed me to stay and continue the work I'm engaged in. I'm thankful that I have enough energy and health so that I can continue to do my part. I hope I can hang around long enough to get it all done."[16]

As if to underscore the point, six days later, President Ballard and Elder D. Todd Christofferson were in New England. Their first stop was the quiet rural setting of Sharon, Vermont, which is unheralded by most but incredibly significant to the two Church leaders. President Ballard explained:

> We're at the birthplace of a prophet of God. . . . Here on December 23, 1805, a baby with the responsibility of restoring to the earth the fulness of the everlasting gospel was born. . . . I can't get anywhere near this birthplace without having deep affection and love for the Prophet Joseph Smith. I feel obligated to do everything I can to declare and to teach that the gospel is once again on the earth.[17]

"What a special privilege it is to be with President Ballard, to be on assignment together," Elder Christofferson told the *Church News* at the time. "The Restoration and the beginnings of the work in this dispensation are not that far in the past." Then, referring to President Ballard's relationship with the Prophet Joseph and Hyrum Smith, he added, "We're connected to all of it by someone who is living today."[18]

President Ballard and Elder and Sister Christofferson spent about an hour walking around the original Smith home site and strolling down a wooded path to view the foundation of the home where Solomon Mack, the father of Lucy Mack Smith, resided. But it was the granite monument memorializing the birth of the Prophet Joseph

Smith, dedicated by President Joseph F. Smith on December 23, 1905, that most captured President Ballard's attention: "I hope when that day comes, if I get a chance to meet Joseph Smith on the other side, that I can tell him that even sitting at the fireplace of the cottage where he was born was a very important spiritual time in my life."[19]

Before leaving the area, President Ballard and Elder Christofferson addressed 3,200 missionaries in nineteen missions in a broadcast from the visitors' center in Sharon.

The Apostles then traveled to Boston, where they met with government and Church leaders, including Governor Charlie Baker, the governor of Massachusetts; attended sacrament meetings; and spoke to a gathering of young single adults. On Sunday, October 20, they addressed a gathering of 12,000 Latter-day Saints and guests at the DCU Center in Worcester, Massachusetts. Their words were broadcast to Church meetinghouses throughout the New England states of Connecticut, Maine, Massachusetts, New Hampshire, Rhode Island, and Vermont. In his address, President Ballard invited all to "join a new movement," explaining:

> I plead with you this evening to pray for this country, for our leaders, for our people and for the families that live in this great nation founded by God. . . . Our nation was founded on prayer, it was preserved by prayer, and we need prayer again. . . . This country was established and preserved by our founding fathers and mothers who repeatedly acknowledged the hand of God through prayer. We must stand boldly for righteousness and truth, and must defend the cause of honor, decency, and personal freedom.[20]

After the devotional, President Ballard and Elder Christofferson bid farewell to their New England friends and returned to Salt Lake City.

Walking Where Jesus Walked

Historic sites central to the Restoration had long been deeply meaningful to President Ballard. On his way home from his first mission to the British Isles in 1950, he had visited many key Restoration sites in New York. He knew he was walking in the footsteps of his own progenitors, but he also felt the wooded area near Joseph and Lucy Mack Smith's home in Palmyra township was sacred because of the appearance of the Father and the Son to Joseph Smith in 1820.

As his ministry as a General Authority unfolded later in life, President Ballard became familiar with other Church history sites in Ohio, Missouri, Illinois, Nebraska, and Utah. He played a significant role in drawing Church members' attention to them and worked diligently to beautify them, often in cooperation with the leaders of the Community of Christ Church.

In one sense, these sites were part of America's Holy Land. Not only had the Lord appeared and spoken in some of these places, but the angels of God had there conferred priesthood authority and keys, and faithful and dedicated men and women had gathered to build Zion and to listen to a prophet's voice as he shared the Lord's word and will with them.

The Holy Land in the Old World also drew his attention. On his way home from one assignment in 1991, he stopped there for a short visit. It was a wonderful introduction to that special land and helped him appreciate the New Testament more fully.

A few years later, during the 1993 Christmas holidays, Elder and Sister Ballard had organized a family trip to the Holy Land for their adult children and their spouses. The trip provided the family important private time together and allowed them to visit sites associated with the life and ministry of the Savior. But for years after, he had the desire to return again. The pressures of his schedule combined with Barbara's final illness kept this from happening.

A visit to the Holy Land

But then, after Barbara's death, President Ballard decided it was time to make the journey to Jerusalem again. He wanted it to be a personal visit to the Holy Land, without a schedule of meetings and other appointments. Richard Neitzel Holzapfel, an Area Seventy and retired BYU professor who had spent much of his academic career teaching and publishing about the New Testament and traveling to the Holy Land, accompanied him.

Since President Ballard's earlier visit to the Holy Land in 1993, several archaeological discoveries had been opened to visitors, including the traditional site of Jesus's baptism north of the Dead Sea, the town of Migdal (home of Mary Magdalene) on the west side of the Sea of Galilee with its first-century synagogue, the cave where an ancient olive press complex was discovered—literally *Gethsemane* ("olive press") at the foot of the Mount of Olives, and the site in Jerusalem where Jesus met Pilate on His final day on earth.

In Jerusalem, they visited the traditional sites of the Upper Room, the Garden of Gethsemane, Golgotha, and the empty tomb.

In Galilee, President Ballard climbed Mount Arbel, a mountain near the city of Tiberias, with high cliffs and views of Mount Hermon in the Golan Heights. Here he read about the Savior's visit with His eleven disciples after His Resurrection, as recorded in the final chapter of Matthew: "Go ye therefore, and teach all nations, baptizing them in the name of the Father, and of the Son, and of the Holy Ghost: Teaching them to observe all things whatsoever I have commanded you: and, lo, I am with you alway, even unto the end of the world. Amen" (Matthew 28:19–20). He couldn't help but focus on the reality that this commission, given originally to the Savior's Apostles, rests today upon the shoulders of the First Presidency and Quorum of the Twelve Apostles.

President Ballard has taken this responsibility seriously. Though he was on a personal pilgrimage, he shared the gospel as opportunities were open to do so. He formed a connection with a German pastor who was on a bicycle tour with his son. They ran into each other at several different sites, and, by the time they were finished, they had exchanged names and addresses. Later, President Ballard sent his new friend a copy of his book *Our Search for Happiness*.

One site touched President Ballard in a special way. Located on the northern shore of the Sea of Galilee, Tabgha is two miles west of Capernaum and may be the site of the story preserved in John 21 when "Jesus stood on the shore: but the disciples *knew not* that it was Jesus."[21] Jesus asked the disciples if they had caught anything through the night. John noted:

> They answered him, No.
>
> And he said unto them, Cast the net on the right side of the ship, and ye shall find. They cast therefore, and now they were not able to draw it for the multitude of fishes.
>
> Therefore that disciple whom Jesus loved saith unto Peter, It

is the Lord. Now when Simon Peter heard that it was the Lord, he girt his fisher's coat unto him, (for he was naked,) and did cast himself into the sea.

And the other disciples came in a little ship; (for they were not far from land, but as it were two hundred cubits,) dragging the net with fishes.[22]

No one else was present on the shore on the beautiful day when they read the full account in John 21. President Ballard observed after a few moments of silence, "He may have stood here with that great catch of fish flopping around."[23]

He later recalled, "I don't think I have visited that site before. I was really impressed and deeply touched by the story. I felt a connection with Peter and the other Apostles who were command by the Lord to feed His lambs and sheep."[24]

So when they had dined, Jesus saith to Simon Peter, Simon, son of Jonas, lovest thou me more than these? He saith unto him, Yea, Lord; thou knowest that I love thee. He saith unto him, Feed my lambs.

He saith to him again the second time, Simon, son of Jonas, lovest thou me? He saith unto him, Yea, Lord; thou knowest that I love thee. He saith unto him, Feed my sheep.

He saith unto him the third time, Simon, son of Jonas, lovest thou me? Peter was grieved because he said unto him the third time, Lovest thou me? And he said unto him, Lord, thou knowest all things; thou knowest that I love thee. Jesus saith unto him, Feed my sheep.[25]

After returning home from the Holy Land on November 29, 2019, President Ballard jumped back into the work doing just that, feeding the flock. But the methods for doing so were about to change dramatically.

The Worldwide Pandemic

During his more than forty-five years as a General Authority, President Ballard was used to sitting "knee to knee" with local Church leaders around the world. Members had come to enjoy being taught personally by him in priesthood leadership councils, mission tours and conferences, area and stake conferences, youth, temple, and Church school devotionals, and in a myriad of other settings. His personal yet direct style communicated love as well as confidence that those who knew the truth would embrace it and teach it themselves.

Through the years he shook the hands of thousands, tens of thousands, perhaps more; but with ever-increasing numbers of Saints gathered to hear him speak, President Ballard found himself inviting the audience to stand at the conclusion of a meeting and put out their hands in the air. He did the same, and, as he shook his hand, he asked them to shake their hands. He said, "You now have shaken hands with President Ballard!"

His ministry was about to change even more dramatically as a result of a worldwide health crisis that erupted in 2020. The COVID-19 pandemic, with its social distancing, limited numbers at gatherings, travel restrictions, and closed borders made his typical in-person ministry impossible.

After months of pandemic-related adjustments in the way President Ballard and the senior Brethren administered the Church, he told the *Church News* that "we are in a different world. But even though the pandemic hit the world, the Lord provided us a system whereby we could still stay in touch with our people."[26]

That "system" included the use of Zoom, Microsoft Teams, and other videoconferencing capabilities that make it possible to communicate via technology.

"It is what we are doing now—every day," President Ballard said. "In fact, this morning we held our Quorum of the Twelve meeting—half of

Conducting a meeting via Zoom

us were on the fifth floor, and the other half were home getting on via Zoom or in their offices via Zoom.

"We are meeting with missionaries, with priesthood leaders, with sister leaders, in combined leadership conferences with both the men and the women," President Ballard said. "And we don't get on an airplane to do it."

Naturally, President Ballard and other Church leaders would prefer to conduct conferences, devotionals, and other instruction in person and to interact directly with the Saints, he said. But through videoconferencing technology, participants can still see and hear each other and interact in conversational and question-and-answer settings.

"It is not like being in the same room where you can see their faces and shake their hands. But it is wonderful that you can do it, when you can get to them any way you can."

A Historic General Conference

The April 2020 general conference was historic in many ways. Because of the pandemic, it was held virtually, with only those participating in each specific session gathered in the main auditorium of the Church Office Building for the broadcast. The Tabernacle Choir at Temple Square did not perform live.

But other events of greater significance went forward despite the restrictions. President Russell M. Nelson announced and explained a new Church symbol in the Saturday evening session of conference. President Ballard, as the Acting President of the Quorum of the Twelve, was integrally involved with the creation of the new symbol, working with the First Presidency. In the past, the Salt Lake Temple, the angel Moroni, or other visual identifiers had been used as symbols. The new symbol was designed as "a continuation of the effort . . . to focus on the Church's divinely revealed name." The logo was described to the public this way:

> This new emblem emphasizes the name of Jesus Christ and His central role in all the Church does. The name of the Church is contained within a rectangular shape that represents a corner-stone. This idea has biblical roots. The Apostle Paul, employing a construction metaphor in a letter to the first century Saints in Ephesus, wrote that the Church is built upon the foundation of apostles and prophets—Jesus Christ Himself being the chief cornerstone. The center of the symbol is a representation of Thorvaldsen's marble statue, the *Christus*. Jesus stands under an arch as a reminder of His emergence from the tomb three days after His death.
>
> "[The symbol] portrays the resurrected, *living* Lord reaching out to embrace all who will come unto Him," President Nelson said. "This symbol should feel familiar to many, as we have long identified the restored gospel with the *living*, resurrected Christ. . . .
>
> "The symbol will now be used as a visual identifier for official literature, news, and events of the Church. It will remind all that this is the Savior's Church and that all we do, as members of His Church, centers on Jesus Christ and His gospel."[27]

Finally, the April general conference was historic because President Nelson announced a new proclamation, "The Restoration of the Fulness of the Gospel of Jesus Christ: A Bicentennial Proclamation to the World by the First Presidency and Council of the Twelve Apostles." Along with his brethren, President Ballard was involved in preparing the document for publication.

The document was read by President Russell M. Nelson as part of his message on April 5, 2020. The proclamation outlines core Latter-day Saint beliefs, including the supremacy of Jesus Christ in salvation, the divinity of Joseph Smith's revelations and the Book of Mormon, the unique mission of The Church of Jesus Christ of Latter-day Saints, and the ongoing nature of the Restoration that began with Joseph Smith's First Vision of Deity in 1820. It invites people everywhere to know for themselves that God speaks and that this Restoration of truth is occurring to help them prepare for the Second Coming of Jesus Christ.

Ministering to the Saints

As the pandemic continued, so did the ministering of the Twelve continue in unique ways. When President Ballard conducted a leadership conference for those in Cusco, Peru, he made note of the ways in which communication and instruction from Church headquarters continued. Leaders and members residing more than 4,500 miles from Salt Lake City, high in the Peruvian Andes Mountains, joined President Ballard, Elder Patrick Kearon of the Presidency of the Seventy, and Elder Jorge T. Becerra, a General Authority Seventy and counselor in the South America Northwest Area.

From the fifth floor of the Church Administration Building, President Ballard and the others sat in front of several large video screens filled with subscreens of meeting participants, with highlighted viewing windows keying on individuals speaking or asking questions.

Stake, district, and ward council members from six stakes

headquartered in the Peruvian cities of Cusco, Juliaca, Puno, and Sicuani, along with five neighboring districts, attended the Saturday leadership session on August 29, 2020.

The Sunday member devotional on August 30 continued the theme of the leadership session—building faith and confidence in the Lord Jesus Christ and His Atonement during the uncertainties and fears the Cusco-area Latter-day Saints were facing.

Referring to President Spencer W. Kimball's historic and prophetic April 1974 talk, "When the World Will Be Converted," given to General Authorities and regional representatives, President Ballard noted that President Kimball envisioned handheld devices to help others understand the gospel in their native tongues as well as advances of globe-spanning satellite technologies.

Through it all, President Ballard noted that Church leaders were learning a new way to communicate. "The expediency of being able to pull together a group of priesthood leaders or sister leaders and to see that group and teach them, and not have to take, say, three days to get to New Zealand and three days to get back and to be able to sleep in your own bed—that's not too bad."

Concerning the revolutionary events of 2020, President Ballard observed, "I think it will be like everything else—we'll look back on this and say, 'The Lord knew what we needed. He is always ahead of us.'"

Personal Ministry

In addition to utilizing Zoom for Church leadership and member gatherings, President Ballard did not let the pandemic stop his personal ministry.

He had been in the habit of joining people in the hospital, in their homes, and in his office for a visit or blessing. The pandemic virtually stopped that one-on-one ministry. So President Ballard used his phone, iPad, and computer to continue ministering to the one.

An example of his outreach occurred in late July 2020, when President Ballard contacted Avis Clinger. She, her husband, Shane, and their four daughters, Relina, Faith, Abby, and Shae, had been involved in a single-vehicle rollover in northern Utah. Youngest daughter Relina had died on the way to the hospital. Avis's husband, Shane, had been taken to Salt Lake City for emergency care.[28]

During the call, President Ballard listened, ministered, and shared his testimony and counsel. He also took the opportunity to emphasize the plan of salvation and what he had learned about "accidents."

President Ballard commended Sister Clinger for her faith and observed, "We can hear in your voice your testimony." As the visit came to an end, President Ballard said gently, "Continue holding on to the iron rod, as it will lead you to where you want to go." He then asked her to call him back when her husband was in a position to talk. A few hours later, Avis called back, and a similar conversation ensued.

Though his desk was full of letters, notes, and minutes needing attention, and there were any number of General Authorities waiting in line to counsel with him on one matter or another, President Ballard believed that visiting individual members and their families, in person or through technology, was what his ministry was really about.

He had observed many times that, when ministering to the one, the giver always receives more than he or she gives. Whether it be in a refugee camp in Greece or Ethiopia or in a palace or place of government, the giver learns that people are resilient and courageous.

While President Ballard was visiting his son Craig in the hospital after he had been injured in a bicycle accident, one of Craig's therapists asked if he had time to walk down the hall and visit a young woman who had been involved in a tragic automobile accident resulting in the loss of both of her legs. The young woman was Sarah Frei.

President Ballard readily agreed and went to Sarah's room to meet her. In Sarah, he found a strong, confident, faith-filled young woman, and he was touched by her faith and determination. Before leaving, he

With Sarah Frei

gave Sarah a blessing and then maintained regular contact while she was in the hospital. As they finished their phone calls, President Ballard would ask her, "What do I want you to do?" Sarah would repeat, "Keep up your courage and hang in there!"

From his first experience in full-time ministering as a missionary to the British Isles, to his labors as a bishop, mission president, and General Authority, President Ballard often pondered the significance and meaning of the Savior's teachings in Matthew 25:

> Then shall the King say unto them on his right hand, Come, ye blessed of my Father, inherit the kingdom prepared for you from the foundation of the world:
>
> For I was an hungred, and ye gave me meat: I was thirsty, and ye gave me drink: I was a stranger, and ye took me in:

Naked, and ye clothed me: I was sick, and ye visited me: I was in prison, and ye came unto me.

Then shall the righteous answer him, saying, Lord, when saw we thee an hungred, and fed thee? or thirsty, and gave thee drink? When saw we thee a stranger, and took thee in? or naked, and clothed thee? Or when saw we thee sick, or in prison, and came unto thee?

And the King shall answer and say unto them, Verily I say unto you, Inasmuch as ye have done it unto one of the least of these my brethren, ye have done it unto me.[29]

In many ways, the pandemic that began in 2020 drew the importance of ministering into sharp focus.

"From the beginning of history there have been circumstances similar to this one," President Ballard said. "Somehow, they got through them, and we are going to get through this one.

"The Lord Jesus Christ loves us with a love beyond our ability to comprehend. The kingdom of God will continue to roll forth. Everything is going to be just fine as we turn our hearts to our Father in Heaven and look to Him and to the Savior as the Redeemer of all mankind."[30]

An Enduring Legacy

Despite world circumstances, President Ballard pressed on. "As an apostle of the Lord Jesus Christ," he declared, "I have a solemn duty to bear witness of the Lord and deliver his message. His words often include words of encouragement and expressions of love. They also include words of warning."[31]

And so it will continue, he said, until the Lord determines otherwise.

"I've seen my dad walk through the door very weary," said President Ballard's daughter Stacey Murdock. "I have wondered if he could take another step. It is then I see him pull from his wallet a tiny picture of the Savior and pause to remember Gethsemane. Somehow this helps him to keep going."[32]

Fatigue notwithstanding, President Ballard has no intention of taking a day off or planning out his funeral arrangements. "We [in the Twelve] kid him that it might be time to consider a headstone with the inscription 'Brethren, keep it simple,'" jokes Elder Jeffrey R. Holland.[33] Knowing his determination to press on, Elder Dieter F. Uchtdorf wrote, "You have our prayers and support as you go forward in the work of the Lord."[34]

With his forward emphasis, it is difficult for him to pause and reflect upon his legacy to the Church and kingdom of God. But those who work with him daily are quick to reflect on his unique style of leadership.

"President Ballard will certainly be remembered as one who knows to counsel in councils in an inspired and inspiring way," said Elder Uchtdorf.[35] Elder D. Todd Christofferson said, "President Ballard can be credited with almost singlehandedly reestablishing the use of councils in Church government at every level."

"The need to spread the gospel seems to just eat at him," says Elder Dale G. Renlund.[36] Elder Holland agrees and adds, "He lives, thinks, and breathes missionary work all the time. . . . If we were all as missionary minded as Russell Ballard, we would be adding millions to the Church each year, not just hundreds of thousands."[37] Elder David A. Bednar said:

> There are four words that characterize President Ballard to me. He is *wise*. He does not rush to a conclusion. His wisdom is knowing that the Lord is at the helm and he is willing to wait upon Him. President Ballard is *steady*—unflappable. He often says, "Just relax. This will work out." He is *practical,* not in the pedestrian sense. He knows how to take the complex and translate it into day-to-day terms that bless members throughout

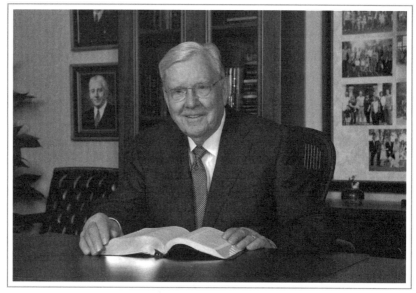

President M. Russell Ballard

the world. His legacy is, he is the *link* to the earliest days of the Restoration. There is a portrait of Joseph Smith in the temple where we hold our meetings. As I look at the portrait and then at President Ballard, I realize that we are not far removed from the early days of the Church. To me President Ballard is the "Grandpa of the Church" in appearance, demeanor, love and affection for everyone.[38]

President Ballard is grateful for the love of his brethren in the Twelve, but from his point of view, any talk of legacy begins and ends with his testimony of Jesus Christ and the Restoration of the gospel through the Prophet Joseph Smith:

> I want all of my family, children, grandchildren, great-grandchildren, and their companions in the generations yet to be born, and my friends throughout the world, to know that as I have experienced life with its trials and successes, my testimony of our Father in Heaven and the life and ministry of His Beloved Son, the Lord Jesus Christ, has progressively grown stronger.

I know of no gift that I could leave to those I love that will be as important and precious as my sure witness that the gospel of Jesus Christ has been restored to the earth through the Prophet Joseph Smith, my testimony that the holy priesthood has been restored with the power to bless and perform all the essential ordinances of eternal salvation. I consider it one of the great blessings of my life to have been able to bless and perform all priesthood ordinances, including sealing to their companions, for my seven wonderful children and many of my grandchildren.

My testimony that the Book of Mormon is the word of God and another testament of Jesus Christ has been borne to the many nations of the earth because of the wonderful privilege that has been mine to serve as a General Authority of the Church. I have worked side by side with prophets and apostles of this, the last dispensation of time. My association with these remarkable men of the apostleship as well as those who have served in the Presiding Bishopric and the Quorums of the Seventy around the world has been a blessing beyond my capacity to express in words.

It is the will of our Father in Heaven, through His Beloved Son, the Lord Jesus Christ, that this mighty work moves forward. This is His gospel. He stands at the head—holy, divine, supreme, full of power, majesty, grace, and truth. He lived for us, and He died for us, because He loves us. I love Him more deeply and powerfully than I can find words to express. He is my Lord, my Savior, my Redeemer, and my friend. I know that Jesus Christ is the Son of God our Eternal Father. He lives and directs His Church today through His prophet and His Apostles. His great work will continue to roll forth until it fills the whole earth.

This is my testimony in the name of the Lord Jesus Christ, amen.

—M. RUSSELL BALLARD

SELECTED
WRITINGS

Classic Talks by M. Russell Ballard

"Making Your Influence Felt," BYU–Idaho Commencement, April 11, 2008

"That the Lost May Be Found," General Conference, April 2012

"Let Us Think Straight," BYU Devotional, August 20, 2013

"Be Still, and Know That I Am God," CES Devotional for Young Adults, May 4, 2014

"Stay in the Boat and Hold On!" General Conference, October 2014

"Women of Dedication, Faith, Determination, and Action," BYU Women's Conference, May 1, 2015

"God Is at the Helm," General Conference, October 2015

"To the Saints of the Utah Salt Lake Area," Salt Lake City Multi-stake Conference Broadcast, September 11, 2016

"To Whom Shall We Go?" General Conference, October 2016

"Questions and Answers," BYU Devotional, November 14, 2017

"The Vision of the Redemption of the Dead," General Conference, October 2018

"Watch Ye Therefore, and Pray Always," General Conference, October 2020

Books by M. Russell Ballard

Our Search for Happiness: An Invitation to Understand The Church of Jesus Christ of Latter-day Saints, 1993

Suicide: Some Things We Know, and Some We Do Not, 1993

Counseling with Our Councils: Learning to Minister Together in the Church and in the Family, 1997, revised 2016

The Law of Sacrifice—What Came from Kirtland, 1998

When Thou Art Converted: Continuing Our Search for Happiness, 2001

As Women of God, 2002

Daughters of God, 2009

One Drop at a Time: A Message for Women, 2013

Yesterday, Today, and Forever: Timeless Gospel Messages with Insights from His Grandfathers, Melvin J. Ballard and Hyrum Mack Smith, 2015

Our Family Council Journal, 2016

His Daughters, His Disciples, 2019

NOTES

CHAPTER ONE
Family Matters

1. Susan Easton Black, "How Large Was the Population of Nauvoo?" *BYU Studies Quarterly,* vol. 35, no. 2.
2. Karl Ricks Anderson Letter, June 19, 2020.
3. Emma Smith Bidamon Letter, December 2, 1867; "Notes," MRB Journal #13.
4. "Notes," MRB Journal #11.
5. Karl Ricks Anderson Letter, June 19, 2020.
6. *Church News,* August 10, 1995; "Notes," MRB Journal #13.
7. *Church News,* August 10, 1995; "Notes," MRB Journal #13; *Ensign,* November 1991. Elder Ballard later added, "When I go to Nauvoo, the temple is overwhelming and it's marvelous to behold and participate in, but there's something that happens when I walk onto the family cemetery plot, and there lie the remains of Joseph and Hyrum and Emma and Joseph Smith Sr., and Lucy Mack and Samuel and others of the Smith family. It's a sacred place, and we have raised the necessary funds to ensure that it remains beautiful" ("Smith Family Heritage," M. Russell Ballard Oral History, Updated Volume, 2005).
8. Karl Ricks Anderson Letter, June 19, 2020.
9. Thomas S. Monson Interview, June 29, 2006.
10. M. Russell Ballard, "What Matters Most Is What Lasts Longest," *Ensign,* November 2005.
11. M. Russell Ballard, quoted in Carolyn Hyde, *On the Lord's Errand: A Biography of Elder M. Russell Ballard of the Quorum of the Twelve Apostles* (Salt Lake City: M. Russell Ballard, 2007), 31.

12. M. Russell Ballard Interview, June 6, 2019; Hyde, *On the Lord's Errand*, vii.
13. Ann Keddington Interview, August 23, 2006.
14. Information from notes taken by Heber G. Wolsey during a personal interview with Melvin R. Ballard, June 8, 1967. Heber G. Wolsey, "Religious Broadcasting by the LDS Church," MA thesis, Northwestern University.
15. G. Homer Durham, quoted in Hyde, *On the Lord's Errand*, 39. Nate Wade said of Elder Ballard's mother, "His mother was a real lady. Very quiet, but beautiful and kind. She never learned to drive." Nate/Bonnie Wade Interview, January 26, 2006.
16. Utah, Select County Marriages 1887–1966.

CHAPTER TWO

"Something Special Going on Here"

1. Ann Keddington Interview, August 23, 2006.
2. Carolyn Hyde, *On the Lord's Errand: A Biography of Elder M. Russell Ballard of the Quorum of the Twelve Apostles* (Salt Lake City: M. Russell Ballard, 2007), 33–34.
3. M. Russell Ballard Interview, June 6, 2019.
4. Ann Keddington Interview, August 23, 2006.
5. Hyde, *On the Lord's Errand*, 32.
6. M. Russell Ballard Interview, August 7, 2006.
7. M. Russell Ballard Interview, August 7, 2006.
8. Hyde, *On the Lord's Errand*, 27.
9. Hyde, *On the Lord's Errand*, 26; M. Russell Ballard, *Yesterday, Today, and Forever: Timeless Gospel Messages with Insights from His Grandfathers Melvin J. Ballard and Hyrum Mack Smith* (Salt Lake City: Deseret Book, 2015), 111; M. Russell Ballard, *When Thou Art Converted: Continuing Our Search for Happiness* (Salt Lake City: Deseret Book, 2001), 205–6.
10. M. Russell Ballard, "Building Kinder, Gentler Homes," Salt Lake Holladay Regional Conference, January 22, 1989.
11. Ballard, *When Thou Art Converted*, 9–10.
12. The Nash 10 Point Award was based on (1) Capital, (2) Floor Space, (3) Location, (4) Identification, (5) Appearance, (6) Service, (7) Parts, (8) New Car Showroom, (9) Used Car Display Facility, and (10) Accounting ("Congratulations to Ballard Motor Co. 633 South Main on receiving the Nash 10 Point Award," in MRB Scrapbook #39, January 2016 through December 2016).
13. B. C. Forbes and O. D. Foster, *Automotive Giants of America: Men Who Are Making Our Motor Industry* (Jersey City, NJ: Forbes Publishing, 2003), 211–13.
14. Hyde, *On the Lord's Errand*, 26–27.
15. M. Russell Ballard, "Let Us Think Straight," Brigham Young University Devotional, November 29, 1983. Elder Jeffrey R. Holland said, "[Elder Ballard] has a quote that he loves from his Grandfather Ballard which says, 'Brethren, let us think straight.' That's Russell Ballard. . . . I have said he has good street smarts. He has good instincts. . . . I have seldom known anyone who could get to the heart of

the matter more quickly and more precisely than President Ballard does in examining any issue, however complex it may be. He has uncommon good judgment" (Jeffrey R. Holland Interview, May 2, 2006; Jeffrey R. Holland Letter, September 24, 2019). Elder Neil L. Andersen wrote to Elder Ballard, "I love the quote you have in your office from your Grandfather, Elder Melvin J. Ballard, "Above all else, Brethren, let us think straight." Your Grandfather would be proud of how you bring that quality to the Quorum of the Twelve" (Neil L. Andersen Letter, October 8, 2009).

16. M. Russell Ballard Interview, February 6, 2020.

17. Hyde, *On the Lord's Errand*, 29.

18. M. Russell Ballard Interview, February 6, 2020.

19. Ann Keddington Interview, August 23, 2006.

20. Ann Keddington Interview, August 23, 2006.

21. Ann Keddington Interview, August 23, 2006.

22. Ballard, *Yesterday, Today, and Forever*, 166–67.

23. Hyde, *On the Lord's Errand*, 33.

24. Hyde, *On the Lord's Errand*, 37.

25. James E. Faust, quoted in Hyde, *On the Lord's Errand*, 33.

26. M. Russell Ballard Interview, June 6, 2019.

27. Ann Keddington Interview, August 23, 2006.

28. His high school friends became his lifelong friends and formed a study group that met often. Elder Ballard said, "We take great interest in one another's welfare and support of one another as well as each other's families" (M. Russell Ballard Interview, August 7, 2006).

29. Hyde, *On the Lord's Errand*, 26.

30. Elder Ballard shared this story with his seventeen-year-old daughter who had been studying for a chemistry test and wanted his help. After telling of his experience in a chemistry class, Elder Ballard said to his daughter, "We are in real trouble. The only thing I know that I can do in the timeframe that you have left is we could go into the office and kneel down and ask the Lord to bless you. . . . We did not ask for a miracle. We simply asked that Heavenly Father enlighten her mind and that somehow by the power of the Holy Ghost, bring back to her remembrance what she had studied for 35 hours that she might be successful in the test that she was to take the next day. . . . She got the third highest score in the whole class" (M. Russell Ballard, "The Divine Nature of the Human Soul," Monument Park 11th Ward Sacrament Meeting, January 20, 1980).

31. M. Russell Ballard Interview, February 6, 2020.

32. M. Russell Ballard Interview, February 6, 2020.

33. "Notes," MRB Journal #4.

34. M. Russell Ballard Interview, February 6, 2020.

35. *Deseret News*, April 16, 1946; "Notes," MRB Journal #1.

36. In January 1991, Elder Ballard was honored as a "Significant Sig" at the Sigma Chi Fraternity reception held at the Huntsmans' Lodge in Deer Valley, Utah. On that occasion, Murray K. McComas said, "Our fraternity is indeed fortunate to

have alumni such as you. Your personal achievements outside of Sigma Chi have brought great honor to the Fraternity and I am delighted that you are now among the ranks of Significant Sigs" ("Notes," MRB Journal #17).

CHAPTER THREE
A Mission to England

1. "Notes," MRB Journal #4. Elder Ballard spoke at the funeral service for Elder G. Homer Durham on January 14, 1985. He said on that occasion, "I had the opportunity to choose from many different sources those whom I would like to speak at my farewell when I left the University Ward to go to England on my mission. Often Homer and I talked about that experience where he spoke at my farewell. I am grateful to have the privilege to speak at his today" ("Notes," MRB Journal #5).
2. M. Russell Ballard Interview, January 21, 2020.
3. Carolyn Hyde, *On the Lord's Errand: A Biography of Elder M. Russell Ballard of the Quorum of the Twelve Apostles* (Salt Lake City: M. Russell Ballard, 2007), 121–22.
4. M. Russell Ballard, "Success through Faith in Christ and Obedience," Missionary Training Satellite Broadcast, August 28, 1998.
5. Hyde, *On the Lord's Errand*, 122.
6. Hyde, *On the Lord's Errand*, 122.
7. M. Russell Ballard British Mission, Missionary Journals, April 11, 1948; Ballard, "Success through Faith in Christ."
8. M. Russell Ballard, *When Thou Art Converted: Continuing Our Search for Happiness* (Salt Lake City: Deseret Book, 2001), 180–81; Ballard, "Success through Faith in Christ."
9. Hyde, *On the Lord's Errand*, 124.
10. MRB Journal, April 25, 1948.
11. M. Russell Ballard, *Yesterday, Today, and Forever: Timeless Gospel Messages with Insights from His Grandfathers Melvin J. Ballard and Hyrum Mack Smith* (Salt Lake City: Deseret Book, 2015), 1.
12. "Dear Hugh: Your companionship then and your friendship these many years are precious to me" (M. Russell Ballard Letter, February 1, 2011).
13. Hyde, *On the Lord's Errand*, 124–25.
14. Hyde, *On the Lord's Errand*, 125–26.
15. "Pres. Ballard, Congratulations! I'm not sure how to express my feelings about your new assignment [Acting President of the Quorum of the Twelve Apostles]; having watched your change of responsibilities in the leadership of the church over the years, to say the least, it has been very exciting; and continues to be. It seems awesome, overwhelming, only you will know; but, you are prepared. I must say, 'I trained you well.' I am no John the Baptist; but, as your mission forerunner, I should have recognized you more definitely when we were Elders in England; I am seeing more clearly now" (Keith E. Tibbitts Letter, January 30, 2018).

16. M. Russell Ballard, "The Great Blessing of the Comforter," Preston England Temple Dedication, June 8, 1998.
17. MRB Journal, May 11, 1948.
18. MRB Journal, May 11, 1948.
19. MRB Journal, May 15, 1948.
20. MRB Journal, May 16, 1948.
21. M. Russell Ballard Interview, January 21, 2020.
22. MRB Journal, May 20, 1948.
23. Hyde, *On the Lord's Errand*, 139–40.
24. MRB Journal, May 20, 1948.
25. MRB Journal, July 10, 1948.
26. Harold B. Lee Letter, July 28, 1948; "Notes," MRB Journal #25.
27. Selvoy J. Boyer, "British Mission Today," *Millennial Star*, vol. 111, no. 7 (July 1949): 196.
28. MRB Journal, August 7, 1948.
29. MRB Journal, August 9, 1948.
30. MRB Journal, August 10, 1948.
31. MRB Journal, August 26, 1948.
32. MRB Journal, September 7, 1948.
33. M. Russell Ballard, "There Is Great Strength in the Women of the Church," Preston England Temple Dedication, June 9, 1998.
34. MRB Journal, February 26, 1949.
35. M. Russell Ballard, *Our Search for Happiness: An Invitation to Understand The Church of Jesus Christ of Latter-day Saints* (Salt Lake City: Deseret Book, 1993), 7–8.
36. Hyde, *On the Lord's Errand*, 139; Ballard, "Success through Faith in Christ."
37. Salt Lake Temple Minutes, January 7, 1919; *Melvin J. Ballard, Crusader for Righteousness* (Salt Lake City: Bookcraft, 1966), 65–66; Ballard, *When Thou Art Converted*, 12; Ballard, *Our Search for Happiness*, 19.
38. M. Russell Ballard Interview, January 21, 2020.
39. M. Russell Ballard Interview, June 6, 2019.
40. MRB Journal, January 16, 1949.
41. Elder Ballard said, "For many years basketball was used to advantage in placing the name of the Church before sporting fans of the world. The London team has won the national senior basketball championship of England and Wales for the past two years" ("Notes," MRB Journal #1).
42. MRB Journal, April 28, 1949.
43. "Geraldine Anthony emigrated decades ago with her husband Tom and $1.00 in her pocket. . . . She said the dollar was given to her by a young missionary, Elder Russell Ballard" (Jeff O'Driscoll Letter, January 15, 1999; "Notes," MRB Journal #25).
44. Ballard, "There Is Great Strength in the Women."
45. MRB Journal, May 5, 1949.
46. MRB Journal, July 11, 1949.

47. Ballard, "Great Blessing of the Comforter."
48. MRB Journal, October 9, 1949; Ballard, *Our Search for Happiness*, 24.
49. Ballard, "Great Blessing of the Comforter."
50. Ballard, "Great Blessing of the Comforter."
51. Hyde, *On the Lord's Errand*, 145.
52. MRB Journal, November 2, 1949.
53. "New Member of Mission Presidency Announced," *Millennial Star*, December 1949.
54. Ballard, "There Is Great Strength in the Women."
55. Hyde, *On the Lord's Errand*, 147.
56. Hyde, *On the Lord's Errand*, 147.
57. Hyde, *On the Lord's Errand*, 147.
58. Hyde, *On the Lord's Errand*, 148.
59. Hyde, *On the Lord's Errand*, 148.
60. MRB Letter, January 1, 1950; "Notes," MRB Journal #25.
61. MRB Journal, February 19, 1950.
62. M. Russell Ballard Interview, June 6, 2019.
63. Ballard, "Great Blessing of the Comforter."
64. M. Russell Ballard Interview, August 7, 2006; M. Russell Ballard, "The Hearts of the Children," Logan Temple Rededication, March 14, 1979.
65. Ballard, "Hearts of the Children"; M. Russell Ballard, "My Heart Has Been Turned to My Fathers," Boise Temple Dedication, May 27, 1984.
66. Hyde, *On the Lord's Errand*, 153.
67. Hyde, *On the Lord's Errand*, 154.
68. M. Russell Ballard Interview, June 6, 2019.
69. M. Russell Ballard Interview, June 6, 2019.
70. "Notes," MRB Journal #14.
71. "Notes," MRB Journal #20; M. Russell Ballard, "May We Make Right Choices," Fresno California Temple Dedication, April 9, 2000.
72. Chaunie Larson Interview, August 23, 2006.
73. Hyde, *On the Lord's Errand*, 154.
74. Hyde, *On the Lord's Errand*, 154; Ballard, "My Heart Has Been Turned."

CHAPTER FOUR

Courtship and Marriage

1. M. Russell Ballard, "Following Up," *Ensign*, May 2014.
2. "Sister Barbara Bowen Ballard, Wife of President M. Russell Ballard, Dies at 86," *Church News*, October 1, 2018.
3. Carolyn Hyde, *On the Lord's Errand: A Biography of Elder M. Russell Ballard of the Quorum of the Twelve Apostles* (Salt Lake City: M. Russell Ballard, 2007), 44.
4. Ballard, "Following Up."
5. Hyde, *On the Lord's Errand*, 44.
6. "Sister Barbara Bowen Ballard."

7. Hyde, *On the Lord's Errand*, 44.
8. 1940 US Federal Census.
9. M. Russell Ballard Interview, June 6, 2019.
10. Russell baptized Arthur W. Jackson, a friend at the University of Utah. "Notes," MRB Journal #26.
11. Thomas S. Monson Interview, June 29, 2006.
12. Patriarchal Blessing, October 11, 1950.
13. M. Russell Ballard Interview, May 14, 2020. He added: "I wish I knew what happened to that sweater set. We should have put it in a frame and hung it on a wall, it was such a sweet part of our story."
14. Barbara Ballard, "People of Vision" Award Video, November 17, 2003.
15. Barbara Ballard, "Our Life's Values," Montpelier Idaho Regional Conference, June 3, 2000.
16. M. Russell Ballard Interview, June 6, 2019.
17. "Sister Barbara Bowen Ballard"; M. Russell Ballard Interview, June 6, 2019.
18. M. Russell Ballard, *When Thou Art Converted: Continuing Our Search for Happiness* (Salt Lake City: Deseret Book, 2001), 7–8.
19. Hyde, *On the Lord's Errand*, 45.
20. M. Russell Ballard recollection of discussion with Allen MacKay Acomb, in MRB Scrapbook #30.
21. M. Russell Ballard Interview, May 12, 2020.
22. Utah Select Marriage Index 1887–1985. M. Russell Ballard and Barbara Bowen married August 28, 1951, in Salt Lake City.
23. M. Russell Ballard, address at Utah North Multistake Conference, October 28, 2018.
24. M. Russell Ballard Interview, January 21, 2020.
25. "Notes," MRB Journal #2; Hyde, *On the Lord's Errand*, viii; "Sister Barbara Bowen Ballard."

CHAPTER FIVE

Starting a Career

1. US Certification of Military Service, March 13, 1953; Army of the United States Military Certificate, March 9, 1953.
2. Carolyn Hyde, *On the Lord's Errand: A Biography of Elder M. Russell Ballard of the Quorum of the Twelve Apostles* (Salt Lake City: M. Russell Ballard, 2007), 42. Russ eventually became a first lieutenant and served faithfully as an army reserve officer until he was honorably discharged on March 11, 1960.
3. "Our Favorite Facebook Posts from Church Leaders This Year," *LDSLiving*, November 14, 2017.
4. Hyde, *On the Lord's Errand*, 22.
5. "Righteous Expectations: Elder Ballard Speaks at Salt Lake Institute," *Church News*, January 31, 2016.
6. M. Russell Ballard, "O Be Wise," Young Single Adult Fireside, February 2006.

7. Thomas S. Monson Interview, June 29, 2006.
8. US City Directories, 1822–1995, Salt Lake City Utah Directory, 1953.
9. Frederick J. Bell quote, in "Notes," MRB Journal #1.
10. M. Russell Ballard Interview, May 21, 2020.
11. On July 19, 1992, Kay Stoker died. At the time, he was president of Gateway Mining Company and the La Teko Mining Company. "Notes," MRB Journals #14 and #15.
12. Hyde, *On the Lord's Errand*, 45.
13. US City Directories, 1822–1955, Salt Lake City Utah Directory, 1956, 1958.
14. M. Russell Ballard Interview, May 21, 2020.
15. Hyde, *On the Lord's Errand*, 60.
16. FindAGrave. James Russell Bowen.
17. M. Russell Ballard Interview, January 19, 2020.
18. "Notes," MRB Journal #12; M. Russell Ballard, *When Thou Art Converted: Continuing Our Search for Happiness* (Salt Lake City: Deseret Book, 2001), 70–72.
19. "Notes," MRB Journal #12; M. Russell Ballard, *Yesterday, Today, and Forever: Timeless Gospel Messages with Insights from His Grandfathers Melvin J. Ballard and Hyrum Mack Smith* (Salt Lake City: Deseret Book, 2015), 51.
20. Ballard, *Yesterday, Today, and Forever*, 50.
21. "Notes," MRB Journal #12.
22. "Notes," MRB Journal #12; M. Russell Ballard, "In Search of Spiritual Strength," University of Utah Institute of Religion, September 28, 1980.
23. Nate/Bonnie Wade Interview, January 26, 2006.
24. "Obituary," *Deseret News*, August 25, 2019. President Ballard spoke at the funeral of Nate Wade on September 4, 2019, saying of him: "He was a good man, lived a good life, and I say goodbye for a short season. . . . We can rejoice that Nate was a faithful member of the Church. Whenever there was a need at a welfare farm or the temple he was willing to volunteer to do his part. Nate and I knelt in prayer hundreds of times which is a precious remembrance to me of my dear friend. Nate's business philosophy was 'A fair deal must be good for both sides.'"
25. "Obituary," *Deseret News*, August 25, 2019.
26. Elder Jeffrey R. Holland said, "One time we were in a meeting wrestling with some difficult challenges, and [Elder Ballard] stopped and said, "Well, now, brethren, this isn't nearly as hard as selling used cars" ("People of Vision" Award Video, November 17, 2003).
27. *Salt Lake Tribune*, March 4, 1990.
28. Nate/Bonnie Wade Interview, January 26, 2006.
29. Thomas S. Monson Interview, June 29, 2006.
30. M. Russell Ballard Interview, August 7, 2006.
31. M. Russell Ballard, *Counseling with Our Councils: Learning to Minister Together in the Church and in the Family* (Salt Lake City: Deseret Book, 2012), 8.
32. M. Russell Ballard Interview, August 7, 2006.
33. Nate/Bonnie Wade Interview, January 26, 2006; Remarks of President Ballard at the funeral of Nate Wade, September 4, 2019.

34. Statement of L. Kouns, western regional sales manager of Ford Motor Company, in "Notes," MRB Journal #1.

35. M. Russell Ballard Interview, July 25, 2019; M. Russell Ballard, "Let Us Think Straight," Brigham Young University Devotional, November 29, 1983.

36. M. Russell Ballard, *Our Search for Happiness: An Invitation to Understand The Church of Jesus Christ of Latter-day Saints* (Salt Lake City: Deseret Book, 1993), 85–86.

37. Nate/Bonnie Wade Interview, January 26, 2006.

38. Ballard, "Let Us Think Straight."

39. Hyde, *On the Lord's Errand,* 49; Ballard, *Our Search for Happiness,* 86.

40. Hyde, *On the Lord's Errand,* 50.

41. Hyde, *On the Lord's Errand,* 50.

42. M. Russell Ballard Interview, January 19, 2020.

43. The Holladay Twelfth Ward was formed by a division of the Holladay Seventh Ward. On January 17, 1960, the ward boundaries were again changed. Families residing west of Wasatch Boulevard were invited to attend the Holladay Fifteenth Ward. The boundary change led to Glendon M. Whitmore becoming first counselor and Boyd Nielson, second counselor to Bishop M. Russell Ballard. "Notes," MRB Journal #1.

44. "Notes," MRB Journal #1; Ballard, *When Thou Art Converted,* 103.

45. Ballard, *Counseling with Our Councils,* 127; M. Russell Ballard Interview, June 6, 2019.

46. M. Russell Ballard, "Safely Dead, With Testimonies Burning Brightly," Denver Colorado Temple Dedication, October 28, 1986.

47. "Notes," MRB Journal #21.

48. "Notes," MRB Journal #21; "Deacons of the Holladay 12th Ward, Olympus Stake," *Church News,* April 1, 1961; "Deacons of Quorum 100%ers," *Church News,* October 5, 1996.

49. M. Russell Ballard Interview, June 6, 2019.

50. "Notes," MRB Journal #25. The *Church News* of July 3, 1999, reported a reunion held on June 13, 1999, for the "youth" of the ward. They mingled with the priesthood leaders who had so much influence on their lives, but now the former youth were bishops themselves, stake presidents, high councilors, Relief Society presidents, and mission presidents. As Elder Ballard put it, "They are the fruit of one ward's determination to nurture its youth."

51. Hyde, *On the Lord's Errand,* 63.

52. Hyde, *On the Lord's Errand,* 67–68.

53. Hyde, *On the Lord's Errand,* 78.

54. M. Russell Ballard, "The Role of the Spirit in Missionary Work," New Mission Presidents' Seminar, June 22, 1993.

55. Ballard, "Role of the Spirit in Missionary Work"; Hyde, *On the Lord's Errand,* 66.

56. Ballard, *Counseling with Our Councils,* 16–18.

57. Ballard, *Counseling with Our Councils,* 16–18.

58. Ballard, *Counseling with Our Councils,* 67–68.

59. Nate/Bonnie Wade Interview, January 26, 2006.
60. Hyde, *On the Lord's Errand*, 64–65; Ballard, *When Thou Art Converted*, 104–5.
61. Hyde, *On the Lord's Errand*, 68.
62. M. Russell Ballard Interview, June 6, 2019; Hyde, *On the Lord's Errand*, 76–77; M. Russell Ballard, *Daughters of God* (Salt Lake City: Deseret Book, 2009), 2–3.

CHAPTER SIX

Young Man in a Hurry

1. Art Linkletter statement for "Helping Hand" Award, September 25, 2002; M. Russell Ballard, *Yesterday, Today, and Forever: Timeless Gospel Messages with Insights from His Grandfathers Melvin J. Ballard and Hyrum Mack Smith* (Salt Lake City: Deseret Book, 2015), 164.
2. Linkletter statement for "Helping Hand" Award.
3. US City Directories, 1822–1995, Salt Lake City Utah Directory, 1965.
4. Valley Music Hall, *Camelot* production program; "Notes," MRB Journal #1.
5. "Scores of Famous Stars to Attend Grand Opening Valley Music Hall," *Salt Lake Tribune,* July 4, 1965.
6. Thomas S. Monson Interview, June 29, 2006.
7. M. Russell Ballard Interview, June 6, 2019.
8. Thomas S. Monson Interview, June 29, 2006.
9. Thomas S. Monson Interview, June 29, 2006.
10. Boyd K. Packer Interview, April 26, 2006.
11. LeGrand Richards, quoted in Carolyn Hyde, *On the Lord's Errand: A Biography of Elder M. Russell Ballard of the Quorum of the Twelve Apostles* (Salt Lake City: M. Russell Ballard, 2007), 68; M. Russell Ballard, "When Someone Cares," Church Employees Devotional, February 27, 1981.
12. M. Russell Ballard, "Having Great Desires to Know the Mysteries of God," Missionary Fireside, Orem, Utah, September 26, 1996.
13. M. Russell Ballard Interview, June 6, 2019.
14. Hyde, *On the Lord's Errand*, 69.
15. M. Russell Ballard, *When Thou Art Converted: Continuing Our Search for Happiness* (Salt Lake City: Deseret Book, 2001), 140.
16. Ballard, *When Thou Art Converted*, 141–42.
17. Years later, one of his priests, Steve Holbrook, recalled, "He would take each of us out to lunch when we would get our mission calls. It was at Fred's Burger Chalet, which was right next to his office." Scott Lloyd, "Part of a Rich Family Legacy," *Church News,* February 11, 2018.
18. M. Russell Ballard Interview, June 6, 2019.
19. Hyde, *On the Lord's Errand*, 79.
20. M. Russell Ballard, "The Eternal Perspective of the Family," Reno Nevada Temple Dedication, April 23, 2000.
21. Brynn Ballard Huntsman, 2006, in M. Russell Ballard Papers.
22. Clark Ballard, quoted in Hyde, *On the Lord's Errand,* 102.

23. Hyde, *On the Lord's Errand,* 114.
24. Hyde, *On the Lord's Errand.*
25. Meleea Ballard, quoted in Hyde, *On the Lord's Errand,* 85.
26. Hyde, *On the Lord's Errand*; Clark Ballard comments in "People of Vision" Award Video, November 17, 2003.
27. Stacey Ballard Murdock Letter, December 13, 1981; "Notes," MRB Journal #4. Son-in-law Paul Clayton said of his father-in-law, M. Russell Ballard, "He is an amazing example of being a father. He will be gone for a week or ten days on a Church assignment and that night or the next morning telephone each of his children to make sure everyone is all right. It is not just checking the box for him, he is concerned." Paul Clayton Interview, October 4, 2019.
28. Linkletter statement for "Helping Hand" Award, September 25, 2002.
29. M. Russell Ballard Interview.
30. Robert Pedersen, quoted in Hyde, *On the Lord's Errand,* 57.
31. Ballard, "The Eternal Perspective," address in Guam, 1977.
32. M. Russell Ballard, *Our Search for Happiness: An Invitation to Understand The Church of Jesus Christ of Latter-day Saints* (Salt Lake City: Deseret Book, 1993); Ballard, *Yesterday, Today, and Forever,* 165–66; M. Russell Ballard Interview, June 6, 2019; Ballard, "Eternal Perspective," Guam.
33. *Church News,* November 10, 1970.
34. *Church News,* August 8, 1970; "Notes," MRB Journal #1.
35. M. Russell Ballard Letter, April 15, 1971; "Notes," MRB Journal #1.
36. M. Russell Ballard Letter, April 15, 1971; "Notes," MRB Journal #1.
37. Thomas S. Monson Interview, June 29, 2006.
38. Julie A. Dockstader, "Lord Has a Way of Turning Adversity to Good," *Church News,* February 9, 1991.
39. Dockstader, "Lord Has a Way."
40. In 1974 it became Nate Wade Subaru, which continues today (2019) as America's oldest Subaru dealership. "Obituary," *Deseret News,* August 25, 2019.
41. MRB dictation for biography, August 7, 2006; Ballard, *When Thou Art Converted,* 209–11.

CHAPTER SEVEN

President of the Canada Toronto Mission

1. M. Russell Ballard speech at the Provo Utah Chamber of Commerce, March 1983, as reported in the *Daily Herald,* March 24, 1983; "Notes," MRB Journal #3.
2. "Elder M. Russell Ballard, Jr. of the First Quorum of the Seventy," *Ensign,* May 1976.
3. Thomas S. Monson Interview, June 29, 2006.
4. Carolyn Hyde, *On the Lord's Errand: A Biography of Elder M. Russell Ballard of the Quorum of the Twelve Apostles* (Salt Lake City: M. Russell Ballard, 2007), 157.
5. First Presidency Letter, April 9, 1974.

6. Parley P. Pratt, *Autobiography of Parley Parker Pratt* (Salt Lake City: Deseret Book, 1938), 130–31.

7. Hyde, *On the Lord's Errand*, 157.

8. Scrapbook, M. Russell Ballard Family, Canada Toronto Mission, 1974–1977.

9. Chaunie Larson Interview, August 23, 2006.

10. Scrapbook, Ballard Family, Canada Toronto Mission.

11. M. Russell Ballard, *Counseling with Our Councils: Learning to Minister Together in the Church and in the Family* (Salt Lake City: Deseret Book, 2012), 131; "First Presidency Calls Four More Mission Presidents," *Church News*, 1974.

12. Richard Dunstan, "Mormons Say Gospel Returned in 1830," *The Daily Times* [Brampton, Ontario], July 26, 1975.

13. Stan Poulsen, "A Memory from Elder Ballard."

14. "Farewell and Departure and How We Will Miss You," in Scrapbook, Ballard Family, Canada Toronto Mission.

15. Ballard, *Counseling with Our Councils*, 131–32.

16. "Counselors in Toronto," dictated by M. Russell Ballard, September 25, 2005.

17. "Mormons Get New Leader," *Toronto Sun*, August 2, 1974; "New President Gave Up Profitable Auto Business to Lead Mormons," *Etobicoke Gazette*, August 15, 1974; "District Mormons to Hold Conference Here, Sunday," *Orillia Daily Pucket and Times*, August 10, 1974.

18. M. Russell Ballard, "Overview and Expectations," Mission Presidents' Seminar, June 25, 2006.

19. Hyde, *On the Lord's Errand*, 164.

20. "Mission Motto," in Scrapbook, Ballard Family, Canada Toronto Mission.

21. "Missionary Work Is Aided: Canadian National Exhibit," *Church News*, summer 1974; "Hillsdale Artist Paints Mural at CNE," in Scrapbook, Ballard Family, Canada Toronto Mission. The latter article explains that Grant Hillman, president of the Orillia Branch and local artist, painted the largest work of his career for no compensation. The painting was a sixteen- by twenty-two-foot mural.

22. Hyde, *On the Lord's Errand*, 181–82.

23. M. Russell Ballard, "The Making of a Missionary," *Ensign*, November 1976; M. Russell Ballard Interview, July 2, 2019.

24. M. Russell Ballard, "Panel Discussion," Seminaries and Institutes of Religion Satellite Broadcast, August 3, 2010.

25. Great Seal of Ontario—Proclamation from Lieutenant Governor of the Province of Ontario. "Voice of the People—Religious Leaders Urged Family Month, He Says," *Toronto Star*, May 30, 1975.

26. M. Russell Ballard, *When Thou Art Converted: Continuing Our Search for Happiness* (Salt Lake City: Deseret Book, 2001), 79–80.

27. Elder Ballard recalled, "About a year and a half later in the Ogden Temple I officiated at the sealing for that mother and father with their three sons as they knelt at an altar in the temple, all dressed in white" (M. Russell Ballard, "Think, Think, Think," Full-Time Missionary Meeting, Harlingen, Texas, January 21, 1990).

28. M. Russell Ballard, "The Peaceable Things of the Kingdom," *Ensign*, May 2002.

29. Hyde, *On the Lord's Errand*, 179.
30. Anonymous elder, quoted in Hyde, *On the Lord's Errand*, 199.
31. Elder Bradford J. Brower, quoted in Hyde, *On the Lord's Errand*, 190–91.
32. Boyd K. Packer, quoted in Kathleen Lubeck, "Elder M. Russell Ballard, True to the Faith," *Ensign*, March 1986. Of Elder Packer, Elder Ballard said, "He is one of my dearest friends in the Quorum of the Twelve. He was very approachable for me. I spent a lot of time at his home and sitting with him down by the pond. We talked about what we needed to do to try to get the gospel into the hearts of the people. It was a tremendous loss when he died." Elder Ballard spoke at his funeral on July 10, 2015 (M. Russell Ballard Oral History, June 14, 2017; Boyd K. Packer Interview, April 26, 2006).
33. Thomas S. Monson Interview, June 29, 2006.
34. The film was produced by Karl Konnry and sponsored by the Public Affairs Council of Toronto. See William G. Hartley, "Documentary on Church Will Premier in Canada," *Church News*, June 1975.
35. Thomas S. Monson Interview, June 29, 2006.
36. Thomas S. Monson Interview, June 29, 2006.
37. Thomas S. Monson Interview, June 29, 2006.
38. J. Bruce Smith Letter, May 5, 2020.
39. M. Russell Ballard, "Developing Personal Spirituality," Missionary Training Center, February 21, 1984.
40. Hyde, *On the Lord's Errand*, 189.
41. Hyde, *On the Lord's Errand*, 189–90.

CHAPTER EIGHT
An Unexpected Assignment

1. "Elder Melvin Russell Ballard, Jr., of the First Quorum of the Seventy," *Ensign*, May 1976.
2. M. Russell Ballard and President N. Eldon Tanner met in the Church Office Building at 50 East North Temple due to extensive remodeling on the Administration Building at 47 East South Temple.
3. Carolyn Hyde, *On the Lord's Errand: A Biography of Elder M. Russell Ballard of the Quorum of the Twelve Apostles* (Salt Lake City: M. Russell Ballard, 2007), 237.
4. Jack E. Jarrard, "Greatest Period of My Life: Servicing a Mission Termed Top Work," *Church News*, April 1976.
5. "New Scriptures Voted: Four Authorities Called," *Church News*, April 1976.
6. Hyde, *On the Lord's Errand*, 238.
7. M. Russell Ballard, "Learn Obedience and Service," *Ensign*, May 1976.
8. "Elder Melvin Russell Ballard, Jr."
9. Kenneth Edwin Shoesmith Interview, May 20, 2019.
10. MRB dictation for biography, August 7, 2006.
11. M. Russell Ballard, "How Glorious Is the Voice We Hear from Heaven," Raleigh North Carolina Temple Dedication, December 18, 1999.

12. M. Russell Ballard, "Prepare Today for the Needs of the Church in 1988," Ricks College Devotional, 1978.

13. M. Russell Ballard, *Yesterday, Today, and Forever: Timeless Gospel Messages with Insights from His Grandfathers Melvin J. Ballard and Hyrum Mack Smith* (Salt Lake City: Deseret Book, 2015), 134–35; M. Russell Ballard, *When Thou Art Converted: Continuing Our Search for Happiness* (Salt Lake City: Deseret Book, 2001), 37–39; Ballard, "Prepare Today."

14. M. Russell Ballard Interview, May 29, 2020.

15. Telegram Message, April 2, 1976, in Scrapbook, M. Russell Ballard Family, Canada Toronto Mission, 1974–1977.

16. M. Russell Ballard, "The Making of a Missionary," *Ensign*, November 1976.

17. M. Russell Ballard Letter, December 1976, in Scrapbook, Ballard Family, Canada Toronto Mission.

18. M. Russell Ballard, *Our Search for Happiness: An Invitation to Understand The Church of Jesus Christ of Latter-day Saints* (Salt Lake City: Deseret Book, 1993), 23.

19. Hyde, *On the Lord's Errand*, 191–92; Ballard, *Our Search for Happiness*, 24–25.

20. "Elder Melvin Russell Ballard, Jr."

21. Hyde, *On the Lord's Errand*, 201–2.

22. Scrapbook, Ballard Family, Canada Toronto Mission.

CHAPTER NINE

First Quorum of the Seventy

1. Carolyn Hyde, *On the Lord's Errand: A Biography of Elder M. Russell Ballard of the Quorum of the Twelve Apostles* (Salt Lake City: M. Russell Ballard, 2007), 240.

2. Thomas S. Monson Interview, June 29, 2006.

3. M. Russell Ballard Letter to Marsha Elrod, December 16, 1977; "Notes," MRB Journal #2.

4. Dean L. Larsen, "The Challenges of Administering a Worldwide Church," *Ensign*, July 1974.

5. M. Russell Ballard, *Counseling with Our Councils: Learning to Minister Together in the Church and in the Family* (Salt Lake City: Deseret Book, 2012), 39.

6. Elder Bednar later said, "As a stake president, I was taught by and learned from many General Authorities. However, the spiritual uplift I received from the Holy Ghost through Elder Ballard was indeed remarkable. Today as a General Authority as I interact with priesthood leaders, one of my primary objectives is to lift and strengthen those brethren the way I, as a young priesthood leader, was edified and inspired by Elder M. Russell Ballard" (quoted in Hyde, *On the Lord's Errand*, 249–50).

7. Neil L. Andersen Letter, October 8, 2009; Neil L. Andersen Email, August 2019.

8. M. Russell Ballard, *When Thou Art Converted: Continuing Our Search for Happiness* (Salt Lake City: Deseret Book, 2001), 73.

9. Ballard, *When Thou Art Converted*, 74.

10. Ballard, *When Thou Art Converted*, 74–75.
11. Ballard, *When Thou Art Converted*, 75; M. Russell Ballard, "You, the Leaders in 1988," Brigham Young University Devotional, May 16, 1978.
12. Ezra Taft Benson Letter, May 4, 1978; "Notes," MRB Journal #2.
13. Thomas S. Monson Interview, June 29, 2006.
14. Wayne B. Lynn Interview, July 31, 2019.
15. Andrzej Janiszewski Letter, July 13, 1984.
16. LeGrand Richards Letter, May 16, 1978; "Notes," MRB Journal #2. On November 20, 1979, Elder LeGrand Richards wrote to Elder Ballard, "I can't tell you how much I love you and your family, including your father and grandfather, and your sweet wife and your children. The beautiful poem 'We Plow the Fields and Scatter the Good Seed on the Ground' . . . is what you and I are doing and have been doing for years" ("Notes, MRB Journal #2).
17. Mark A. Benson Letter, June 9, 1978; "Notes," MRB Journal #2.
18. M. Russell Ballard, "Beginnings and Progress in the Caribbean," Caribbean Satellite Broadcast, January 28, 2007.
19. Doctrine and Covenants, Official Declaration 2.
20. Ballard, "Beginnings and Progress in the Caribbean."
21. M. Russell Ballard, "Spiritual Development," *Ensign,* November 1978.
22. MRB dictation; "Notes," MRB Journal #2.
23. "We extended the invitation to President Carter to sign the National Family Week proclamation in Atlanta, and eight months later through many meetings and a great deal of effort on the Atlanta, Georgia, Saints, President Carter arrived in Salt Lake City" ("Notes," MRB Journal #2).
24. President Jimmy Carter. Filed with the Office of the Federal Register, 10:29 a.m., October 23, 1978, Washington, DC.
25. Carter, Filed with the Office of the Federal Register.
26. Herb Scribner, "Jimmy Carter's Prayer at the Salt Lake Tabernacle," *Deseret News,* November 9, 2016.
27. Scribner, "Jimmy Carter's Prayer."
28. Spencer W. Kimball Letter, November 27, 1979; "Notes," MRB Journal #2.
29. "Dedicatory Prayer of Jamaica offered by Elder M. Russell Ballard"; "Notes," MRB Journal #2.
30. "Notes," MRB Journal #2.
31. "Dominican Republic," M. Russell Ballard Oral History (Updated Volume, 2005).
32. A plaque that marks the site of the dedicatory prayer reads, "Lugar de Dedicacion de la Republica Dominicana para la Predicacion del Evangelio por El Elder M. Russell Ballard Diciembre 7 De 1978 La Iglesia de Jesucristo de Los Santos de Los Ultimos Dias." "Dedicatory Prayer of Santo Dominican Republic" offered by Elder M. Russell Ballard; "Notes," MRB Journal #2.
33. The temple in the Dominican Republic was dedicated on September 17, 2000, by President Gordon B. Hinckley.
34. "Notes," MRB Journal #2.

35. Member of the Leadership Department Letter, January 6, 1979; "Notes," MRB Journal #2.
36. On September 30, 1982, Elder Ballard was honored as a retiring member of the Chamber of Commerce Board. "Lifestyle," *Salt Lake Tribune,* October 6, 1982.
37. Boyd K. Packer Interview, April 26, 2006.
38. Elder Ballard's assignment on the board of directors of the Freedom Foundation of Valley Forge began in the winter of 1979. The nineteen members on the board represented a cross section of American citizens and included education, business, and media leaders. Near the same time, Elder Ballard also served as chairman of the capital campaign fund for the Pine Canyon Ranch for Boys. "Notes," MRB Journal #2.
39. Anonymous Letter, November 4, 1979; "Notes," MRB Journal #2.
40. Robert G. Pedersen Letter, December 13, 1979; "Notes," MRB Journal #2.
41. Ballard, *When Thou Art Converted,* 186–87.
42. Ballard, *When Thou Art Converted,* 188.
43. Ballard, *When Thou Art Converted,* 189.
44. On September 24, 1979, the missionary wrote to Elder Ballard, "Everything is great out here in the mission field. I love it." "Notes," MRB Journal #2.

CHAPTER TEN
Presidency of the Seventy

1. Released from the Presidency of the First Quorum of the Seventy at that time were Elders A. Theodore Tuttle, Marion D. Hanks, Paul H. Dunn, and W. Grant Bangerter. "Notes," MRB Journal #4.
2. MRB Journal #4; "Presidency of the First Quorum of the Seventy Reorganized," *Church News,* February 28, 1980.
3. "Notes," MRB Journal #4.
4. Elder Derek Cuthbert was the executive administrator in England, and at that time Africa was part of the area that belonged to England. Elder Ballard and Elder Cuthbert were in Nigeria for two weeks. M. Russell Ballard Oral History, March 1985.
5. Brother LaMar S. Williams was sent from the Church to meet with Brother Obinna. Ballard Oral History, March 1985.
6. Ballard Oral History, March 1985.
7. Ballard Oral History, March 1985; M. Russell Ballard, "Do Things That Make a Difference," talk given to the Salt Lake Area Young Adults, October 18, 1981.
8. Ballard Oral History, March 1985.
9. M. Russell Ballard, "The Savior's Touch," *Ensign,* November 1980.
10. M. Russell Ballard, "Abide in the Light of the Gospel," BYU Devotional, October 21, 1980.
11. M. Russell Ballard, "Abide in the Light of the Gospel."
12. "Notes," MRB Journal #4.
13. First Presidency Letter, January 21, 1981; "Notes," MRB Journal #4.

14. On March 18, 1982, the First Presidency announced three new executive councils. MRB dictation for biography, August 7, 2006.

15. M. Russell Ballard, *When Thou Art Converted: Continuing Our Search for Happiness* (Salt Lake City: Deseret Book, 2001), 144.

16. Ballard, *When Thou Art Converted*, 144.

17. Ballard, *When Thou Art Converted*, 145–46; M. Russell Ballard, "Choose to Serve," BYU 15-Stake Fireside, January 5, 1986.

18. MRB dictation for biography, August 7, 2006.

19. Stacey Ballard Letter, December 13, 1981; "Notes," MRB Journal #4.

20. M. Russell Ballard, "Young Single Adults Face-to-Face," November 19, 2017.

21. M. Russell Ballard, *Yesterday, Today, and Forever: Timeless Gospel Messages with Insights from His Grandfathers Melvin J. Ballard and Hyrum Mack Smith* (Salt Lake City: Deseret Book, 2015), 43.

22. Ballard, *Yesterday, Today, and Forever*, 43; M. Russell Ballard, "The Light of Christ," Salt Lake Monument Park Stake, December 1, 1983.

23. M. Russell Ballard Interview, June 6, 2019; see also M. Russell Ballard, *Our Search for Happiness: An Invitation to Understand The Church of Jesus Christ of Latter-day Saints* (Salt Lake City: Deseret Book, 1993), 78; M. Russell Ballard, "Joseph F. Smith and the Importance of Family," Church History Symposium, March 2, 2012.

24. First Presidency Letter, September 1983; MRB Journal #3.

25. Ballard, *Our Search for Happiness*, 78.

26. First Quorum of the Seventy testimony meeting, January 20, 1983; "Notes," MRB Journal #3.

27. First Quorum of the Seventy testimony meeting.

28. First Quorum of the Seventy testimony meeting; Ballard, *Our Search for Happiness*, 61–63.

29. First Quorum of the Seventy testimony meeting.

30. M. Russell Ballard Interview, June 6, 2019.

31. M. Russell Ballard Interview, June 6, 2019.

32. M. Russell Ballard, "Exercising Righteous Dominion," Bountiful Utah South Stake Conference, March 1, 1987.

33. M. Russell Ballard Interview, June 6, 2019.

34. Carolyn Hyde, *On the Lord's Errand: A Biography of Elder M. Russell Ballard of the Quorum of the Twelve Apostles* (Salt Lake City: M. Russell Ballard, 2007), 245.

35. D. Todd Christofferson Letter, September 2019.

36. "Safely Dead, With Testimonies Burning Brightly," Denver Colorado Temple Dedication, October 28, 1986.

37. Richard D. Alsop Letter, December 6, 1984; "Notes," MRB Journal #4.

38. M. Russell Ballard, "Write Down a Date," *Ensign*, November 1984. At the Brigham Young University–Hawaii devotional on January 25, 2001, President Eric B. Shumway said of Elder Ballard, "He is the one who put into the vocabulary of the Church, "Set a Date" in terms of finding someone to hear the gospel. But I, from personal experience, know that is not just talk, not just rhetoric.

He lives the way he talks and is one of the great missionaries of the Church"
(M. Russell Ballard, "That We Might Know," Brigham Young University–Hawaii
Devotional, January 25, 2001).

39. Hyde, *On the Lord's Errand*, 217–18.
40. *Salt Lake Tribune*, April 5, 1985.
41. First Presidency Letter, January 11, 1985.
42. Ballard Oral History, March 1985.
43. Ballard Oral History, March 1985.
44. "Notes," MRB Journal #4.
45. Elder Ballard had checked Church records to see if any members of the Church
were living in Ethiopia. He had located the name of one member, a man from
Seattle, Washington, named Harry Hadlock. He was in Addis Ababa doing
consulting work for Ethiopian Airlines (Glenn L. Pace, *Safe Journey: An African
Adventure* [Salt Lake City: Shadow Mountain, 2003], 27).
46. Ballard Oral History, March 1985.
47. Pace, *Safe Journey*.
48. Pace, *Safe Journey*, 29–30.
49. Pace, *Safe Journey*, 30.
50. Ballard Oral History, March 1985.
51. Ballard Oral History, March 1985.
52. Ballard Oral History, March 1985.
53. Ballard Oral History, March 1985.
54. Ballard Oral History, March 1985.
55. Ballard Oral History, March 1985.
56. Ballard Oral History, March 1985.
57. In the year 2018, Humanitarian Services of The Church of Jesus Christ of Latter-
day Saints worked in 141 countries and territories on 2,885 projects with more
than 1,900 partners to serve millions of people. Since 1985, over $2.2 billion
in assistance has been provided through Humanitarian Services to those in need
(M. Russell Ballard, "Prepare to Serve," *Ensign,* May 1985).
58. Elder Bruce R. McConkie, "The Purifying Power of Gethsemane," *Ensign,* May
1985.
59. On September 26, 2005, Elder M. Russell Ballard spoke at the funeral of Amelia
Smith McConkie, the widow of Elder Bruce R. McConkie.

CHAPTER ELEVEN
An Apostle of the Lord Jesus Christ

1. Carolyn Hyde, *On the Lord's Errand: A Biography of Elder M. Russell Ballard of the
Quorum of the Twelve Apostles* (Salt Lake City: M. Russell Ballard, 2007), 264.
2. Kathleen Lubeck, "Elder M. Russell Ballard: True to the Faith," *Ensign,* March
1986.
3. M. Russell Ballard, "Part of a Family—on Both Sides of the Veil," Caracas
Venezuela Temple Dedication, August 20, 2000.

4. Lubeck, "Elder M. Russell Ballard: True to the Faith."

5. *Deseret News,* October 7, 1985. Elder Russell M. Nelson wrote, "It is a privilege for us to sustain you as our colleague and friend" (Russell M. Nelson Letter, February 24, 1986); "Notes," MRB Journal #6. Elder L. Tom Perry said, "We needed strong leadership when Bruce [R. McConkie]'s life was shortened, much too soon, too early" (L. Tom Perry Interview, May 9, 2006). Elder Ballard's sister Chaunie Larson said, "I can remember the day he was made an Apostle and how thrilling that was and I just think he is kind of a magnificent man" (Chaunie Larson Interview, August 23, 2006).

6. M. Russell Ballard, "In Response to the Call," *Ensign,* November 1985.

7. *Deseret News,* October 7, 1985.

8. MRB dictation for biography, August 7, 2006. According to D. Arthur Haycock, secretary to President Spencer W. Kimball, this was the last priesthood ordinance that President Kimball participated in prior to his death on November 5, 1985. It was President Kimball who called M. Russell Ballard to be a mission president, a member of the First Quorum of the Seventy, a member of the Presidency of the First Quorum of the Seventy, and a member of the Quorum of the Twelve.

9. MRB dictation for biography, August 7, 2006; M. Russell Ballard, *Our Search for Happiness: An Invitation to Understand The Church of Jesus Christ of Latter-day Saints* (Salt Lake City: Deseret Book, 1993), 59.

10. Ballard, *Our Search for Happiness,* 59.

11. M. Russell Ballard, *When Thou Art Converted: Continuing Our Search for Happiness* (Salt Lake City: Deseret Book, 2001), 139–40.

12. Craig Ballard Interview, October 1, 2019.

13. Dallin H. Oaks Interview, May 4, 2006.

14. "Notes," MRB Journal #16. Nate Wade said, "When he speaks at conference or other places, he doesn't preach. It doesn't come across that way. It comes across from the heart" (Nate/Bonnie Wade Interview, January 26, 2006).

15. M. Russell Ballard, *Counseling with Our Councils: Learning to Minister Together in the Church and in the Family* (Salt Lake City: Deseret Book, 2012), 10.

16. M. Russell Ballard, "The Kingdom Rolls Forth in South America," *Ensign,* May 1986.

17. "Notes," MRB Journal #8.

18. Ballard, *When Thou Art Converted,* 56–57; M. Russell Ballard, *Yesterday, Today, and Forever: Timeless Gospel Messages with Insights from His Grandfathers Melvin J. Ballard and Hyrum Mack Smith* (Salt Lake City: Deseret Book, 2015), 127–28.

19. M. Russell Ballard, "Do Not Underestimate the Price Paid by the Forerunners to the Restoration," Provo Missionary Training Center Devotional, January 22, 2002.

20. *Church News,* December 26, 1987; "Notes," MRB Journal #7.

21. M. Russell Ballard, "Trials Can Strengthen Our Faith," Centerville Utah Regional Conference, March 1, 1998.

22. Orson F. Whitney, quoted in Spencer W. Kimball, *Faith Precedes the Miracle* (Salt Lake City: Deseret Book, 1972), 98.

23. *Church News,* February 6, 1988.

24. "Notes," MRB Journal #8.
25. "Notes," MRB Journal #7.
26. M. Russell Ballard, "Schedule Time, No Matter the Distance, to Visit the Temple," Dallas Texas Temple Dedication, March 5, 1989.
27. M. Russell Ballard, "Duties, Rewards, and Risks," *Ensign,* November 1989; "Notes," MRB Journal #9.
28. "Notes," MRB Journal #10.
29. "Notes," MRB Journal #10.
30. M. Russell Ballard, "When We Call upon Him, He Hears and Answers Those Prayers," Monument Park Thirteenth Ward, December 23, 1990.
31. Ballard, "When We Call upon Him."
32. Ballard, "When We Call upon Him."
33. Ballard, "When We Call upon Him."
34. The two Peruvian missionaries were shot and killed on the outskirts of Huncayo, Peru. Elder Ballard flew to Peru in company with Elder Angel Abrea and Elder Charles Didier. "Notes," MRB Journal #9 and #11.
35. Executive secretary note; "Notes," MRB Journal #11.

CHAPTER TWELVE

The Work Goes Forward

1. MRB Journal #11.
2. In 2014, when doctors found that Holly Ballard Clayton had breast cancer, the family gathered together in the spirit of fasting and prayer. This time it was her father, M. Russell Ballard, who offered the prayer (Holly Ballard Clayton Interview, October 4, 2019).
3. "One time Jon was still hooked up to an IV when we took him out," President Ballard recalled during an interview in early 2020. "By the time those two died, we had eaten a lot of frozen yogurt together."
4. About two years later, after Jon Huntsman had himself returned home from an operation, President Hunter and Elder Ballard telephoned him and said, "It's time we took you out for a drive so we can have some frozen yogurt together." Jon Huntsman wrote, "Away we went. The three of us always enjoyed one another immensely and had great times together, spiritually as well as socially" (Jon M. Huntsman, "Thoughts on Elder M. Russell Ballard").
5. First Presidency Letter, January 14, 1987; "Notes," MRB Journal #7.
6. MRB dictation for biography #2, August 7, 2006.
7. MRB dictation for biography #2, August 7, 2006.
8. Jon M. Huntsman, Sr., *Barefoot to Billionaire: Reflections on a Life's Work and a Promise to Cure Cancer* (New York: Overlook Duckworth, 2014), 250–51.
9. Huntsman, *Barefoot to Billionaire,* 252.
10. Ronald A. Rasband Interview, December 2006.
11. Elder Ronald A. Rasband recalled that M. Russell Ballard was "a most trusted advisor to Jon Huntsman" (Ronald A. Rasband Interview, September 5, 2019).

12. M. Russell Ballard, "Stay Anchored to the Approved Program," Seminar for New Mission Presidents, June 21, 1991.
13. Jon Huntsman, "Thoughts on Elder M. Russell Ballard."
14. "Notes," MRB Journal #11.
15. Ronald A. Rasband Interview, December 2006.
16. Ronald A. Rasband Interview, December 2006.
17. M. Russell Ballard, "Open Your Mouth and Speak to Everyone," Missionary Training Center, August 12, 1988.
18. Gary E. Stevenson Letter, September 30, 2019.
19. "Notes," MRB Journal #10.
20. "Nine Missions Announced, Four Lands Dedicated in the Americas," *Church News*, June 1990.
21. Carolyn Hyde, *On the Lord's Errand: A Biography of Elder M. Russell Ballard of the Quorum of the Twelve Apostles* (Salt Lake City: M. Russell Ballard, 2007), 343.
22. "Notes," MRB Journal #11.
23. Bruce Olsen Letter, November 15, 1989; "Notes," MRB Journal #9.
24. President Ballard said, "We are coming out of darkness because of our reach" (M. Russell Ballard Interview, September 20, 2019).
25. M. Russell Ballard Oral History (Updated Volume, 2005).
26. Jeffrey R. Holland Interview, May 2, 2006; Jeffrey R. Holland Letter, September 24, 2019.
27. Jeffrey R. Holland Interview, May 2, 2006; Jeffrey R. Holland Letter, September 24, 2019.
28. M. Russell Ballard, *Counseling with Our Councils: Learning to Minister Together in the Church and in the Family* (Salt Lake City: Deseret Book, 2012), 1–2; Ballard Oral History (Updated Volume, 2005).
29. Ballard, *Counseling with Our Councils*, 1–2.
30. Sheri Dew Interview, September 12, 2019.
31. "Notes," MRB Journal #10.
32. "Notes," MRB Journal #11.

CHAPTER THIRTEEN

The Family, the Country, the World

1. William G. Hartley, "Joseph Smith and Nauvoo's Youth," *Ensign,* September 1979.
2. "Notes," MRB Journal #17.
3. M. Russell Ballard, "Missionary Work on Both Sides of the Veil," Mt. Timpanogos Ordinance Worker Devotional, January 20, 2012.
4. "Notes," MRB Journal #17.
5. Ralph Hardy Jr. Letter; "Notes," MRB Journal #17. "A particularly touching moment came when Elder Ballard, in front of the congregation, embraced Lachlan MacKay, a direct descendant of Joseph Smith and director of the Kirtland Temple.

. . . Descendants of the Prophet and his brother Hyrum were united in the sacred temple setting" (*Church News,* December 4, 1993).

6. "Notes," MRB Journal #20.

7. Ballard, "Missionary Work on Both Sides of the Veil."

8. M. Russell Ballard, "Brothers Bound by Love and Faith," Carthage Jail address, 150-year commemoration of the martyrdom, June 27, 1844–June 16, 1994.

9. "Notes," MRB Journal #14 and #16.

10. "Notes," MRB Journal #16.

11. *U.S. Congressional Record,* Honorable John T. Doolittle of the U.S. House of Representatives, July 30, 1992; "Notes," MRB Journal #15.

12. Elder Ballard was unable to attend the luncheon in his honor. His son Craig Ballard accepted the award on his father's behalf. *Church News,* November 27, 1993; "Notes," MRB Journal #17.

13. M. Russell Ballard, "Religion in a Free Society," Provo Utah Freedom Festival Devotional, July 5, 1992.

14. *Church News,* November 20, 1993; "Notes," MRB Journal #17.

15. "Notes," MRB Journal #16.

16. M. Russell Ballard, "There Is No Gift Greater Than the Atonement," Monument Park Thirteenth Ward Sacrament Meeting, December 20, 1992.

17. M. Russell Ballard, "Keep Your Families Solid," Bountiful Utah Regional Conference, March 3, 1995.

18. First Presidency Letter, January 21, 1993; "Notes," MRB Journal #16.

19. Sheri Dew Interview, September 12, 2019.

20. Sheri Dew Interview, September 12, 2019.

21. Cory Maxwell, an editor at Deseret Book, wrote: "I had planned to just read a chapter or two a day until I had finished the book, but once I got started, I felt impelled to keep reading it, and finished in less than two days. . . . Even though it is written simply, your message comes through powerfully" (Cory Maxwell Letter, November 5, 1993); "Notes," MRB Journal #17.

22. M. Russell Ballard Interview, July 29, 2019.

23. M. Russell Ballard Interview, September 10, 1994.

24. M. Russell Ballard, "The World Does Not Know," Columbia South Carolina Temple Dedication, October 16, 1999.

25. Conversation with Jerry Cahill, Don LeFevre, and Joseph Walker, April 20, 1992.

26. The cable-television program *Perspectives: Faith in Our Times* was shown on March 2 and 26, 1994, on the Faith and Values channel. *Church News,* April 2, 1994; "Notes," MRB Journal #17 and #18.

27. M. Russell Ballard, "Bringing the Church Out of Obscurity," LDS Public Affairs Professionals, May 2, 1998.

28. Carolyn Hyde, *On the Lord's Errand: A Biography of Elder M. Russell Ballard of the Quorum of the Twelve Apostles* (Salt Lake City: M. Russell Ballard, 2007), 339.

29. Hyde, *On the Lord's Errand,* 339.

30. See 3 Nephi 11:15; 3 Nephi 17:21.

31. M. Russell Ballard, "The Power of a Memory," Bountiful Utah Regional Conference, March 3, 1995.

32. Hyde, *On the Lord's Errand*, 294.

33. Hyde, *On the Lord's Errand*, 294–95.

34. Hyde, *On the Lord's Errand*, 295.

35. Donald Doty Journal, August 1, 1995, quoted in Hyde, *On the Lord's Errand*, 296.

36. Stephen M. Studdert Interview, September 30, 2006.

37. Jon M. Huntsman, "Thoughts on Elder M. Russell Ballard."

38. Doty Journal, August 1, 1995.

39. Hyde, *On the Lord's Errand*, 298–99.

40. Hyde, *On the Lord's Errand*, 295.

41. Wallace B. Smith Letter, August 2, 1995; "Notes," MRB Journal #20.

42. Thomas S. Monson Interview, June 29, 2006.

43. M. Russell Ballard Interview, July 2, 2020.

44. "The Family: A Proclamation to the World," *Ensign*, November 2010.

45. M. Russell Ballard Interview, February 13, 2020.

CHAPTER FOURTEEN

Celebrating History

1. "Notes," MRB Journal #13.

2. "Notes," MRB Journal #21.

3. "Notes," MRB Journal #21. Elder Ballard played a key role in planning the 1896 Statehood Inaugural Ceremony in the Tabernacle on Temple Square as well as centennial displays at the Salt Lake International Airport, Utah history fairs, and other festive events (Harold Schindler, "Celebrating the Utah Centennial, 1896–1996," *Salt Lake Tribune,* December 16, 1994).

4. Utah Centennial Celebration, March 1996, news-of-the-church, ChurchofJesus Christ.org.

5. MRB dictation for biography, August 7, 2006; *The Story of This Is the Place Heritage Park* (Salt Lake City: This is the Place Foundation, 2011), 4, 6, 8.

6. Stephen M. Studdert Interview, September 30, 2006.

7. M. Russell Ballard, Remarks at the Dedication of the *Journey's End* Monument at This Is the Place State Park, July 24, 1999.

8. Carolyn Hyde, *On the Lord's Errand: A Biography of Elder M. Russell Ballard of the Quorum of the Twelve Apostles* (Salt Lake City: M. Russell Ballard, 2007), 4.

9. M. Russell Ballard Interview, February 11, 2020.

10. "Bridge Building," in M. Russell Ballard Oral History (Updated Volume, 2005).

11. M. Russell Ballard, "You Have Nothing to Fear from the Journey," *Ensign,* May 1997.

12. MRB Scrapbook #23.

13. Stephen M. Studdert Interview, September 30, 2006.

14. Ballard Oral History, June 14, 2019.

15. Stephen M. Studdert Interview, September 30, 2006.
16. Clifford Wallace Letter; MRB Scrapbook #23.
17. Earl C. Tingey Letter, July 28, 1997; "Notes," MRB Journal #22.
18. Gordon B. Hinckley Letter, August 17, 1997; MRB Scrapbook #23.
19. Jeffrey R. Holland Letter, October 22, 1997; "Notes," MRB Journal #21.

CHAPTER FIFTEEN

A Problem Solver

1. Richard J. Maynes Interview, August 8, 2009.
2. Nate/Bonnie Wade Interview, January 26, 2006.
3. MRB Scrapbook #24.
4. President James E. Faust Letter, May 26, 1998; "Notes," MRB Journal #24.
5. M. Russell Ballard Interview, January 25, 2020.
6. Nate/Bonnie Wade Interview, January 26, 2006.
7. Notes on Elder M. Russell Ballard's service as Chair of the Board of Education's Executive Committee.
8. Notes on Elder M. Russell Ballard's service as Chair of the Board of Education's Executive Committee.
9. The Brigham Young University Athletic Complex was completed in July 2003 and included a 106,000-square-foot enclosed practice facility west of the Smith Fieldhouse. The facility also houses athletic storage, a training/taping area, and an overflow practice area. The Student-Athlete Center, directly north of the fieldhouse, houses a student-athlete academic center, training facilities, locker rooms, conference rooms, and offices.
10. M. Russell Ballard Interview, January 25, 2020.
11. Of "The Living Christ" and "The Family: A Proclamation to the World," Elder Ballard said, "[They] are going to become progressively more and more stand-alone doctrines as the Church stands alone" ("Notes," MRB Journal #25).
12. Excerpts from "The Living Christ: The Testimony of the Apostles, The Church of Jesus Christ of Latter-day Saints."
13. The mural is located on the main floor of the Church Office Building in Salt Lake City.
14. As of July 2019, since 1830 there have been more than 1.47 million full-time missionaries who have served, taught, and testified of Christ in more than 60 languages and in more than 160 sovereign states around the world. Of the 193 countries recognized by the United Nations, 162 are within the boundaries of a mission (Jordan Kesler Email, July 2019).
15. M. Russell Ballard, "Special Witnesses of Christ," *Ensign*, May 2001.
16. In 2019 Moldova had 412 members, 4 congregations, and one Family History Center.
17. Ronald A. Rasband Interview, August 4, 2020.
18. Carolyn Hyde, *On the Lord's Errand: A Biography of Elder M. Russell Ballard of the Quorum of the Twelve Apostles* (Salt Lake City: M. Russell Ballard, 2007), 272.

19. Ronald A. Rasband Interview, August 4, 2020. In 1840, John Benbow and his wife and four others were baptized by Wilford Woodruff immediately after hearing him preach about the gospel.
20. Ronald A. Rasband Interview, August 4, 2020.
21. "A Hopeful Alliance for Unity," *Deseret News* editorial, September 18, 2001.
22. M. Russell Ballard Interview, July 17, 2020.
23. "Hopeful Alliance for Unity."
24. M. Russell Ballard, "The Doctrine of Inclusion," *Ensign,* November 2001.
25. M. Russell Ballard Interview, July 17, 2020.
26. Elder Ballard shared the spotlight with longtime friend Dale Tingey, who also received an honorary doctorate, and with community activist Pamela Atkinson, who received a Presidential Citation from Brigham Young University ("Notes," MRB Journal #29).
27. "Notes," MRB Journal #29.
28. President and CEO of the Friends for Sight Organization at that time was Colleen Malouf ("Notes," MRB Journal #29).
29. BYU–Idaho President David A. Bednar, introductory remarks ("Notes," MRB Journal #28).
30. "Notes," MRB Journal #28; Barbara Ballard, "That We Might Know," BYU–Hawaii Devotional, January 25, 2001.
31. "Notes," MRB Journal #24.
32. M. Russell Ballard Interview, September 20, 2019.
33. "Notes," MRB Journal #28.
34. Dallin H. Oaks Interview, May 4, 2006. Sheri Dew metaphorically said, "President Ballard has a talent for pulling people into a tent and inviting them to contribute. He seems to have a kitchen cabinet around him and calls on individuals to use for the benefit of the Church. He has a talent for recognizing the skill sets of others" (Sheri Dew Interview, September 20, 2019).
35. Richard Heaton Interview, July 30, 2019.
36. M. Russell Ballard, "The Greatest Generation of Missionaries," *Ensign,* November 2002.
37. Gordon B. Hinckley, "To the Men of the Priesthood," *Ensign,* November 2002.
38. Gordon B. Hinckley, "Missionary Service," Worldwide Leadership Training Meeting, January 11, 2003.
39. Benjamin Hyrum White, "The History of *Preach My Gospel*," *Religious Educator*, vol. 14, no. 1 (2013): 129–58; Reid L. Neilson and Fred E. Woods, eds., *Go Ye into All the World: The Growth and Development of Mormon Missionary Work* (Provo, UT: Religious Studies Center, Brigham Young University, and Salt Lake City: Deseret Book, 2012), 151–88.
40. F. Michael Watson to M. Russell Ballard and the Missionary Executive Council, memorandum, June 12, 2003.
41. Quentin L. Cook Interview, August 8, 2019.
42. Quentin L. Cook Interview, August 8, 2019.
43. M. Russell Ballard Interview, July 29, 2019.

44. Thomas S. Monson Interview, June 29, 2006.
45. Richard Heaton Interview, July 30, 2019.
46. M. Russell Ballard Interview, July 29, 2019.
47. Gordon B. Hinckley, Missionary Training Satellite Broadcast, October 15, 2004.
48. Shaun D. Stahle, "Preach My Gospel," *Church News,* November 6, 2004.
49. Richard G. Scott Letter; "Notes," MRB Journal #28.
50. L. Tom Perry Interview, May 9, 2006.
51. Neil L. Andersen Letter, October 8, 2009.
52. Quentin L. Cook Letter; "Notes," MRB Journal #28.

CHAPTER SIXTEEN

In Defense of Truth

1. M. Russell Ballard Oral History, June 23, 2017.
2. M. Russell Ballard, "The Banner of the Lord Revealed," Regional Conference, St. George, Utah, March 22, 1998.
3. Chaunie Larson Interview, August 23, 2006. Elder Ballard said of Chaunie, "She was wonderful. She was giving, and had three great children. The last of her life, health-wise, was difficult. She lived in the downstairs of my sister Ann's home, where she died on Christmas day 2018." Her funeral was held on January 3, 2019. Ballard Oral History, May 10, 2019.
4. Orrin G. Hatch Letter, February 3, 2006; MRB Scrapbook #33, August 2007 through August 2008.
5. M. Russell Ballard Interview, February 11, 2020.
6. "Joseph F. Smith: Beloved by Members, Strangers," *Church News,* March 11, 2012.
7. Steven J. Merrill Email, July 2019; MRB Scrapbook #33; Jason Swensen, "Message-laden Tour," *Church News,* March 10, 2007.
8. Email from Chaplain, Colonel USAF (retired) Steven J. Merrill, July 2019.
9. Elder Gary E. Stevenson expressed similar feelings about M. Russell Ballard: "If he were still in the business world, he would be comfortable and capable of leading any number of Fortune 500 companies . . . but his rare attribute is to lead like the Savior. . . . He is truly one of the greatest leaders that I know" (Gary E. Stevenson Letter, September 30, 2019).
10. Email from Chaplain, Colonel USAF (retired) Steven J. Merrill, July 2019.
11. Email from Chaplain, Colonel USAF (retired) Steven J. Merrill, July 2019.
12. Swensen, "Message-laden Tour."
13. Jon Huntsman died on February 2, 2018. His funeral was held on February 10, 2018. "Most of the summers we traveled around the world; he would do his work for the company, and I would do my work for the Church," President Ballard said. "We preached many sermons in the same meetings together." Elder Ballard also said of Huntsman, "He was as close to being a brother as I had in my lifetime. We watched out for each other and gave blessings to each other. He was a Renaissance man who comes along every once in a while, not very often—visionary,

courageous. I've seen him in Church leadership, and I've seen him in industrial leadership. He's just terrific. Of course, I miss him very, very much" (Ballard Oral History, April 30, 2019). Two days before Brother Huntsman's passing, President Ballard and Elder Ronald A. Rasband gave him a blessing. "We knew he would not make it," President Ballard said. "He knew he would not make it. We pled with the Lord to take away the pain" (Tad Walsh, "A True Believer: Remembering the Faith and Works of Jon Huntsman Sr.," *Deseret News,* February 10, 2018).

14. Walsh, "A True Believer."
15. Walsh, "A True Believer."
16. "Explain Gospel Doctrine in Simple Terms, Advises Elder Ballard," *Deseret News*; MRB Scrapbook #34, September 2008 through December 2009; M. Russell Ballard, "Give Equal Time to the Lord," Denver Colorado Temple Dedication, October 28, 1986.
17. Ballard, "Give Equal Time to the Lord."
18. Jamshid Askar, "Treasure Truth and Prepare for the Future," *Church News,* February 13, 2010; MRB Scrapbook #35, January 2010 through August 2011; Lucy Schouten, "LDS Interfaith Outreach Efforts Aim to Make Friends, Solve Issues," *Deseret News,* October 13, 2013.
19. Ballard Oral History, 2009.
20. Ballard Oral History, 2009.
21. M. Russell Ballard, "Prophecies of the Last Days," BYU–Idaho Student Fireside, January 30, 2010.
22. Ballard Oral History, 2009.
23. Ballard Oral History, 2009.
24. Ballard Oral History, 2009.
25. M. Russell Ballard and Quentin L. Cook, "The Restoration and Following the Spirit—Part 1," 2015 Seminar for New Mission Presidents, June 27, 2015.
26. Ballard and Cook, "The Restoration and Following the Spirit."
27. Ballard and Cook, "The Restoration and Following the Spirit."
28. Ballard and Cook, "The Restoration and Following the Spirit"; Quentin L. Cook Interview, August 8, 2019.
29. M. Russell Ballard Interview, February 11, 2020.
30. Translation copy of Elder Ballard's appearance on Al-Jazeera, in possession of Elder Quentin L. Cook.
31. M. Russell Ballard Interview, February 11, 2020.
32. "Church Leaders Attend President Obama's Inauguration"; MRB Scrapbook #34; "Pres. Uchtdorf, Elder Ballard to Attend Inauguration," *Deseret News,* January 27, 2009; "LDS Leaders Feel Deep Emotion at Inauguration," *Deseret News,* January 22, 2009.
33. Dieter F. Uchtdorf Email, August 2019.
34. "LDS Leaders Feel Deep Emotion at Inauguration."
35. Ballard Oral History, 2014.
36. Ballard, "Prophecies of the Last Days," BYU–Idaho Student Fireside, January 30, 2010.

37. Ballard Oral History, 2014.
38. "Under the Spotlight on 'Mormon Night,'" *Church News,* August 25, 2009.
39. Ballard Oral History, June 14, 2017.
40. Jeffrey R. Holland Letter, March 14, 2012; MRB Scrapbook #36, September 2011 through December 2012.

CHAPTER SEVENTEEN
To All the World

1. See Mark 16:15.
2. M. Russell Ballard Interview, February 13, 2020.
3. Spencer W. Kimball, "When the World Will Be Converted," Regional Representatives' Seminar, April 4, 1974.
4. Information from notes taken by Heber G. Wolsey during a personal interview with Melvin R. Ballard, June 8, 1967 (Heber G. Wolsey, "Religious Broadcasting by the LDS Church," MA thesis, Northwestern University).
5. "Proceedings at the Dedication of the Joseph Smith Memorial Monument," December 23, 1905, 19, 25; "Joseph's Family, Vermont—200th Birthday Commemoration Fireside," December 23, 2005, Sharon, Vermont.
6. David A. Bednar Letter; MRB Scrapbook #40, January 2017 through July 2017.
7. Derek A. Marquis, Personal Journal, June 3, 2007.
8. Marquis, Journal, June 3, 2007.
9. Owen S. Rich, "The Miracle of Radio and the Birth of KBYU-FM," BYU-FM 40th Anniversary Lecture Series, September 21, 2000, 16–17, Brigham Young University. In Derek A. Marquis, "The History of BYU Television, 1946–2017."
10. Derek Marquis noted, "In the ensuing decades, the KBYU audience did grow but the channel was limited in reach by virtue of its FCC license limiting its broadcasts to Utah. Furthermore, as the station migrated into a Public Television Service (PBS) member station, the programming on the channel skewed the audience to young children and senior citizens" (Derek Marquis Interview, October 1, 2019).
11. John Reim Interview, August 1, 2006, quoted in Marquis, "History of BYU Television."
12. Marquis, "History of BYU Television."
13. Gordon B. Hinckley, "Keep the Chain Unbroken," Brigham Young University Devotional, November 30, 1999.
14. John Reim Interview, August 1, 2006.
15. Marquis, "History of BYU Television."
16. Marquis, "History of BYU Television."
17. Rex and Ruth Maughan, quoted in Marquis, "History of BYU Television."
18. Rex and Ruth Maughan, quoted in Marquis, "History of BYU Television." On October 25, 2017, a BYU Broadcasting Scholarship luncheon was held to honor Elder and Sister M. Russell Ballard.
19. Marquis Journal, December 6, 2006.

20. Marquis Journal, December 6, 2006.
21. Marquis Journal, December 6, 2006.
22. Marquis Journal, December 6, 2006.
23. Marquis Journal, December 6, 2006.
24. BYU Broadcasting Building, Groundbreaking Ceremony, May 7, 2009. MRB Scrapbook #34, September 2008 through December 2009; Emily Stone, "Bringing BYU Broadcasting under One Roof," *The Daily Universe,* May 8, 2009; Scott Taylor, "BYU Breaks Ground for Broadcast Building," *Deseret News,* May 8, 2009; Marianne Holman, "Technology Blesses Lives," *Church News,* August 29, 2011.
25. Sara Israelsen-Hartley, "BYU Broadcasting," *Deseret News,* November 29, 2010.

CHAPTER EIGHTEEN

Anxiously Engaged in a Good Cause

1. Doctrine and Covenants 58:27.
2. M. Russell Ballard Oral History, April 30, 2019.
3. Ballard Oral History, June 14, 2017.
4. M. Russell Ballard, "Finding Joy through Loving Service," *Ensign,* May 2011.
5. William D. Price, "The Doctrine of Charitable Service," April 24, 2015; in Richard J. Maynes Papers.
6. Neal A. Maxwell, *A Time to Choose* (Salt Lake City: Deseret Book, 1972), 63–64.
7. JustServe, National Report, JustServe.org, June 2018.
8. Larry Richman, "JustServe.org Helps You Find Community Service Opportunities," *Church News,* April 14, 2018.
9. M. Russell Ballard, "Be Anxiously Engaged," *Ensign,* November 2012.
10. William and Sidney Price, "JustServe Overview Report, NAN Area Directors of Public Affairs," April 22, 2017.
11. R. Scott Lloyd, "JustServe.org: Connecting Volunteers with Community Needs," *Church News,* March 30, 2018.
12. William and Sidney Price Letter, February 1, 2014; in Richard J. Maynes Papers.
13. William and Sidney Price Letter, April 9, 2012; in Richard J. Maynes Papers.
14. Price and Price, "JustServe Overview Report."
15. "JustServe: A Community Service Resource Update," January 2014; JustServe.org.
16. William and Sidney Price Letter, January 30, 2013; in Richard J. Maynes Papers.
17. William and Sidney Price Letter, October 23, 2014; in Richard J. Maynes Papers.
18. Amy Conway, "JustServe," *Ensign,* August 2018.
19. Price and Price, "JustServe Overview Report."
20. Rebecca Bennion, "JustServe Invites Disciples of Christ to Serve as He Would," *Church News,* October 12, 2018.
21. Bennion, "JustServe Invites Disciples."
22. "Why Should I Volunteer?" JustServe.org.
23. "Mormons' JustServe Program Helps the Helpers Find Place to, Well, Help," *Salt Lake Tribune;* in MRB Scrapbook #40, January 2017 through July 2017;

"JustServe.org: Connecting Volunteers with Community Needs," *Church News,* October 6, 2012.

24. Gerry Avant, "Elder Ballard Visits with Refugees," *Church News,* November 29, 2015; Tad Walsh, "Elder Ballard Praises Germany for Accepting Refugees," *Deseret News,* November 25, 2015; M. Russell Ballard Oral History, June 14, 2017.

25. Ballard Oral History, June 14, 2017.

26. Ballard Oral History, 2019.

27. Ballard Oral History, June 14, 2017.

28. M. Russell Ballard, "Finding Joy through Loving Service," *Ensign,* May 2011.

29. Ballard Oral History, April 30, 2019.

30. Ballard Oral History, April 30, 2019.

31. Ballard Oral History, April 30, 2019.

CHAPTER NINETEEN

Acting President of the Quorum of the Twelve

1. Elder Ronald A. Rasband speaks of President Ballard's ability to "work through an illness." Ronald A. Rasband Interview, September 5, 2019.

2. M. Russell Ballard Oral History, May 10, 2019.

3. Ballard Oral History, April 30, 2019; May 10, 2019; Jason Swensen, "Inside the Quorum of the Twelve Apostles: The Ministry of President M. Russell Ballard and His Brethren," *Church News,* June 20, 2018.

4. In his first public address as President of the Church, President Nelson spoke on January 16, 2018, in a live telecast from the Salt Lake Temple waiting room. During the telecast, he announced that his counselors would be Dallin H. Oaks and Henry B. Eyring. President Ballard said of the First Presidency, "We've got a First Presidency comprised of great men. I'll have to hurry to keep up with them" (Swensen, "Inside the Quorum").

5. President Nelson was assisted in the setting apart of M. Russell Ballard as Acting President of the Quorum of the Twelve Apostles by Presidents Dallin H. Oaks and Henry B. Eyring of the First Presidency, and Elders Jeffrey R. Holland, Dieter F. Uchtdorf, David A. Bednar, Quentin L. Cook, D. Todd Christofferson, Neil L. Andersen, Ronald A. Rasband, Gary E. Stevenson, and Dale G. Renlund of the Quorum of the Twelve Apostles (Scott Lloyd, "A Divine Plan of Succession: New Leaders will 'Seek to Know His Will,'" *Church News,* January 2019).

6. The setting apart blessing of Melvin Russell Ballard as Acting President of the Quorum of the Twelve Apostles of The Church of Jesus Christ of Latter-day Saints, January 14, 2018.

7. Jeffrey R. Holland Letter, January 16, 2018.

8. M. Russell Ballard, "Precious Gifts from God," *Ensign,* May 2018.

9. Ballard Oral History, April 30, 2019.

10. Ballard Oral History, April 30, 2019,

11. Ballard Oral History, June 14, 2017.

12. Gerrit W. Gong Email, August 28, 2019.

13. Ulisses Soares Email, September 3, 2019.

14. Ballard Oral History, June 14, 2017.

15. Ballard Oral History, May 10, 2019.

16. M. Russell Ballard Interview, September 20, 2019.

17. Ballard Oral History, May 10, 2019; M. Russell Ballard Interview, September 20, 2019. The First Presidency wrote to President Ballard on February 13, 2018, "Please know of our sincere love and appreciation for your devotion to the work of the Lord and for your leadership of the Quorum of the Twelve at this important time in the history of the Church" (First Presidency Letter, February 13, 2018).

18. Ballard Oral History, April 30, 2019.

19. Swensen, "Inside the Quorum."

20. Ballard Oral History, May 10, 2019.

21. Ballard Oral History, May 10, 2019.

22. Jeffrey R. Holland Letter, January 14, 2018; Jeffrey R. Holland Letter, September 24, 2019.

23. Dieter F. Uchtdorf Email, August 2019.

24. Neil L. Andersen Letter, August 28, 2019.

25. D. Todd Christofferson Letter, September 23, 2019.

26. D. Todd Christofferson Letter, September 23, 2019.

27. Ronald A. Rasband Interview, September 5, 2019. Elder Rasband has had a close working relationship with President Ballard for more than forty years.

28. Dale G. Renlund Email, August 2019.

29. Ballard Oral History, May 10, 2019.

30. M. Russell Ballard, "The Importance of a Name," *Ensign*, November 2011.

31. M. Russell Ballard Interview, February 13, 2020.

32. Doctrine and Covenants 115:4.

33. M. Russell Ballard Interview, February 13, 2020.

34. M. Russell Ballard Interview, February 13, 2020.

35. First Presidency Letter, March 1, 2018. The Houston Texas Temple was originally dedicated by President Gordon B. Hinckley on August 26–27, 2000.

36. Joining him at the dedication of the Houston Texas Temple were Elder Larry Y. Wilson, Elder S. Gifford Nielsen, and Elder Stanley G. Ellis, emeritus. Ballard Oral History, April 30, 2019; Jason Swensen, "A Simple, Different Rededication," *Church News*, April 29, 2018.

37. M. Russell Ballard, "We ask Thee, Heavenly Father, for protection over Thy temple," Houston Texas Temple Rededicatory Prayer; Jason Swensen, "Reopening a Beloved Temple: A Key Moment in Hurricane Harvey Recovery," *Church News*, April 29, 2018.

38. Gary E. Stevenson Letter, September 30, 2019.

39. Ballard Oral History, May 10, 2019.

40. Ballard Oral History, May 10, 2019; Jason Swensen, "A Family Home Evening for Thousands," *Church News*, June 3, 2018.

41. Jason Swensen, "Put Down Your Smartphones and Connect with Heaven, President Ballard Counsels during Visit to Pacific," *Church News*, May 31, 2018.

42. Ballard Oral History, May 10, 2019.

43. Ballard Oral History, May 10, 2019.

44. M. Russell Ballard, "There Is Great Strength in the Women of the Church," Preston England Temple Dedication, June 9, 1998.

45. M. Russell Ballard, "True to the Faith," General Authority Wives' Luncheon, May 30, 2016; "Sister Barbara Bowen Ballard, Wife of President M. Russell Ballard, Dies at 86," *Church News,* October 1, 2018.

46. Barbara Ballard, "Our Life's Values," Montpelier Idaho Regional Conference, June 3, 2000.

47. Stacey Ballard Murdock Interview, October 1, 2019.

48. M. Russell Ballard (Dad) Letter, May 2, 2018.

49. Jeni Broberg Holzapfel Interview, September 27, 2020.

50. Ballard Oral History, May 10, 2019.

51. Conversation with Sheri Dew, May 2018.

52. M. Russell Ballard, "Giving Our Spirits Control over Our Bodies," *Ensign,* November 2019.

53. Ballard Oral History, May 10, 2019; April 30, 2019.

54. Kathy Andersen Letter, October 29, 2018.

55. Dieter F. Uchtdorf Email, August 2019. Sheri Dew said, "When Barbara Ballard walked into a room and shook your hand, it was as if there was no one on the planet that she would rather talk to than you" (Sheri Dew Interview, September 20, 2019).

56. Tammy Ballard Brower Letter, June 28, 2012; Tammy Ballard Brower Interview, October 4, 2019.

57. Paul Clayton Interview, October 4, 2019.

58. Brynn Ballard Huntsman Email, October 7, 2019.

59. M. Russell Ballard, "The Vision of the Redemption of the Dead," *Ensign,* November 2018.

60. Ballard, "Giving Our Spirits Control."

CHAPTER TWENTY

At Home and Abroad

1. M. Russell Ballard Oral History, June 23, 2017.

2. Ballard Oral History, April 30, 2019.

3. Ballard Oral History, April 30, 2019. At the passing of President Thomas S. Monson, John C. Wester, archbishop of Santa Fe, wrote to President Ballard of his "genuine sadness" at his passing and penned, "I am praying for you especially, Russell, my dear friend. . . . May the Lord hold you close to his comforting and merciful heart. We in the Southwest will keep you and all your brothers and sisters in prayer" (John C. Wester Letter, January 5, 2018).

4. At the April 23, 2015, BYU Commencement, Robbie George spoke on "Faith and Reason: The Appropriation of Knowledge and Truth."

5. On June 2, 2018, His Eminence Cardinal Donald Wuerl, archbishop of

Washington, DC, was honored by the BYU Management Society at the Marriott Crystal Gateway Hotel in Arlington, Virginia (Ballard Oral History, April 30, 2019).

6. Sarah Jane Weaver, "President Ballard: Preserved Religious Liberty Is Essential," *Church News,* October 6, 2012.
7. Ballard Oral History, April 30, 2019.
8. Ballard Oral History, April 30, 2019.
9. Ballard Oral History, May 10, 2019.
10. Ballard Oral History, May 10, 2019.
11. Ballard Oral History, May 10, 2019.
12. "Rome Italy Temple Is Dedicated," *Church News,* March 10, 2019; "The Rome LDS Temple Dedication in Photos," *Daily Herald,* March 11, 2019; Tad Walsh, "President Nelson Refers to Apostles Peter, Paul during Rome Temple Dedication," *Deseret News,* March 10, 2019; Sarah Jane Weaver, "President Nelson Dedicates Rome Italy Temple 170 Years after Church 'Opened a Door Which No Man Shut,'" *Church News,* August 9, 2019.
13. Sarah Jane Weaver, "President Nelson Calls Rome Temple Dedication 'A Hinge Point' in Church History," *Church News,* March 15, 2019.
14. M. Russell Ballard Interview, September 20, 2019.
15. Children and Youth Worldwide Broadcast, September 29, 2019.
16. Jason Swensen, "A Look at North Carolina's Church History and Why the Temple Rededication Is a 'Game Changer' for Latter-day Saints," *Church News,* October 2019.
17. Danielle Christensen, "Video: President Ballard, Elder Christofferson Testify of the Restoration at Joseph Smith's Birthplace," *Church News,* October 20, 2019; Sarah Jane Weaver, "Modern Apostles Visit the Prophet's Birthplace," *Church News,* October 6, 2019; Sarah Jane Weaver, "What It Really Means to President Ballard, Elder Christofferson to Be at Joseph Smith's Birthplace," *Church News,* October 20, 2019.
18. See *Church News* videos "Brothers in the Gospel" and "A Baby Was Born," thechurchnews.com.
19. Weaver, "Modern Apostles Visit."
20. Sarah Jane Weaver, "'A New Movement': Pray for the Country, Its Leaders, Church Official Urges Latter-day Saints," *Deseret News,* October 20, 2019.
21. John 21:4; emphasis added.
22. John 21:5–8.
23. M. Russell Ballard Interview, September 27, 2020.
24. M. Russell Ballard Interview, September 27, 2020.
25. John 21:15–17.
26. Scott Taylor, "When Church leaders can't interact with members personally like they used to, 'they are doing it through Zoom,'" *Church News,* September 20, 2020.
27. "The Church's New Symbol Emphasizes the Centrality of the Savior," https://newsroom.churchofjesuschrist.org/article/new-symbol-church-of-jesus-christ.

28. David Louis, "Road trip ends in single-vehicle rollover tragedy for LaVerkin family," *St. George News,* July 12, 2020.

29. Matthew 25:34–40.

30. Sarah Jane Weaver, "The world will win the war on COVID-19, President Ballard says," *Church News,* March 26, 2020.

31. Weaver, "The world will win."

32. Stacey Ballard Murdock Interview, October 1, 2019.

33. Jeffrey R. Holland Letter, September 24, 2019.

34. Dieter F. Uchtdorf Email, August 2019.

35. Dieter F. Uchtdorf Email, August 2019; Dieter F. Uchtdorf Letter, June 26, 2018.

36. Dale G. Renlund Email, August 2019.

37. Jeffrey R. Holland Letter, September 24, 2019.

38. David A. Bednar Interview, October 8, 2019.

INDEX